The
Farm Management
Handbook

Sixth Edition

The
Farm Management
Handbook

by

Robert A. Luening, M.S.

and

William P. Mortenson, Ph.D.

University of Wisconsin–Madison
College of Agricultural and Life Sciences

THE INTERSTATE
Printers & Publishers, Inc.
Danville, Illinois

THE FARM MANAGEMENT HANDBOOK, Sixth Edition.
Copyright © 1979 by The Interstate Printers & Publishers, Inc.
All rights reserved. Prior editions: 1948, 1954, 1960, 1963,
1972. Printed in the United States of America.

Library of Congress Catalog Card No. 79-84906

ISBN 0-8134-2082-2

We dedicate this book to the thousands of farmers of today and tomorrow who are striving to adjust their farming operations to the changing economic conditions that lie ahead.

Preface to the Sixth Edition

This book is being presented as the sixth edition of *The Farm Management Handbook*. Actually, the changes and additions made are so pronounced that, in many respects, it is virtually a new book. There has been a major reorganization of the book with greater emphasis on farm business management; farm records and business analysis; resource acquisition; farm business organization and business arrangement; budgeting; and getting started in farming. Less emphasis has been placed on specific production technology, but information on this is available from other books published by The Interstate Printers & Publishers, Inc.

Less than a half million farms have a gross income of over $40,000. These comprise about 16% of all farms but account for about 80% of the total cash receipts. Farmers who gross over $20,000 receive some 90% of the cash receipts and comprise more than 28% of the total number of farms. Much of the growth in farm size and income, and the reduction of the number of farms, has come about within the past 30 to 35 years.

Operators of these larger farms today are true business persons. Successful farmers understand and utilize the same business principles and practices used by non-farm business persons. In a real sense, up-to-date farmers practice sound business management and combine it with modern production management technology.

In brief, the farm manager's job is to manage land, labor, and capital so as to obtain the greatest returns consistent with the family's goals and values. These basic management principles and practices apply to all farm businesses in all parts of the United States.

Effective farm operators will continue to spend a greater proportion of their time managing the farm's business affairs. In fact, the skill of business management is the most important ability farm operators will need if they are to succeed or even to survive in the years ahead.

We are confident that the changes and additions to this sixth edition will aid students as well as operating farmers in gaining a fuller grasp of the management process, regardless of what part of the United States they happen to live in.

A Farm Management Course Is Valuable for Young People Who Leave the Farm

Many young men and women reared on farms may not be able to follow a farming career for one reason or another. For them, a course in farm management will be extremely valuable. It will help them qualify for the many career opportunities in agri-business, as well as help them manage their own personal business affairs.

The combination of their rural backgrounds and formal agricultural training will place them in a strong competitive position for excellent jobs in the vital agricultural industry. With their knowledge of farming, they will be able to speak the farmer's language and will know more about the science of farming than do many operating farmers. Some training beyond high school, or even a college degree, will be most helpful if not essential for jobs in tomorrow's agriculture.

Note to Instructors

Farm business and financial management is one of the more difficult subjects to teach because it requires logical thinking and application rather than memorization. You are dealing with principles, concepts, and methodologies, all of which are more or less abstract.

The teaching of farm management actually consists of *two separate parts*: (1) presenting basic economic principles of farm business management and (2) weaving these in with materials from the production sciences. Using this approach, Parts One, Two, and Five may be taught alone. All the other parts have some chapters which may be taught alone. But they all become much more realistic if they are related to, or integrated with, the various phases of farm production subjects. Part Four can be looked upon as a "block" with the specific planning processes coordinated—to some extent—with appropriate farm type and enterprises of the locality.

Farm management principles, concepts, and methods will become more clear as these items are woven into the production practices. The point should be made that learning production sciences is only half the job. It is equally important that the economic impact of the use of the technology be evaluated at the individual farm level. As an illustration, no matter how effective a certain pesticide may be, it is of little value to the farmer if its cost is greater than the additional returns from its use. Likewise, in feeding livestock, a specific ration may produce a higher rate of gain (or pounds of milk) than other rations, but if its cost is too high, it may be less profitable than other rations. Using the same reasoning, bright, shining farm machinery might work well and be well engineered, but it may be the most costly way to do a job. Well-designed, solidly constructed buildings may perform well but be the most costly way to house livestock and equipment.

Before deciding on the particular production items to be used, it is important to evaluate both the returns and the cost of each. This is another way of saying that the science of production must be integrated with the techniques of business management in order to bring about the maximum financial result! You will find, as have the authors, that this is a constant challenge, but it is interesting and highly rewarding.

R. A. Luening
W. P. Mortenson

Contents

APPENDICES

PART ONE

Things to Consider Before
Starting Farming

Before starting to farm, one must consider his or her talents and training, along with the availability of an opportunity in farming. There are many non-farming agricultural career opportunities which require or can profitably use training in farm business management.

CHAPTER 1

Goals and Values of the Farm Family

Highlights of Chapter

No two people have the same goals and values in life. This is true of farmers as well as others. Some farmers are extremely ambitious and anxious to earn as much money as possible, regardless of the amount of hard work it takes. Others prefer to take life more easy, even though they know that it will mean a lower income and less security in old age.

There are also conflicts in goals among various members of the family. Dad may want to pay off the debt on the farm as rapidly as possible, but Mother might like to spend some money on improving the house; the children always seem to want, and need, more money for clothing and other items. Teamwork is necessary among family members in order for the farm manager to have enough funds to provide for family living, pay operating expenses, service debt, maintain and improve the business, and still provide a reasonable return to all the resources employed.

In farming, the farm operator and the family work for themselves; thus, they are largely free to establish their own goals and set their own pace in an attempt to reach those goals. No two farm families have the same goals in life. Some attempt to manage their farms to obtain the greatest possible amount of income, even though it means constant hard work and limited recreation for them. We sometimes refer to them as being too hungry for money to enjoy living.

At the opposite extreme, a few will place much more emphasis on leisure than on work. They would rather work less and accept a lower level of living than work harder and have more money to spend. Some refer to these people as being "easygoing." Others use the more common language and say they are "just plain lazy." Such farmers are usually too short of funds to buy the things that the family wants and needs. For them, old age is generally glum. As they advance in years, they become too old to work, and yet they are too poor to retire.

Most Farmers Live a Balanced Life

While we find a few farmers with the extreme points of view just referred to, the great mass of our successful farmers are somewhere between these extremes. They lead a *balanced life*, and all members of the family have some voice in how the family income should be spent. Their goal is to bring about a three-way balance. First, they manage the farm well enough and work hard enough to maintain a good level of living at present and for old age; second, they spend enough of their income to have a favorable level of living; and third, they take enough time off for fun and recreation so as to enjoy life as they go along.

Conflicts Within the Family
Bring Complications

Even though a family attempts to decide on general goals, there are always certain conflicts of interest among the different members. They cannot all agree on how much money should be saved, how much should be spent, and what it should be spent for. Most farmers—especially during their earlier years—owe money on their farm, and Dad is usually the first one to point out that the quicker they get the farm paid for, the sooner they get away from paying the bill for the interest on the money they owe.

But since farms are getting larger and larger, capital requirements are going up rapidly. Perhaps paying for the large modern farm each generation is asking too much. However, well-managed, productive farms should return enough money to pay labor as well as provide a fair return to capital. But this may not be easy, as we shall see.

Mother, who may do most of the housework, is anxious to have as many conveniences as possible to lighten her work load. Natu-

Fig. 1-1. The profitable management of farms like these would be an excellent goal of a prospective young farmer.

rally, she urges that the family put aside money for the purchase of things such as a better washing machine, a new vacuum cleaner, or an improved kitchen.

Frances, who is 16, doesn't worry much about paying for the farm or even getting a better washing machine. Instead, she insists that she needs new dresses, a new coat, and dozens of other items. "Dad," she says, "all the other girls in school have new clothes and I've got to dress as well as they."

Henry, who is 18, not only wants new clothes but also puts pressure on Dad to give him money to help buy a used automobile. "Can't you pay half of the money, Dad, if I pay the other half?" asks Henry.

So this conflict of interest goes on. Each member of the family wants something different—and it all costs money, which has to come out of the farm income.

Teamwork Is Necessary to Operate a Farm

Naturally, the first consideration of every farm manager is to operate the farm so as to make as high an income as possible. To make the maximum income would require a certain setup which not many farmers have. It would require, for example, sufficient funds to construct the needed farm buildings, to buy the required farm machinery and productive livestock, and to have sufficient operating capital available, as well as funds for family living. But few farmers have sufficient funds available for all these purposes. The job of the farm manager becomes one of seeing that the farm produces enough income to bring about a well-balanced life for the entire family while providing cash flow to meet operating expenses, capital purchases, and debt servicing. This is no simple problem, as any experienced farmer will tell you.

All members of the family need to talk over the problems and reach an agreement on the important goals for which they are striving. Among these might be to have (1) good food, (2) well-chosen, but not elaborate, clothing, (3) health and dental care, (4) a home that is comfortable, (5) proper education for the children, and (6) some savings for retirement. These are some basic goals.

Other goals might include recreation, financial support for their church, community involvement, and other things that make for happy, fruitful family living.

Fig. 1-2. When making a farm plan, the whole family should be consulted. Here the father discusses business management with his two sons.

Family Must Choose Between Present
Satisfactions and Longer-Term Values

No family, whether they live on the farm or in the city, can afford to buy everything they want. People have to pick and choose. In this picking and choosing they go without many things they would like to have. It is never an easy task to decide how much to spend to satisfy present desires and how much to spend for something that is less exciting at the moment but provides longer-term values. If one overemphasizes the satisfying of present desires at the expense of longtime permanent values, one is almost sure to pay the penalty later on.

Fig. 1-3. Women have always been an important part of the farm business. This woman manages this farm with cash crops and a dairy herd. (Courtesy, *Wisconsin Agriculturist*)

Success in Farming Has Its Reward

The true story which follows was adapted from an article by F. D. Farrell, past President of Kansas State University.

"Many years ago one of the stops on my farm milk route was the farm of Andrew and Mary, then in their early 30s. Without even suspecting the fact, Andrew and Mary were beginning to develop into a striking example of the importance of the *human factor*. They were 'poor,' as were their neighbors, but their hearts were high and they were happy.

"After an absence of more than 30 years, I revisited Andrew and Mary. The entire area had greatly changed. But Andrew and Mary's farm had changed more than anything else. Their small cottage that they lived in 30 years ago was now a storehouse at the rear of the farmstead. It had been replaced by a spacious two-story brick residence which stood on a site well landscaped with trees, shrubs, and flowers. Mary proudly called attention to the modern conveniences in the home. Comfort, convenience, and leisure characterized their farm home.

Neighborhood Contrasts. "The contrast between Andrew's position and that of several of his nearby neighbors was both painful and inspiring: painful, because it represented human tragedy for those who had failed; inspiring, because it suggested that most of the tragedy might have been averted. Andrew and Mary operated their farm and farm home under essentially the same conditions as had surrounded their neighbors who had failed. They had the same soil and the same climate. They were subject to the same federal, state, and local laws, regulations, and taxes. Their educational facilities— which were excellent—were equally available to everybody in the neighborhood.

"But obviously there was one great difference, a dominating one. It was the *human factor*. That factor is easy to name but difficult to explain. Andrew and Mary 'had what it takes,' while their less successful neighbors did not. What did it take? What qualities and practices of Andrew and Mary stand out sufficiently to set them apart from those of their neighbors that failed?

Qualities Essential for Success. "I should place first their *intense love for the land*. They looked upon their farming and rural life as a lifelong enterprise, a business combined with a way of living. With no thought of leaving the land, they made their plans on a long-range basis and adhered to them. The soil became more productive, the cows produced more milk, the fields brought larger yields of better crops as time went on.

"Another essential quality was *simplicity combined with good money management*. They pretty well followed the dictum for consumer goods, 'Pay as you go, and if you can't pay, don't go.' However, they used credit in the business where it was profitable to do so. In time, these practices enabled them to indulge pleasantly in owning many modern conveniences—all paid for.

"A third quality was a *veritable fondness for productive work*. They accepted work, not as a curse but as a blessing. Further, they spent time in managing the farm business.

"A fourth quality was a *persistent desire to learn*. Andrew and Mary regularly went to educational events sponsored by the state college. They belonged to a farm organization, to the crop improvement association, and to the dairy herd testing association. They belonged because active membership helped them to learn to do a better job and to work effectively with others in enterprises requiring group action.

"*Sustained intellectual interest* was a fifth quality. They were interested in national issues, in international questions, in history, philosophy, and science."

Fig. 1-4. These young people have completed a successful project year "earning while learning." (Courtesy, *Wisconsin Agriculturist*)

There were other qualities and practices, but those mentioned will suffice as examples. Those five qualities illustrate the way in which the human factor functions in making some farm families succeed while their neighbors, with identical environments, fail.

When we see, as we often do, a strikingly successful farm family separated from an obviously unsuccessful one by nothing visible except a barbed-wire fence, we usually are warranted in suspecting that the human factor is the basic cause of the difference. More than three centuries ago Shakespeare recognized the importance of this factor as applied to human affairs when he wrote:

> "Men at some time are masters of their fates:
> The fault, dear Brutus, is not in our stars.
> But in ourselves, that we are underlings."

Questions and Problems for Class Discussion

1. What are the important adjustments the various members of a farm family need to make so each one will have the things necessary for happy living and so there will still be enough money to service debt on the farm and to buy the equipment and other things necessary to operate the farm efficiently? Discuss fully in class.

2. What are six of the most important goals that a family should strive toward in an attempt to have a well-balanced program and a happy life for the *entire family*? What are your goals and values?

3. Do you agree with the general program and goals that Andrew and Mary followed through the years in building up their farm?

4. In your judgement, did they overstress the longtime (future) satisfactions?

5. As you read the account of their success, does it appear that they had unusual abilities or qualities? If so, what were they?

CHAPTER 2

Education and Training—
Keys to Success

Highlights of Chapter

Most young people reared on the farm have a choice of making farming their life work or going into non-farm vocations. Those who decide to leave the farm will need to determine rather carefully what kind of job they want and how much training and education will be needed to qualify for it. It would be unfortunate if one left the farm for the city, unqualified for anything but common labor.

In order to obtain the well-paying and desirable city jobs, one not only needs to have good training and education but also must have much more than average capability. However, this is also true for those who want to be successful farmers.

No engineer could hope to succeed without good training. But, in farming, training is equally essential. Today's agriculture is highly complex and exceedingly competitive. The successful farmer has to be well versed in production management technology and skills as well as in business and financial management techniques.

Farm operators need to be able to select and apply appropriate methods to obtain good crop yields without depleting the soil. They must, for example, be able to manage various livestock enterprises effectively and operate and service complicated equipment. All this must be done with top economic efficiency. Further, the farm operator must understand net worth statements, farm earnings statements, cash flow reports, estate planning, farm business arrangements, and a host of other things associated with farm business and financial management. This means that a successful farmer has to be well versed on many subjects.

Only the Better Farmers Will Succeed

Today, farming is a highly competitive business. Top-notch farmers will be successful, but average ones will barely get by, and many of the poorly informed and less able farmers will fail. Here is where your vocational training in agriculture will fill a basic need. It will provide much of the basic training necessary to make you a highly successful farm manager. However, you will need to continue to learn throughout your farming career if you are to remain competitive.

Vocational Agriculture Applies Science to Modern Farming

You have often heard it said that experience is the best teacher. We agree that experience may be an effective teacher, but it is also an expensive teacher. In fact, it may be extremely expensive to learn by experience only. It is a "hit-or-miss" method, and you generally "miss" as often as you "hit." Experience may keep you from making the same mistake twice, but you may make new ones which you might avoid if you had good training.

Where would farmers have been today if it had been necessary for each one to learn individually—by experience—how to test soil, how to determine the fertilizer and lime needed, how to set up a strip cropping system, how to practice contour farming, or how to determine economical feeding rations for livestock, to mention only a few problems in farming! Information on these subjects was developed after years of experimental effort by individual farmers, state experiment stations, the U.S. Department of Agriculture, and many private organizations.

Anyone who starts farming today without taking advantage of this vast store of knowledge is inviting trouble and may even be headed for failure. Modern farming cannot be successful on a self-experience hit-or-miss basis. It has to be approached on a scientific method where today's farmer cashes in on the experience of past generations of farmers and of organizations which have carried on research over the years. Actually, a person starting farming today

Fig. 2-1. The hog enterprise on this farm was assigned to these boys. This is one way to give farm youth experience and a start in farming. (Courtesy, National 4-H Service)

has the opportunity to benefit from the organized thinking and knowledge acquired over a long period of years.

The basic purpose of vocational agriculture is to give students the advantage of this tremendous background. Your instructors are specially trained in the basic production sciences and business practices needed to provide them a broad background in agriculture.

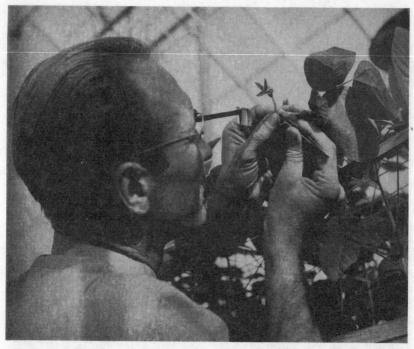

Fig. 2-2. People in agricultural research find their work stimulating and rewarding. But good education and training, which require several years of college work, are necessary. The goal is certainly a worthy one. (Courtesy, *Better Farming Methods*)

Vocational Training Gives the Basis
for a Good Start

When you enrolled in the vocational agriculture course you made your first decision to learn more about farming, farm management, or agri-business and agri-industry. Not only will you be learning in your classes and laboratory, but you will be carrying a project of your own where you will get practical experience under the direction of a well-trained instructor. This is a highly effective type of education. Most students in vocational agriculture join the Future Farmers of America, or FFA, an organization which adds interest to school work and provides many new stimulating experiences.

In many instances vocational agriculture gives young men and women their first start in farming. It is common for students to continue to increase the size of their project(s) until they gradually grow into a farming operation. Often it becomes the basis of a business arrangement with the family on the home farm. Later the home farm may be enlarged by acquiring more land or by intensifying the type of farming on the existing acres of the farm. "To large trees little chestnuts grow."

Young People Taking Vocational Agriculture
Have Decided Advantages

Young people choosing to take courses in agriculture will have a triple advantage when they start farming.

1. They will have a good classroom educational background covering many phases of the way science and business practices are applied to agriculture.

2. They will have the personal supervision of their project by a well-trained instructor.

3. They will have an opportunity to see how new methods can be applied to the home farm or a laboratory farm. For example, they

Fig. 2-3. Upon completion of a successful year, this young man received an award for outstanding performance. His vo-ag teacher (center) smiles proudly. (Courtesy, Ken Allen)

can analyze the farm to determine if it has the right amount and the right kinds of livestock and crops, and they can determine if the livestock is being fed the proper rations. They will learn what pesticides to use for different weeds, insects, and plant diseases. They will learn what kind of fertilizer is adapted to their soil and crops, the amount to use, and how to apply it. This training in the science of agriculture will give them an insight into the reasons why they must follow certain practices for success.

Today's Successful Farmer Must Be an Able Business Person

Years ago, farmers were sometimes pictured as people with weather-beaten faces and uncombed hair, wearing patched shirts and overalls. Such pictures left the impression that farmers were limited in intelligence and business ability. Here and there we still find people with similar ideas of today's farmers. This is extremely unfortunate, because nothing could be further from the truth. Typical farmers of today are well-trained, intelligent business persons. They must be well trained and capable to be successful. Their success is determined by their ability to make the right decisions in managing the farm. No one today can make money farming without having a grasp of modern production practices, as well as an understanding of the economics involved in the various phases of farming and good judgement!

Modern Farms Are Becoming Big Business Firms

In many instances, the total amount of capital invested in a farm, including machinery, livestock, buildings, and land, will add up to more than $175,000. On larger farms it will be still greater. Of course, most farmers have to borrow a considerable portion of this capital. But there is the same responsibility of managing a large and costly operation, whether or not it is fully paid for. Even the expense of household equipment is considerable, including such items as electric refrigerators and freezers, washing machines, and T.V. sets—to mention only a few items.

The Future Offers an Opportunity
in Farming

In these changing times, some farm operators are doing very well; others are less successful. Many are taking part time employment off the farm.

About 90% of all agricultural products are produced by less than 30% of the farmers. The other 70% produce only some 10% of the agricultural products. The increase in the size of farms is likely to continue, but at a slower rate. In the future we will see an increase in the number of acres per farm and a greater capital investment in the successful farms of tomorrow. An investment of $175,000 to $250,000 in a farm, in machinery, and in livestock will be required on many farms, and on some farms the investment will be even more.

A successful farm business should be so organized and managed that the yearly *gross income* should equal 30 to 35% of the capital investment in land, equipment, and livestock. Thus, in the years ahead, many family farms will need a gross income of $50,000 to $100,000 annually. There will be more specialization in particular kinds of crops and livestock and less diversification. The rate of earnings between the high and low efficiency farms will continue to widen. The family-sized farm will still predominate in agriculture for some time, but it will be a larger operation.

There will be good opportunities for young, aggressive farmers in the future. However, they will need considerable financial backing and business management as well as production management ability.

Larger Farms Will Require Costly
Farm Machinery

New kinds of labor-saving and cost-saving farm equipment and machines will be developed at a rapid rate in the future. For the most part, they will be relatively expensive, and farm managers will have to decide what kind of farm machinery can be used to advantage.

An important way to reduce the operating cost of a machine is to use it as extensively as possible. That is why modern machines generally pay out better on large farms than on small ones. If the farm you are operating is too small to make the best use of cost-saving machinery, it may pay to buy or rent more land so as to make more efficient use of modern equipment and machinery, or perhaps you can work out arrangements so several farmers can use the more costly machines and share the expense.

Fig. 2-4. Large, modern, costly farm machinery such as this requires large acreages. (Courtesy, John Deere)

Today's tractor, with both speed and power, naturally makes it possible for farmers to plow or cultivate more land or harvest more grain in a day than they could with smaller and poorer machinery drawn by horses. The result is that fewer farmers are needed to produce the total crops to feed the nation than were needed under a system using less advanced technology.

Some Changes Come Rapidly

No one can predict what is ahead, but it is certain that there will be a real future for the person who can adjust to the changing situation. However, the young person starting farming in the future will likely be faced with new problems. It is hoped that this course in farm management will help him or her to keep in step with the changing world of farming. There have always been farmers who made money when their neighbors were in financial trouble. That will likely be even more true in the future because of the rapid changes expected.

Some Young Folks on Farms Will Move
to City Jobs

Not all young people who are born and reared on the farm will want to stay there, partly because they believe that life in the city is preferable, or because they lack the necessary financial backing to obtain a farm large enough to provide a good living. If these young folks are able to get the necessary education and special training for a good job in the city, they may do better than they would on the farm. This would be especially true if they could train themselves to qualify as doctors, lawyers, or other professionals.

The choice of one's life occupation requires more careful thought than ordinary decisions because one's whole future may be at stake.

Suggestions to Help in Choosing
an Occupation

What are some of the things which may help a young person to decide whether to choose farming as a lifetime occupation or to take up some occupation in a city? First, you must find out what opportunities may be open. Here are some of the things you can do:

1. You may go to the city and attempt to get a job at common labor in a factory, a railroad, or a mining company. Sometimes a young person may leave the farm and start work with almost no delay, but these jobs are not rewarding.

2. You may go to a nearby town or village and get a job as a store clerk, a bus or taxi driver, a helper in a filling station, or an assistant mechanic in a garage. Other jobs which require more specialized training include positions as bookkeepers, stenographers, file clerks, and the like; you may, however, go into a business on your own.

3. You may go to the city, learn a trade, and become a machinist, carpenter, bricklayer, painter, or plumber. People with these skills are in demand, and the wages are good to excellent.

4. You may elect to get technical training in areas such as electronics or computer technology. Employers eagerly seek persons with technical skills.

5. After finishing high school, you may go to a college or a university for special training. For example, you may train yourself

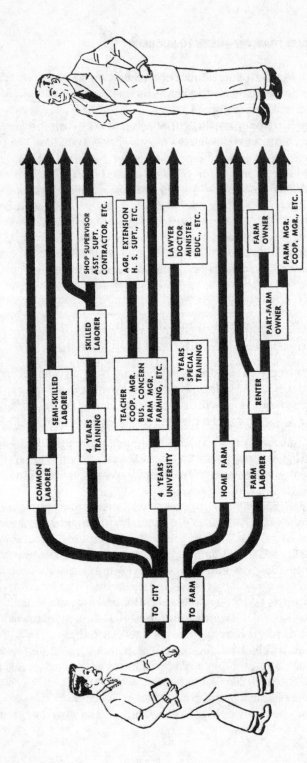

Fig. 2-5. Are you training yourself for one of these opportunities? Which one?

to become a teacher of agriculture, a county agricultural agent, or a forester, or to work with the many ag-related industries. A farm background will be a big asset.

6. College training could prepare you as a professional, such as an engineer, a medical doctor, a lawyer, a musician, or a minister.

Advantages of Non-farm and Farm Compared

Farm youths who want to find out how much they might be able to earn if they should go to the city should not consider the salaries of those with specialized training or with financial backing who receive the higher incomes; rather, they need to ask themselves these questions: "Considering my training, financial condition, and general background, what kind of a job can I reasonably expect to get? Am I in a position to spend the time, money, and effort to train myself to become a skilled worker, or a professional person, such as a doctor, a lawyer, an engineer, a forester, a county agricultural agent, or a high school or college teacher? Can I reasonably expect to get into a salaried position as an officer of a bank or into a key position, as, for instance, in a manufacturing plant, a wholesale house, or a brokerage company? Can I start a business of my own? Or, on the contrary, if I should decide to leave the farm for the city, will it be necessary for me to take a job at common labor, or at best, at semi-skilled labor?" Vocational counselors can be of assistance to young people in exploring many career opportunities, including non-farm but farm related occupations.

If we compare the average income per person of all people living in the city with the income per person of all those who live on farms, we would find that the income of those in the cities is somewhat higher than it is for farmers. But, in comparing incomes of two groups—farm and city—it is not sufficient to compare only money incomes. One has also to consider the expense—that is, actual cash outlay—of the city family compared with the family on the farm. City persons must buy all their food and fuel. Farmers produce some of their food and may get some of their fuel from the woodlot. Food, rent, fuel, and transportation to and from work are all major items in a city person's budget. They are less of a cost to the farmer because some of the food and fuel is produced right on the farm. But this difference is not as great as it was a generation ago.

How Can Young Persons Determine Their
Special Abilities?

A young person between 16 and 18 years of age may have an intense interest in becoming a doctor. Another at the same age may be equally anxious to become an electrical engineer. A third young person may have decided on law as a profession. Besides a liking for a certain profession or occupation, they all may think they have unusual natural ability along their own lines of interest. They may in fact be correct. Again, they may be entirely wrong in believing that they have an outstanding ability along a certain line just because they have an interest in it. The real difficulty is that they have no dependable way of finding out. Their high school work may be somewhat helpful in determining to what extent they really are unusually capable along particular lines, but it provides only a limited amount of evidence. It certainly furnishes no definite proof of such ability or talent. Practically all people have some particular interest. Such interest may or may not change from year to year; ordinarily it does.

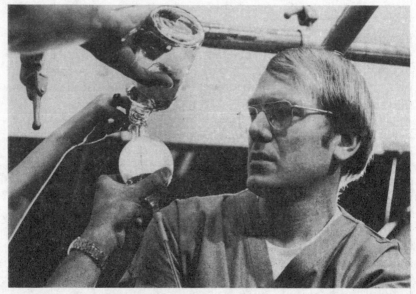

Fig. 2-6. This young veterinarian is working on a research project involving reproductive physiology. Hard work and many years of education are required to become a vet.

Sadly enough, a young person's interest in some particular thing at some particular period of youth is no positive indication that the person will continue to maintain that same interest. Nor does it furnish any convincing proof that the person has an outstanding talent along that line. To illustrate, many high school graduates have told the authors that they wanted to go to college and train to become mechanical engineers. We usually ask, "Why do you think you will like engineering?" To this question the most common answer is "I like to repair farm machinery and run Dad's automobile and tractor!" The next question usually asked is "Do you enjoy mathematics and do you have good grades in it?" Very few youths see any connection between this question and the question of becoming a mechanical engineer. "Why do you ask me that question?" they inquire. We try to explain that the principles of mechanical engineering are based largely on mathematics, and unless one has a liking for and considerable ability in mathematics, that person is not likely to be very successful as an engineer, no matter how much he

Table 2-1. Experienced Civilian Labor Force by Occupation (Distribution by Percentage)

	Percentage	
Occupation	1966	1974
Professional and technical workers	12.5	14.4
Managers and administrators (except farm)	9.9	10.0
Sales workers	6.2	6.3
Clerical workers	16.1	17.6
Craft and kindred workers	13.1	13.0
Operatives	19.2	16.1
Non-farm laborers	5.1	5.3
Private household workers	2.6	1.3
Service workers (except private households)	10.2	12.5
Farmers and farm managers	2.8	1.7
Farm laborers and supervisors	2.2	1.6
	100[1]	100[1]
Total number (1,000's)	75,299	91,796

[1]Due to rounding, these columns do not total 100%.

or she enjoys repairing and operating a tractor. The fact is that most young people—especially young men—like to work with automobiles and tractors. This is probably because they like to see action and power!

The important point is that a young person may have leanings toward a particular occupation because of some distorted idea of what it involves. Young people may think they can become great engineers by operating a powerful machine. Actually, however, engineers generally become great because of their ability to work out complex mathematical formulas, not because they can operate a powerful machine after a well-trained and capable engineer has designed and built it.

On a modern large farm the owner-operator spends little time in the actual field operations.

Jim Kelly (not his real name) operates a 3,000-acre farm (more than 5 sections). Here is a sample of his activities for one day. At 8:00 in the morning he hops into his pickup truck and drives around his wheat, corn, and sugar beet farm to check the progress of the crops. Along the way he checks the various fields and then pulls out his pocket calculator to determine just how much pesticide and irrigation water will be needed.

This information is passed to one of his boys or to a hired man, who provides the amounts of these necessary to maximize the crop income for the season.

After lunch the operator enters his small office to plan the farm operations for the days ahead.

Successful farmers operating these huge farms are well educated and trained to control vast amounts of capital, adding up to, say, $2 million or $3 million!

But a farm doesn't have to be that large for a family to make an excellent living. Many well-operated, medium-sized farms are paying good returns.

Questions and Problems for Class Discussion

1. What particular training or education would you have to have in order to get and hold the city job you would like?

2. How long would this training and education take, and how much do you estimate it would cost?

3. Discuss the important advantages or disadvantages of farming compared with the particular type of non-farm job for which you think you may qualify.

4. What do you consider some important advantages of staying on the farm instead of moving to the city?

5. What do you think would be some important advantages of leaving the farm and going to the city? How does this fit with your goals, values, and capabilities?

6. What sort of a program of training and experience are you planning for yourself? Do you have the funds needed to carry it out?

CHAPTER 3

Agriculture in the United States[1]

Highlights of Chapter

Not all the vast U.S. land mass is cropland. Much of it is forest and grassland.

Over the years certain types of farming have become dominant in specific areas of the United States. A certain type of farming is developed because it gives the most satisfactory returns to the farmers in that area.

Wheat and other small grains are grown primarily in the Great Plains States. Hogs are grown in the Central States, where corn is highly productive. Cotton is grown in the South, where the climate is favorable. It is a general principle that farmers will produce the crops and grow the kind of livestock that have the greatest comparative advantage in their area.

Many forces influence the type of farming, the most important of which are:

1. Physical factors—chiefly climate, topography, and soil.
2. Economic factors—such as the price of land, distance to market, transportation facilities, and labor requirements.

The United States has a rich and varied agriculture. From the Canadian border to the Gulf of Mexico and from the Atlantic to the Pacific, U.S. farmers are actively engaged in producing food and fiber for our use and for export.

In the United States less than 1 acre of every 5 is used as cropland. The total number of acres in grassland is noticeably greater than the number in cropland, amounting to almost one-third of

---

[1]Note: The maps and data in this chapter are the most recent census data available. General trends of agricultural production areas change very slowly.

MAJOR USES OF LAND

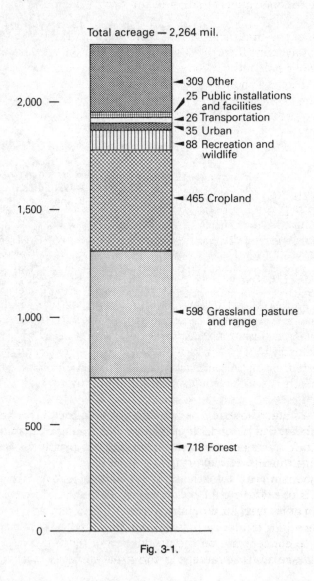

MIL. ACRES
2,500 —

Total acreage — 2,264 mil.

2,000 —

◄ 309 Other

25 Public installations
and facilities
◄ 26 Transportation
◄ 35 Urban
◄ 88 Recreation and
wildlife

◄ 465 Cropland

1,500 —

1,000 —

◄ 598 Grassland pasture
and range

500 —

◄ 718 Forest

0 ——

Fig. 3-1.

the total acres of the nation. More than one-third is in forest, and the balance is used for various other purposes as shown in Fig. 3-1.

The land in farms is not evenly distributed throughout the United States. (See Fig. 3-2.) However, the cropland is more concentrated. The upper central part of the United States has the greatest concentration of some of the best cropland in the world. (See Fig. 3-3.)

One of the measures of size in farming is the amount of gross sales. Today many farm families have income from off-farm sources. In fact, over half of the income to farm families comes from off-farm sources. Fig. 3-4 shows that only 6.6% of the farms produce about 54% of the gross sales. When we consider farms with over a $40,000 gross, we see that about 21% of those farms produce over 78% of the value of sales.

Comparative Advantage

In any given area most of the farmers follow nearly the same pattern and practices of crop and livestock production. This results in a particular type of farming within a region which becomes quite fixed. This means that a farming type area has been established after many years of effort put forth by individual farmers to adjust their capital, labor, and managerial ability to get the greatest net return. Those products which have been the most profitable over the years are being produced in larger amounts while the less profitable ones have gradually faded out.

To illustrate: Some decades ago many sheep were kept on New York farms. But gradually the demand for fluid milk in the eastern city markets made dairying more profitable than sheep raising, so dairying gradually came in. You could say the cows drove the sheep out of the state. Sheep raising is now established in the range region where sheep can be raised to better advantage than any other type of livestock. In that area sheep raising has a greater comparative advantage than it would have in any other area.

Wisconsin was once a great wheat state, but dairying has pushed it out. Instead of producing wheat, the land is now used mostly to grow feed for the dairy herds.

There is a tendency of any economic unit—farm, region, or nation—to concentrate on the production of those items for which that unit's relative advantage is the greatest or its relative disad-

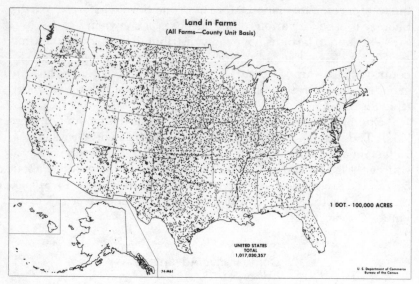

Fig. 3-2.

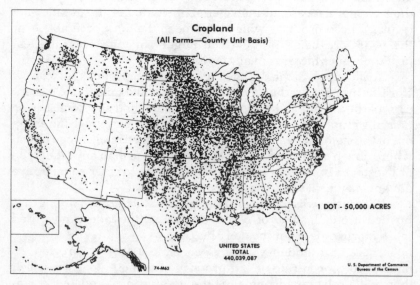

Fig. 3-3.

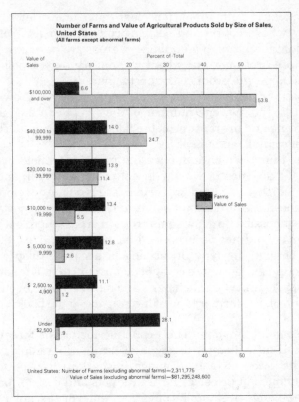

Number of Farms and Value of Agricultural Products Sold by Size of Sales,
United States
(All farms except abnormal farms)

Fig. 3-4.

vantage is the least. For this reason economic units specialize and trade with other nations for what they want.

The dominance of a certain type of farming does not mean that other types do not also exist in that area. There are only a few areas where a single farm enterprise, such as dairying, is carried on to the exclusion of all other enterprises.

Factors or Forces Affecting Types of Farming

1. Physical Factors. The physical factors include mainly climate, topography, and soil. These three factors have more to do with the type of farming followed in any given area than any other consideration. You have little or no control over these physical factors, so you adjust your farming to them. It is clear that climate determines the boundary where cotton and certain fruits and vegetables can be grown profitably. Rough mountainous areas are best used for grazing. In these areas corn or wheat will not pay out. A soil which is slightly alkaline will produce the best alfalfa.

Climatic conditions influence length of the growing season—that is, the average number of days between the last killing frost in spring and the first one in the fall, the degree of sunshine, the amount of rainfall, and the like.

Other things which influence the type of farming include the presence or absence of weeds, insect pests, and crop and animal diseases which are found in certain areas. The development of hardier and disease-resistant seeds and earlier maturing varieties has made it possible to grow some crops in areas where old varieties and strains could not be produced economically. This, of course, tends to change the type of farming in an area. Crop or animal diseases or pests have often compelled farmers to shift to some other enterprise. Again, when such pests and diseases have been brought under control, the former type of farming has come back.

2. Economic Factors. The economic factors or forces have a pronounced influence on the type of farming. Examples of these include the price of land, distance to market, transportation facilities, changes in prices of farm products and costs of producing them, the relative profitability of various enterprises, labor requirements, and available supply and cost of labor.

These economic forces influence the farmers' decisions on whether they will produce a certain product. Normally, farmers are interested in the answer to the question: "Will it pay?"

3. Other Considerations. Persons who expect to start farming will want to attempt to satisfy their personal likes and dislikes; that is, they will want to select the area where the type of farming they prefer is carried on.

A few people have tried to practice a type of farming which does not fit an area, but in almost every case, they have found it an uphill job. Of course, in areas where the type of farming is not clear-cut, there will be fewer disadvantages to overcome. In fact, there are many instances where the type of farm is determined more by market conditions than by all the combined factors we have just discussed. For example, milk may be produced for city markets in areas which are by no means dairy areas, but the advantage of nearness to market is so great that it outweighs many disadvantages.

CROPS

The factors just discussed affect the location of the production of various crops. Let us now look at some of the major crops produced in the United States.

Corn

Corn is king of all the crops grown. Fig. 3-5 shows the concentration of corn in what are called the "Corn Belt" States. This area, especially the central part of it, has a combination of climate, soil, and topography ideal for growing corn. It has a long growing season and warm (or hot) days and nights. The soil is rich and deep, and the surface of the soil is well adapted for large-sized farm machinery. These are the ideal conditions for production of a large yield of corn at low cost. However, even with all these advantages for growing corn, it is generally not produced on much more than half of the crop

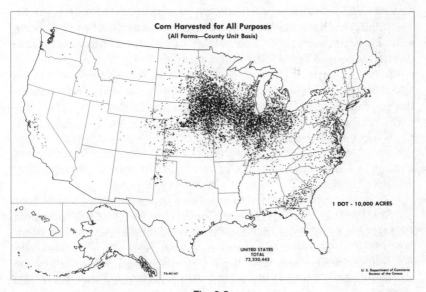

Fig. 3-5.

acreage. Soybeans, wheat, oats, hay, and other crops are used in rotation with it.

Sorghum

Sorghum is another important crop. As you can see by the map in Fig. 3-6, most of the sorghum is grown slightly southwest of the Corn Belt and in Texas. Sorghum can stand hotter and drier conditions than can corn. In these areas, sorghum will do better comparatively than will corn.

Wheat

There are two main wheat areas in the United States—the winter wheat area and the spring wheat area. The hard winter wheat area consists of Oklahoma, Kansas, Nebraska, and eastern Colorado. The most influential factor for production of wheat in this area is climate, which includes rainfall and temperature. The lack of rain and rapid evaporation in summer months limit the growing of corn. In the place of corn you will find grain sorghums. Some grazing is practiced where conditions are more favorable for this than for raising a large acreage of wheat.

The other large area is the spring wheat area of North Dakota and adjoining portions of the states of Montana, Minnesota, and South Dakota. Flax is a common crop grown in the rotation with wheat in this area.

Wheat is also grown in the rotation with corn and other grains in the southern Corn Belt extending eastward. This is the soft winter wheat region known as the corn and wheat region, corn being the more important crop. (See Fig. 3-7.)

Soybeans

Soybean production has increased dramatically over the past years. You will note that soybeans are grown in many of the same areas as is corn, but slightly further south. (See Fig. 3-8.) Also note the heavy production area along the Mississippi River. Soybeans are sometimes planted as a second crop following another early type of crop.

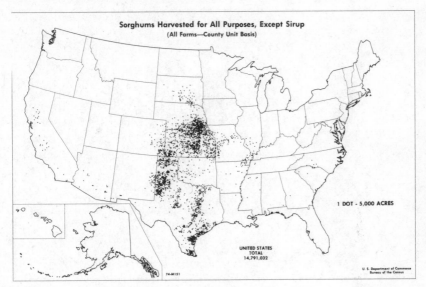

Fig. 3-6.

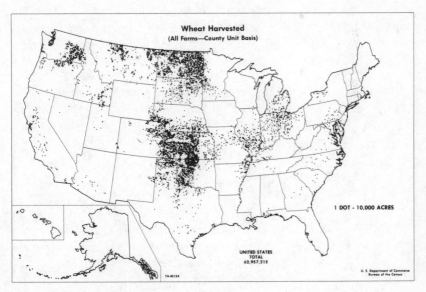

Fig. 3-7.

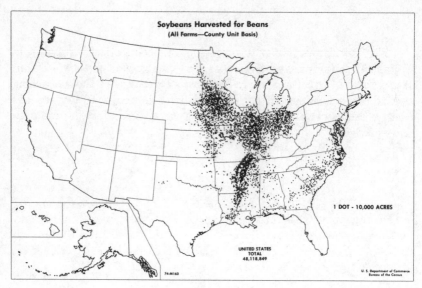

Fig. 3-8.

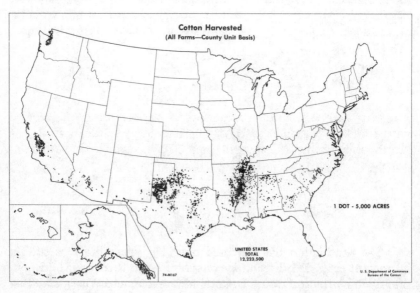

Fig. 3-9.

Cotton

Fig. 3-9 shows that cotton production is concentrated mainly in Texas, Mississippi, and Arkansas, but it is grown in over a dozen states from North Carolina to California. Because of the increasing use of large equipment where level land is necessary, there has been a decided shift from the hilly areas to more level areas with larger fields.

Rice

Rice production is concentrated in Arkansas, Louisiana, Texas, California, and Mississippi. (See Fig. 3-10.) The United States produces only a small fraction of the world production, but rice is an important cash crop in the five states mentioned.

Peanuts

Peanuts are produced in only a few states, including Virginia, North and South Carolina, Florida, Oklahoma, and Texas, with the main concentration in Georgia and Alabama. (See Fig. 3-11.)

Barley

The barley area is most important to the northwest of the central oat-producing region. (See Fig. 3-12.) The main producing states are North and South Dakota, Montana, Idaho, California, and Minnesota.

Oats

Oat production has declined over the years but it is still an important crop. Production is concentrated in the upper Midwest, mainly in North and South Dakota, Minnesota, and Wisconsin. (See Fig. 3-13.)

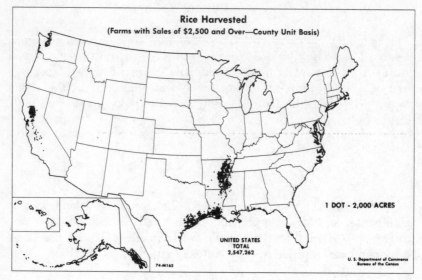

Fig. 3-10.

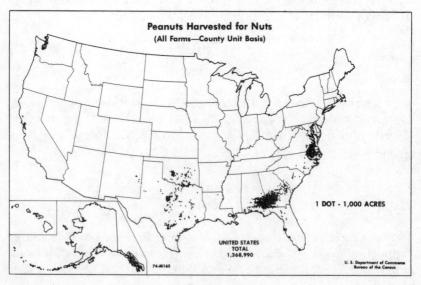

Fig. 3-11.

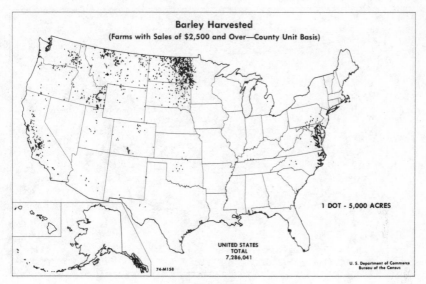

Fig. 3-12.

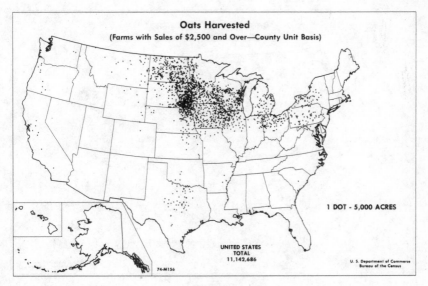

Fig. 3-13.

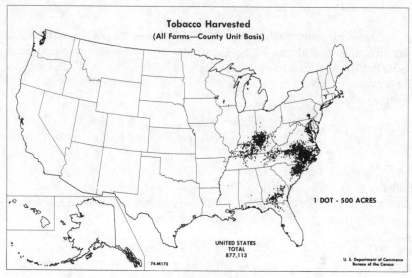

Fig. 3-14.

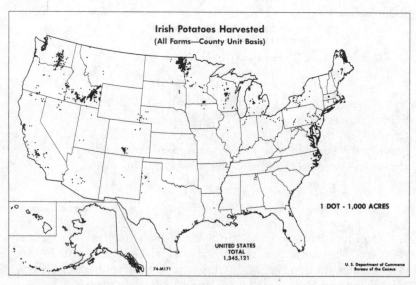

Fig. 3-15.

Tobacco

Tobacco requires a good deal of hand work. It is generally a small-scale operation. The heavy tobacco areas are in North and South Carolina, Kentucky, and Virginia. (See Fig. 3-14.) Each type of tobacco is grown in a specific area of the tobacco-growing sections of the country.

Irish Potatoes

Potatoes are an important cash crop in several concentrated areas. Fig. 3-15 shows pockets of potato-growing areas scattered throughout the United States. Special soil, water, and climatic conditions are vital for profitable potato production.

Hay

Hay is an important crop, especially on land not suited to intensive row cropping. It is a vital feed in ruminant livestock nutrition. Land in hay is well protected from the ravages of erosion and thus helps conserve soil. As can be seen in Fig. 3-16, hay is grown in all areas of the country where there is cropland. Compare this map to Fig. 3-3.

Vegetables

Vegetables are an important part of a balanced human diet. Vegetable production is highly specialized. Most major vegetable production is close to processing plants—canning, freezing, and drying—or where markets are readily accessible. Vegetables require very specific soil, water, and climatic conditions. Fig. 3-17 shows the location of major vegetable-producing areas.

Orchards

Orchard crops would include citrus fruits, apples, pears, cherries, etc. The major concentrations are in California and Florida, with important production in states such as Washington, Oregon, Michigan, and New York, as well as other states. (See Fig. 3-18.)

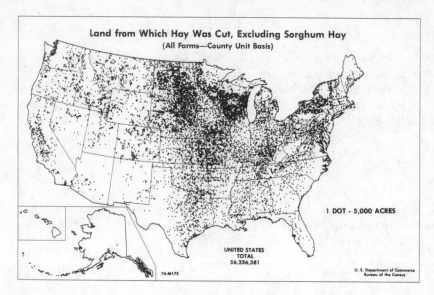

Fig. 3-16.

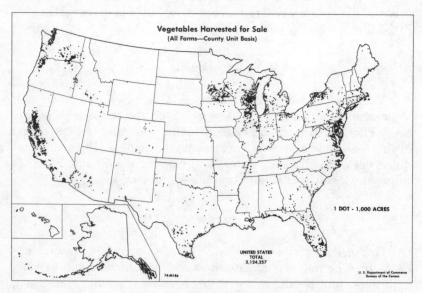

Fig. 3-17.

Fig. 3-18.

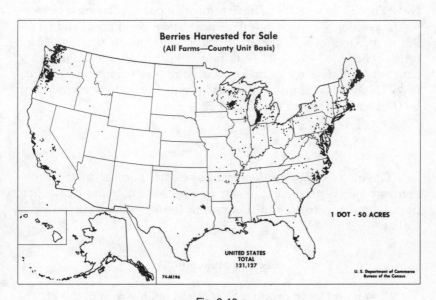

Fig. 3-19.

Berries

Berries are important in selected areas but are grown throughout the United States. The states along the Pacific, the states along the Atlantic, Wisconsin, and Michigan are the main producing areas. (See Fig. 3-19.)

LIVESTOCK

Livestock production is generally found in areas which produce crops that can be used as livestock feed. Thus, the type of livestock farmed in an area is closely tied to the crop production characteristics of the area. Let us look at the location and distribution of various kinds of livestock.

Cattle

Fig. 3-20 shows the distribution of all cattle and calves. Note this is quite similar to the distribution of the hay-producing areas shown in Fig. 3-16. But Fig. 3-21 shows that milk cows are concentrated in states such as Wisconsin, Minnesota, California, Pennsylvania, and New York. While all states have some milk cows, dairying is becoming increasingly concentrated in those specialized areas shown on the map. Beef cow distribution closely follows the location of hay production. (See Fig. 3-22.) But finished cattle production is highly concentrated near the corn- and sorghum-producing areas. Texas, Iowa, Nebraska, Kansas, California, and Colorado are important beef-producing states. (See Fig. 3-23.)

Hogs and Pigs

The major swine-producing areas closely parallel the most concentrated corn-producing areas. In Fig. 3-24, note the heavy hog population is in Iowa and Illinois and the immediate surrounding states.

Sheep and Lambs

Sheep and lamb production is found mainly west of the Missis-

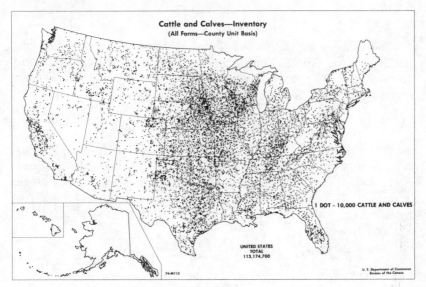

Fig. 3-20.

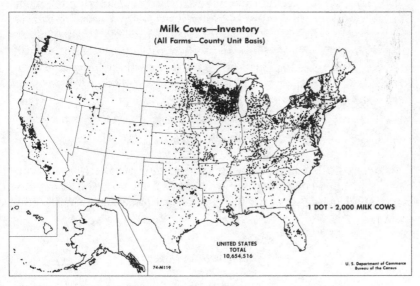

Fig. 3-21.

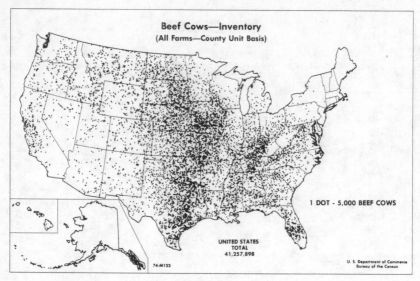

Fig. 3-22.

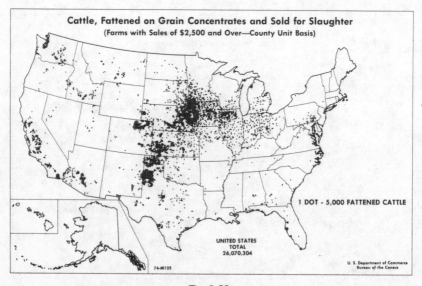

Fig. 3-23.

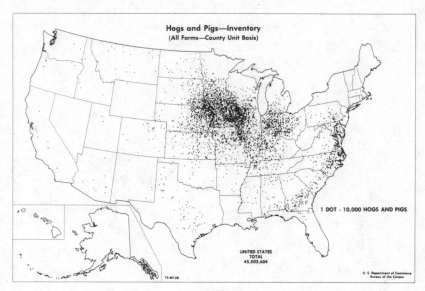

Fig. 3-24.

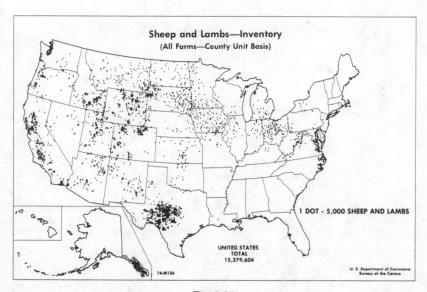

Fig. 3-25.

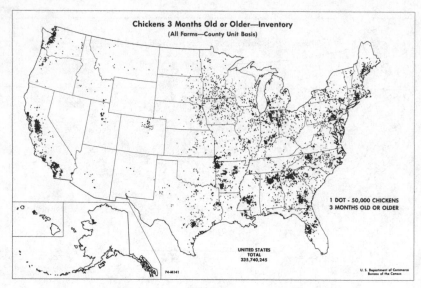

Fig. 3-26.

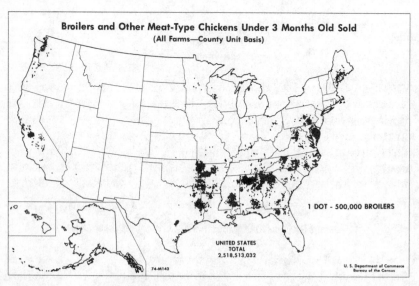

Fig. 3-27.

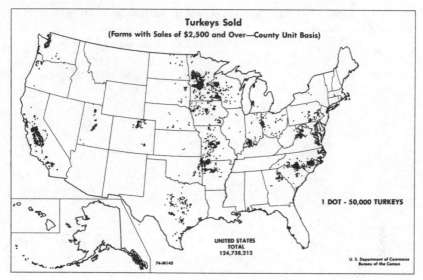

Fig. 3-28.

sippi River. Texas, Colorado, California, Wyoming, South Dakota, Idaho, Utah, Oregon, Montana, and Iowa are especially noted for sheep and wool production. (See Fig. 3-25.)

Poultry

Figs. 3-26 and 3-27 show the location of the chicken industry. It is broken into two categories: (1) the chickens kept for eggs and (2) the broiler and meat-type chickens. The latter are heavily concentrated in southeastern states, while the former are somewhat more widely distributed throughout the United States. Turkey production is concentrated mainly in Minnesota, California, and Wisconsin, with other pockets of production in several other states. (See Fig. 3-28.)

Questions and Problems for Class Discussion

1. What types of crops and livestock do you produce on your farm? Or what types of crops and livestock do you expect to produce on your farm?

2. Explain why certain crops and livestock production occur in the same location.

3. What is comparative advantage? How does it apply to your area?

4. What are important factors which determine the type of farming in your area?

CHAPTER 4

The Nature of the Management Job and Decision Making

Highlights of Chapter

The role of management is becoming increasingly important. Farm managers must use organized decision making and must understand the nature of the management job to arrive at appropriate business decisions. Farm managers operate their farms to make money or to attain other specified goals. They must effectively manage their land, labor, and capital to succeed.

There is a difference between a successful farm and a successful farmer. A farmer may be financially successful by taking over the home farm, or by acquiring one through marriage with no debts, or by inheriting one from a rich uncle! Often such farmers follow methods and practices which would not meet interest and principal payments on a mortgage if these had to be paid along with family living and operating expenses.

Farm business management is the coordination and supervision of the farm business for long-run maximum profits or other specified goals.

A good farm manager must know something about agricultural production sciences, production economics, marketing, purchasing, personnel management, financial management, estate planning, farm business arrangements, and world affairs. These must be integrated into a total farm business management program. The farm manager must make decisions concerning the use of farm resources in crop and livestock production. Further, the manager must coordinate and supervise the implementation of these decisions. Farmers must manage their land, labor, and capital and attempt to reach their goals with their various enterprises.

Business and Financial Management Is Growing More Important

The process of farm management is becoming more important with every passing year. This is due to a variety of reasons.

Profit margins per unit of output have been narrowing, and we can expect this to continue. New technology has been increasing at a rapid rate, so successful farmers must spend more time learning new technology. They also must learn to decide which technology is profitable for their individual set of circumstances. With increasing farm size, narrower profit margins, and new technology, there is a need for larger and larger amounts of capital. Use of more capital in the business requires greater knowledge of financial strategies. The transfer of the farming business from one generation to another is a management problem that calls for increasing skills. Farmers want and deserve the same standard of living enjoyed by people in other occupations utilizing the same amount and kind of resources. It takes efficient management of land, labor, and capital to do these things.

Nature of the Management Job

Management of the farm is a continuous and challenging process because it is affected by many changes. Fluctuations in weather conditions and prices of farm products, diseases, and technological innovations are constantly taking place. In addition, government programs, changes in credit policies, tax structure, and the general economic climate are usually in somewhat of a turmoil. All these factors, along with changing values and goals, force farmers continually to make decisions and to be on the alert.

Some typical management decisions deal with what combination of crops to grow, what combination of livestock to produce, what resources to devote to a specific unit, how to substitute resources for each other, what the best size of operation or enterprise is, and how production and marketing should be timed. Because of the difference between farmers and their farming resources there is

Fig. 4-1. These farmers are getting help from their county agent in forage testing and ration balancing. (Courtesy, *Wisconsin Agriculturist*)

no one answer. *Farmers must therefore become skilled decision makers.*

For several reasons, all decisions are different. Some are made only once. Some may be postponed. Equal knowledge about the decisions is not always available, and some decisions—once they are made—cannot be changed. All decisions are not of equal importance; some hinge on others.

You, as a manager and decision maker, have certain goals for your family and your business. You are the one who has the control so you must make decisions, take the risks associated with them, and deal with the consequences.

As a family person you are concerned with providing a decent standard of living for yourself and your family, and you are interested in how your income compares with those for other occupations. As a farm business person you are concerned with your return to land, capital, and labor, as well as your competitive position with other farmers having similar resources.

Management is not a manual skill, nor is it a recipe-type skill. There are no simple textbook-type answers to management problems. Good managers need to be good thinkers! They need concepts, principles, and theories to guide them in the application of farm management skills.

The Decision-making Process

Many decisions are made on the basis of habits, customs, or hunches. But to be an effective manager you must base decisions on logic. There are several simple direct steps in the decision-making process using logic. We will list these and make a few comments about each step.

1. *Determine your goals and values*—All people have certain things they want to accomplish. Earning a comfortable living is a key goal. But certain other values are important even though it may be difficult to measure them.

2. *Appraise your resources*—Here you need an inventory of your land, buildings, machinery, livestock, and capital. Look at the capacity and condition of all these resources. You also need to look at your labor supply, including yourself and your family. Most important, you have to look at your own management ability.

3. *Define the problem*—Good managers have to look at their situations closely to see what problems they have, in order to outline specifically what problem they are attempting to solve.

4. *Recognize the alternatives*—Most problems have different ways and means of being solved. You must recognize the different methods of solving them.

5. *Get all relevant facts about the different alternatives*—Once you have recognized the various alternative ways of solving the problem you must gather facts about the different alternatives.

6. *Compare outcomes of alternatives*—Here you must carefully analyze each alternative to see what the expected outcome would be if you selected that alternative.

7. *Decide by selecting the best alternative*—Having analyzed

Fig. 4-2. A farm couple should use their farm records as the basis for making logical decisions based on facts for the farm business. (Courtesy, *Wisconsin Agriculturist*)

each alternative, you can now decide how these outcomes compare with your goals and values. Finally, select the alternative which comes closest to your goals and values from Step 1.

8. *Implement the decision*—Once a decision is made it is necessary to put it to work if progress is to be made. Failing to implement a decision is like making no decision at all.

9. *Accept the consequences*—When managers make their decisions and implement them, they must deal with the consequences.

10. *Evaluate the decision*—Each decision must be reviewed to see if it was a good one. Doing this will help you gain experience and will make other decisions easier and will probably improve future decisions.

As a brief summary, to successfully manage a farm, you must be a good decision maker. Farm management is concerned with the decisions that affect the profitability of the farm business. So we take our scarce resources of land, labor, and capital and manage or allocate them to the best alternative uses in an attempt to reach the goals consistent with our values.

What to Expect from a Farm

To be financially successful, a farm should produce an income large enough to (1) pay all farm operating expenses, (2) maintain inventories, (3) maintain capital items, (4) provide reasonable returns to equity capital, (5) provide a reasonable return to the operator's unpaid labor and management, (6) provide a reasonable return to unpaid family labor, and (7) allow for reasonable debt servicing.

The successful management of a farm depends upon the ability of farm operators to organize their resources (land, labor, and capital) that are at their command. They must also follow improved methods and economical practices of crop and livestock production that will result in a nearly maximum annual income.

A farm is the place where you must fit together the production of several crops and animals in their proper relationship. To do this requires much ability. If some methods and practices are followed perfectly while others are neglected, the chances for success are reduced. There are close relationships among many of these practices, because one may affect another.

There are general principles of farm management which determine the extent of success, but let us stress that no two farms are alike; neither are any two operators alike. Therefore, the methods and practices being followed on one farm will be quite different from those followed on an adjoining one. It is equally true that some animals must be handled differently from others, even in the same herd or flock. Success on any particular farm depends very much on the individual operator, but only to the extent that certain methods and practices are followed. People must think for themselves on their individual farms. You are the one who must decide how well the practices you have in mind will work on your farm.

Farm management then is knowing what factors affect farm profit and controlling the important factors so that returns are high.

The average person has five senses: sight, taste, smell, touch, and hearing. The successful farm manager has one more: common!

Questions and Problems for Class Discussion

1. What is farm business management?

2. Why is business and financial management growing more important?

3. Describe the nature of the management job.

4. What are the steps in the decision-making process? Apply them to a specific situation.

5. What seven things should a financially successful farm provide?

CHAPTER 5

Economic Principles and Concepts in Farm Business Management[1]

Highlights of Chapter

Economic principles and concepts can aid farm managers in arriving at the best decision for a given set of circumstances.

To understand these principles and concepts, one first needs to learn the meaning of some words associated with them.

This chapter deals with the law of diminishing returns, the equimarginal principle, the opportunity cost concept, the substitution principle for inputs and outputs, cost relationships, risk and uncertainty, and the time value of money concept.

These economic principles are an important aid in making organized decisions in the easiest manner possible.

Before going further in our discussion of farm management, we should discuss a few basic and very important economic principles. These can help you understand the process of successful farm management and can guide your decision making.

Some Words We Will Need to Know

To begin with, we first need to define some terms. These terms will be used throughout this book. You also will use these terms in thinking and talking about managing your farm business.

---

[1]Authors' note to instructors: Chapter 5 will require some extra time and effort in teaching, but the material can be comprehended and used by the class. These basic economic principles are vital to a sound understanding of farm management.

1. *Economic principle*—A law which has wide application to the allocation of scarce resources (land, labor, and capital) to the best, or optimal, alternative ends. Principles are a very convenient means of using available information. Principles save time and work as they are basically common sense which can be used in logical decision making. The use of principles helps get to the right answers to management questions.

2. *Inputs, resources, and factors*—An input is an ingredient used in the production of a product. Alternative names are *resources* or *factors*. Examples: tons of fertilizer, dollars of capital, hours of labor.

3. *Outputs, products, and commodities*—An output results when inputs are combined in a production process. Alternative names are *products* or *commodities*. Examples: bushels of corn, pounds of milk, tons of hay, pounds of pork.

Note: An *output* may also be an *input*. Fertilizer is used to produce corn and corn is in turn used to produce pork. Therefore, corn can be termed both an *input and an output*. It is an *output* of the corn enterprise and an *input* of the hog enterprise.

4. *Classification and definition of inputs*—Inputs are commonly classified into one of four categories: (a) *land*, (b) *capital*, (c) *labor*, and (d) *management*.

a. *Land* is natural wealth used in production. It is created without use of human resources. Besides soil, land also includes native trees, minerals, and wild animals.

b. *Capital* is wealth used in production. It differs from land in that it is man-made rather than found in nature. Examples of capital include machinery, fertilizer, and buildings.

c. *Labor* is the physical human energy used in production.

d. *Management* is the mental human energy used in production. Management is primarily concerned with *decision making* and *risk bearing*.

5. *Physical and economic relationships*—

a. A *physical relationship* refers to associations between inputs and/or outputs in their *physical* (non-monetary) states. For example, a *physical* relationship between fertilizer and corn could be expressed as 40 pounds of fertilizer per 80 bushels of corn.

b. An *economic relationship* refers to associations between inputs and/or outputs in *monetary* terms. For example, it may take 3 cents' worth of concentrates to produce 15 cents' worth of milk.

6. *Marginal* or *added*—Refers to the *last* or additional unit of either an input or an output. In physical terms, if we apply an *additional* 100 pounds of fertilizer per acre, then 100 pounds is the marginal input. If this 100 pounds of fertilizer *increases* production per acre by 10 bushels of corn, then the *marginal* or *added* physical product is 10 bushels. *Marginal* also refers to monetary terms. The concept of marginalism underlies many economic principles, and it should be thoroughly understood.

7. *Fixed costs*—Refers to those costs which do not vary with the level of production for a given planning period. These fixed costs are associated with inputs which have been committed to the production process by previous planning. Typically, these are Depreciation, Interest, Repairs, Taxes, and Insurance, often called the D.I.R.T.I. five. Fixed costs then are those costs which would occur whether we produce something or not. They remain essentially the same regardless of the production level reached.

8. *Variable costs*—Refers to those costs which change with the level of production. They change as output, or production, changes and only occur when production takes place. Examples are fuel, pesticides, seed, feed, fertilizer, etc. Some *variable costs* become fixed, once they are put into the business. Pesticides once applied to the crop become *fixed costs* to that crop.

9. *Short run*—Refers to a period of time short enough so that some inputs are fixed. Generally we think of this as one production planning period.

10. *Long run*—Refers to a period of time long enough that all inputs can vary in quantity. But we generally think of the long run as several or a series of production planning periods.

This should give us enough of a fundamental vocabulary to begin our discussion of these vital economic principles of use to the farm manager. Indeed, these principles can be useful in all businesses, including the business of running a household.

Economic Principles Under Conditions of Certainty

To start we will look at these economic principles, assuming we live in a certain world where we can predict things with accuracy. Later we will relax this assumption and deal with risk and uncertainty.

The Law of Diminishing Returns

The law of diminishing returns states that as marginal (additional) units of a variable input are added to a fixed quantity of some other inputs, the resulting output will first increase then decrease, and finally may become negative, when all other inputs are fixed. That may sound like a long, complicated statement, but in reality it is quite simple and logical.

Let us take an example of fertilizer applied to corn with the quantity and quality of all other resources held constant. Table 5-1 shows the physical input (fertilizer) and physical output (corn) response on one acre (the fixed input) of corn.

Table 5-1. Physical Input–Output Data: Fertilizer on Corn (Hypothetical Data)

Line No.	(1)[1] Total Lbs. of Fertilizer	(2)[1] Added or Marginal Lbs. of Fertilizer	(3)[2] Total Bu. of Corn (T.P.P.)	(4)[3] Added or Marginal (M.P.P.) Bu. of Corn	(5)[4] Bu. of Corn per 100-Lb. Unit of Fertilizer (A.P.P.)	
1	0	0	40	0	0	
2	100	100	44	4	44	Stage I
3	200	100	90	46	45	
4	300	100	120	30	40	
5	400	100	140	20	35	
6	500	100	150	10	30	Stage II
7	600	100	156	6	26	
8	700	100	158	2	22.6	
9	800	100	159	1	19.9	
10	900	100	158	− 1	17.6	Stage III

[1]Col. 1 is the actual input (fertilizer) used. Col. 2 is the added fertilizer used and is computed by subtracting Line 1, Col. 1, from Line 2, Col. 1, to equal Line 2, Col. 2, and so on down the column.

[2]Col. 3 is the actual number of bu. or physical amount produced. It is the Total Physical Product (T.P.P.).

[3]Col. 4 is the added or marginal bu. of corn produced and is called the Marginal Physical Product (M.P.P.). It is the difference between the T.P.P. in the prior line and the T.P.P. in the same line, or Line 2, Col. 3, minus Line 1, Col. 3, equals Line 2, Col. 4, and so on down the column.

[4]The average Physical Product (A.P.P.) is the T.P.P. (Col. 3) divided by the units of the variable input used (Col. 1 fertilizer).

We added a variable input (fertilizer) to a constant quantity of all other inputs it takes to produce corn. The marginal output (corn, Col. 4) first increased and then decreased for each added 100 pounds of marginal input (fertilizer). Finally, if too much fertilizer is added, yields may actually drop.

Now that we have looked at the physical response, the economic, or dollar, response must be considered. (See Table 5-2.) Assume fertilizer costs $6 per 100 pounds and corn is worth $2 per bushel. Column numbers 1 through 4 in Table 5-2 correspond with those column numbers in Table 5-1. However, Table 5-2 shows the dollar values.

From the physical response data in Table 5-1, we cannot determine how much fertilizer to apply to reach the *maximum profit point*. When dollar values are put on the inputs and outputs we can find that point. Obviously you would not apply over 800 pounds, as you would be losing bushels. If it is profitable at all to fertilize, you

Table 5-2. Economic Input–Output Data for Corn, Using Physical Response Data from Table 5-1

Line No.	(1)[1] Total Value of Fertilizer	(2)[1] Added or Marginal Cost of Fertilizer	(3)[2] Total Value of Corn	(4)[3] Marginal Value Product of Corn	
1	$ 0	$0	$ 80	$ 0	
2	$ 6	$6	$ 88	$ 8	Stage I
3	$12	$6	$180	$92	
4	$18	$6	$240	$60	
5	$24	$6	$280	$40	
6	$30	$6	$300	$20	Stage II
7	$36	$6	$312	$12	
8	$42	$6	$316	$ 4	
9	$48	$6	$318	$ 2	
10	$54	$6	$316	$−2	Stage III

[1]Col. 1 is the dollar value (100 lbs. × $6/cwt. = $6) of the input used. Col. 2 is the dollar value of the *added* input used and is computed by subtracting Line 1, Col. 1, from Line 2, Col. 1, to equal Line 2, Col. 2, and so on down the column.

[2]The total value is the price per unit times the units of the T.P.P., i.e., $2/bu. × 40 bu. = $80.

[3]The marginal or added value of corn is the M.P.P. times the price per unit, or 46 bu. × $2/bu. = $92.

would always fertilize where the output is increasing at an increasing rate—that is, *up to 200 pounds*. But at what level *between 200 and 800 pounds* would you fertilize for maximum profit?

That can only be answered by looking at Table 5-2 with the economic data. You only need to consider the range between 200 and 800 pounds. Remember, profits will *increase* as long as the added returns from the use of another unit of variable input (fertilizer) are greater than the added costs ($6 per cwt.). Profits are maximized when the added returns equal the added costs. Therefore, even if the second $6 of fertilizer (Line 3) added $92, it is *not* the maximum profit point. The maximum profit point is between Line 7 and Line 8. At 600 pounds the added $6 of fertilizer yields $12 in corn. At 700 pounds the added $6 of fertilizer only yields $4 in corn.

Thus, we can see we need *both physical* and *economic* information to make the most profitable decision. We only need the information in Table 5-2, Col. 2 and Col. 4, to make the correct decision. But, let us prove this another way. (See Table 5-3.) When the return above fertilizer cost is calculated, we can see that again the maximum profit point is at a little beyond the 600 pounds or $36 level but not up to the $42 level.

This information can also be shown graphically. (See Fig. 5-1.)

Table 5-3. Total Value of Fertilizer and Corn, and Return Above Fertilizer Cost

Line No.	(1) Total Fertilizer Cost	(2) Total Corn Value	(3)[1] Return Above Fertilizer Cost	
1	$ 0	$ 80	$ 80	
2	$ 6	$ 88	$ 82	
3	$12	$180	$168	
4	$18	$240	$222	
5	$24	$280	$256	
6	$30	$300	$270	
7	$36	$312	$276	←— Maximum Profit Point
8	$42	$316	$274	
9	$48	$318	$270	
10	$54	$316	$262	

[1]Col. 3 equals Col. 2 minus Col. 1.

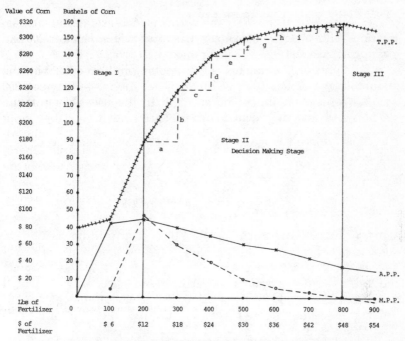

Fig. 5-1. Total Physical Product (T.P.P.), Marginal Physical Product (M.P.P.), and Average Physical Product (A.P.P.). Graph of data in Tables 5-1 and 5-2.

In Stage I, if it pays to produce at all, you will at least produce up to the maximum in this stage. The efficiency of the variable input (fertilizer) is increasing. That is, the T.P.P. increases at an increasing rate. This means that the marginal corn output is increasing as additional units of fertilizer are being applied.

In Stage III, the T.P.P. is going down so one would not produce in this stage or go beyond 800 pounds of fertilizer.

Stage II is the decision-making stage. Here the efficiency of the variable input is increasing at a decreasing rate. Note that in Fig. 5-1 the lines b, d, f, h, j, and l get successively shorter with each succeeding added 100 pounds of fertilizer shown by lines a, c, e, g, i, and k. It is somewhere in this stage that the maximum profit point exists. But that is determined only when the economic information is applied as in Tables 5-2 and 5-3.

You may want to try different values for corn and fertilizer to see how this would change your decision as to where the maximum profit point is located.

Finally, remember these key points:

1. Profits are *not* necessarily maximum when the total physical product is greatest.

2. Profits are *not* maximized when the physical efficiency (the A.P.P.) is greatest.

3. Profits maximization *does* depend on the prices of inputs and outputs and how they relate to physical productivity.

Now we are ready to look at another closely related economic principle.

The Equimarginal Principle

Closely tied to the law of diminishing returns is the principle of *equimarginal returns*. This principle says we should allocate a resource among its several uses in such a way that the marginal (added) returns *are equal in all uses*. In other words, with *limited* resources one should divide land, labor, and capital among different enterprises or other *fixed* factors to produce the *greatest* income from that resource.

This can be illustrated by using capital as a limited resource. Suppose we have only $600 of capital which can be spent for fertilizer to be applied on corn, hay, and oats. Table 5-4 shows the dollar outputs from each of these crops for each additional (marginal) $100 of fertilizer used.

How would you invest in fertilizer? Remember, the law of diminishing returns would tell us to put $600 of fertilizer on corn, $500 of fertilizer on hay, and $400 of fertilizer on oats to reach the maximum profit point. But, here we are *limited* to $600 that can be spent on fertilizer. The equimarginal principle tells us to put our limited resources (in this case dollars or capital) into that enterprise where it can yield the greatest income. Thus, one would spend the first $100 on hay, the second $100 on corn, the third $100 on corn, the fourth $100 on hay, the fifth $100 on oats, and the sixth $100 on corn. This would produce a total return to fertilizer of $325 + $300 + $285 + $275 + $250 + $240, or $1,675. (See Table 5-5.) This is $400 greater than if all the fertilizer had been put on corn.

In total, more than the cost of fertilizer would have been recovered by putting the $600 of fertilizer on any one of these three

Table 5-4. Returns per Dollar Invested in Fertilizer (Hypothetical Data)

Line No.	Fertilizer Investment	Returns from Crops		
		Corn	Hay	Oats
1	1st $100	$ 300	$ 325	$250
2	2nd $100	$ 285	$ 275	$225
3	3rd $100	$ 240	$ 225	$175
4	4th $100	$ 200	$ 175	$100
5	5th $100	$ 150	$ 100	$ 75
6	6th $100	$ 100	$ 50	$ 25
7	Total return from $600 of fertilizer	$1,275	$1,150	$850

Table 5-5. Selection of the Most Profitable Use of $600 Fertilizer Capital and the Maximum Profit Point (M.P.P.)

Line No.	Fertilizer Investment	Corn	Hay	Oats
1	1st $100	2. $ 300	1. $ 325	5. $250
2	2nd $100	3. $ 285	4. $ 275	$225
3	3rd $100	6. $ 240	$ 225	$175
4	4th $100	$ 200	$ 175	M.P.P. $100
5	5th $100	$ 150	M.P.P. $ 100	$ 75
6	6th $100	M.P.P. $ 100	$ 50	$ 25
7	Total return from $600 of fertilizer	$1,275	$1,150	$850

crops. But in managing a business the objective is to have the *most profitable return, not just a profitable return.*

Table 5-5 ties together the two economic principles—*diminishing returns* by showing the maximum profit point and the *equimarginal principle* by showing how to *most profitably* invest $600 in fertilizer.

If an unlimited amount of capital were available, it would be most profitable to apply $600 of fertilizer to corn, $500 to hay, and $400 to oats, or $1,500 in total. But where capital is limited to only $600, then the most profit is obtained by applying $300 of fertilizer to corn, $200 to hay, and $100 to oats.

Finally, when a resource is limited, it should be used not only in a *profitable* way but also in the *most profitable* way if the highest profit is to be obtained from the farm.

Opportunity Cost

The opportunity cost principle ties in very closely with the equimarginal principle. By opportunity cost we mean the value of a resource in its best alternative use. To say this another way, opportunity cost is the value of the product or output that was *not* produced because resources or inputs were used for a different purpose.

Again, some examples should help us to understand this vital concept. Assume we have one acre of land capable of growing continuous corn, hay, or oats. After *all* costs including labor are paid, *except* the cost of land, and after *all* income is calculated, we reach the figures listed in Table 5-6.

Table 5-6. Returns to Land from One Acre of Various Crops

(1) Crop	(2) Acres	(3) All Income from Crop	(4) All Costs from Crop Other than Land Cost	(5) Return to Land (3 − 4)
Corn	1	$240	$165	$75
Hay	1	$200	$130	$70
Oats	1	$140	$ 75	$65

Then the return to land of $75 for corn sets the cost of the value of land for growing any of the other crops adaptable to that one acre of land, that is, corn, hay, or oats. Thus, the opportunity cost for this acre of land is $75.

One other example might help. Suppose a farmer wanted to buy a tractor and had to pay 9% interest on the money. This then is the farmer's cost of capital. If, however, the farmer could invest this capital in another way, say in fertilizer, and receive a 20% return to capital, then 20% is the opportunity cost of the capital.

The opportunity cost of any one single input is determined by its value in the production of another product or output. From this it can be seen that opportunity cost is indeed the value of a scarce resource at its best alternative use.

The Substitution Principle for Inputs

Many inputs in the farming business can be substituted for each other. For example, machinery can be substituted for labor, silage for hay, soybean meal for cottonseed meal, No. 1 grade corn for No. 2 grade corn, and many others.

In nearly any production process in the farm business, one can use different combinations of inputs or resources to produce a given product or output. Some resources substitute for each other at a *constant* rate, for example, No. 1 corn for No. 2 corn. Others substitute for each other at *diminishing* rates, as grain for hay in a dairy ration.

If No. 2 corn is 98% of the feeding value of No. 1 corn in feeding hogs, then 100 pounds of No. 2 corn substitutes for 98 pounds of No. 1 corn. This is true for the first 100 pounds used, as it is for any other amount used. Thus if No. 1 corn is worth $.04 per pound then No. 2 corn is worth $.0392 (98% × $.04) per pound. This illustrates the *constant* rate of substitution.

The rule to follow when inputs substitute for each other at a *constant* rate is simple. Substitute one input for another as long as the cost of the added input is less than the cost of the replaced one. This assumes output is constant. In the preceding example one would substitute No. 2 corn for No. 1 corn as long as 100 pounds of No. 2 corn costs less than 98 pounds of No. 1 corn. An interesting fact about constant substitution is that one uses either all of one input or all of the other input.

Many resources substitute for each other at *diminishing* rates. That is, as one input is substituted more, it will take the place of less and less of the input which it is replacing.

Let us look at one example of this in hog feeding. Here are some hypothetical physical input data concerning the amount of concentrate in combination with corn needed to produce 100 pounds of pork. See Table 5-7 for both physical and economic data.

Table 5-7. Combinations of Concentrate and Corn Required to Produce 100 Lbs. of Pork, and Cost per 100 Lbs. of Pork at Various Prices for Concentrate and Corn—Physical and Economic Data (Hypothetical Data)

	Physical Data			Economic Data[2]		
	Possible Combinations of Corn and Conc.			Feed Cost of Producing 100 Lbs. Pork with Corn and Conc. at Various Prices		
	(1)	(2)	(3) Lbs. Corn Replaced by 1 Lb. Conc. (M.R.S.)[1]	(4)	(5)	(6)
Line No.	Lbs. Conc.	Lbs. Corn		Corn, 2¢; Conc., 6¢	Corn, 2¢; Conc., 8¢	Corn, 3¢; Conc., 6¢
1	0	600	0	$12.00	$12.00	$18.00
2	10	400	20	$ 8.60	$ 8.80	$12.60
3	20	300	10	$ 7.20	$ 7.60	$10.20
4	30	220	8	$ 6.20	$ 6.80	$ 8.40
5	40	180	4	$ 6.00	$ 6.80	$ 7.80
6	50	150	3	$ 6.00	$ 7.00	$ 7.50
7	60	130	2	$ 6.20	$ 7.40	$ 7.50

[1]M.R.S. stands for Marginal Rate of Substitution. The M.R.S. is the amount of an input which may be replaced as a result of adding an additional unit of another input in order to maintain the same level of production, or:

$$\text{M.R.S.} = \frac{\text{amount of input replaced}}{\text{amount of input added}}$$

For example, M.R.S. is calculated by subtracting Line 2, Col. 2, from Line 1, Col. 2, and dividing that result by Line 2, Col. 1, or $600 - 400 = 200$. $200 \div 10 = 20$, which is Line 2, Col. 3. This only provides the physical data. We also need to know the cost of concentrate and corn to make the most profitable management decision.

[2]Calculations for above cost information.

Line No.	1	2	3	4	5	6	7
Corn, 2¢	$12.00	$ 8.00	$ 6.00	$4.40	$3.60	$3.00	$2.60
Conc., 6¢	0	.60	1.20	1.80	2.40	3.00	3.60
Total Cost	$12.00	$ 8.60	$ 7.20	$6.20	$6.00	$6.00	$6.20
Corn, 2¢	$12.00	$ 8.00	$ 6.00	$4.40	$3.60	$3.00	$2.60
Conc., 8¢	0	.80	1.60	2.40	3.20	4.00	4.80
Total Cost	$12.00	$ 8.80	$ 7.60	$6.80	$6.80	7.00	$7.40
Corn, 3¢	$18.00	$12.00	$ 9.00	$6.60	$5.40	$4.50	$3.90
Conc., 6¢	0	.60	1.20	1.80	2.40	3.00	3.60
Total Cost	$18.00	$12.60	$10.20	$8.40	$7.80	$7.50	$7.50

We see that in Col. 4, Line 6 is least cost, in Col. 5, Line 5 is least cost, and in Col. 6, Line 7 is least cost. It is a great deal of work to figure out the cost of all combinations, but there is an easier way. First, we would look at the price ratios of the two inputs—corn and concentrate. From Col. 3, Line 2, we see that 20 pounds of corn substitutes for 1 pound of concentrate, so the substitution ratio is 20 to 1 (200 ÷ 10). Following down Col. 3, we see the substitution ratio at 10 to 1, 8 to 1, 4 to 1, 3 to 1, and 2 to 1.

Next, we look at the price ratios of concentrate to corn. In Col. 4 the ratio is 6 cents to 2 cents, or 3 to 1. In Col. 5 it is 4 to 1 and in Col. 6, 2 to 1.

With this information we can say if the substitution ratio

$$\left(\frac{\text{amount of input replaced}}{\text{amount of input added}} \right)$$

is equal to the *inverse* of the price ratio

$$\left(\frac{\text{price of input added}}{\text{price of input replaced}} \right)$$

we are at the low cost point. To say it another way, when the price of the input added times amount of input added equals the price of the input replaced times the amount of the input replaced, then we are at the low cost point.

Thus, Line 7, Col. 6, shows price (6 cents) of input added times amount (10 lbs.) input added equals 60 cents. This should equal price (3 cents) times amount (20 lbs.) input replaced, or 60 cents. Again, the substitution ratio equals the inverse of the price ratio. The substitution ratio (2/1) equals the inverse of the price ratio (2/1). This is our low cost point.

Thus, we can say costs are minimized, once the physical substitution ratio of one input for another input equals the opposite or inverse ratio of their prices. In other words, it pays to substitute one input for another as long as more is subtracted from total costs than is added—that is, as long as the marginal rate of substitution is *greater* than the price ratio.

A good manager is always alert to the possibility of substituting one input for another to maximize profit.

The Substitution Principle for Outputs

The idea of substitution applies to outputs as well as to inputs. So we can apply the substitution principle to outputs or products produced by the farm business.

This substitution principle says we should substitute one output for another as long as the value of the added output is greater than the value of the output being replaced and the costs of the inputs remain unchanged. To say this another way, the added returns from any proposed enterprise should exceed the reduced returns from the replaced enterprise.

There are three general types of enterprises or outputs—supplementary, complementary, and competitive. A *supplementary* enterprise is one which does not compete with or add to production of another. An example of this would be a small poultry operation using surplus labor, unused buildings, and some waste feed. There are very few cases where enterprises or outputs are supplementary. They are not of great concern to the farm manager.

The *complementary* enterprise adds to another enterprise when resources are limited. Or, a complementary enterprise is one that increases the output of one enterprise as the output of others increase. For example, the nitrogen fixed by alfalfa increases the yield of the following corn crop. However, this complementarity does not exist over a long time. Further, two enterprises are never complementary over all combinations.

The most important type of enterprise for the farm manager to consider is the *competitive* enterprise. Almost all enterprises are competitive, as an increase in one enterprise produces a decrease in another. For example, corn and soybeans compete for row cropland. If you raise one extra acre of corn, you sacrifice one acre of soybeans.

Perhaps a diagram can help you understand these three types of enterprises. (See Fig. 5-2.)

In the range between A and B, both corn and alfalfa total production is increased, while between B and C the quantity of alfalfa produced has no effect on corn production. However, between C and D (the competitive range) any increase in alfalfa production causes a decrease in corn production.

Thus, at first (between A and B) alfalfa and corn have a complementary relationship for a short time and then (between B and C)

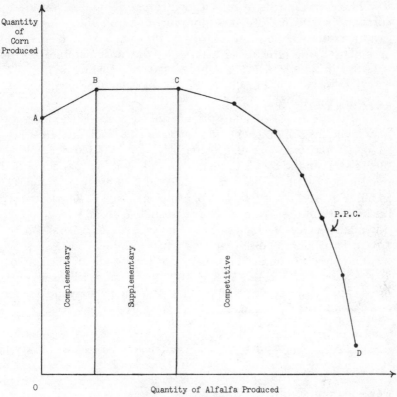

Fig. 5-2. Production Possibilities Curve (P.P.C.).

a supplementary relationship. Then an increasing amount of corn is sacrificed for each pound of hay gained.

The exact combination of enterprises or outputs which is most profitable is determined by the rate the enterprises substitute for each other (physical) and the ratio of prices and per unit costs. Enterprises or outputs can substitute for each other at increasing or constant rates as can inputs.

The *increasing* rate of substitution can be illustrated by the alfalfa-corn example. At first a short complementary relationship existed, followed by a supplementary relationship. Then an increasing amount of corn was sacrificed for each pound of hay gained. We would stop increasing alfalfa production when the added returns from the alfalfa are equal to the reduced returns from the corn.

The *constant* rate of substitution can be shown by considering corn and soybeans as competitors for row cropland. If one could produce either 120 bushels of corn or 40 bushels of soybeans on an acre of land, the substitution ratio called the Marginal Rate of Product Substitution (M.R.P.S.) would be 120 bu. ÷ 40 bu., or 3.

In other words, 3 bushels of corn is sacrificed for each bushel of soybeans produced.

Next, we must look at the price ratio, but costs of producing corn and soybeans are different, so we will need to look at the *net* price ratio. If our total cost of growing soybeans is $180 per acre (40 bushels), then the cost is $4.50 per bushel. With our expected $5.00 per bushel price we have a net price of $.50 per bushel ($5.00 − $4.50). Further, if our total cost of growing corn is $240 per acre (120 bushels), then the cost is $2.00 per bushel. With an expected $2.20 per bushel price we have a net price of $.20 per bushel ($2.20 − $2.00). Thus, our net price ratio is 2.5 (.50 ÷ .20).

Our substitution principle says that profits will increase as long as the substitution ratio (M.R.P.S.) is *less* than the inverse of the price ratio. In other words, the price ratio must go beyond 3 before you should grow soybeans instead of corn. The equation is:

$$M.R.P.S. = \frac{\text{amount of output replaced}}{\text{amount of output added}}$$

For maximum profit:

$$M.R.P.S. = \frac{\text{net price of added output}}{\text{net price of replaced output}}$$

Thus, we continue to replace corn with soybeans as long as the M.R.P.S. (3) is greater than the price ratio (2.5).

If soybeans increased 10 cents per bushel in price, our ratio would be exactly 3 (.60 ÷ .20), or if corn dropped 3⅓ cents per bushel, the price ratio would be 3. At this point one would be indifferent as whether to produce soybeans or corn. Risk, uncertainty, labor distribution, and machinery capacity could also affect the decision on whether to produce corn or soybeans.

Farm managers must be constantly alert to changes in cost of producing outputs and to price changes so that they might select the highest profit mix of outputs from their bundle of resources.

Cost and Revenue Relationships

In our definitions earlier, we defined fixed and variable costs. There are some other cost relationships we need to consider. They are:

1. Total costs—the sum of the fixed and variable costs.
2. Marginal cost—the addition to total costs which results from producing one more unit of output. This is a variable cost.
3. Average total cost—total costs divided by the units of output.
4. Average fixed cost—total fixed costs divided by the units of output.
5. Average variable cost—total variable costs divided by the units of output.

Further, there are some revenue ideas to consider. These are:

1. Total revenue—the number of outputs times the price per unit of output.
2. Average revenue—the total revenue divided by the units of output. It is the price of the output.
3. Marginal revenue—the addition to total revenue from selling one more unit of output. It too is the price of the output.

To start with, look at Table 5-8 and consider Col. 1, 2, and 3. Note fixed costs remain the same regardless of the level of production. But the variable costs increase as production increases. Fig. 5-3 illustrates this graphically.

Now look at these costs (fixed, variable, total) on an average basis in Table 5-8 (Col. 5, 6, 7). Note the average fixed cost drops as production goes up, while the average variable cost drops for awhile and then increases. Increasing production will result in increased efficiency to a point but will then decrease. Average total cost also decreases for awhile before finally increasing. But after the average variable cost has increased, the average fixed cost continues to decrease. Marginal cost at first declines but then quickly starts to increase.

Fig. 5-4 shows these cost relationships graphically. Note the M.C. curve first declines and then increases, cutting the A.T.C. and A.V.C. curves at their low points. The A.F.C. curve declines and keeps on declining while the A.V.C. curve declines for awhile and then turns up. The A.T.C. also drops until it reaches its low point where the M.C. curve cuts through it. This is the low cost point per

Table 5-8. Cost Relationships for Producing One Acre of Corn (Hypothetical Data)[1]

Line No.	(1) Bu. of Corn/A[1]	(2) Total Fixed Cost/A	(3) Total Variable Cost/A	(4)[2] Total Costs/A	(5)[3] Average Fixed Cost/Bu.	(6)[4] Average Variable Cost/Bu.	(7)[5] Average Total Cost/Bu.	(8)[6] Marginal Cost/Bu.
1	40	$100	$ 65	$165	$2.500	$1.625	$4.125	—
2	44	$100	$ 71	$171	$2.273	$1.614	$3.886	$1.50
3	90	$100	$ 78	$178	$1.111	$0.867	$1.978	$0.15
4	120	$100	$ 90	$190	$0.833	$0.750	$1.583	$0.40
5	140	$100	$100	$200	$0.714	$0.714	$1.428	$0.50
6	150	$100	$110	$210	$0.667	$0.733	$1.400	$1.00
7	156	$100	$118	$218	$0.641	$0.756	$1.397	$1.33
8	158	$100	$125	$225	$0.633	$0.791	$1.424	$3.50
9	159	$100	$132	$232	$0.629	$0.830	$1.459	$7.00

[1] Also see Tables 5-1 and 5-2.
[2] Col. 2 plus Col. 3.
[3] Col. 2 divided by Col. 1.
[4] Col. 3 divided by Col. 1.
[5] Col. 4 divided by Col. 1.
[6] (Line 2, Col. 3, minus Line 1, Col. 3) divided by (Line 2, Col. 1, minus Line 1, Col. 1) and so on down the columns.

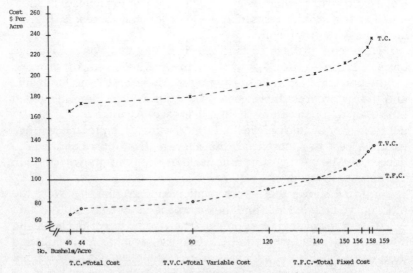

Fig. 5-3. Total cost relationships—one acre of corn.

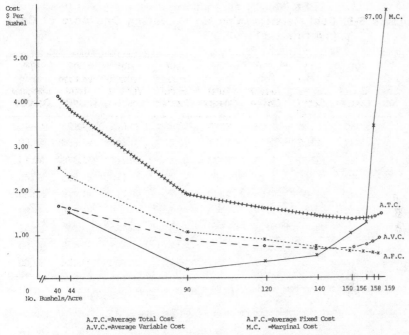

Fig. 5-4. Average cost relationships—one acre of corn.

A.T.C.=Average Total Cost   A.F.C.=Average Fixed Cost
A.V.C.=Average Variable Cost   M.C. =Marginal Cost

bushel of production and represents the point of highest production efficiency. But profits are *not* necessarily highest at this point.

Thus, it is *not most profitable* to produce at a higher level, nor is it most profitable to produce where the A.V.C., A.F.C., and M.C. are lowest. This might best be illustrated with Table 5-9. While a profit is made throughout the range of 90- to 159-bushel yield, the *most* profit is made at about the 156-bushel level. Here the M.C. is still a bit lower than the M.R. The highest profit point is where M.C. = M.R. Thus, to make the best economic decision, you only need to know the marginal cost and the marginal revenue. In other words, go to Fig. 5-4 and put a ruler horizontally across it at the $2.00 price level, and you will see that it cuts the M.C. line over the 157-bushel production level. With $1.00 corn it cuts the M.C. line at the 150-bushel level. In any one planning period (short run) the manager is only concerned with variable costs, particularly the marginal cost, in decision making.

Is there a point where the manager should decide not to produce? Yes, there is! But *only if the total revenue is less than variable*

Table 5-9. Profitability of Producing the One Acre of Corn[1]

Line No.	(1) Bu. of Corn/A	(2) Total Cost/A	(3)[2] Total Revenue/A	(4)[3] Profit/A	(5)[4] Marginal Revenue/A	(6)[5] Marginal Cost/A
1	40	$165	$ 80	$−85	—	—
2	44	$171	$ 88	$−83	$ 8	$ 6
3	90	$178	$180	$+ 2	$92	$ 7
4	120	$190	$240	$ 50	$60	$12
5	140	$200	$280	$ 80	$40	$10
6	150	$210	$300	$ 90	$20	$10
7	156	$218	$312	$ 94	$12	$ 8
8	158	$225	$316	$ 91	$ 4	$ 7
9	159	$232	$318	$ 86	$ 2	$ 7

[1] Based on data in Table 5-8.
[2] Based on $2 corn.
[3] Col. 3 minus Col. 2.
[4] Additional bu. of corn per acre times $2, i.e., (Line 2, Col. 1 − Line 1, Col. 1) × $2 = (44 − 40) × $2 = 4 × $2 = $8, or Line 2, Col. 5.
[5] Table 5-8, Col. 8, times number of additional bu. of corn per acre.

costs for that production period. As long as the total revenue is greater than variable costs you will be better off to produce for that planning period. You will minimize loss this way. Look again at Table 5-8, Line 5, Col. 6. For any one production planning period you will be better off producing corn at the 140-bushel level if the price is 72 cents per bushel or above. You at least have something to apply towards fixed costs which go on regardless of the level of production.

Further, once inputs are committed into an enterprise they become fixed or "sunk" costs. Therefore, if disaster strikes a crop and yields are drastically cut, you will still be better off to harvest as long as the variable cash costs of harvest are less than the value of the crop to be harvested.

Careful consideration of cost and revenue relationship can help the manager make better business decisions.

Risk and Uncertainty

Up to now we have assumed all the data we have been using are

known with perfect certainty. They are not in the real world! Prices
and yields change. How then do we cope with risk and uncertainty?

First we need to define these two terms:

1. *Risk*—You, the manager, know what the future outcomes
could be and the probabilities associated with them. Examples are
fire, hail, wind, and some floods. You can insure against these risks.

2. *Uncertainty*—You may not be aware of different outcomes
and cannot assign any probabilities to these outcomes. Generally
you cannot reasonably insure against uncertainty. You have to examine your own personal goals and values and your business situation to make adjustments for uncertainty.

Some managers will gamble on high risk, high payoff prospects. Others may want to choose lower payoff alternatives with
lower risk.

There are different types of risk and uncertainty. Some deal
with prices for both inputs and outputs. Others deal with yields of
crops and livestock. Changes in agricultural technology make fixed
assets become obsolete rapidly when whole new production systems are adopted. The government and other institutions can
change tax laws, credit programs, farm programs, and other factors
relating to the farm business. And there are always the weather and
pests to contend with.

The farm manager must use the best tools of effective production, business, and financial management to combat risk and
uncertainty.

The presence of risk and uncertainty has a cost to both the
farmer and all of society. It results in inefficiencies from bad planning, too much conservative planning, and a deliberate change from
the economically best combination of resources to prepare for or
reduce the uncertainty or risk.

A good manager needs to deal effectively with risk and uncertainty to be successful.

One way to deal with risk is to ask the question: "What does it
cost me if I am wrong?" and "What are the consequences of being
wrong?"

The Time Value of Money

The last concept we must consider is the time value of money or capital. There are two procedures for computing this. They are *compounding* and *discounting*.

Compounding is the process of finding the future value of a present amount of money. The equation and an example follow:

Future value = present value $(1 + \text{interest rate})^{\text{number of time periods}}$

or simply:

$$F.V. = P.V. (1 + i)^n$$

If you have $100 to invest today, what will it grow into in 10 years at a 6% interest rate? Answer: $179.08.

$$F.V. = \$100 (1 + .06)^{10}, \text{ or } F.V. = 100 \times 1.7908, \text{ or } F.V. = \$179.08$$

Therefore, money does have a time value. You would rather invest the money at some interest rate than put it under the mattress where it would not draw any interest. See Fig. 5-5 to see how the money grows over the 10 years with a 6% interest rate. Higher or lower interest rates would change the answer.

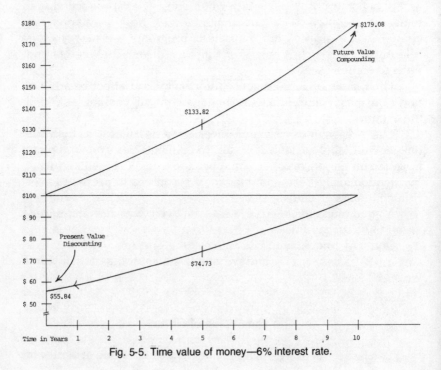

Fig. 5-5. Time value of money—6% interest rate.

The reverse of compounding is discounting. We have all heard the saying, "A bird in the hand is worth two in the bush." In other words, possessing something today is generally worth more than possessing it in the future.

Discounting is the process of finding the present value of a future amount. The equation and an example follow:

$$\text{Present value} = \frac{\text{future value}}{(1 + \text{interest rate})^{\text{number of time periods}}}$$

or simply:

$$\text{P.V.} = \frac{\text{F.V.}}{(1 + i)^n}$$

If you want $100 in 10 years, what will you have to invest today at 6%? Answer: $55.84.

$$\text{P.V.} = \frac{100}{(1 + .06)^{10}} \quad \text{or P.V.} = \frac{100}{1.7908} = \$55.84$$

Look at Fig. 5-5 to see discounting illustrated and compared to compounding. Money has a time value, and time decisions affect farm management decisions in many ways. Do you buy a $5,000 secondhand tractor with a useful life of 5 years, or should you invest $8,000 in a tractor which will last 10 years? Should you buy a farm now or rent for a few years? Would it be better to buy 10 producing dairy cows for $6,000 or 10 bred heifers for $4,500 and wait 9 months for a return while incurring their costs? Should you build a machine shed with a 50-year life for $18,000 or build one with a 25-year life for $16,000? If we know something about the capital position of the farm manager and have reasonably reliable information about the future, these questions can be answered.

The important principle to remember is to invest in a durable input (a capital asset) such as machinery, buildings, breeding livestock, etc., *only when the sum of the discounted future revenues is greater than the cost of the input.*

Let's take an example by going back to a question asked earlier—should you build a machine shed with a 50-year life for $18,000 or build one with a 25-year life for $16,000? If the cheaper building is replaced in 25 years at the same price, the total investment requirement is $32,000. Which building is less expensive?

If interest rates are 8% on long-term money and the manager has access to the needed capital, we can answer the question this way. By buying the cheaper shed, the farmer would have to put $2,336.29 away at 8% interest [$16,000 ÷ $(1 + .08)^{25}$ or $16,000 ÷ 6.84847] to generate another $16,000 at the end of 25 years. Or, $2,336.29 compounded at 8% would equal $16,000 [$2,336.29 × $(1 + .08)^{25}$ or $2,336.29 × 6.84847]. The $16,000 plus $2,336.29 would be greater ($18,336.29) than $18,000 and thus the more expensive choice. Thus, the $18,000 shed is the better choice.

If you had an opportunity cost of money of, say 15%, then the answer might be different. Calculate it.

$$\frac{16,000}{(1 + .15)^{25}} = \frac{16,000}{32.918} = \$486$$

In this case $16,000 plus the $486 will be the better choice.

However, you also need to consider changes in building costs in this time period. Further, carefully consider changes in technology which may make the old building technologically obsolete before it is worn out.

Another item to take into consideration is inflation. If we have an inflation rate of 6%, $1,000 will only have a value of $233 [$1,000 ÷ $(1 + .06)^{25}$ or $1,000 ÷ 4.29186] at the end of 25 years.

Every farm manager is faced with time comparison decisions. The knowledge of discounting and compounding can help in making better financial decisions.

Principles Help

Once you have thoroughly mastered these economic principles, your job as a farm business manager will be easier. You will also arrive at better, more profitable decisions. These principles and concepts can apply to business other than just the challenging business of farming.

Questions and Problems for Class Discussion

1. Does maximum production from a given crop or class of livestock always mean maximum profit? Why?

2. When your capital is limited do you use it in the first enterprise where you find it will return a profit? Why?

3. What is opportunity cost and how does it apply to the farm business?

4. How do inputs and outputs substitute for each other?

5. What is the difference between fixed and variable costs?

6. Discuss the different cost relationships of marginal cost, average total cost, average variable cost, and average fixed cost. How do they relate to decision making?

7. What is the difference between risk and uncertainty? How do they affect farm business decision making?

8. What is the difference between discounting and compounding? Explain their use in decision making.

PART TWO

Getting Started in Farming

Part Two will take up the subject of getting started in farming: farm appraisal, sharing agreements, leases, partnerships, corporations, estate planning, and part time farming.

CHAPTER 6

Considerations and Strategies for Getting Started in Farming— Entry, Growth, and Exit

Highlights of Chapter

Farming has become more of a "life style" than a "way of life." Most U.S. farms are family farms and will likely remain that way for some time to come. Farmers have a difficult time in separating their business and personal lives but should attempt to do so, especially in multi-person business agreements. Before selecting the most appropriate form of farm business organization and arrangement, the people and the business must be evaluated. Do the people have the required personal characteristics and training needed for a farming career? Has the business, or does the business have the potential for, adequate profitability, solvency, and liquidity-cash flow? Written agreements are extremely important.

The family and the farm business life cycle move together. Three phases—entry, growth, and exit—characterize this business cycle. The appropriate farm business arrangement can correlate with the different stages of business evolution. The stages can include testing, short-term joint operation, long-term joint operation, or separation. The old traditional "agricultural ladder" (that is, hired hand, renter, and owner) has changed with further options. Various methods can be used to transfer the farm business. Appropriate tax planning should be done when buying and selling a farm. Good business planning can prevent personal and business tragedies.

Farming is no longer just a way of life. Many farm families are realizing this or have realized this for some time. Farming, like other occupations, has a "life style" to it, as does being a plumber, a doctor, an electrician, a computer programmer, an electronic technician, or any other vocation—even being a college professor!

One of the characteristics of the farming occupation life cycle is the difficulty in separating the business life from the family life. Because of this it is very important that the business part of farming be handled in a formal, businesslike manner complete with written legal agreements and other formal business arrangements.

Most U.S. farms are family farms—that is, most of the labor and management and a good share of the capital are furnished by the farm family. Some family farms are very large farms where several family members have pooled their resources of land, labor, management, and capital into a larger-sized unit. Others are smaller and some may provide only part time employment. The form of farm business organization selected and the method of transferring these farm assets will be heavily dependent upon the amount and type of resources controlled and the objectives, goals, and values of the family involved. Therefore, the plans selected will differ from farm to farm and family to family.

Not all young farm people will have an opportunity to farm. Along with the personal qualifications and training needed, one has to consider the required replacement rate for farmers. A farmer's son or daughter does not have the inherent right to farm. Neither does a carpenter's child automatically have the right to a career in carpentry. Similarly, the doctor's or lawyer's children do not have the right to follow those professions. It will depend on the current demand for these abilities, along with the talent and training involved.

Before selecting an appropriate business organization and eventual transfer plan, you must consider two very important factors—the *people* involved and the *business* under consideration.

The People

In a multi-person business arrangement the people involved need to have the desire and ability to get along with one another. Satisfactory housing should be provided, although it need not be luxurious. Housing should allow for each family and each family member to have the needed privacy and separation from one another and from the business. Many times personal relationships become strained if people are too close to each other every day in their business and personal lives.

All family members entering into a business relationship need to realize that they are not destroying or changing their family relationship, but are adding a second relationship—that of business and professional associates. These two should be kept as separate as possible to avoid conflicts and promote understanding. In a two- or three-generation business all generations should recognize the unique contributions each can make to strengthen the business. Those of the older generation have much to offer in the way of experience and wisdom gained over their lifetimes. Further, they also offer the leverage the young generation needs to be able to start in the business. Members of the younger generation can offer their youthful enthusiasm, new creative ideas, and energetic labor supply. Indeed, the multi-generational contributions complement each other in many ways. Capitalize on this strength! Do not let it become competitive or destructive. Members of different generations should recognize they need each other because of their unique contribu-

Fig. 6-1. A father and his son are talking over plans and making decisions together, rather than the father ignoring the son in the management problems. (Courtesy, Ken Allen)

tions to the farm business. Similarly, members of the same generation can contribute their special abilities and training to the business.

The parties in any business, including farming, must have managerial and business competence and must be good production managers. Financial and business management can be learned and effectively practiced at all ages. There should be joint participation in the management function. The older generation must let the younger generation be a part of the decision-making process. Of course, some mistakes may be made, but you can keep these to a minimum. Let the beginner make a few minor errors. It is part of the learning process. More major decisions amounting to larger dollar values can be controlled. In fact, you will be pleasantly surprised to find that many young people are good decision makers. Having more than one decision maker can help establish a stronger business. People have a chance to specialize. One can be the crop manager and another the livestock manager, while a third may be the business manager.

People are the most important part of any business endeavor. By recognizing the contribution each person has to make, you can make the appropriate decisions to provide for orderly continuation of the business.

The Business

The business must be well managed if it is to be successful. It must have adequate size, productivity, efficiency, and organization to provide a decent living for each person and family involved. The best, most equitable business agreement in the world is doomed to failure without adequate income. On the other hand, adequate income can mask some inequities. Therefore, not only should the business agreement be equitable but it also should be applied to a well-managed business which is making a profit.

The agreement, whatever form it takes, should be *written*! An *attorney* should be consulted for the drafting of the arrangement. The written agreement puts the arrangement on a businesslike basis. The separation of business affairs from family affairs must be considered. The written agreement enables the parties to discuss and work out potential problems before they occur. The details of the terms of the agreement can be worked out. This helps in preventing misunderstandings later. We are all subject to "selective recall." That is, we remember those things which further our interests. A written agreement guards against this.

Difficulties at termination or death can be avoided if all the termination provisions are spelled out in the agreement. In fact, it is a good idea to write the termination clause first. This helps to get at many of the problem areas early and enables all parties to have a reasonably graceful exit should that occasion arise. The agreement should be reviewed periodically and changed when necessary.

The farm must have an adequate records system which is kept up-to-date. The records system can be the foundation upon which the agreement is based. It should be available to all business associates at all times for their inspection.

Banking arrangements must be set up so there is a sound financial footing for the agreement. It is best to keep farm business funds and family funds separate. All persons should have their own personal funds so they may manage their personal and household expenses as they see fit without interference from others.

A buy-sell agreement should be worked out in the written agreement. This can provide a method for the orderly continuation of the business should a member of the business die or choose to leave the business. The buy-sell agreement simply outlines a procedure of how and at what terms the assets of the business can be disposed of by the person (or the person's heirs) to the people remaining in the business or to others.

Many times, insurance, particularly term insurance, can be used to help fund the buy out by a survivor. This is especially true for business arrangements involving members of the same generation. For example, if two brothers are in a partnership and one dies, what happens? With a two-way term policy (each party has a term policy on the other's life), the surviving party has the capital or leverage to buy out the other's assets. The surviving members of the decedent's family get the needed cash, and the surviving partner can continue the business. The policy need not be so large as to cover the entire purchase but should be large enough to provide the needed leverage so the remainder of the capital can be borrowed. As equity increases, the need for insurance decreases. In some cases none would be desirable.

Roles of the People in the Business

Each business has contributions of labor, capital, and management. In the farm business these inputs are generally supplied by the same person. In large businesses this is generally not true. The officers of a company know they are management, stockholders know they are capital, and assembly line workers know they are labor. Farmers are all three.

Being all three (labor, management, and capital) can be a frustrating experience, as each supplier of the different inputs has different goals and objectives. At times it is difficult to determine which role you are playing in the farm business. The manager desires high profitability, the capitalist wants a competitive return to capital, and the laborer wants top wages and ideal working conditions. Therefore, you, as a supplier of labor, want the most modern facilities and equipment and ease of working conditions. But, you, as a supplier of capital, have a limited capital supply which should be spent where it obtains the highest return. This may not be on the most modern labor-saving equipment, especially if you have an excess fixed labor supply. As a supplier of management you desire a high profit. This goal many times conflicts with the goals of the laborer and capitalist.

If different people are supplying different amounts of these inputs, certain philosophical and business differences may arise. The young generation supplying a major portion of the labor will have different investment priorities from the older generation supplying less of the labor but more of the capital. All of this must be carefully discussed, and procedures for dealing with it should be outlined.

Perhaps farmers can best visualize this by having three hats: (1) a nice big Stetson as their manager's hat, (2) a dark conservative homburg as their capitalist's hat, and (3) their seed corn company cap as their laborer's hat. Then they can decide which hat to have on when making certain decisions. This might help you look at which role you are playing as a decision maker.

Once you have decided you have the necessary competent people and you have a business with adequate income-generating potential, you are ready for the next step, which is deciding which form of business organization is appropriate for your situation. Then tie that to the total business and to the transfer plan.

The Farm and Family Life Cycle

The majority of U.S. farms are operated as sole proprietorships.

The life cycle of the business is tied to the life cycle of the family. It can be broken down into three general categories—entry, growth, and exit. (See Fig. 6-2.)

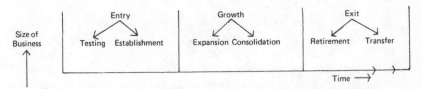

Fig. 6-2. Typical family/farm life cycle of individually operated business. (From N.C.R. 50, *Farm Business Arrangements: Which One For You?* by K. Thomas and M. Boehlje)

Each of these three categories has two subdivisions. The entry part consists of the testing stage where the beginning farmer decides if a sufficient opportunity exists to get into farming and the stage where the farmer begins to get established.

The growth part consists of expanding the business into a viable profitable economic unit and then consolidating it into a going business. Toward the end of this stage the business might have a tendency to stagnate and perhaps fall a bit behind competitively.

The third part, exit, consists of retirement and transfer of the business to others. Entry and exit are the two most difficult times and require a great deal of thought and effort to implement successfully. Bringing in a member of the next generation at the appropriate time can ease that new person's entry as well as provide for an orderly transfer for the retiring generation.

The farming generation (parents) may have developed a very successful operation, as shown by line 1 (Fig. 6-3), or may not have been quite as successful, as shown by line 2. As stated earlier, the farm business must have adequate income potential. If that exists, then bringing in the beginning generation (the son or daughter) some time midway into, or even toward the end of, the growth period can smooth out the cyclical pattern.

The business of farming can no longer stand the dismantling of businesses built over a lifetime every generation only to be rebuilt again. Perhaps one of the greatest tragedies is the disbursement of a successful farm business with future potential in a one-day sale. In the short space of less than a day, the fruits of 30 to 50 years of work and planning are broken into small pieces only to be reassembled by

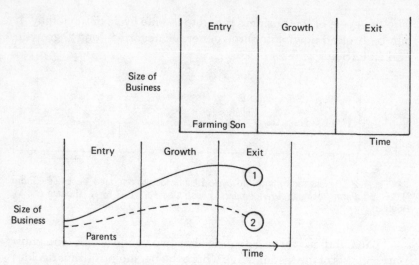

Fig. 6-3. Merging family/farm life cycles of parents and farming son. (From N.C.R. 50, *Farm Business Arrangements: Which One For You?* by K. Thomas and M. Boehlje)

the beginning farmer. Good planning, using the appropriate business arrangement and transfer plan, can help prevent this tragedy from occurring. Of course, in a few cases a reasonable transfer may not be feasible. If the business lacks potential, transfer may not be desirable. But in many situations, provision for starting the beginning farmer will be of benefit not only to the beginning farmer but also to the established or existing farmer.

The timing of the beginning generation's entrance into the business is crucial. If the farming generation has several more years of an active career, then the business must be large enough to accommodate two families. Otherwise, other income-generating activities must be used. This could include some off-farm work by either or both of the parties.

Selecting the Most Appropriate Arrangement
for Your Situation

Fig. 6-4 illustrates a decision-making framework you may consider. Chapter 7 discusses the various forms of farm business organization and business arrangements which may be used.

Earlier we discussed the *people* and the *business*. This diagram

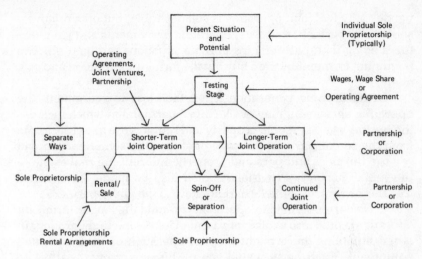

Fig. 6-4. Alternative business arrangements and the decision framework. (From N.C.R. 50, *Farm Business Arrangements: Which One For You?* by K. Thomas and M. Boehlje)

starts with the *business* side, with the assumption that well-qualified *people* are available. Here the present farm business situation must be evaluated, and the potential of that business for accommodating more people must be considered. Generally we are starting from a sole proprietor type of business. Where the *people* and the *business* are will determine where to start in the diagram. In some cases the testing stage has already occurred, and in others some operations are down to the continual joint operation. But we will walk through all the steps.

In entry the first step is testing. This step should be of relatively short duration—no less than a year but perhaps no longer than three years. It should be characterized by simple arrangements which can be easily started and quickly and painlessly terminated, and it should have the characteristics which will enable it to evolve into the more permanent, longer lasting relationship.

It may well be determined in the testing stage that things will not work out satisfactorily. The agreement can then be terminated, and all parties will go their separate ways. Straight wages (for one year or two at the most), a wage share, or an operating agreement would be appropriate at this stage.

When the testing stage has been successfully completed, the

parties may feel joint operation is still desirable, but on a relatively short-term basis. In this case, operating agreements and joint ventures along with partnerships in some situations can be used. The beginning farmer may then buy out the farming generation and go it alone.

If the farming generation is not too close to retirement, the operating agreement may evolve into a partnership which includes the business and personal property and rental of the farm real estate from the senior partner. At retirement time the senior partner can sell the business and personal property and rent the real estate to the junior partner. Provisions should also be made for eventual transfer or control of the farm real estate to the junior partner.

The shorter-term joint operation (as could the longer-term joint operation) could also evolve into a spinoff or complete separation. In other situations there might be joint operation of field work and equipment. Each party would control his or her own real estate package and livestock operation, but they would have a partnership (or joint venture) with the field operations.

The short-term joint operation may well evolve into a long-term business arrangement for continued joint operation. Generally, but not necessarily, in this case more formal and sophisticated arrangements are used. These would include partnerships (general and limited) or corporations (Subchapter C and Subchapter S).

Under some conditions a combination of the various business arrangements may be used. (See Chapter 7 for a discussion of the various forms of farm business organization and arrangements.) Legal, tax, and accounting help should be sought, and plans for transfer should be made.

The Agricultural Ladder

Traditionally, the steps to becoming established in farming were taken on the "agricultural ladder." There were three steps on this ladder— hired hand, tenant, and owner. These steps on the old "agricultural ladder" are becoming further apart. It is much more difficult, and in some cases impossible, to make these steps successfully. Other ladders with different steps might be used.

Earlier we discussed the testing, short-term, and long-term business arrangements. One can go through these stages or steps not only in the family farm environment but also in non-family situations. In some cases people with non-farm upbringing go into farming. In others a farm is inherited. The people inheriting the farm go into farming, manage the farm, hire someone to manage it for them, or sell it. Other people retire early from one career and take up farming as a career. Some go into farming on a part time basis or are part of the "back-to-the-land" movement.

So one can see there are many routes to take or ladders to climb to getting established in farming. But in all cases it takes *people* with the required characteristics and qualifications along with a *business* which can provide the needed income.

Transferring the Farm Business

The form of farm business arrangement selected should provide a mechanism for eventual transfer of the assets.

Each form of business organization presents its own difficulties and opportunities for transfer. Corporations in many cases are the most convenient to transfer because of their shares. The sole proprietorship is usually the most difficult because it is either in one lump—the whole business—or in two lumps—the personal property and real estate. Partnership interests can be transferred relatively easily, but usually a new partnership agreement must be drawn. If the business evolves through the steps discussed earlier, partial transfers can be made as the business evolves. If the business owner waits until death for transfer, then the inheritance route is used. The buy-sell arrangement can facilitate transfer. Some find that using the land contract, gifts, or trusts facilitates transfer.

Most situations call for a combination of transfer methods. It will depend upon the individual fact situation and goals of the people. Also, one has to make allowance for income tax and death tax considerations. On farms where more than one generation is involved, the family members need to particularly consider the method which not only provides for security for the outgoing generation but also gives the incoming generation a reasonable opportunity for success. Equitable treatment of other family members is also important.

Long-range planning is important, as many things can be done over a period of years which cannot be accomplished in a short time span. Waiting until retirement time is a poor way to meet goals and objectives.

BUYING A FARM

In buying a farm you will be handicapped right from the beginning if you start with a farm which costs too much when compared with your available capital. However, a poor, cheap farm may be the most expensive in the long run. You will always need to guard against an unwise and unprofitable deal, even in your own community where you think you know local conditions.

When you are ready to buy a farm—investigate before you invest. It will pay good dividends. Check with some good farmers in the area. Call on the local banker and others who know the farm. Find out how good the crops have been the last few years. Take several samples of soil over the farm and have them tested. Find out if there are erosion problems. Examine a recent soil map and plan from the Soil Conservation Service (S.C.S.). What about noxious weeds? How good is the water supply? If there is more than one farm for sale in the area, which is the best buy? Which one best fits your needs? Look at the farm when crops are growing. Winter is the worst time to buy a farm in an area with which you are not ac-

Fig. 6-5. This rice being harvested is an example of a southern cash crop. (Courtesy, John Deere)

quainted. A qualified farm appraiser can be of great help in determining the true market value of a farm. (See Chapter 9.)

It should also be remembered that there are many owners of small farms who have only part time jobs and, as a result, small incomes. The ownership of a farm does not insure one an adequate income. The farmers of today have become more efficient in handling crops and livestock, and competition is growing keener. The ones with the most ability will survive. Leasing may be the best alternative in some cases.

Type of Farming to Follow

Before you look around and get too serious about buying a farm, be sure you know the type of farming you wish to follow. Do you prefer to be a livestock or cash crop farmer? You may wish to be both. Whatever type of farming you choose, be sure you locate in a region which is adapted to that type of farming. You will not want to keep all kinds of livestock or grow all kinds of crops.

Areas differ in their combination of crops and livestock best adapted, largely due to topography, climate, and economic conditions. Usually the most successful farmers in any community are following the type of farming which pays best in that area.

Location. The most usual situation is for a young person to desire to buy the home farm or one within a few miles of it. If one buys in the home community, the kind or type of farming in which he or she will engage has generally already been decided upon.

Young farmers who go outside their own locality should realize that a change in soil and climatic conditions may necessitate a change from the kind of crops they have been used to growing. They may have come from a region where cotton grows readily, but this other area has a soil type on which cotton will not thrive. Usually one should not try to farm land on which others have failed. It is best to try to get a going business.

There is little that can be done about a given location—you take the farm or you don't. The advantage of being near home and in a community with which you are well acquainted may be more important to you than some of the disadvantages of location. The farm should be on an improved road, with access to schools, churches, and markets. With the use of the automobile, school bus, and truck, it is not as much of a handicap as it used to be to live some distance

Fig. 6-6. This farm is set up as a dairy farm and is a type of livestock farming common in the North Central States. (Courtesy, *Wisconsin Agriculturist*)

from these facilities. If you are on a good road, it is only a matter of a few more minutes and you are there.

Climatic Conditions. There are season-to-season changes to contend with. You may have a dry year followed by a wet one, but there is no assurance that this will happen. It is important to note rainfall patterns and amounts. The kind of weather to expect is about average, but be prepared to have it go one way or the other— it will probably seldom if ever happen to hit an exact average.

The number of days between late killing frosts in the spring and early killing frosts in the fall determines the kind of crops which are adapted to certain regions. Alfalfa that will thrive in southern

Fig. 6-7. Large, level fields with a good soil type are more valuable than those small fields on hilly, stony land. (Courtesy, Allis Chalmers)

Kansas will not withstand the cold winters and late springs in northern Wisconsin. The same variety of corn that will mature in the southern United States will not mature in the northern United States.

Topography. It is more difficult and expensive to work a hilly, rolling farm than a level one. Much of the modern labor-saving machinery cannot be used efficiently on farms with rough topography and irregular boundaries. Erosion is another factor to contend with. It is becoming more acute in many areas. You do not have to travel many miles in most states to see all the disadvantages brought about by adverse topography and conditions of the land surface. The hills and knolls are dry with poor crops growing; the low lands are wet and many times cut up by a meandering stream. Any of these conditions will cut down farm profits.

Soil. A good fertile soil is essential for economic crop production. A fairly deep topsoil should be underlain with a good subsoil. It should not be so light that it becomes droughty. On the other hand, it should not be so heavy that it has poor drainage. Soil productivity may change on a farm due to depleted fertility, erosion, and weed infestation. If this has resulted from poor management, perhaps it can be brought back into economic production without too much expense and too many years of labor.

Soil surveys have been made for every state showing the type of

Fig. 6-8. Highly specialized farms require special equipment and facilities. (Courtesy, *Wisconsin Agriculturist*)

soil, depth of topsoil, kind of subsoil, slope, and degree of erosion. A recent soil test will show the available phosphate, potash, and organic matter and the need for lime. Obtain one of these maps from your county agent, your state college of agriculture, or the S.C.S. office.

Character of the Farm. A good location will never compensate for a poor soil. Soil types differ widely in each state and even within counties. It is possible to buy a poor, run-down farm in a good soil area. It is too costly and too slow a process to build up a worn-out soil. Try to get the best type you can and, if possible, a deep, rich, and well-drained soil.

Farm improvements, such as buildings, fences, drainage tile, irrigation water, and electric systems, differ from farm to farm. It is cheaper in the end to buy good buildings and other improvements with a farm than to attempt to build new ones or repair old ones later. Buildings are of somewhat greater importance and cost on livestock farms than on crop farms. However, many farm buildings are obsolete and need replacement or extensive remodeling to make them useful.

How Will the Farm Debt Be Retired? You will want to buy as cheaply as possible. If you are convinced that you are paying a premium in order to get in while high prices are still being paid for farm products, pay this extra amount in cash. You cannot afford to go into debt for the premium price. There is no real trouble with premium prices until they appear in the mortgage.

If you find a farm which looks satisfactory in most respects, there still remains the question as to how much you should pay. Since the value of the farm will depend on what it will produce, the best procedure is to estimate what the farm production will be, one year as compared with another—how much will be sold and at what value at normal prices. After all the income items have been computed, estimate the farm expenses. Make a list of all costs and allow for repairs to buildings and equipment, replacements of equipment, and livestock. (See Chapters 14, 15, 16, and 17.)

Most times it will pay you to hire an experienced appraiser to look at the farm you are thinking of buying. Contact your state chapter of the American Society of Farm Managers and Rural Appraisers for a list of qualified rural appraisers in your state.

Legal Matters to Consider. You, as a farmer, will want to get acquainted with your legal relationships to your neighbors and their relationships to you. You will want to learn how our system of law works; where we get legal rights and legal duties; how they develop; and how they come to pass under the civil law, the criminal law, and the law of courts. What is the relationship of the farmer to the public with respect to damages done by the farm animals? What is the relationship between owner and tenant? Many other questions of this kind pertain to agriculture.

Today we have a great deal of law that requires us to watch our step. For that reason, we should learn about the law of animals, the law of fences, the law of land owner and tenant relationships, and the law of contracts. A farmer is an owner of property, a producer of property, an employer, a buyer, and a seller. All lines of human endeavor and human capacity are present on the farm. It is a business on just about as broad a scale as any city business.

When Buying a Farm, Secure a Merchantable Title. There are some safeguards that one should have in mind when buying or selling a farm. Now, while this may be more important from the standpoint of the buyer, it is helpful to the seller as well, because every seller must know, or should know, what the wise buyer is apt to demand, and everyone wants to be a wise buyer. What is the objective of the average buyer, whether it be of a farm, a home, or any type of property? As a matter of fact, it is the buyer's purpose and objective to become an owner of that piece of property, and the buyer can become the owner only if able to secure from that seller a good merchantable title. One may become the owner with a defective title, but that is not very safe, because there is a chance of losing the farm.

A title should commence with original ownership by the United States government as the first link in the chain of title. It should show each transaction that has taken place down to the present. The buyer wants to know that the transfer of conveyance in each case has been regular, has been complete, and has complied with the law. Some day you, as the owner, will want to transfer or sell that property to somebody else, and they no doubt will demand from you, before they buy, a good merchantable title that they in turn can pass on. Have an attorney help you with this.

What Goes with the Sale of a Farm? What items of property go with the sale of a farm, and what items do not? In the case of selling real property, everything that is real property usually goes with the sale. The cows, other livestock, and the farm machinery are purely personal property. No question about this. When you sell a farm, those items do not go with the sale. But the question is not as simple as that. How about the T.V. aerial? Is that real property, or is it personal property? If it is personal property, it does not go with the farm sale. If it is real property, it does. How about the barn cleaner, the silo unloader, the bulk tank? Are those personal property, or are they real? How about the portable hog house or the brooder houses on that farm? One could go on and enumerate many other items. In other words, there are items of property that fall in the "danger zone" from the viewpoint of the buyer and seller of a farm; they are doubtful items. So wise buyers, when they buy the farm, or are "dickering" to buy the farm, have an understanding with the people selling that farm as to just what is and what is not going with the sale.

There has been much waste and useless litigation in our courts when such items are not listed. Often where people get together and sell a house or a farm with no agreement as to what goes and what does not go with the sale, they end up in court. Buyers should also know, when they go into possession, about the taxes for the current year. Is the seller going to pay all the taxes, is the buyer going to pay all, or are they going to prorate them? How about insurance? Is that going to be assigned to the buyer? Or is the seller going to cancel the insurance and get a refund from the insurance company and let the buyer get a new policy? These are problems that you have to take into consideration.

The Contract. Whether you buy or sell a farm, you are entering into a contract. Every business person should know that in the law of contracts there are two stages of importance from the legal viewpoint: the first, the negotiation stage, and the second, the contract stage. Keep in mind that a contract arises from an offer and acceptance.

How about insurance, taxes? These matters and others should have been covered in the negotiation stage. At the close of your negotiation stage, you request the seller to make you an offer covering all the points that you covered in the negotiation stage. If the seller's offer is not the way you want it, make the seller change it, if you can, to the way you want it. After you have reduced that offer of the negotiation stage to writing in the shape of a contract, then you are in a position to accept that offer. It is so simple to do. Take, for instance, what property goes and what property does not go with the sale: the bulk tank, the portable hog house, the tobacco poles, the laths on which the tobacco is speared, and other doubtful or danger zone items. You should have the help of an attorney for all contracts, which should be in writing.

The Deed. There are many kinds of deeds, such as tax deeds, trustee deeds, administrator deeds, and executor deeds, but the general run of deeds is the warranty deed or the quit-claim deed.

What kind of deed do you want? Do you want a warranty deed or a quit-claim deed? So far as efficiency in the matter of conveyance is concerned, one deed is just as efficient as the other. If you have a perfectly good merchantable title with respect to a given piece of land and you are given a quit-claim deed, it is perfectly good. You will then have a good merchantable title. A quit-claim deed merely says: "Take it. I am giving you all that I have, but I guarantee nothing." This title is perfectly good, but the average business person does not take a quit-claim deed. Most want and insist on a warranty deed. The warranty deed not only conveys as a quit-claim deed, but it warrants that the seller has a good merchantable title, and if that seller is financially irresponsible, this is good to have.

How do you want the property conveyed to you? Do you want it in your name, or do you want it in joint tenancy with your spouse, or do you want it as tenants in common? Be sure to consider the estate planning aspects when you decide how to take title.

Record the deed immediately with your county registrar of deeds. *Your attorney should help and advise you in each of these steps.*

The Land Contract

Few people have money enough to buy a farm for cash. Either they make a fairly sizable down payment, such as 40 to 60% of the purchase price, and carry the balance as a longtime mortgage, or they buy on a land contract with a relatively small down payment—perhaps 5 to 20%. In recent years, the investment in a farm, in machinery, and in livestock has been so great that more beginning farmers have purchased on a land contract because of the smaller down payment which is needed.

A land contract is a legal arrangement whereby the seller holds the title to the farm. The buyer takes possession and operates the farm much the same as if it were his or her own. The buyer pays for it on the installment basis—usually over a long period, such as 20 to 40 years. When the farm is fully paid for, the seller turns the deed over to the buyer, showing that the buyer owns the farm.

When one buys a farm under this plan, the interest cost during the first year of payment is often larger than the payment on the principal. Many times this problem is avoided by using an amortized level repayment plan—that is, having equal installments over the life of the contract. The first installment is primarily interest; the last primarily principal. In some cases a 30-year amortized plan is selected, but there is a balloon payment at the end of 10 years.

Land contracts, with low down payments, frequently qualify as installment sales for income tax purposes. Buyers should check with their tax advisors about this.

Fig. 6-9. This young man is looking over his farm which he purchased on a land contract. (Courtesy, Soil Conservation Service, USDA)

Usually, the only contract provision for flexibility of payment is one under which payments may be made in advance. This provision is highly recommended and should be included in all land contracts. Deferment of payments in the event of crop failure, sickness, accident, etc., is usually not provided for in a land contract.

Special provisions may be made in the contract to allow the buyer to obtain the deed before the farm has been fully paid for. When half or more of the purchase price for the farm is paid, it may pay the buyer to end the land contract, and refinance the farm—perhaps with a mortgage. Such a change will result in greater security for the purchaser.

Before one buys a farm on a land contract (or under any other arrangement, for that matter), the abstract of title should be brought up-to-date and examined by a lawyer. Serious trouble may be avoided if an up-to-date abstract is available and approved by a lawyer at the time the farm is purchased. The reason for this is that the ownership rights of the parties to a large extent are fixed at the time of signing the contract, even though a deed is not to be delivered until later. If there is a title defect, it should be cleared up before the buyer starts making payments. In some cases title insurance is available to make sure the title is marketable and to defend the purchaser against claims made against the title.

Some Things to Consider When Buying a Farm

Paying for a farm takes many years, so a prospective buyer needs to give consideration to things such as the following:

1. Is the farm of adequate size and productivity for the type of operation planned?

2. Are the buildings, fences, drainage, and water supply usable and suitable?

3. What is the estimated debt-paying capacity of the farm under my management?

Some questions buyers should ask about themselves and their families are as follows:

1. Will I be able to manage and operate this farm efficiently?

2. Do I have enough machinery and livestock to operate the farm efficiently?

3. Do I expect to have to work off the farm during the first two or three years after purchase? If so, will this hamper my farming operations to the extent that I would not show a profit from the farm?

4. Will my family be willing to live on this farm?

5. Will my family be willing to assume the debt, the debt payments, and the personal sacrifices involved in buying this farm?

The terms of the sale contract will have an effect on buyers and their families for quite a number of years. The buyer should, therefore, do everything possible to insure that the terms are as satisfactory as possible. It should be realized, however, that with a low down payment, sellers must have adequate security, and that they cannot expect the terms to be as lenient. Some of the questions about a sale contract that should be considered are as follows:

1. Under the terms of this contract, will I be able to make payments in advance?

2. Does the contract permit refinancing the farm with another lender?

3. Will the time of making payments coincide fairly well with the time at which I will receive my highest income?

4. Will the payments be too high for my income?

5. What is the length of the grace period for the deferment of payment in cases of unexpected difficulties?

6. Have I retained a lawyer to check on the abstract and advise me about the sale contract before I sign it?

Income Tax—Buying and Selling

Buying or selling a farm has short- and long-term significant income tax consequences. As tax laws change from time to time and there is a variance from state to state, we cannot be too detailed in our discussion. So you should consult your own tax advisor for details.

When you buy farm assets, you also are buying a tax situation. By careful planning it can become an asset. Poor planning will result in a liability. Tax management at this time provides opportunities to make or lose money.

The first step is to make a list of all the farm assets. Land should be broken down into cropland; pasture land; woodland; and waste, roads, building sites, etc. Standing timber and gravel deposits also need to be inventoried. Real estate improvements such as drainage tile, wells, irrigation ditches, conservation structures, etc., also should be listed. Each building and building improvement, including personal houses and improvements, also should be listed separately. The same goes for machinery, equipment, and breeding and dairy livestock. Purchased breeding and dairy livestock should be listed separately from raised animals. Stored or harvested crops, growing crops, and held-for-sale livestock (for example, feeder hogs, cattle, or lambs) must also be inventoried.

Once a complete detailed inventory is made, sellers determine their adjusted tax basis for each item. The total selling price must be allocated among all assets sold. This allocation must be reasonable. The portion of the price to be allocated to each asset should be based on the relative fair market value of each asset at the time of sale. Then appropriate gains, losses, depreciation recapture, and investment credit recapture can be computed. Buyers also need these figures to determine their beginning cost or basis for the purpose of computing depreciation, determining gain or loss upon sale, or settling their estate.

Expert help at this time can save both the buyer and the seller time, money, and headaches. Competent tax help will save much more than its cost.

A Final Note

Many personal and financial tragedies have occurred over the years because people have neglected to take care of the business side of farming. The FFA calf too often becomes Father's cow. Promises of future gifts and inheritances ring hollow after the funeral and the estate is divided up with no solid written agreement. If no written satisfactory agreement is reached early (within one to two years), it is best to part company or at least to insist on and receive competitive wages.

Questions and Problems for Class Discussion

1. What characteristics should individuals have if they expect to be successful in farming by working in a multi-person business arrangement?

2. What characteristics should the business have in a multi-person farm situation?

3. Why are written agreements so important?

4. Describe the family and business life cycle.

5. What forms of farm business arrangements fit in the testing stage? For short-term joint operation? For long-term joint operation?

6. What are some methods of transferring the farm business?

7. Discuss the land contract.

8. Why is income tax planning important in buying and selling a farm? What information do you need?

CHAPTER 7

Forms of Farm Business Organization and Business Arrangements

Highlights of Chapter

Changes in farming have prompted a great deal of interest in the various forms of farm business organization and arrangements. Many progressive farm managers realize it may not be desirable or feasible to own all the resources they need to successfully operate their farm businesses. Some wish to merge into larger units with others who also have some farm resources. More multi-person or multi-family units are appearing. There is no one answer as to which is the best form of farm business organization or arrangement to select. There are many alternative methods from which to select, including some combinations of these methods. The alternatives range from cash wages to corporations and include wage incentive enterprise agreements, sharing agreements, joint ventures, leases, rentals, partnerships, and corporations. Methods for determining an equitable arrangement are discussed. As in all legal matters, an attorney should be consulted, and qualified tax and accounting help should be sought.

Tax (income, estate, or inheritance) regulations, legal requirements, larger farms, higher capital requirements, the changing economic climate, greater expectations from the farming business, and changing goals and values require more sophisticated and different forms of farm business arrangements. These could include wage incentives, enterprise agreements, sharing agreements, joint ventures, leases (cash, variable cash, crop share, and livestock share), rentals (buildings, machinery, and livestock), custom or contract farming, partnerships (general and limited), corporations

(Subchapter C and Subchapter S), or some combination of these. Careful economic and legal analysis must be made of these forms of farm business arrangements so that the appropriate ones for a specific situation will be selected.

All legal business arrangements should be made with the guidance and counsel of an attorney familiar with the farming business. One who acts as his or her own attorney has a fool for a client!

Written Agreements

It is highly recommended that all business arrangements be in writing. As with all legal matters, an attorney familiar with agricultural law and farm problems should be retained to write the agreement and assist in monitoring it over the life of the arrangement.

A written agreement puts things on a businesslike basis, helps the parties to think through potential problem areas, helps prevent misunderstanding, and aids in settling matters at termination time. It is best to think through and develop the termination part of the agreement first. This enables the parties to more effectively develop other parts of the agreement. A clear method for arbitration should also be included in the agreement.

Budget the Business Arrangement

Another crucial item to consider is an economic analysis of the agreement. Past performance of the business can be a guide. But a total long-range budget and a transitional budget should be developed to determine the profitability, liquidity-cash flow, and solvency characteristics of the business. Adequate income is vital to all parties concerned. Equitable agreements which are well written by qualified people are of little help if the business is a failure.

THE CONTRIBUTIONS APPROACH TO AN EQUITABLE AGREEMENT

The contributions approach to an equitable agreement can be the primary methodology to use in developing many of the forms of business arrangements. It is a methodology of using absolute numbers to arrive at appropriate relative numbers or percentages for use in the business agreement.

The worksheet (Table 7-1) with an example should help you understand this method. While the worksheet only shows two sets of columns, additional columns may be added to accommodate more than two individuals.

Inventory and Valuation of Assets

The first step is to make a physical inventory of all the assets each party will contribute. These would include things such as land, buildings, machinery, equipment, livestock (breeding or dairy), labor and management, inventory items, and special other considerations.

The second step is to place an appropriate dollar value on each item. The value can range from the adjusted tax cost basis (acquisition cost plus improvements minus depreciation) to fair market value. In a strict business deal, the fair market value would be the most appropriate figure. In a situation where one of the contributors wanted to give the other person(s) a break (as in a family situation), lower values might be selected. This might be especially true for land values. But be careful—too much of a break may trigger gift tax consequences.

What Rate of Return Is Appropriate?

The third step involves selecting an appropriate rate (%) of return to the assets. The cost assigned to depreciation should reflect wear and tear as well as functional and economic obsolescence. Buildings, machinery, and equipment will depreciate, while land will not. If breeding and/or dairy livestock inventories remain constant through the raising of replacements by your business, then no depreciation would be charged.

Interest rates selected might well reflect the cost of borrowing money to purchase the asset, typical returns to that asset, or the nature of the asset (that is, appreciating or depreciating). For example, owners of land (which generally is an appreciating asset) might be content with a lower return (5 to 6% instead of 8 to 10%) than would owners of buildings, equipment, and machinery (depreciating types of assets). Remember, on depreciable assets, to take the

Table 7-1. Contributions Approach Worksheet and Example

Contribution	Landlord or Farming Generation			Tenant or Starting Farming Generation		
	Value	Rate	Value of Annual Contribution	Value	Rate	Value of Annual Contribution
	($)	(%)	($)	($)	(%)	($)
LAND						
Interest		6.0				
Taxes		2.0				
(Total Value)	$175,000	8.0	$14,000	0	0	0
BUILDINGS						
Depreciation		5.0				
Interest		4.0				
Repair						
Taxes		3.0				
Insurance						
(Total Value)	$ 65,000	12.0	$ 7,800	0	0	0
MACH. AND EQUIP.						
Depreciation		10.0				
Interest		4.5				
Repair		3.0				
Taxes		None				
Insurance		0.5				
(Total Value)	$ 55,000	18.0	$ 9,900	0	0	0
LIVESTOCK (Breeding and Dairy)						
Depreciation		None			None	
Interest		8.0			8.0	
Taxes		0.5			0.5	
Insurance		0.5			0.5	
(Total Value)	$ 50,000	9.0	$ 4,500	$10,000	9.0	$ 900
LABOR AND MANAGEMENT			$12,000			$12,000
OTHER CONTRIBUTIONS			None			None
TOTAL CONTRIBUTIONS $61,100	TOTAL ANNUAL CONTRIBUTION		$48,200	TOTAL ANNUAL CONTRIBUTION		$12,900
	PERCENT TOTAL CONTRIBUTION		78.9%	PERCENT TOTAL CONTRIBUTION		21.1%

interest rate, you select and multiply it by the average value of the asset over its lifetime. An easier way to do this is to use 50% of the appropriate interest rate. Thus, if you select 8% as the rate, use 4% of the total investment.

Repair costs refer to those costs which are fixed and do not change in the short run or by level of use, such as the barn roof, a paint job, etc. Determine the value of taxes and insurance by using the current costs for these contributions.

Figuring Labor and Management

The value of the labor and management the parties contribute should be determined by mutual understanding as to who provides what quantity of labor and how management will be shared. You might consider typical farm wage rates for the labor input. And you could select a certain percent of the value of farm production as an appropriate management rate.

Other contributions would reflect any special assets contributed

Fig. 7-1. These two boys and their father have worked out a business arrangement where they are paid for their contributions to the business. (Courtesy, *Wisconsin Agriculturist*)

to the business. You can determine their value by using some of the same methods used above.

The Value of Annual Contribution

Enter the "value," "rate (%)," and "value of annual contribution" in the appropriate columns for each of the contributors to the business. If there are more than two people involved, make additional columns. Then total the "value of annual contribution" column for each contributor and add the totals to get a gross value of all contributions. Divide the total "value of annual contribution" of each person by the total of all "values of annual contribution" to arrive at a percent of total contributions.

Based on this percentage figure, all costs and returns not accounted for in the above analysis are shared on the basis of the percentage determined. This should provide an equitable agreement if you used appropriate figures in your analysis.

Final Test

One further test is to apply this agreement to a well-organized, sound business of adequate size, good productivity, and high efficiency. This can be done by applying the terms of the agreement to past years' records or by using a forward planning budget. Use both methods if possible.

No matter how fair the agreement is or how well it is written, it will not be successful if income is not sufficient for all parties to share. Thus, before consummating an operating agreement, thoroughly examine your business's past and future profitability, liquidity, and solvency. Take corrective action needed and plan for working within the framework of the proposed operating agreement.

The Worksheet and Example

Table 7-1, "Contributions Approach Worksheet and Example," illustrates a two-generation sharing agreement example for a 70-cow dairy unit. The farming generation is supplying 78.9% of the inputs, while the starting farming generation is supplying 21.1% of the inputs. This can be rounded to 80-20. Or if the farming generation wants to help the starting farming generation, it could be set at 75-25. This would constitute a beginning sharing arrangement.

All the listed costs associated with the land, buildings, and machinery are paid for by the farming generation. The starting farming generation will pay their own interest, taxes, and insurance on their livestock. Receipts from sales of livestock owned by each will be kept by the respective owners. But all calves born will be owned 75-25 if that is the split selected. Operating expenses such as feed, seed, fertilizer, fuel, oil, etc., and operating income such as milk, calves, crop sales, etc., will also be shared 75-25. Within a few years (about five) the herd will be owned 75-25.

The starting generation may even begin to buy machinery and equipment or additional land. In a few years (two to three) the agreement may no longer be equitable. Therefore, this arrangement should be reviewed and changed at that point. Perhaps, if the business relationship is working out, a more formal long-term agreement should be entered into at that point.

This example can also show what cash rent might be appropriate for the farm—at least from the landlord's point of view. If the landlord wants to full cost the rental rate, then $21,800 ($14,000 plus $7,800) per year would be the rental rate. Landlords may also want to add a charge for their management effort. If the landlord furnished lime or grass seed, the cost of these items would be added.

This example also could illustrate a livestock share agreement. If the landlord furnishes the land, the building, half of the livestock, and $6,050 of labor and management, a 50-50 livestock share lease would be equitable. The tenant would furnish all the machinery and equipment, half of the livestock, and $17,950 of labor and management. Of course, in all the agreements mentioned here, there is room for bargaining.

The contributions approach is valuable to determine the equity of a business arrangement. It shows how to allocate the returns between the landlord and the tenant, based on their respective contributions. The ideal arrangement will also attempt to attain the maximum economic efficiency of resource use.

Wage Incentive Programs

One way to get started is with a wage incentive agreement. Here the employee furnishes only the labor and receives a base wage, some fringe benefits, and a wage incentive. This generally should be a relatively short-term arrangement. This gives beginners a chance to see if they like farming and can take responsibility, as well as showing if the parties can work together.

The wage incentive should *not* substitute for a reasonable wage. There are two approaches for a wage incentive—payments based on physical output (pigs weaned per litter, crop yields per acre, pounds of milk sold per cow) or based on profits or gross income. (See Appendix A-1c for suggestions.) The wage incentive program provides for sharing of profits but not losses.

The wage incentive must be carefully outlined. All terms must be thoroughly defined. A written agreement describing its purpose, employee responsibilites, calculation methods, arbitration methods, and payment methods should be made. The goals must be reasonably reached and be large enough to be worthwhile. The employee must have some control over the variables which affect the payment size.

Wage incentives have a good deal of appeal but present several difficulties. Incentives based solely on physical output of one enterprise may encourage uneconomic production practices or the neglect of other important factors. Incentives based on "profit" present problems of defining "profit." Perhaps the employee's incentive will become too dependent on past decisions, such as overinvestment in fixed facilities, income tax strategies, selection of enterprise combinations, or other decisions beyond the employee's control. In some cases the employer will be unwilling to open up the farm business accounts to the degree necessary to calculate profit.

Developing clear and simple arrangements which all parties thoroughly understand is difficult. Much thought and planning must be done before a program such as this can be implemented successfully.

Enterprise Working Agreements

In an enterprise working agreement the employee furnishes some personal property such as machinery or livestock along with labor. Generally the employee will make major decisions related to the enterprise but will not make major decisions affecting the whole business. This type of arrangement should generally be viewed as a short-term arrangement.

The fixed contributions to the selected enterprise by each party are allocated as in the contributions approach to arrive at the desired percentage share arrangement. Other enterprise costs are shared on this percentage basis. Generally the employee is guaranteed a minimum allowance for wage and fringe benefits.

A complete farm budget should be made to analyze the profitability, liquidity-cash flow, and solvency characteristics of this arrangement.

Sharing Agreement—Joint Venture

The sharing agreement can be based on the contributions approach as outlined earlier. In that situation an 80-20 or 75-25 ratio seemed appropriate. This provides an excellent vehicle for starting a beginner.

In some cases two parties may have a joint venture with the field machinery and carry on cropping activities together. The land, buildings, and livestock are owned or rented, and managed independently. In other situations, the parties may be together for a livestock enterprise but carry on other separate independent farming activities.

LEASES

With rapidly increasing capital inputs into the farm business, more farm operators are turning to leases as an alternative method of controlling resources. Leasing is one method of gaining control without the capital outlay or debt associated with purchasing. In some states more land is operated on lease arrangements than is owned by operators. Leasing is one way a beginner can get started in farming with limited capital. Many farmers remain tenants all their lives and are very successful financially. The authors have seen farms where the second- and third-generation tenants are working with second- and third-generation landlords in mutually beneficial agreements.

One of the main disadvantages of renting is the short year-to-year lease arrangement. This may make it necessary for many tenants to pull up and move to another farm at a tremendous cost to both the tenant and the landlord. Good leases can help prevent this.

In some areas this has brought about depletion of the soil and

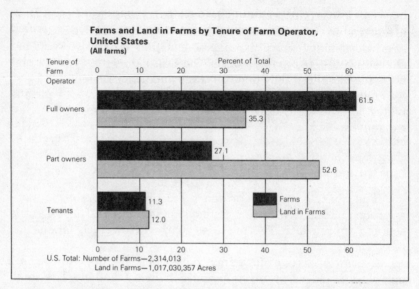

Fig. 7-2. The largest number of farms is operated by full owners but over 50% of the land is operated by part owners; that is, they own part and rent part of the land they operate. Full tenants are a minority of farmers.

run-down farm buildings. In other sections tenant farms are the most productive farms in the community, with very satisfactory conditions for tenant and landlord.

Even with certain shortcomings in the system of renting, the advantages of renting outweigh the disadvantages for the person with a small amount of capital who does not wish to go heavily into debt. Not all tenants can or will become farm owners. In fact, ownership provides no assurance of success and in some cases is the downfall of the beginner.

Almost every state college of agriculture has lease forms available which will fit local situations much better than a standard lease. These are more or less only guides for farmers to use to meet their own situations. An attorney should be consulted to draw up the lease.

Most landlords and tenants wish to develop a leasing arrangement which is economically sound and which is equitable to all parties. Thus, a lease arrangement can be said to have two primary objectives: (1) attainment of the maximum economic efficiency in resources used and (2) equality or fairness in allocating the returns between landlord and tenant based on their respective inputs. Both of these important considerations should be carefully incorporated into the leasing arrangement. Optimum farm organization as well as profit maximizing production practices should be attainable under an economically efficient lease. To be equitable, the lease must provide the mechanism to reward suppliers of the business inputs with outputs in the same proportion to those inputs.

There are several distinct interests or rights an individual can hold in property. Taken together, they represent a "bundle of rights" which can be compared to a cable with several strands— each strand represents a distinct interest or right. The total cable represents complete ownership. The complete or "fee simple" owner has the right to possess it; use it; sell it; give it away; devise it to heirs; mortgage it; grant easements on it; enter into contractual agreements involving its use or disposition; and lease some of these rights to others. These ownership rights are limited by government through taxation, police power, eminent domain, and zoning. By *leasing* the owner or landlord gives some of the strands in the cable to the operator or tenant in exchange for a rental fee.

The contributions approach discussed earlier in this chapter can be used to determine the appropriate rent. Custom is not always a good way to determine rent. Technology and economic conditions are changing rapidly, and these conditions may well affect leasing arrangements. Good farms with good landlords attract good tenants. In many cases the quantity either of available farms or of tenants may put some party in a stronger bargaining position. Therefore some "dickering" or "bargaining" will take place. But remember, a lease which is unfair to either party encourages dishonesty.

Make your lease fair, written, clearly understandable, and in tune with modern technology. Such leases make for better understanding, better working relationships, and better farming, all of which should make for better incomes. All parties involved must have the opportunity to make money from this business arrangement.

Cash Leases

In a cash lease the landlord generally furnishes the land, buildings, management, legal arrangements for a written lease, and, in some cases, the grass seed and lime. The tenant generally furnishes the labor, management, machinery, livestock, and operating expenses, including a rent payment to the landlord. This rent payment may be monthly, quarterly, semiannually, or annually, depending on the type of farming and the needs of the parties involved. Landlords pay all costs associated with their contributions, while tenants pay all costs associated with theirs. The landlord does *not* share in the tenant's profits or losses.

The cash rental fee may be determined by three methods or a combination of these three plus some "bargaining." The first method is the "market" approach. The market approach observes what is currently happening in the marketplace and generally should reflect what tenants and landlords are willing to agree to in rental terms. It does not specifically analyze the variables affecting local rental rates.

The second method is the "cost" approach. Landlords would like to recover all their ownership costs or fixed costs. In some cases this is not feasible, especially if area land values are substantially above their income-generating value or if there is a limited demand for land. Imprudent overinvestment in fixed assets such as buildings can also affect how much of the fixed cost the landlord might recover. The discussion of the contributions approach can give you some guidance. At least owners must recover their cash costs in the short run and a reasonable return to all contributions in the long run or they will not generally be content to retain their ownership. The cost approach is of somewhat more concern to the landlord than to the tenant.

The third method—the "income" approach—is more appropriate for the tenant. Here the total value (cash and non-cash) of the tenant's inputs is subtracted from the total value of production (cash and non-cash). The difference is the maximum the tenant can pay. One could question letting the residual accrue to real estate rather than to some other input such as management. But, once the figures have been calculated, some adjustments can be made.

Armed with these three analyses, the landlord and tenant can bargain as to the final lease terms. Both parties will consider items such as length of lease, quality of farm, ability of tenant, characteristics of landlord, risk, availability of farms and tenants, technology, and economic conditions.

Another method of determining rent is the variable cash lease approach. There are so many variations of this that farmers would want to see which specific methods are used in their own area for their farm type.

In periods of increased profit potential, rapidly changing prices, locally poor weather conditions, changing tax and social security regulations, and other variable factors, both landlords and tenants may want a flexible cash rental rate. Most of the variations of this revolve around price and yield risk factors or some combination thereof. In some cases the tenant pays the value of a fixed physical amount, for example, 30 bushels of No. 2 shelled corn per acre. In others the tenant pays a fixed percent of the crop value, for example, 30%. Still others provide for a base cash rent times an index of yields and/or prices. Some have a sliding scale arrangement.

The flexible or variable cash lease should not try to accomplish what a share rent could do better. But this method could help solve the problem of annually determining rental rates and could provide some risk protection to both parties.

Share Rents—Livestock

In a livestock share lease the landlord generally furnishes all the land and buildings, and a percent of the livestock, management, inventory, and operating expenses. Landlords furnish all the costs associated with their contributions. Tenants generally furnish all the labor and machinery and associated expenses, and a percent of the livestock, management, inventory, and operating expenses. The appropriate percent figures are generally determined by the contributions approach and by bargaining. The tenant and landlord then share their joint expenses and their farming income on the basis of the agreed upon percentage.

In the share rental determination analysis procedure, careful consideration must be given to extraordinary weed problems, soil fertility problems, grain harvesting and handling changes, irrigation, drainage, large and highly capitalized livestock facilities, custom in the area, and the parties' respective bargaining positions.

Share Rents—Crop

In a crop share lease the landlord generally furnishes all the land and buildings, and a percent of the management, inventory, and operating expenses. Landlords furnish all the costs associated with their contributions. Tenants generally furnish all the labor and machinery and associated expenses, and a percent of the management, inventory, and operating expenses.Again, the appropriate percent figures are generally determined by the contributions approach and by bargaining.

The same items outlined under "Share Rents—Livestock" should also be considered. The tenant and landlord then share their joint expenses and their farming income on the basis of the agreed upon percentage.

Tenants who have a house furnished, use some livestock buildings, use some cropland for livestock, use pasture lands, or have other assets furnished to them from which the landlord obtains no income will pay a cash rent. This is sometimes called "privilege" rent.

Other Rental or Lease Arrangements

In some situations the cash or share leases do not consist of the total farms. Individual fields are rented on a field basis, on either a cash or share basis. In some cases share agreements will only cover a livestock enterprise. The same analytical procedures as previously outlined can be used to arrive at an appropriate rental agreement.

Custom farming is becoming more popular in some areas of the country. This may involve the hiring of a custom operator for a specific operation on a specific crop such as custom cotton picking, corn combining, wheat combining, corn planting, pesticide spraying, etc. In other situations the complete cropping procedure is hired on a custom or contract basis. This agreement many times has a stipulation as to the timing and quality of work done with incentives and penalties associated with it.

Building Rental

Sometimes buildings are cash rented. This is a bit more difficult to analyze because of local conditions. Two indicators of fair rental value are (1) building ownership costs and (2) the contribution of buildings to farm returns. The owner looks at (1) and the renter looks at (2). Here the supply-demand situation comes into play. In many areas farm consolidation has produced a surplus of farm-

Fig. 7-3. Large, high capacity machines can cover many acres in a day. To spread fixed costs, many farmers depend on a custom operator for harvest. (Courtesy, New Idea)

steads. Retiring farmers who continue to live on their farms and cash rent their land also generally have surplus buildings. The state of technology in the area must also be considered. The rental value of corn cribs is very low if not nonexistent in areas where all the corn is harvested as shelled corn. Location, convenience, and up-to-date design also affect rental values.

Owners are better off to rent the buildings out so long as their returns are greater than their variable costs. Renters are better off to rent if their rental costs are below their ownership costs. Thus, it gets down to a bargaining situation to finally arrive at the terms of the lease. For a fair initial agreement, some middle ground must be determined. Owners should receive at least enough to cover repairs, taxes, and insurance, or they would be better off to destroy the buildings. Tenants should be willing to pay some sort of reasonable price if the earnings from the buildings warrant use at all.

Machinery Rental

Machinery leasing is becoming more popular and available. It is especially suited for moderate- or small-sized operations. It is easy to calculate whether this is a good plan. One uses a break even analysis. This is the formula:

$$\text{Break even acres or hours} = \frac{\text{total annual fixed costs}}{\left(\begin{array}{c}\text{lease rate per acre}\\\text{or hour}\end{array}\right) - \left(\begin{array}{c}\text{variable cost per acre}\\\text{or hour}\end{array}\right)}$$

Thus, if lease rates were $8 per hour and variable costs were $3 per hour and the total annual fixed costs were $500, the break even hours are 100:

$$\frac{\$500}{\$8-\$3} = \frac{\$500}{\$5} = 100$$

Thus, leasing would be the best alternative up to 100 hours. After that, ownership would be cheaper.

Fig. 7-4. For highly specialized crops the short-term lease of a machine may be the most economical way to get the harvesting done. (Courtesy, International Harvester)

Livestock Rental

In some cases livestock (breeding and dairy) rental can be an advantage to owners and tenants. In arriving at an equitable agreement the same analysis procedures should be used as outlined earlier in this chapter.

Some possible advantages to renters are (1) use of capital for other purposes, (2) control of more resources, (3) sharing of risk, (4) increased volume of business, (5) cash flow advantages, and (6) potential tax advantages.

Possible advantages for owners are (1) having "rental" income for Social Security advantages, (2) securing retention and maintenance of the breeding herd without having to provide labor and other inputs, (3) having a return on a productive investment, and (4) having a vehicle for transferring ownership and phasing out of the business.

Generally, however, investment strategies for tenants and other operations would suggest that the ownership of breeding or dairy livestock is the best alternative. But all parties should carefully analyze the profit opportunities before making a decision.

Final Lease or Rental Comments

As you can see, the variation of lease agreements are many. Owners and operators need to carefully analyze their contributions to arrive at an appropriate lease arrangement which is mutually beneficial. Then a written agreement should be drawn up with the help of an attorney.

PARTNERSHIPS

Partnerships are generally a somewhat more involved form of business organization than the ones discussed earlier. A partnership can be described as a group or aggregation of business owners. Two or more people contribute business assets to the partnership. They then share in the operation, management, and profits and losses of that business.

There are two kinds of partnerships—general and limited. The general partnership is more familiar. Here all general partners are full participants in the business. This makes them liable for the actions of all the other partners. All the general partners then stand liable for the actions of all partners, within the scope of the partnership framework.

In a limited partnership the limited partners are not bound by obligations of the partnership beyond their own financial contributions. But the limited partners cannot participate in management and in most cases cannot contribute services, cannot have their names in the partnership name, and cannot recover their capital contributions until outside creditors are satisfied. In other words, the limited partner is just an investor, not a participant except for financial contribution. But the limited partner shares in profits and losses. There must be at least one general partner in a limited partnership. That person handles the management of the partnership debts and obligations. In both types of partnerships the partners should share according to their total contributions in the business.

A separate informational income tax form is filed for both types of partnerships, but the partners report their shares of the partnership profits or losses and capital gains or losses on their own income tax forms. They then pay income tax at their own tax rates. Generally there are no major immediate tax consequences at the formation of a partnership, but there can be later on. All partners should keep all the records pertaining to assets transferred into the partnership. This would include original cost basis, date of acquisition, adjusted tax basis, and investment tax credit.

The partnership is dissolved either by agreement or by law. Dissolution by law occurs at the death of a partner. Other causes could include bankruptcy, unlawful activity, court order due to incompetency, breaches of the partnership agreement, or the ability of the business to operate only at a loss. The partnership can also be dissolved if the agreed upon length of life is reached, if all partners decide on a dissolution, if a partner is expelled, or if a partner requests dissolution when no agreed upon term is stated.

It is important to have a written partnership agreement which clearly outlines the contributions of each party, the methods of calculating costs and returns and of sharing profits and losses, the way management decisions will be made, the kind and amount of insurance to be carried, the manner of arbitrating disagreements, the limits on business activity, and the provisions for termination, including buy-sell agreements. Partnerships sound deceptively simple. They are not! Legal, tax, and accounting advice is essential if the partnership is to be properly formed, operated, and dissolved. This is not an activity for amateurs!

The partnership can provide the advantage of the pooling of resources such as land, labor, capital, and management; provide for flexibility in the operation and organization of the business; and provide for a flexible management arrangement. But, the partnership involves unlimited individual liability, makes for difficulty in determining the value of each partner's interest, complicates some accounting procedures, has an uncertainty of term in some cases, and lacks uniformity in business operation and organization. It is, however, somewhat simpler than the corporation and is somewhat easier to start and dissolve. Many of the disadvantages of the partnership can be overcome by a carefully thought out and implemented partnership agreement. (See Table 7-2, "Comparison of Farm Business Organizations.")

CORPORATIONS

The corporation is an artificial legal entity created under state laws. It is separate from its owners. The owners are called shareholders, as they own the shares of the corporation. The corporation, as a separate individual, is generally subject to the same type of actions as a natural person, for example, it can sue and be sued.

Farm corporations may be classed as "closely held" or as "publicly owned." Closely held corporations are owned by a small number of shareholders, often by members of the same family or by relatives. Usually shares of stock are not made available to outsiders. This is the more common type of farm corporation.

Publicly owned corporations may have many hundred owners, located in all parts of the country. This type of corporation is, however, not nearly as common in farming as in other types of business. A corporation has two distinct advantages, namely, (1) each shareholder of the corporation is liable for only the amount of the shares owned, and (2) in a corporation each shareholder can purchase any number of shares, and the shares are easily transferrable. The limited liability *may not* be a big advantage when the corporate owners must sign individually and personally for debt obligations, as is frequently the case.

There are two general types of corporations—the regular or Subchapter C, and the Subchapter S, sometimes called tax option, small family, psuedo, small business, and various other names. The Subchapter S corporation option came into being in 1958 through federal law.

The Subchapter S elects to be taxed as partnership. Each

Table 7-2. Comparison of Farm Business Organizations[1]

	Sole Proprietor	Partnership	Corporation
Nature of entity	Single individual.	Aggregate of two or more individuals.	Legal person separate from shareholder-owners.
Life of business	Terminates on death.	Agreed term; terminates on death of a partner.	Perpetual or fixed term of years.
Liability	Personally liable.	Each partner liable for all partnership obligations.[2]	Shareholders not liable for corporate obligations.
Source of capital	Personal investment; loans.	Partners' contributions; loans.	Contributions of shareholders for stock; sale of stock; bonds and other loans.
Management decisions	Proprietor.	Agreement of partners.	Shareholders elect directors who manage business through officers elected by directors.
Limits on business activity	Proprietor's discretion.	Partnership agreement.	Articles of incorporation and state corporation law.
Transfer of interest	Terminates proprietorship.	Dissolves partnership; new partnership may be formed if all agree.	Transfer of stock does not affect continuity of business—may be transferred to outsiders if no restrictions.
Effect of death	Liquidation.	Liquidation or sale to surviving partners.	No effect on corporation. Stock passes by will or inheritance.

Income taxes[3]

Income taxed to individual; 60% deduction for long-term capital gains. Capital gains may be "preference" income and subject to special tax.

Partnership files an information return but pays no tax. Each partner reports share of income or loss, capital gains and losses as an individual. Capital gains may be "preference" income and subject to special tax.

REGULAR CORPORATION (Sub. C)

Corporation files a tax return and pays tax on income; salaries to shareholder-employees deductible.

Capital gains offset by capital losses; no 60% deduction for capital gains.

Rate: The rate structure for corporations for tax years after Dec. 31, 1978, is:

$ Taxable Income	Percent
0—25,000	17
25,000— 50,000	20
50,000— 75,000	30
75,000—100,000	40
Over 100,000	46

Shareholders taxed on dividends paid to them.

TAX-OPTION CORPORATION (Sub. S)

Corporation files an information return but pays no tax. Each shareholder reports share of income, operating loss, and long-term capital gain.

[1] Adapted from N.C.R. 11, *The Farm Corporation.*

[2] See discussion of limited partnership.

[3] Federal income taxes.

shareholder includes his or her share of ordinary corporate gains or losses on the personal income tax. Capital gains are also reported and are eligible for the 60% deduction. Capital losses do not pass through to the shareholders, but the investment tax credit does.

To qualify for Subchapter S treatment, all shareholders must consent to the Subchapter S election. There can only be one class of stock outstanding, and there can only be 15 shareholders. Co-owned stock by husband and wife is considered a single ownership. All shareholders must be individuals or estates, and no more than 20% of the gross income can come from rent, royalties, dividends, interest, and sales or exchange of stocks or securities.

The Subchapter C or regular corporation pays taxes like an individual except that it has no personal or non-business deductions. Both the Subchapter C and the Subchapter S report business income (such as crop sales, livestock sales, etc.) and business expenses (such as seed, employee fringe benefits, feed, fertilizer, interest, depreciation, etc.) as do sole proprietor farmers. But they also include expenses such as salaries, rents, and interest paid to shareholders as business expenses. Wages paid to employees, including shareholder employees, are subject to Social Security taxes. Here is where the similarity ends. The Subchapter S situation has

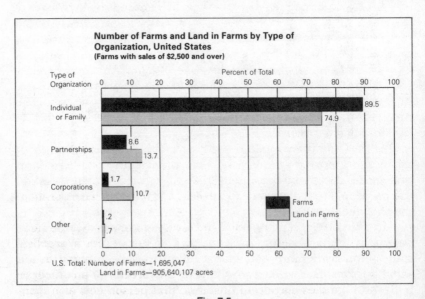

Fig. 7-5.

already been outlined. The Subchapter C pays income tax as does an individual. But, capital gains treatment for qualified capital asset sales is *not* subject to the 60% deduction, and capital gains are offset by capital losses. The shareholders cannot take advantage of the corporation's capital gains or losses. The Subchapter C has a special tax rate, and dividends paid out are taxed to the individual stockholder receiving the dividend. These dividends are taxed at the shareholder's own personal tax rate. They are not tax-deductible to the corporation. An operating loss by the Subchapter C corporation cannot be used by the shareholders to offset their personal incomes.

You need to check your state laws and tax regulations. All the tax laws regarding corporations are complicated and are changing. Many income tax problems arise because of the complex tax relationship between the corporation and the shareholders. Many tax regulations are aimed at preventing tax evasion by dealings between the corporation and the shareholders. You will need competent professional legal, tax, and accounting help for this. (See Table 7-2, "Comparison of Farm Business Organizations.")

Persons wishing to form a corporation make application to the proper agency in their state. Each state determines the general purposes for which a corporation may be formed and the procedure which must be followed to establish a corporation.

When clearance has been received from the proper officials of the state, shares of stock are issued to the persons who are to be the owners of the corporation. A share of stock represents a share of the total worth of the business of the corporation. It is *not* an interest in individual assets. Shareholders own the corporation, but the corporation operates the farm and carries on the business. The shareholders elect a board of directors to manage the corporation. The directors elect the officers, who are generally responsible for the day-to-day operation of the corporate business.

Separation of ownership and management is characteristic of the corporate form of business. Sole proprietors own their farm businesses and make the management decisions. In a partnership, the partners are the owners and decision makers. In a corporation, the shareholders are the owners but not the managers.

In a small corporation, however, it often happens that the same person is a shareholder, director, and officer. From a practical standpoint, ownership and management may be merged in the same persons. But when a shareholder is a director or an officer or both, and handles corporate business, that person acts as a manager, not as an owner. The separation of ownership and management always exists legally, even though the owners elect themselves managers.

As the number of shareholders increases, it is likely that some of the shareholder-owners will participate in corporate activities only through their power to vote for the directors.

Once the corporation has been formed and directors have been elected, the carrying out of the requirements is not complicated. Day-to-day operations of the farm corporation are very similar to those of a farm partnership. The main difference is that certain meetings and some records are required by law. The state requires that annual reports be sent in, that the shareholders meet annually, and that the directors hold periodic meetings and keep written minutes of these meetings.

The transferring of ownership of a farm to the next generation always presents problems and, under certain circumstances, may be costly. In a corporate form of organization, shares of stock provide a simple and convenient way to make lifetime as well as death transfers.

A share of stock may be sold, given away, or transferred by will or under the state inheritance laws at death. Transfer of shares of stock results in the shift of ownership interests in the farm corporation without necessarily disrupting the continuity of the business. Although it is theoretically possible to transfer small, undivided interests in the assets of a business regardless of the form of business organization, shares of stock make the transfer easier.

Transfer of shares by gift is one way of minimizing state inheritance and federal estate taxes. Gifts of stock in a family farm corporation have been made by parents to equalize advantages given to children for education, getting started in a business, etc. Stock has been distributed by gift or sale as a means of dividing ownership in proportion to labor, capital, and management contributions to the business.

The ease of orderly and gradual transfer of a going farm business by transfer of shares of stock can provide for a progressive shift in ownership and management. Control arrangements are very flexible. In the simplest case, retention of 51% of the stock preserves control, even though the other 49% may have been given away. However, more refined arrangements are possible to divide ownership and control. For example, a particular family corporation might issue two or more classes of stock. All states permit nonvoting stock or preferred stock, or both. These stocks may be used to give special or preferential dividend rights to a shareholder. (The Subchapter S corporation may have only one class of stock outstanding.) Or a widow's stock could be exchanged for bonds or notes to make her a creditor instead of an owner. Such arrangements are useful in keeping voting rights within the circle of experienced managers.

Corporate real and personal property are subject to the regular property taxes in each state. Shares of stock in the hands of the shareholder may also be personal property subject to tax in some states. State law may provide some form of offset so that the property tax does not fall on the property owned by the corporation and also on the share of stock which represents an interest in corporate property.

Sometimes, however, these taxes can be more severe after incorporation. The tax may reach property interests of a corporation that would escape taxation in the hands of an individual. It may happen that the total tax on the corporation and the shareholders is greater than the tax would have been on an individual alone.

Before entering into a corporation one needs to carefully consider the reasons for incorporating. In many situations it is *not* the best alternative, as other simpler methods can be used to accomplish the desired results. Future plans for the business, the characteristics of the people involved, the income tax situation, estate planning goals and objectives, type and size of business, legal and accounting requirements, the number of people involved, and dissolution plans must all be considered and evaluated carefully. *A plan for perpetuity is worthless if there is not a viable business with qualified people to carry it on. People run businesses—a pile of corporation papers does not!*

Insist that your attorney, tax practitioner, and accountant thoroughly explain the corporation so you understand what it involves. If you then decide to move ahead, you will do a better job of using this tool. In many cases the corporation will be the best available tool. Properly set up and operated, it can be of help to many farm businesses.

Which Arrangement Should I Choose?

This will depend upon the people and the business situation. The goals and objectives of the people and the business, size and type of business, length of planning horizon, profitability of the business, and age and ability of the people involved are all factors to consider. Chapter 6 should help you make your decision. But remember, some goals and objectives are competitive and some compromises will have to be made. Also, you may evolve from one form of business arrangement to another as time and conditions change.

As a final note, remember this chapter does not give detailed information, but rather gives an overview of different arrangements. When you narrow your interest down to a couple of alternatives, study further in those areas.

Questions and Problems for Class Discussion

1. Why have a written agreement?

2. Work out a contributions approach example appropriate for your situation, your area, your farm type, or your area of interest.

3. Describe the differences and similarities between a wage incentive program and an enterprise sharing agreement. What are some advantages and disadvantages of each?

4. What are three main types of farm leases? How are they similar? How are they different?

5. What are some other rental arrangements? How can they be used?

6. Discuss partnerships and how they can be used.

7. Discuss corporations and how they can be used.

CHAPTER 8

Estate Planning and Asset Transfer

Highlights of Chapter

Estate planning has always been important but is becoming more important. In this chapter we will define some terms, outline objectives, discuss the estate planning team, and look at a kit of tools to use in estate planning. The steps in estate planning are outlined. For details on current estate and inheritance rules and regulations you should consult your estate planning team. Estate planning should be done early in life. The plan should be reviewed periodically and updated when necessary.

Estate planning for all families, including farm families, has always been an important family and business concern. It has grown in recent years because of the rapid appreciation of assets and larger farm capital investments which will eventually need to be transferred, massive changes in the Federal Estate Laws, and changes in state inheritance laws. While each state has somewhat different laws regarding estates, and both state and federal regulations change from time to time, several things can be said about estate planning.

Definitions

Before talking about estate planning, we should become better acquainted with some terms.

Estate—A person's property in real estate or personal property, a person's possessions. The extent of one's interest in or ownership of property.

Estate plan—A comprehensive plan designed to create the desired *economic* and *legal* consequences in the disposition of the estate.

Estate laws—Those laws, rules, and regulations pertaining to or governing the disposition of an estate under the federal government.

Inheritance laws—Those laws, rules, and regulations governing the disposition of an estate under the government of your state.

Death taxes—Those taxes levied at the time of a person's death. Estate and inheritance taxes.

Objectives of an Estate Plan

The disposition of your estate is primarily under your control but subject to some guidelines set forth by statutes. To most effectively plan your estate, you should outline your objectives of the estate plan. Planning objectives are competitive, and you will probably have to compromise in some areas to most effectively meet these objectives which should be based on your goals and values.

In an estate plan there are four general objectives for you to consider. You may also develop others to suit yourself.

1. *Establish financial security*—As you have accumulated an estate over your active working lifetime to provide for a pleasant, financially secure retirement or for other purposes, premature disposition of these assets to others could result in unneeded financial stress and problems. Therefore, you should carefully guard against putting yourself in a position where insufficient assets are available for your current and expected use.

2. *Provide for the orderly transfer of assets*—While your financial security is perhaps the overriding objective, the next generation should be provided an opportunity to take over the going farm business intact in an orderly fashion. Careful planning can help both generations achieve this orderly transfer as well as financial security and opportunity.

In the opinion of the authors, these are the two most important objectives. They involve the *people* so they can best meet their personal goals and objectives and the *business* so it can continue with a minimum of disruption.

3. *Be equitable*—This means being fair and not necessarily being equal. Some heirs may have contributed more than others to the

Fig. 8-1. A farm such as this represents a large investment. A good estate plan can help provide the method for an orderly transfer to the next generation. (Courtesy, University of Wisconsin Department of Agricultural Journalism)

creation of an estate, while others due to age or some handicap need special attention. Also, some heirs may have contributed more to the physical and mental well-being of the older generation than others. These situations need to be recognized and dealt with.

4. *Minimize death taxes and probate costs*—Holding these costs to a minimum will result in the maximum conservation of the estate. However, if minimizing these cost results in not being able to satisfactorily meet the other objectives, you will have to make some compromises.

The task of the estate planner is to find the best possible methods of meeting these objectives consistent with the goals and values of the people involved.

The Farm Estate Planning Team

Farm estate planning can be involved. There are many viewpoints on how it should be done. Also, a great deal of very specialized knowledge is required. Therefore, it may be advisable to draw on the experience and knowledge of several qualified people. One of the team could act as the coordinator or captain.

1. *Attorney*—There are certain legal requirements to estate planning. Legal documents need to be drawn up and executed. Therefore, the attorney is a key person on the team. At the outset you should talk about the fees and services involved.

2. *Financial advisor*—Your credit supplier, banker, and bank trust officer should also be on the team. They can suggest effective

financial strategies to use and can provide an institutionalized agent to act during estate settlement. An institution can provide continuity of management in the event that family members are under age, lack business skills, or are unavailable to serve for other reasons.

3. *Tax advisor*—Death taxes can take a big bite out of an estate. Certified public accountants (C.P.A.s) and other qualified tax advisors can aid the estate planner in working out a tax cost minimizing plan which can coordinate with the other parts of the plan. But do not let beating the tax collector make you forget about the people and the business.

4. *Life insurance agent*—Farm businesses are usually "cash poor." Estate settlement time usually brings with it a big demand for cash in a short period. A good insurance program can help provide that needed cash.

5. *Farm management advisor*—While in most cases the same principles of estate planning and business management can be applied to both farm and non-farm situations, farming is unique in many respects. The farm management advisor can bring the needed skills to help plan for the continuity of the business during this time of stress on both the business and the survivors.

6. *You*—This is your plan! You must be the guiding force and final decision maker. You must tell the team what goals, values, and objectives are important to you. This will help you get the best plan to fit your situation.

Tools of Estate Planning

The carpenter uses a kit of tools to build a barn. So also does the estate planner need a kit of tools to build an appropriate estate plan for you. There are five basic tools which can be used. You may not need all of them, but you will probably need at least two or three.

1. *Wills*—This tool should be used by everyone. A will is simply a legal enforceable statement as to what you want done with your property after death. If you die without a will, your state has made provisions as to how the estate will be distributed. There are *very few* cases where these laws will best accomplish what a family needs or wants. Everyone should have a will! An attorney should be consulted for the drafting of a will. After it is completed the will should be reviewed periodically and if necessary changed to keep it

up-to-date. Having no will or having an outdated will has been responsible for many family tragedies.

2. *Gifts*—This tool can be used to transfer money or property (real or personal) during your lifetime. There are three basic requirements for gifts to be recognized. They are: (1) The one giving (donor) must have the gift to give and must deliver it. (2) The one receiving the gift (donee) must accept the gift. (3) The gift cannot be taken back by the donor—that is, the gift must be irrevocable. It is always best to document the gift. The gift can reduce the estate, relieve the donor of management, and promote the financial management abilities of the donee. But do not give away your needed financial security!

3. *Trusts*—This tool is perhaps the least understood and most underutilized of all the tools. It can in many cases be an effective method of transfer. A trust is an arrangement by which the maker of the trust transfers title of the property to a trustee. The trustee manages the property, distributes the income, and in some cases distributes the principal to the beneficiaries. This is done in accordance with the provisions of the trust agreement and other legal documents. The trust can help save on death taxes, income taxes, and administrative costs. It can help to conserve capital assets from mismanagement, provide experienced business management, and provide management for those who will not or cannot assume the management burden. Further, it can be used for gifts and for providing flexibility in estate planning. There are generally two kinds of trusts—living and testamentary. The living trust is set up to take effect during your lifetime and can be revocable or irrevocable. The testamentary trust takes effect after death. Talk to your estate planning team, especially your bank trust officer and attorney, about this tool which offers so much potential.

4. *Insurance*—Life insurance can help provide that needed cash at the time when cash can be especially short. But do not just use a large insurance policy for the entire estate plan! You need to ask three questions about insurance: (1) How much? (2) What kind? (3) From whom? As to Question 1, you need to list the financial requirements at death and subtract from that the existing resources. The remainder is what you need. Question 2 is answered by determining how much you want to use life insurance as a savings vehicle. Determine how much you wish to save and check to see what size straight life policy this would take. The rest of the insurance require-

ment can be met with term insurance. Question 3 is more difficult to
answer. You will need to be a careful insurance shopper to get your
policies from the top rated, financially sound companies which offer
the policies which best meet your requirements. Then determine
which company gives you the best deal.

5. *Form of business organization*—The type of farm business
you select will affect the day-to-day operation of the business as well
as the way it can best be transferred. (See Chapter 7 for a discussion
of the various forms of farm business organization.) Also consider
the use of installment sales, buy-sell agreements, and annuities.

Steps in Estate Planning

Estate planning can follow an orderly procedure. There are
some things you can and should do before getting your estate planning team together. Then get their professional help. You should
expect to pay a reasonable fee for this. It is well worth the cost.

Fig. 8-2. A poor estate plan with no provision for the continuity of the business can
result in the dispersal of the business by auction. (Courtesy, University of Wisconsin
Department of Agricultural Journalism)

Where should you get started on an estate plan? This should be done early. As soon as you own a life insurance policy, an auto, 4-H or FFA project assets, and other assets, you need an estate plan. You start an estate plan at accumulation time. Do *not* wait for disposition time!

There are six steps in developing and implementing an estate plan.

1. *Inventory property*—This is one of the things you can do. Your farm records system as outlined in Chapter 11 can be of help. Make a list of all your property and its present fair market value. This could include the farm assets as well as other property, such as automobiles, life insurance, savings, notes due you, etc. Then write down the questions you want to ask your team.

2. *Determine how property passes to heirs*—In this step you determine what type of ownership you have in the property. Your attorney can tell you what assets will have to be probated. Trusts are reviewed, changed, or created. All assets are classified as to how each will pass to your heirs. A longer-term look should also be taken as to how the assets will transfer in the next estate. This is particularly true for husband and wife.

3. *Determine and study problem areas*—Every estate generally has one or more problem areas. These could include type of ownership problems, final expenses, probate and transfer costs, death taxes, debts, and liabilities. The smooth continuation of the business and the welfare of the survivors also need to be considered. Buy-sell agreements, primary and secondary beneficiaries, and ownership of life insurance are other factors needing attention. The problems should be resolved in the best possible way consistent with the goals, values, and objectives of the plan.

4. *Make a rough draft*—After a rough draft of the total plan has been made, you can thoroughly review the plan and make any needed changes.

5. *Prepare final documents*—The final documents should at a minimum contain an up-to-date will. Ideally, the whole estate plan will be put together using all the tools listed earlier in this chapter.

6. *Put the plan in a safe place and review it periodically*—The plan can be put in your safety deposit box, left with your attorney, or put in some other safe but accessible place. The plan should be reviewed periodically and/or whenever family and economic conditions change.

Estate and Inheritance Laws and Regulations

As these laws, rules, and regulations and their interpretations are continually being changed, we will not attempt to outline them. The 1976 Federal Tax Reform Act made sweeping changes in this area. Modifications will be made to that act, and several years will pass before most of the provisions will have been tested in court. Therefore, you will need to refer to your team to keep up-to-date.

A Final Word

Many young people become involved in the family business, such as farming, on an informal basis. Often the business arrangement is never formalized with a written business agreement coupled with an estate plan. The authors have seen numerous situations which ended in personal and financial tragedy. In some cases only a few years and a few thousand dollars were lost. In many cases a lifetime of work and savings was destroyed because of no planning or poor planning. Young people need to be interested and concerned with estate planning as it affects their future and their family's future. We urge you to take action now!

Questions and Problems for Class Discussion

1. What are the objectives of an estate plan? How do they affect you?
2. Who should be on the estate planning team? Why?
3. What are the tools the estate planning team can use?
4. List the steps in estate planning.
5. Discuss and outline an estate plan which could fit your farm and family situation.

CHAPTER 9

Appraising the Farm

Highlights of Chapter

Appraisal is an art as well as a science. Appraisers use three approaches to estimating the value of a piece of property. They are (1) cost or inventory approach, (2) market or comparable sales approach, and (3) earnings, income, or use value approach. Appraisers are skilled professionals who subscribe to a vigorous code of ethics. Farm appraisals are done for various reasons to aid the property owner in decision making.

Appraisals of farm property are made for many purposes. You may want to estimate the value of farm assets for purchase, sale, loans, insurance, property tax, gift and estate purposes, eminent domain, and feasibility studies. Qualified farm appraisers, such as members of the American Society of Farm Managers and Rural Appraisers, are people who are highly trained and who subscribe to a vigorous code of ethics. Selection of a qualified appraiser is an important task if one is to obtain a reliable appraisal. (See Fig. 9-1.)

Appraisal is an art as well as a science. To have value, an item must have *utility* and *scarcity* and the buyer must have *money*. Price is a measure of *value* in terms of money.

Appraisers typically use three approaches to estimating "fair market value"[1] of property. "Fair market value" is usually defined as what a willing buyer will pay a willing seller in terms of money, given reasonable time and adequate knowledge, for a piece of

[1]Rural appraisers do not create the "fair market value," but report their best estimate of how the market for farm assets is performing. The appraisal is a written, definite, relatively detailed opinion of the value of the property at a given date, based on the three approaches.

Fig. 9-1. Determining the fair market value of the land, buildings, livestock, machinery, and inventory of a modern farm requires the services of a highly trained and experienced appraiser. (Courtesy, University of Wisconsin Department of Agricultural Journalism)

property. The three approaches to estimating value are (1) the cost or inventory approach, (2) the market or comparable sales approach, and (3) the earnings or income or use value approach. Generally, the objective is to arrive at a reasonable estimate of the "fair market value" of the subject property using these appraisal techniques.

Why Own Farm Assets?

People want to own farms for several reasons, which may be either monetary or non-monetary. Some might want to own farms as a means of earning a living, as an investment, or as a hedge against inflation. Others may want to hold land as a place to live and raise a family, as a means of living in a rural area, as a source of pride of ownership, or for other personal reasons. These factors, both tangible and intangible, have a bearing on the value of the property. They give rise to value for a particular farm asset.

The Cost or Inventory Approach

The cost or inventory approach uses the concept of either replacing or replicating the subject property (the property being appraised) in a similar area. The appraiser is asking, "How much will one have to pay to get land similar to the subject land?" With a building the question is "What would it cost to replace this building with the same building, or to construct a different building which serves the same function?" Then the appraiser subtracts the amount of physical deterioration and functional and economic obsolescence.

Perhaps an example would help explain this. If we have a 24' × 48' machine shed with 40% physical deterioration and 20% obsolescence, how would we estimate its fair market value with the cost approach?

Table 9-1. Cost Approach—Machine Shed Example

Reconstruction cost, 24' × 48' shed:	
1,152 sq. ft. @ $3.10 per sq. ft.	$ 3,571
Less physical deterioration (40%)	−1,428
Estimated structural value	$ 2,143
Less obsolescence (20%)	−714
Estimated contributory value of shed	$ 1,429

One may also want to value the buildings for reasons other than the cost approach. Some of these would include the adjusted tax basis, insured value, assessed value, loan value, liquidation value, and value in use. In some cases bare land will sell for as much as improved land due to building obsolescence. In other cases, value in use may equal or exceed the contributory value.

Market or Comparable Sales

This approach to estimating value involves analyzing sales of property similar to the subject property. Then adjustments have to be made for factors which may not be similar to the subject property. These would include things such as size, location, buildings, soil, time of sale, and conditions of sale.

The sale prices of the comparable sale farms should reflect all origins of value into their sale prices. The appraiser then makes the necessary adjustments in the comparable sales data to reflect the differences between the subject property and the comparable sales properties.

Again, an example might be helpful.

Table 9-2. Comparable Sale Approach—Example

Sale No.	Sale Price	Sale Condi- tions	Time	Size	Loca- tion	Soil	Build- ings	Indi- cated Value
				Adjustments				
1	$550	0	$+125	$−40	$−10	$+30	0	$ 655
2	$800	$−50	0	0	$−50	0	$−25	$ 675
3	$650	0	$+ 50	$−30	$−35	$+15	$+20	$ 670
4	$700	0	$+ 25	$−20	$+25	$−20	$−50	$ 660
5	$800	0	0	$+15	$−40	$−85	$−25	$ 665

$3,325 ÷ 5

Indicated value per acre $ 665

You can see that the sale prices vary greatly, but when they are adjusted, the indicated values come together quite closely. The appraiser can then either average the sales as shown in the example or make some judgements as to which are the most appropriate sales.

Income Capitalization or Use Value or Earnings Approach

This approach rests on two basic numbers: (1) the expected annual net income stream from the subject property and (2) a capitalization rate. The expected annual net income stream (A) divided by the capitalization rate (r) equals the estimated value (V). Thus, the formula:

$$\text{Value} = \frac{\text{annual net income}}{\text{capitalization rate}}$$

or simply:

$$V = \frac{A}{r}$$

Table 9-3. Calculation of Annual Net Return (A) to Real Estate—
Example

Item	Amount
Cash operating income[1]	$50,000
Capital sales	None
Interest paid out	8,000
Inventory adjustment (+)[2]	2,000
Capital goods adjustment (+)[3]	None
Subtotal	$60,000
Cash operating expenses	$30,000
Inventory adjustment (−)[2]	None
Capital goods adjustment (−)[3]	5,000
Interest on non-real estate capital	7,000
Value of unpaid labor and management	12,000
Subtotal	$54,000
Return to real estate (A)	$ 6,000

With a 6% capitalization rate, value would be $100,000, or $6,000 ÷ .06 = $100,000. Note: you need to carefully select the capitalization rate appropriate for your specific situation. 6% is only used as an example.

[1]For convenience, the full amount of breeding livestock sales are included in this figure.

[2]This includes changes in feed, grain, supplies, market livestock, accounts payable, and accounts receivable.

[3]This includes depreciation and boot money paid for capital purchases. ("*Boot*" *money* is cash paid in addition to the value of an asset or assets traded in.)

In working the income approach, "typical" prices, values, and coefficients of production should be used. "Typical" can be defined as that which most frequently exists or occurs in the particular situation under consideration. A common error is to overestimate a typical operation.

Further, this capitalization formula is very sensitive to the capitalization rate selected. The capitalization rate is an interest rate which reflects many factors. These could include factors such as what holds money in an investment, the opportunity cost of money, current market rates, risk, rates of return on similar investments, expectations of the future, personal preference, competition, rates of inflation or deflation, and recapture of the investment.

Generally, the capitalization rate is selected by determining the origins of the value of money or by deriving a rate from the market using comparable sales for value (V) and calculating the annual return (A). Thus, $r = A \div V$.

Annual net returns can be affected by changes in technology, rates of inflation or deflation, and general economic changes, as well as by the kind of farm business organization selected.

It will suffice to say that this approach is the most demanding and calls upon the farm management skills, as well as upon the ability of the appraiser.

This approach to value can also provide the farm manager and lender a great deal of relevant information upon which to base financial management and loan decisions.

The Appraisal Process

The appraisal process can be briefly outlined in seven steps:

1. Define the problem. Here the property is identified by legal description and address, and the property rights are outlined. The date and purpose of the appraisal are determined.

2. Make a preliminary survey. This involves making a site analysis, along with an analysis of improvements and neighborhood area. Then an estimate of data, sources of data, personnel required, time required, costs, and a reasonable appraisal fee is made. At this point a written agreement with the client should be made so both parties understand what is involved.

3. Plan the appraisal. Here the appraisal is outlined and a determination is made on how to proceed to gather the relevant data and organize it into a complete appraisal report.

4. Apply the cost approach.

5. Apply the income approach.

6. Apply the comparable sales approach.

7. Correlate the three approaches and make a final estimate of value. Here the appraiser must analyze all the data obtained in light of the purpose of the appraisal and reasonably narrow down the figures from the three approaches to decide on the final value estimate. The adequacy and reliability of the data must be reviewed. Then the final report must be written.

The Appraisal Report

A complete appraisal report will have the following sections:

1. Title page
2. Table of contents
3. Letter of transmittal
4. Purpose of appraisal
5. Summary of relevant facts and conclusions
6. Descriptions and interpretations of pertinent economic factors
7. Area and neighborhood analysis
8. Site analysis
9. Soils analysis
10. Improvement analysis
11. Market approach analysis
12. Cost approach analysis
13. Earnings approach analysis
14. Correlation of values
15. Final estimate of value
16. Contingent and limiting conditions
17. Qualifications of appraiser
18. Addenda—such as maps, statistical data, and other documentation of facts in the body of the report

In many cases an appraisal is made without as complete a report as just outlined. But to arrive at a reliable estimate of value, it is necessary for the appraiser to go through the organization, data gathering, and analytical process as specified here. When dealing with valuable farm assets, it is foolish to depend on unqualified people to advise on important matters such as the fair market value of these assets. Select a qualified person, pay a reasonable fee, and be sure. For a detailed comprehensive discussion on farm appraisal, see *The Appraisal of Farm Real Estate* by Robert C. Suter, available from The Interstate Printers & Publishers, Inc., Danville, Illinois.

Questions and Problems for Class Discussion

1. What are the three approaches to value and how are they used?

2. What uses can the farm manager make of a complete appraisal report?

3. What career opportunities do you think are available for professional rural appraisers?

4. How would you go about making a complete appraisal of a farm?

CHAPTER 10

Part Time Farming

Highlights of Chapter

Part time farming is increasing as a longer-term farming alternative. Some use it as a method of getting in or out of the farming business. The part timer will find there are several advantages and disadvantages to this farming alternative. Part timers use many of the same production and business management practices as commercial farmers. They must adapt these to their own framework of operation because of the smaller size. The prospective part time farmer should ask and answer several questions before making the move. Selecting and combining appropriate crops and livestock calls for careful decision making. So do building selection, machinery use, and marketing.

Part time farming has increased over the past several years. Part time farmers generally (1) live on a farm, (2) work off the farm, and (3) have a major portion of their income from off-farm sources.

Some part time farmers are semi-retired and do not work off the farm. Other part timers may be on small farms which do not provide for full employment but which may be treated by the family as their "full time" occupation. Some use part time farming as a way to retire gradually. Others view it as a method of getting started. But a growing number are treating part time farming as a long-term alternative course of action.

Retiring farmers can use the principles and methods in this book to aid in their farm management decisions in phasing out of the business. Small farm operators may decide to enlarge the business to become fully employed. They too can use the methods and principles outlined in this book to help them develop more profitable

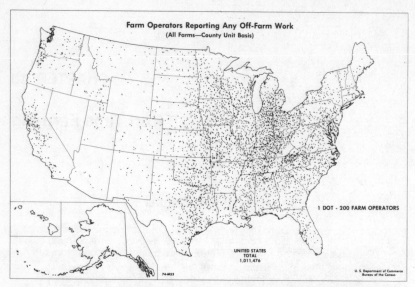

Fig. 10-1. Over one million farm operators in the United States have off-farm work.

businesses of adequate size. Or, using their present resource base, they might become more efficient operators. This chapter will be geared mainly to the longer-term, part time farming operation.

The difference between full time farmers and part time farmers is not as great as one would imagine. But there are some special problems part time farmers face due to the smaller size of the operation. They both have to determine their goals, objectives, and values. They both use the same decision-making methods and principles. But they do this in a somewhat different framework.

Advantages of Part Time Farming

The part time farm provides the opportunity for "country living" and a place to raise a family as well as to teach them responsibility and give them practical life experiences. For some it means better living conditions. Some like the open air and a chance to work off tensions by physical activity. Others view the countryside as a place of privacy. Some like the idea of raising their own food. Others feel the joint farm effort will make the family a more cohesive unit. There are also some who view it as an investment opportunity, while others believe they can see some income tax advantages. For some it is a challenge and chance to change their life style. Some look at it as a recreational outlet for family activities. Perhaps newcomers to the farming activity are looking for an intangible "something" they cannot put their fingers on.

Disadvantages of Part Time Farming

Many part time farmers moving from the city will not find the simple and satisfying life they want or imagine. They will be further away from many services and activities they took for granted. Transportation costs may be higher. An extra car may be needed. Some will get a feeling of isolation, while others may find that the privacy they sought does not exist. They might find it hard to adjust and may find farming a confining activity which competes for time they would wish to spend on other activities. Becoming knowledgeable in the skills of farming may be too big a chore. Learning about crop growing, livestock raising, and farm business management can be a big task. The inevitable losses due to pests, including the loss of livestock, might be traumatic. Some who have had agricultural experience and training may not find all this too difficult. However, if they have been away from farming for awhile, they will have to become retooled. Things have changed down on the farm!

Therefore, prospective part time farmers should ponder the question: "Why am I making this move?" The cooperation of the entire family is essential in making this crucial decision.

Considerations Before Starting

Before making a major investment in a part time farm, you need to consider several factors. Do you have an adequate down payment and can appropriate financing be arranged? Will you have enough cash left to purchase the needed fixed assets such as machinery, equipment, new buildings (or remodeled buildings), and breeding livestock? Can your off-farm employment provide the extra needed cash flow at least in the start up period? Are you willing to make the necessary sacrifices to make a go of it? What about location? Do you have ready access to hospital, medical, and dental services? Are good schools available? What about churches, shopping centers, and social and cultural activities? What about roads? What is the tax situation? Is the climate suitable for you and the type of farming you are planning to do? What about the soil and topography of the farm? Will the residence be adequate as is or will a great deal of remodeling have to be done? What about drainage, the well, and the septic system? All these questions and more should be raised and answered before you get too deeply involved.

Enterprise Selection

Some farm enterprises fit into a part time farming time and resource framework better than others. Selecting the appropriate enterprise combination on the part time farm takes a good deal of thought and planning.

Not all livestock enterprises fit into the part time farmers' work schedule. Staggered work hours by some family members can help on this. In other situations vacation time might be arranged to take care of peak labor demands. But remember, livestock and poultry enterprises are very confining. Attention at least daily and usually more often is required if adequate care is to be given on a timely basis.

For many, crop enterprises provide an attractive alternative. They are less confining on a daily basis than livestock and are less demanding during the off season. But timing for planting, pest control, and harvest is important.

If you are near an urban area, garden vegetables and fruits are attractive enterprises. Pick-your-own operations can be a highly profitable alternative on limited acres suitable for their production if a market is close at hand. Other crops for sale such as corn, soybeans, and specialty crops might be considered.

Crop enterprises as well as livestock enterprises may have such special equipment, buildings, and technological requirements that a small enterprise is not feasible. For some part timers the level of technical expertise required is difficult for them to reach without spending too much time and effort.

Combining Enterprises

It is best to keep the number of different enterprises to a minimum. The livestock enterprises should fit in with the crop enterprises. For example, if the farm requires a high percent of the land in forage, then forage-consuming animals such as cattle, sheep, horses, or goats are the best choice. If feed grains are the predominant crop, then grain-consuming livestock such as hogs and poultry are the best choice. But the combination must fit the available resources of land, labor, capital, and management.

Machinery Selection

Machinery has a high fixed cost associated with it. Therefore, small acreage farmers need to be particularly careful about overinvestment in machinery and equipment. Many times hiring a custom or contract operator for the whole operation is an excellent alternative. Some part time farmers rent out their cropland on a crop share lease. In this way they get a share of the crop for sale or livestock feed and avoid having to purchase machines which will have little use most of the year. In many other cases a minimum of used machinery can be purchased to do most of the work with a custom operator hired to do some of the specialized work requiring expensive equipment. Being able to do some repair work themselves

Fig. 10-2. This building is functional and has flexibility in use for the part time farm operator. (Courtesy, Wick Buildings)

helps hold costs down. Special skills are required to operate, maintain, and repair farm equipment.

Buildings

Part time farmers rarely will find a farm with a set of buildings entirely suitable for their needs. Overinvestment in special buildings can be as big a problem as it is in machinery. In many cases existing buildings can be remodeled economically to be satisfactory for use of the part timer. If new buildings are built, the design should be flexible enough so they can be easily converted to other uses. Smaller buildings are generally more expensive to build on a square foot basis than are larger buildings of the same design. For livestock and poultry enterprises, appropriate housing must be supplied for at least enough protection in inclement weather. Crop storage and machinery storage building space also should be available. Convenience of building layout is important. Good total farmstead planning on a long-range basis will provide for better building use and convenience.

Markets

Most part time farmers market only small quantities of products. Their marketing problems in most instances are more difficult

Fig. 10-3. A roadside market provides an opportunity to sell farm products at retail prices. This is one way to increase the income of a small farm. (Courtesy, George Klingbeil)

than commercial farmers'. Direct marketing to consumers is one attractive alternative. Joining in or pooling commodities with other commercial farmers can also help. Before the production cycle is started, the marketing program should be outlined. In many cases the part time farmer's family itself will be one of the main markets.

A Final Note

Part time farming can be a very attractive alternative for many. Others will find it too demanding and not in tune with their goals and objectives. Careful study should be made before starting. The same methods and principles used by commercial farmers can be used by part time farmers. The smaller size of the operation can be a limiting

Fig. 10-4. A pick-your-own operation fits well on a part time farm. (Courtesy, University of Wisconsin Department of Agricultural Journalism)

factor in enterprise selection, crop enterprises, livestock enterprises, machinery and building selection, and marketing.

Questions and Problems for Class Discussion

1. What are some of the advantages of part time farming?

2. What should the prospective part time farmer consider before
going into that activity?

3. What are some things to consider in machinery and equipment selection?

4. What are some things to consider in buying or remodeling
buildings?

5. What are some things to consider in marketing?

PART THREE

Farm Records, Income Tax Management, Business Analysis, Financial Management, and Credit

Part Three will examine the keeping of farm records and accounts and the utilization of these records as (1) a service tool, (2) a diagnostic tool, (3) an indicator of progress, and (4) a forward planning tool. Financial management and credit will also be discussed, along with farm income tax management.

Farm Records and Accounts

Highlights of Chapter

> A farm is a business organization, and like every other business firm, should keep adequate records of its entire operation. The farm records should not be so elaborate that a great deal of time is required to keep them. But, they must be complete enough to provide adequate information for tax filing and business and financial management. The several types of farm records are listed and discussed.

To properly keep a set of farm records, the manager needs (1) some basic knowledge of accounting and (2) a fundamental grasp of income tax rules so the records meet Internal Revenue Service (I.R.S.) and state income tax requirements. All states have excellent farm account books available from university or private sources. Some are computerized, either monthly or annually, while others depend on hand records.

After you have kept records a few months, it will become a habit and will usually be followed up even during busy seasons.

Requirements of Records

Good farm records should meet three requirements to be most useful for farm managers. First, records must be *complete* enough to

---

[1]Much of the material in Chapter 11 is drawn from North Central Regional Bulletins on "Managing Your Financial Future," Nos. 34-1, 34-2, 34-3, and 34-4, and business and records analysis from University of Wisconsin Extension material prepared by R. A. Luening.

give the managers sufficient information about their business. Second, if the records are to be of any value, they must be *accurate*. And finally, farm records must be *used* if they are to be of real value to the farm manager.

Uses of Records

Farm records have several uses in helping farm managers do a more profitable job of farming. All farmers must file income tax reports and should manage their taxes. A good set of farm records can make this job easier and more accurate and many times can save tax money. Your instructor or county agent can give you the latest information on tax rules. Many young people go into the farming business with their parents. Farm records can provide the basis of the written business arrangement, whether it be a partnership, share arrangement, corporation, lease, or some other form of business. Further, most farm businesses need credit, and your records can help you obtain and manage credit. Also, effective estate planning requires a good set of farm records. Thus, farm records are a *service tool* for farmers.

Farm records can be used as a *diagnostic tool* to help you spot the strengths and weaknesses in your farm business. Your records can help in analyzing the farm business to see what changes need to be made to make more profit. With records you can determine the relative and absolute profitability of your farm business.

The records system can be used as an *indicator of progress*, from both a business management and a financial management standpoint. Using it as a business indicator, the manager can measure changes in size, productivity, efficiency, and organizational factors unique to that particular business and to similar businesses. Managers can measure actual performance in comparison with planned performance and/or standards of performance for their type of business. Using it as a financial indicator, the farm manager can measure the changes in the financial condition of the business as well as measure actual performance with planned performance. Thus, the records system can be used as a monitoring device for the manager to observe actual change with planned change and take steps to make necessary adjustments. This needs to be done on a regular basis so problems can be worked on as soon as they develop.

Finally, records may be used as a *forward planning device* for short- and long-term planning. Past records can be used as a basis for projecting cash flows. The manager can then compare actual performance with the plan. The records system can provide cost information and coefficients of production unique to the situation for budgeting ahead in both the short and long run. They can project short- and long-term credit needs and repayment capacities. Further, managers can schedule purchases of inputs, compare various inputs as to costs and returns, select the kinds and sizes of enterprises, and determine capital generation capacities of different alternatives. They can budget for changes in their business by using as much information on their own farm as is available. Your own records are the best source of information, as they show how you operate your own farm. You may even want to use your records for the new computer linear programming or other computer budgets on your farm. But, your records need to be complete and accurate.

Kinds of Records to Keep

Several types of records are needed to provide a complete farm records system. They break into two main types: (1) income tax records which are required by law and (2) business and financial management records which are essential for management. The following discussion will weave these two types together for a complete system.

The kinds of farm records to keep will depend on how much you want and need to know about your business. But good tax records *must* be kept. If no other records will be used, then no further time and effort need be spent. However, in today's competitive business of farming it is difficult, if not impossible, to successfully manage a business without a complete tax and business management record system.

The records system can be relatively simple. You need not be an expert bookkeeper, but you can follow the directions given in the many adequate farm records systems available. Most account books use single entry accounting. Some larger farm businesses are now moving to double entry accounting. In Chapters 12 and 13 we will explain how to use the records for analysis purposes.

Most farmers keep their farm records using the *cash* system of accounting. By this we mean expenses are considered expenses when they are actually paid and income is income when it is actually

Fig. 11-1. It pays to keep complete and accurate records to be used in decision making.

received. A few farmers use *accrual* accounting. With this method expenses are considered expenses when they are incurred, regardless of when they are paid in cash. Income is income when it is earned, regardless of when it is received in cash. Further, changes in inventory items and changes in breeding and dairy livestock are also considered. Cash accounting is generally regarded as simpler for accounting and tax purposes. However, it can be *very misleading* for management purposes. For management purposes then we will adapt cash accounting to reflect accrual methods.

There are three main basic records every farm business should have. They are (1) the Farm Earnings Statement, sometimes called the Profit and Loss Statement or the Operating Statement, (2) the Net Worth Statement, sometimes called the Financial Statement or the Balance Sheet, and (3) the Cash Flow Statement, sometimes called the Sources and Uses of Funds Report. We will first discuss these "big three" reports and then look at the various other types of records you should have. (See Appendix A for complete forms of the "big three.")

The Farm Earnings Statement

The Farm Earnings Statement is divided into three main sections. (See Table 11-1.) The cash operating statement shows all the cash operating income for the farm from livestock, crops, and all other sources as well as all cash expenses associated with the crops and livestock, along with all other cash expenses. The end result is the Net Cash Operating Income. This tells you how the operating

Table 11-1. General Format of a Farm Earnings Statement

FARM EARNINGS STATEMENT

I. Cash Operating Statement

Income

A. Sale of livestock and livestock products .... $_____

B. Sale of crops .... $_____

C. Other farm income .... $_____

    D. Total Cash Farm Operating Income (A + B + C) .... $_____

Expenses

E. Crop expenses .... $_____

F. Livestock expenses .... $_____

G. Other farm expenses .... $_____

    H. Total Cash Farm Operating Expenses
    (E + F + G) .... $_____

        I. NET CASH FARM OPERATING INCOME
        (I-D − I-H) .... $_____

(Continued)

Table 11-1 (Continued)

FARM EARNINGS STATEMENT (Continued)

II. Adjustments for Inventory Items

	A. Feed and Grain	B. Livestock Held for Sale	C. Supplies and Prepaid Expenses	D. Accounts Receivable	E. Accounts Payable
Ending inventory	$_____	$_____	$_____	$_____	$_____ (Begin.)
Beginning inventory	$_____	$_____	$_____	$_____	$_____ (End.)
Net adjustment	$_____	$_____	$_____	$_____	$_____

F. Total Net Inventory Adjustment .... $_____

G. ADJUSTED NET FARM EARNINGS
(I-I ± II-F) ....$_____

III. Adjustments for Capital Items

	A. Dairy and/or Breeding Livestock	B. Machinery and Equipment	C. Buildings and Improvements	D. Land and Improvements
Ending inventory	$_____ (In I-A above)	$_____	$_____	$_____
Sales	$_____	$_____	$_____	$_____
Subtotal	$_____	$_____	$_____	$_____
Beginning inventory	$_____	$_____	$_____	$_____
Purchases	$_____	$_____	$_____	$_____
Subtotal	$_____	$_____	$_____	$_____
Net adjustment	$_____	$_____	$_____	$_____

E. Total Net Capital Adjustment .... $_____

IV. NET FARM EARNINGS [Return to unpaid labor, management, and equity capital (II-G ± III-E)] ....$_____

cash moves in and out of the business. It further shows the sources, the amount, and the type of income received and expenses incurred.

The second section shifts from cash to accrual accounting so that changes in the values of farm inventory items can be determined. The Net Cash Farm Operating Income plus or minus the Total Net Inventory Adjustment equals the Adjusted Net Farm Earnings. But this still does not tell all of the story.

A further adjustment in the third section is made for capital items to provide a total Net Capital Adjustment. The Adjusted Net Farm Earnings plus or minus the Capital Adjustment equals the Net Farm Earnings.

This is the farmers' return to their three unpaid inputs—labor, management, and equity capital. It is the starting number for many different business analyses and is an excellent measure of the profitability of the business.

The Net Worth Statement

This statement is sometimes called a Financial Statement or Balance Sheet. It is divided into two main parts—Assets and Liabilities. (See Table 11-2.)

The assets are divided into *current* (cash or assets which will be cash in the next 12 months), *intermediate* (those ranging from 1 year to 10 years in life, such as machinery and productive livestock and specialized buildings with less than a 10-year life), and *long-term* (those which have over 10 years of life, such as land or buildings). The liabilities side of the Financial Statement can be constructed by assembling notes, mortgages, accounts payable, etc., and entering them as current, intermediate, or long-term liabilities, using the same time criteria as with the assets.

The problem of selecting appropriate values in the Net Worth Statement is, at best, troublesome. The values used should reflect the *purpose* for which the statement will be used. Thus, if a Net Worth Statement is made to prove one's honesty to the I.R.S., then all assets should be valued at their adjusted tax basis. On the other hand, if the statement is to be used in obtaining credit or in estate planning, the fair market value of all assets should be used. Also, fair market value (minus selling costs and income taxes) should be considered if one wishes to evaluate investment opportunites of the

Table 11-2. General Format of a Net Worth Statement

NET WORTH STATEMENT

ASSETS	LIABILITIES

I. Current

A. Farm .... $_____

B. Non-farm .... $_____

C. Total Current
(A + B) .... $_____

V. Current

A. Farm .... $_____

B. Non-farm ...... $_____

C. Total Current
(A + B) ..... $_____

II. Intermediate

A. Farm .... $_____

B. Non-farm .... $_____

C. Total Inter-
mediate
(A + B) .... $_____

D. Total Current
and Inter-
mediate
(I-C + II-C) .... $_____

VI. Intermediate

A. Farm .... $_____

B. Non-farm ...... $_____

C. Total Inter-
mediate
(A + B) ..... $_____

D. Total Current
and Inter-
mediate
(V-C + VI-C) . $_____

III. Long-Term

A. Farm .... $_____

B. Non-farm .... $_____

C. Total Long-Term
(A + B) .... $_____

VII. Long-Term

A. Farm .... $_____

B. Non-farm ...... $_____

C. Total Long-Term
(A + B) ..... $_____

IV. Total Assets

A. Farm
(I-A + II-A +
III-A) .... $_____

B. Non-farm
(I-B + II-B +
III-B) .... $_____

C. Total Assets
(A + B) .... $_____

VIII. Total Liabilities

A. Farm
(V-A + VI-A +
VII-A) .... $_____

B. Non-farm
(V-B +VI-B +
VII-B) .... $_____

C. Total Liabilities
(A + B) ..... $_____

IX. Net Worth

A. Farm (IV-A − VIII-A) .... $_____

B. Non-farm (IV-B − VII-B) ...... $_____

C. Total Net Worth (A + B) ...... $_____

farm capital in alternative uses. Further, this valuation approach can be used to measure results of investment strategies in the farm assets. This is particularly useful with farm land values.

For management purposes, where the manager is attempting to measure *only* the financial performance of the business, the following valuation scheme would be helpful: land at cost; buildings, depreciable real estate, machinery, and equipment at adjusted tax basis; breeding livestock at conservative market value; and resale livestock, feed, seed, supplies, and other current assets at market value. Further, to make valid comparisons from year to year, breeding livestock values should not be changed materially to avoid paper profits and losses. However, current assets will change in value and, as they are generally converted to cash in the next 12 months, should be valued at expected market value. By using this valuation scheme, changes in net worth are more a reflection of the earning capacity of the farm than of investment strategies or changes in value of assets, particularly fixed assets. But, *do not ignore* examining the market values of the farm assets, particularly for estate planning and credit purposes.

The Net Worth Statement shows how capital is invested in the business, how liabilities are divided, and how net worth is changing. The Net Worth Statement can be viewed as a snapshot of the financial picture of the business at a specific point in time—the day the statement was made.

The Cash Flow Statement

This statement can be viewed as a report of sources and uses of cash. It provides a history of how cash moves in the business. It is simply a summary of cash movement in the business in a definite time frame. (See Table 11-3.) The cash flow is divided into two parts—cash inflows (money coming in) and cash outflows (money going out).

The inflows should be equal to the outflows. If family living and savings records are not available, the difference between the inflows and outflows should equal family outflows.

Cash flow provides a record of cash movement and can help to project future movements, as well as be a monitoring device to measure actual performance with projected performance. It helps connect the Farm Earnings Statement with the Net Worth Statement.

Table 11-3. General Format of a Cash Flow Statement

CASH FLOW STATEMENT

I. Cash Inflows

A. Beginning cash balance .... $_____

B. Farm operating income .... _____

C. Farm capital sales .... $_____

D. Non-farm income .... $_____

Total Cash Inflows (A + B + C + D) .... $_____

II. Cash Outflows

A. Ending cash balance .... $_____

B. Farm operating expenses .... $_____

C. Farm capital expenses .... $_____

D. Principal repayment on debts .... $_____

E. Non-farm expenses .... $_____

F. Income tax and Social Security .... $_____

G. Family living and savings .... $_____

Total Cash Outflows
(A + B + C + D + E + F + G) .... $_____

Now that we have given you an overview of the "big three" statements, let us look at several other important records.

Income and Expense

All farm businesses must keep at least cash income and expense records for income tax purposes. The income and expense record may be kept by either column or page distribution. When the farm income is classified on a single or double page according to the different farm enterprises in column form, it is called column distribution. Fewer mistakes occur when income is separated from expenses. Many farm account books have a double page on which descriptive information about the items of income is entered on the extreme left of the page, and the amount received is entered in the enterprise column provided. This distribution is convenient in determining what each main farm enterprise contributed to the total income. The enterprise contributing this receipt is credited with the amount in the column headed by the enterprise. The columns bring all items of a certain enterprise together where they can be quickly seen and their totals known. Most farm account books usually have helpful suggestions about entering any item of income or expense. Space should be provided for both the physical amount and the dollar value of milk, livestock, crops, poultry, and eggs sold, while with all other receipts, values alone are usually sufficient.

Milk companies send a statement with the check showing the amount of milk and butterfat delivered and the deductions made. One should record the *total* amount received for the milk and other sales before deductions are made and charge the deductions in the proper place on the expense pages. This is also true for livestock and other items.

Milk check deductions for butter and cheese should be charged to food, if a home record is kept. Deductions for hauling milk should be charged to trucking expenses. The purchase of strainer pads should be charged to livestock expenses in the farm record. Assignment of part of the milk check is quite common. This amount should be entered as payment on debts. Skim milk, buttermilk, and dried milk deductions for livestock feed should be charged to feed. Pails and strainers go to equipment expenses.

There are some receipts that do not come from any particular farm enterprise, such as soil conservation checks, pay for work off the farm, gas tax refunds, and other miscellaneous income. These should be entered under other income.

Whenever eggs are traded for groceries, or one animal is traded for another, a sale should be entered on the income page and a purchase entered on the expense page. Any increase in inventory during the year is considered the same as a farm receipt but is not recorded as a cash receipt.

The farm expenses are recorded in the same way as the farm income, using that portion of the farm account book providing for expenses. With column distribution, the items purchased are usually entered on the extreme left of the page and then distributed under the proper column head. Items should be recorded, whether paid for or not, at the full price. If they are not paid for at the end of the year, the amount still due can be inventoried on the page showing bills payable. If old machinery is traded for new, only the "boot" money is recorded. Then on the depreciation schedule the "boot" money is added to the remaining cost (adjusted basis) of the old machine to give the new cost (basis) of the new machine. (See the most recent "Farmer's Tax Guide," I.R.S. Publication No. 225.)

If it seems impossible to determine under what heading some purchase should be entered, one should consult the page listing some of the more common items falling under such a heading. If, then, no place seems to be found, one can always list it under other farm expense. Any decrease in inventory at the end of the year is considered the same as an expense, as is the value of unpaid family labor, but it is not recorded as a cash expense. The value of the purchased items for the board of hired labor is an expense.

Income and expenses should be recorded and totaled on a current basis for greatest accuracy. This provides a running account so problems can be observed while appropriate action may still be taken.

Unpaid Family Labor and Hired Labor

On most farms, members of the family do considerable crop work and livestock work, for which no cash wages are paid. Such work has a money value and is considered a farm expense before the operator's labor income is computed. The farm operator should determine what would have been paid out if no family help were available, and a record should be made of such amounts.

Board to hired labor is another expense which is not paid out in cash to the hired man but which actually adds to the family's cash personal expense. The amount, along with the description "Board to hired labor," should be charged to the farm labor expenses. Some farmers hire married men and furnish an extra house and some farm products. Such houses and farm products furnished are part of labor costs.

Depreciation

Depreciation is the term used to express a loss in value of property due to wear and tear and obsolescence. The depreciation record must be kept for income tax purposes. Depreciation is allowed or allowable. Thus, it *must* be taken for tax purposes. Fences, drains, fixtures, and buildings are real estate assets which are generally depreciated. Land is not depreciated except in some very unusual and definite cases. Therefore, it should not be depreciated.

Fig. 11-2. This farm manager and his wife are studying their farm records in the farm office. (Courtesy, *Wisconsin Agriculturist*)

Machinery, equipment, and purchased dairy, breeding, draft, or sporting animals are generally depreciated. In some cases (particularly the above named livestock) these assets have a salvage value, which is subtracted before computing depreciation. See the most current federal and state income tax regulations for the different types of depreciation and how to properly compute them.

The rate of depreciation is a function of the practice and use of the farmer. If you have doubts as to what rate of depreciation to use, see I.R.S. guidelines. But, generally, the rate is based on the expected useful life in your business, if reasonable.

You should obtain a special Depreciation Schedule record book in which you can keep your depreciation records.

Inventory

The inventory is an important part of the farm record and forms the basis of all farm accounts. It does not show where the gain or loss was made but shows what items were on hand at the beginning and end of the year. There may be a gain or loss for the year which does or does not show up as cash. The number of livestock and the amount of crops on hand change from year to year and will show an inventory gain or loss for the year. Money may be paid out for new machinery, making one very low on cash. An inventory will account for this at the end of the year.

An inventory should be taken at the beginning of the accounting year. Most farmers start on January 1. The inventory taken at the end of the accounting year will be the beginning inventory for the next year. After you start keeping records, one inventory a year is all that is necessary, and it will require a short time to complete.

An inventory includes a list of the real estate, livestock, equipment, feed, supplies, and growing crops, together with a simple description and the estimated value of each item.

Real estate includes the land, buildings, fences, drains, water systems, electric system, and fixtures. Usually the land is divided into cropland, permanent pasture, rotated pasture, woods, and waste land. Waste land includes roads, lanes, yards, and space around the buildings.

Livestock includes a detailed list of all classes of animals. The milk cows are sometimes listed by name or number and are distinguished from the heifers, calves, and bulls. Brood sows and raised market hogs; beef cows and raised feeders; breeding ewes and lambs; and hens, broilers, and other poultry should be listed separately. Livestock purchased for resale (held for sale) have special income tax rules associated with them and should be inventoried separately.

Machinery and equipment includes a list of each different tool and machine on the farm. This also includes portable or movable brooder houses for chickens and colony houses for hogs.

Feeds and supplies on hand when the inventory is taken include all feeds, such as hay, silage, grains, straw, and all mill feeds. Supplies include items such as fertilizer, lime, grass seeds, posts not set, wood, pesticides, and other supplies and materials. (For estimating quantities, see Appendix B.)

Putting values on the physical inventory of assets is difficult.

The one thing to keep in mind is that the record is of little value to the farm operator unless it shows a fair value for the different items. This requires good judgement and careful thought. Whatever method is followed when taking an inventory at the beginning of the year, that same method should be followed when taking the inventory at the end of the year. It is important that the method satisfy the farmer.

Estimating real estate values may be the most difficult part of making the inventory, as farms are so different in soil fertility, condition of buildings, and percentage of land in crops. There may be too few sales of real estate made in any one community to establish values. The cost of replacing the buildings on some farms is more than the farms are worth. The land and each building should be valued separately.

The cost basis of the farm can be used, if the farm has recently been purchased, but even then the farmer may have paid too much or the farm may have been purchased at a forced sale at too low a price. Many farmers use the actual cost of the land and the depreciated value of the buildings.

Livestock values are not so difficult to estimate, as there are enough sales of dairy cows, beef cattle, hogs, and sheep so that one can arrive at a very reliable estimate. The total number of livestock and poultry could be entered at an average value per head.

Equipment on the average farm is made up of some nearly new equipment and some that is practically worn out, with all stages in between, so values of machines and tools differ on each farm. When estimating inventory values, one can consider what such a piece of equipment would bring at a well-attended auction sale. This is a "service-value method." Another method is to use cost price less yearly depreciation from the tax depreciation records, also called the adjusted tax basis (A.T.B.).

(See the discussion under Financial Statement for further information on how to value the farm assets.)

Production

Production records for individual crops, livestock, and other enterprises are essential if managers are to evaluate their performance as production managers. Things such as pounds, bushels, baskets, tons, and crates per acre; and milk sold per cow, pigs

Fig. 11-3. Feed and crop records are an important part of farm record keeping. Keeping track of feed going into storage and being fed can help make for better cropping and feeding efficiency. (Courtesy, Gehl Company)

weaned per litter, eggs sold per hen, etc., can provide insight into the productive capabilities of the farm business. The records can help the manager analyze the production side of the business. Most states have crop and livestock production records books and records systems available.

Feed

Feed is one of the largest inputs for the livestock enterprise. The expense record shows all purchased feeds for the various livestock enterprises. But, a large part of the feed used on most livestock farms is home grown. Almost all home grown feeds have a farm gate value. Managers need to be concerned about feed utilization and efficiency in the various livestock enterprises. A record of home grown feed is also useful in forward planning. A simple monthly record of feed allocation can be kept to be used in summarizing and analyzing the feed input and efficiency of livestock enterprises.

Enterprise Accounts

Accurate enterprise accounting can give the farm manager much useful information needed for effective business management. An enterprise can be defined as a single separate project or undertaking for the purpose of making a profit. A dairy herd of 50 cows would be an example of a livestock enterprise, while 75 acres of corn would be a crop enterprise.

To find out more about the relationship of the farm's various enterprises and to spot strengths or weaknesses in a particular enterprise takes the kind of information found in an enterprise account.

Here are some suggestions for keeping an enterprise account record:

1. Select enterprise categories that fit your farm business.
2. Charge and credit all dollar values to the enterprise involved. When in doubt, ask this question: "Would I have incurred this expense or had this income if this enterprise were not on the farm?"
3. Use non-cash dollar values to charge and credit the enterprise for those items for which no cash was paid, for example, home grown feed, your labor, depreciation, etc.
4. Use the enterprise account as a decision-making and diagnostic tool in your business.

Labor

Labor costs have been going up rapidly over the past several years. Not only must farm managers consider the cost of all hired labor, but they also must consider what their labor would be worth if they were to work at some other job. Thus, there is a cost for all labor used on the farm.

A record of labor used on the farm can help farmers decide if their labor is used prductively and efficiently. They can then compare their labor input with others. Knowing the labor requirements and costs can help farmers decide on how much mechanization they can afford. It can also tell where peak labor loads are. Further, if excess labor is available at certain times, the farmer can schedule vacation time, or, if necessary, take on or expand an enterprise to fully utilize the labor supply.

Equipment

Larger, more expensive, complicated equipment, with its high fixed cost plus large operating costs, calls for special analysis on many farms. Therefore, it may pay for managers to keep an individual set of financial records for these types of machines. This information can serve as a guide as to when to buy, sell, or trade equipment.

Experimental

With exploding technological developments, managers are continually faced with decisions concerning whether technology can be profitably used in their business. Thus, records of trial projects in crop, poultry, and livestock enterprises can provide a guide as to the

Fig. 11-4. Larger, more expensive specialized machines call for better, more complete record keeping for good cost control. (Courtesy, John Deere)

physical and financial performance of that technology for a specific farm situation.

Family Accounts

Family living and savings records should also be kept by the farm family. They should be kept separate from the farm business. The family business and the farm business should be budgeted on a regular basis. A separate household checking account would be most helpful.

Computerized Records

In recent years many fine electronic or computerized records systems have been developed. Some are relatively simple systems which have a main emphasis on income tax accounting, while others are extremely complete. The complete systems not only have tax information but also put a good deal of emphasis on management and financial information. This could include a whole farm business analysis as well as enterprise analysis along with financial management information. Some are monthly mail-in systems. Others depend on annual input from a hand system.

While good complete farm records systems still leave some work for the farm manager, the computer systems can quickly and economically do the busy work of arithmetic. This gives the manager more time to study the records and to use them as a decision-making tool. It will pay most farm businesses to make use of this new tool in their farm management programs.

Summarizing the Records

After the accounting year has been completed and all items have been checked for completeness and accuracy, the records should be summarized. Joint costs which are partly farm and partly personal should be separated. Income and expenses need to be reconciled with bank statements. The summary is done for two purposes—income tax filing and use of the records in business decision making. Chapters 12 and 13 deal with the effective use of records for business analysis.

Many states have farm records associations which help farmers keep complete records and which assist in tax and farm management work.

Questions and Problems for Class Discussion

1. What are three requirements of farm records?
2. What are some uses of farm records?
3. Name the "big three" forms of records and statements and explain how they are useful to the farm manager.
4. By using your farm record book, take an inventory on your home farm.

Analyzing the Farm Business
for Tax Management
and Financial Performance[2]

Highlights of Chapter

Complete, accurate records are needed for income tax management and business analysis.

Income tax management begins with making an estimate and then applying appropriate strategies to maximize after tax income.

There are several ways to measure a farm's financial performance to meet the objectives of profitability, liquidity–cash flow, and solvency. In analyzing the farm's financial performance, the manager needs to first look at the 12 "key" measures or "vital signs" of the business, then decide if these show strength or weakness. The manager then capitalizes on the strengths and takes measures to correct the weaknesses.

The most valuable part of the farm records system is the analysis made from the facts and information it furnishes. Income tax management and financial business analysis are two vital areas to consider.

More than ever before, success in farming depends upon the farmer's promptness in making changes in farm practices and busi-

---

[1]Much of the material in Chapter 12 is drawn from North Central Regional Bulletins on "Managing Your Financial Future," Nos. 34-1, 34-2, 34-3, and 34-4, and business and records analysis from University of Wisconsin Extension material prepared by R. A. Luening.

[2]Note to instructor: You may want to develop your own case farm materials from current record summaries or from a student's home farm.

ness methods to meet changing economic conditions. Farm profits may be increased by making changes in the farm operation and/or organization, but first, the farm manager must analyze the farm business in order to know what changes to make.

Farm Business Studies

Studies of farm businesses over a number of years show that farms which prove profitable have certain characteristics in common which distinguish them from less profitable farms. The ability of the farm operator to adopt the improved methods and practices and to combine the different crops and livestock enterprises into an efficient working unit is one of the most important considerations for successful farming. The farm record furnishes the facts and information for this.

The purpose of the farm analysis is not to prove that farmers are prosperous or not prosperous. The analysis should show actual conditions on farms and point out ways in which these conditions may be improved. Your instructor, county agent, university extension specialist, farm business association field representative, or any other professional trained in farm management can help you with this. Each of these individuals will have access to records and record summaries to help you.

As a family person you will be concerned about providing a decent living for yourself and your family, as well as about your position on the income scale in comparison with other occupations. Your farm records can tell you how much your business is making, and many statistics are available to show what people in other occupations earn. When comparing incomes with other occupations, don't forget to look at some of the advantages of farm life. Also consider the training and other expenses associated with another occupation, as well as your own abilities and desires.

Income Tax Management

As federal and state income tax rules and regulations are continuously changing, we will not discuss specific rules in detail. But, there are some general things to be said about income tax and income management strategies.

Generally, farmers want to minimize the cost of income taxes.

But, they also want to maximize after tax income and increase net worth. Having little or no income will keep taxes low. That is not the real objective! So managers first should look to making a good profit. Then with proper tax management they should attempt to keep the tax bill as low as possible.

You need not be a tax expert to practice income tax management. However, you should know enough about income tax to keep the necessary farm records properly. And you should realize the income tax consequences of the business decisions you make. Also, you need to be able to intelligently discuss your income tax and income tax management problems with your tax consultant.

Tax management is a farm management job and therefore needs to be practiced continually all year long. Almost all farm management decisions have some income tax consequences. As

Fig. 12-1. The purchase of a new machine will have income tax and income tax management effects on the farm business. (Courtesy, Ford Motor Company)

farm businesses become larger, the tax decisions have a greater impact on net income, net worth, and cash flow.

You should obtain the "Farmer's Tax Guide," Publication No. 225, which is published annually by the Internal Revenue Service, and also various up-to-date income tax management publications available from your county agent and other agricultural professionals. This will keep you abreast of the latest changes.

Two to three months before the close of your accounting year, you should prepare an income tax estimate. This is simply done by totaling up the books to date for income and expenses. Then estimate the income and expenses for the rest of the year. This provides your net cash income. From this subtract your estimated depreciation. The result of this subtraction needs to be further adjusted downward by your personal deductions and exemptions. To this you add your Social Security taxes. Using current tax tables, you can complete your estimated tax bill. Finally, subtract any tax credits you have earned. (See Table 12-1.)

When you have a sound estimate of your tax liability (federal

Table 12-1. General Format of an Income Tax Estimation Worksheet

INCOME TAX ESTIMATE

1. Ordinary farm receipts .... $_____
2. Sale of held-for-sale items (minus purchase cost) .. $_____
3. Net taxable gain from capital items .... $_____
4. Other taxable income .... $_____
    5. Subtotal Income (1 + 2 + 3+ 4) .... $_____
6. Ordinary farm expenses .... $_____
7. Depreciation .... $_____
8. Other deductible expenses .... $_____
    9. Subtotal Expenses (6 + 7 + 8) .... $_____
    10. Net Income (5 − 9) ....   (±)$_____

11. Deductions and exemptions .... $_____
12. Computed tax (Tax on Line 10 − Line 11) .... $_____
13. Social Security tax .... $_____
14. Tax credits .... $_____
    15. Estimated Tax Bill (12 + 13 −14) $_____

and state), you can then make some tax management decisions. It is generally best to attempt to maintain income in a steady stream, because of the graduated income tax scale.

If income is above your "normal" tax bracket and you are not expecting income to rise over the next years, there are some strategies for you to use. These would include delaying sales, providing you did not lose more in income than you saved in taxes. The reverse strategy is accelerating expenses. You can also use the faster regular depreciation methods and the additonal first year or "bonus" depreciation where appropriate. In some situations income averaging will help. These tools can be used singly, but in many cases more than one of the tools should be used.

You also need to practice tax management if your income is below "normal." In this case you would delay expenses and accelerate income. Further, you would not use the fast depreciation methods.

Good farm records will give you the information you need to estimate your tax. It is then the manager's job to take this information and apply the appropriate strategies based on the particular situation and current tax regulations. You will also want to consider future years' tax consequences in making your final decisions.

Analyzing the Financial Performance
of the Farm Business

Farm businesses have three primary objectives: (1) profitability, (2) solvency, and (3) liquidity–cash flow.

These objectives can be competitive. Having a great deal of liquidity means that excess cash or quickly salable inventory is held. This has a tendency to reduce profitability. The rapid repayment of debt to improve the solvency position can put a severe bind on liquidity–cash flow as well as divert capital which could increase profitability. Going for maximum profitability could restrict liquidity–cash flow and/or reduce solvency.

Each farm manager will have to make some compromises. These must fit the goals and values of the business and family. There are no pat answers for this. You need to work this out for your farm situation.

The farm manager as a family person is interested in providing an adequate living for the family as well as in comparing farm income with those employing similar skills. The farm manager is also a business person, and thus wants to determine the return to the land, labor, management, and capital employed in the business. Further, business persons want to compare their returns to those with like bundles of resources and enterprises.

To analyze a farm business you need to determine first which factors have an influence on your business performance. Second, a method of calculating these factors must be developed, and third, "standards" of performance must be developed.

If one has most of the types of records discussed in Chapter 11, a complete business and financial analysis can be readily performed. The task of the manager is to develop an orderly method of taking the available records and putting them into an organized format where they can be readily analyzed.

There are so many different numbers one can look at in analyzing the business, it might be helpful to look first at an overview of the business. We could approach this as a doctor examining a patient. The first step after determining the objectives (profitability, solvency, and liquidity–cash flow) and having adequate records is to look at the "key" measures or "vital signs" of the business. From this we can determine where best to look under causes and effects. (The causes and effects are discussed in Chapter 13.)

Perhaps a general diagram of the analysis procedure will be helpful in better understanding it. (See Fig. 12-2.) The objectives, source documents, and "key" measures or "vital signs" can be applied to any type of farm business. However, the cause and effect part of the analysis system under profitability should be individually designed for specific farm types and/or enterprises.

In the diagram, one can visualize the profitability measures generated from the Farm Earnings Statement and Net Worth Statement, the liquidity/solvency measures from the Net Worth Statement, and the cash flow measures from the Cash Flow Statement. The 12 key measures or vital signs can present the manager with a broad overview of the performance of the business for that one accounting period. It, however, does *not* deal with the symptoms and causes of the performance. Further analysis is necessary to do this. We will deal with this in Chapter 13.

A whole farm business analysis, business section, and individual enterprise analyses are necessary to arrive at cost and return measures affecting profitability. Thus, cost and return measures appropriate for the individual farm type and the enterprise making

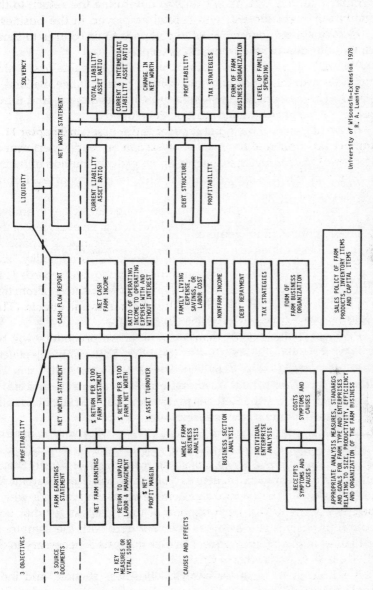

Fig. 12-2. Farm business and financial analysis schema (actual and/or projected).

up that farm type must be developed. These measures must reflect the causes and symptoms of the costs and returns of the various segments of the business.

Before going further, we need to define some terms so we can better understand the analysis procedure and what we are measuring.

GLOSSARY OF TERMS—PROFITABILITY, LIQUIDITY, SOLVENCY

Profitability Measures

Profit—The net proceeds obtained by deducting from the gross proceeds *all* items of expense or outlay. *Profitable*—Yielding or bringing a profit.

Net Farm Earnings or Farm Profit Loss—The returns to unpaid labor, unpaid management, and equity capital *or* cash income, minus cash expenses, plus or minus inventory changes, plus or minus capital item changes.

Return to Unpaid Labor and Management—Net farm earnings minus an assigned or imputed cost of equity capital.

% Return per $ Invested—Returns to farm investment, divided by average farm investment. Returns to farm investment is the net farm earnings, plus farm interest paid, minus an assigned or imputed cost of unpaid labor and unpaid management.

% Return per $ Equity (Net Worth)—Returns to net worth, divided by average net worth. Returns to net worth is the returns to farm investment minus farm interest paid.

Asset Turnover Ratio—Adjusted gross receipts (A.G.R.) divided by the average farm investment. A.G.R. is the sale of farm products, adjusted for changes in inventories of feed, grain, market livestock, and breeding livestock, and for purchase of resale livestock.

Net Profit Margin—Returns to farm investment divided by adjusted gross receipts (A.G.R.).

Liquidity Measures

Liquid Assets—Assets such as cash or those assets which can be promptly converted to cash.

Liquidity—Your business's ability to meet its current obligations in a timely fashion.

Current Liabilities—Those liabilities which must be paid in the next 12 months (not operating expenses).

Current Assets—Those assets which are cash or will be converted into cash in the next 12 months.

Current Liability Asset Ratio—Current liabilities divided by current assets. Percent in debt in short run.

Solvency Measures

Solvent—Able and sufficient to pay all legal debts.

Solvency—Quality or state of being solvent.

Solvency Position—The ability of your farm business to pay all its debts if it were liquidated at this time.

Long-term Assets—Those assets which have over a 10-year useful life in the business.

Long-term Liabilities—The deferred portion of mortgages and land contracts. Generally put in over a 10-year time frame.

Intermediate Assets—Those assets which support production rather than go for sale. Generally put in a 1- to 10-year time frame.

Intermediate Liabilities—Portion of notes and accounts payable that can normally be deferred for periods of 1 to 10 years.

Total Assets—Sum of current, intermediate, and long-term assets.

Total Liabilities—Sum of current, intermediate, and long-term liabilities.

Total Liability Asset Ratio—Total liabilities divided by total assets. Percent in debt.

Net Worth—Total assets minus total liabilities.

Change in Net Worth—Difference in net worth between this accounting period and the last accounting period. This year's net worth minus last year's net worth.

Financial Measures of Performance

Not all farmers think of farm profits in the same terms. You will find some who think in terms of gross cash farm income, others in terms of net cash farm income, and still others in terms of net cash balance accumulated at the end of the year. For management purposes these are *not* the best measures of financial performance.

First let us look at the annual financial information of a farm family which operates a one-family dairy farm of moderate size with 40 cows. We will call him Frank Jones. He is 38 years old, married, and has one daughter, 13, and one son, 10. The same kind of a financial analysis can be done for other types of farms.

This financial information for the Jones farm is given in the "big three" statements in Tables 12-2, 12-3, and 12-4.

With this information on our case farm we are ready to calculate the 12 "vital signs" of the business to measure the profitability, solvency, and liquidity characteristics of this business along with the current year's cash flow characteristics.

Profitability Measures (Six Measures)

Profitability measures answer the question, "Did I make any money last year?" Profitability can be measured by (1) *net farm*

Table 12-2. Farm Earnings Statement

1. FARM EARNINGS STATEMENT

I. Cash Operating Statement

Income

Sale of livestock and livestock products	$50,000
Sale of crops	$ 1,000
Other farm income	$ 1,500
Total Cash Farm Operating Income	$52,500

Expenses

Crop expenses	$ 9,500
Livestock expenses	$13,000
Other farm expenses	$ 9,000
Total Cash Farm Operating Expenses	$31,500
NET CASH FARM OPERATING INCOME	$21,000

(Continued)

Table 12-2 (Continued)

FARM EARNINGS STATEMENT (Continued)

II. Adjustments for Inventory Items

	Feed and Grain	Livestock Held for Sale	Supplies and Prepaid Expenses	Accounts Receivable	Accounts Payable
Ending inventory	$ 18,000	None	$ 1,000	None	$ 1,000 (Begin.)
Beginning inventory	$ 16,500	None	$ 1,500	None	$ 500 (End.)
Net adjustment	$+ 1,500	None	$− 500	None	$+ 500

Total Net Inventory Adjustment . . . . $+ 1,500
ADJUSTED NET FARM EARNINGS . . . . $ 22,500

III. Adjustments for Capital Items

	Dairy and/or Breeding Livestock	Machinery and Equipment	Buildings and Improvements	Land and Improvements
Ending inventory	$ 31,000	$ 31,500	$ 32,000	$80,000
Sales	(Included in livestock sales)	None	None	None
Subtotal	$ 31,000	$ 31,500	$ 32,000	$80,000
Beginning inventory	$ 30,000	$ 32,000	$ 30,000	$80,000
Purchases	$ 500	$ 4,000	$ 3,000	None
Subtotal	$ 30,500	$ 36,000	$ 33,000	$80,000
Net adjustment	$+ 500	$− 4,500	$− 1,000	None

Total Net Capital Adjustment . . . . $− 5,000

IV. NET FARM EARNINGS (Return to unpaid labor, management, and equity capital) . . . . $ 17,500

Table 12-3. Net Worth Statement

2. NET WORTH STATEMENT

ASSETS

	Beginning	Ending
I. Current		
Cash	$ 500	$ 500
Farm[1]	$ 18,000	$ 19,000
Non-farm[2]	$ 2,000	$ 3,000
Total Current	$ 20,500	$ 22,500
II. Intermediate		
Farm[3]	$ 62,500	$ 62,500
Non-farm[4]	$ 1,000	$ 1,500
Total Intermediate	$ 63,500	$ 64,000
Total Current and Intermediate	$ 84,000	$ 86,500
III. Long-Term		
Farm[5]	$110,000	$ 112,000
Non-farm[6]	$ 22,000	$ 22,000
Total Long-Term	$132,000	$ 134,000
IV. Total Assets		
Farm	$191,000	$ 194,000
Non-farm	$ 25,000	$ 26,500
Total Assets	$216,000	$ 220,500

LIABILITIES

	Beginning	Ending
V. Current		
Accounts payable	$ 1,000	$ 500
Farm[7]	$ 6,000	$ 6,000
Non-farm	$ 500	$ 500
Total Current	$ 7,500	$ 7,000

(Continued)

Table 12-3 (Continued)

NET WORTH STATEMENT (Continued)

LIABILITIES

VI. Intermediate

Farm[8]	$ 25,500	$	20,500
Non-farm[9]	$ 1,000	$	500
Total Intermediate	$ 26,500	$	21,000
Total Current and Intermediate	$ 34,000	$	28,000

VII. Long-Term

Farm[10]	$ 73,000	$	70,000
Non-farm	None	None
Total Long-Term	$ 73,000	$	70,000

VIII. Total Liabilities

Farm	$105,500	$	97,000
Non-farm	$ 1,500	$	1,000
Total Liabilities	$107,000	$	98,000

IX. Net Worth	*Beginning*	*Ending*	*Change*
Farm	$ 85,500	$ 97,000	$+ 11,500
Non-farm	$ 23,500	$ 25,500	$+ 2,000
Total	$109,000	$122,500	$+ 13,500

[1]Feed, grain, supplies, and prepaid expenses.
[2]Savings and investments.
[3]Breeding or dairy livestock, machinery, and equipment.
[4]Co-op stock.
[5]Buildings and land.
[6]House and other.
[7]Portion of intermediate and long-term debt due in current year ($3,000 long, $3,000 intermediate, $500 intermediate).
[8]Deferred intermediate debt.
[9]Four-year personal note on household capital items.
[10]Deferred long-term debt.

Table 12-4. Cash Flow Statement

3. CASH FLOW STATEMENT

I. Cash Inflows

Beginning cash balance	$ 500
Farm operating income	$52,500
Farm capital sales	None
Non-farm income	$ 3,000[1]
Total Cash Inflows	$56,000

II. Cash Outflows

Ending cash balance	$ 500
Farm operating expenses	$31,500
Farm capital expenses	$ 7,500
Principal repayment on debts	$ 6,500
Non-farm expenses	None
Income tax and Social Security	$ 1,500
Family living and savings	$ 8,500
Total Cash Outflows	$56,000

[1]Mrs. Jones's off-farm work and other miscellaneous non-farm income.

earnings or profit and loss (returns to unpaid labor, unpaid management, and equity capital), (2) *labor and management returns* (profit and loss − assigned return to equity), (3) *percent return per dollar invested* (return to farm capital ÷ average farm investment), (4) *percent return per dollar of equity or net worth* (return to net worth ÷ owner's net worth), (5) *net profit margin* (return to farm capital ÷ value of farm production), and (6) *asset turnover* (adjusted gross receipts ÷ average farm investment). (See Table 12-5.) Profitability is affected by the whole farm business analysis, as well as by each section or enterprise making up that business.

Solvency Measures (Three Measures)

Solvency measures answer the long-run question, "Will I be able to remain in business in the future, and how strong is the long-run financial condition of the business?"

Table 12-5. Calculations for Profitability Measures

* 1. Net farm earnings	$ 17,500
2. Assigned return to equity (6% × $[(\$85,500 + \$97,000) \div 2])$ ..	$– 5,475
* 3. Returns to unpaid farm labor and management (1 – 2)	$ 12,025
4. Net farm earnings	$ 17,500
5. Farm interest paid	$ 6,800
6. Returns to all capital and unpaid labor and management (4 + 5)	$ 24,300
7. Assigned value to labor ($8,000) and management (8% × $54,000 A.G.R.[1])	$–12,320
8. Return to all capital (6 – 7)	$ 11,980
* 9. Return to average farm investment ($11,980) ÷ $[(\$191,000 + 194,000) \div 2]$	6.2%
*10. Return to net worth ($11,980 – $6,800) ÷ $[(\$85,500 + \$97,000) \div 2]$	5.7%
*11. Asset turnover ratio ($54,000 A.G.R. ÷ $192,500 avg. farm investment)	28.1%
*12. Net profit margin ($11,980 ÷ $54,000)	22.2%

*The six vital profitability measures.

[1]Sale of farm products + inventory change + dairy and breeding livestock changes = $54,000.
   ($52,500)   ($1,000)   ($500)

Solvency is a measure of long-term financial stability of the business and is generally measured by the *total ratio* (total liabilities ÷ total assets). With inflating land values, it is also well to look at the *current + intermediate ratio* (current and intermediate liabilities ÷ current and intermediate assets). (See Table 12-6.) Thus, if this ratio is out of line, one may not be able to get financed for current and intermediate items and thus may tend toward insolvency. Solvency

Table 12-6. Calculations for Solvency Measures

*1. Total farm liability asset ratio (Total farm liabilities ÷ total farm assets) End of year ($97,000 ÷ $194,000)	50%
*2. Current plus intermediate farm liability asset ratio [(Total current + intermediate farm liabilities) ÷ (total current + intermediate farm assets)] End of year ($27,000 ÷ $85,000)	31.8%
*3. Change in farm net worth	$11,500

*The three vital solvency measures.

then is a reflection of the ability of the business to pay all the liabilities with existing assets at any point in time. A solvent business will have a good balance of assets over liabilities. A profitable business will provide for good solvency. Solvency is also affected by the form of business organization as well as by tax strategies. A final measure is how *net worth* is changing over time. This may well be the result of profitability but can also be a function of the level of family spending or changing values of assets, or some combination of these. Downward changes in net worth should generally be viewed with alarm and immediate corrective steps taken.

Liquidity–Cash Flow Measures
(Three Measures)

Liquidity–cash flow measures answer the short-run question, "Was I able to pay for my family living, farm operating expenses, and debt service in a timely fashion last year?"

Liquidity refers to the short-run (for the next 12 months) ability of the business to service debt. One measure is the *current ratio* (current liabilities divided by current assets). This ratio shows how much of the current assets might have to be liquidated to pay the committed current liabilities or debts. (See Table 12-7.) Liquidity is affected by debt structure as well as by profitability.

The cash flow characteristics of the business serve as the connecting link between the profitability and liquidity/solvency characteristics. Cash flow characteristics can be measured by the *ratio of cash operating expense to cash operating income without interest* as well as by the *ratio of cash operating expense to cash operating income with interest* and the *net cash farm income*.

Table 12-7. Calculations for Liquidity–Cash Flow Measures

*1. Current farm liability asset ratio
   (Current farm liabilities ÷ current farm assets)
   End of year ($7,000 ÷ $19,500) 35.9%

*2. Ratio of cash operating expense to cash operating income
   a. Without interest ($24,700 ÷ $52,500) 47%
   b. With interest ($31,500 ÷ $52,500) 60%

*3. Net cash farm income
   ($21,000 − $500 − $4,000 − $3,000) $13,500

*The three vital liquidity–cash flow measures.

Along with profitability, cash flow is influenced by several other factors, such as (1) debt repayment characteristics; (2) sales policy of farm products, inventory items, and capital items; (3) family living expense or labor cost; (4) tax strategies; (5) forms of business organization; and (6) non-farm income.

Even those businesses which may exhibit moderate to excellent profitability characteristics may find themselves in a difficult position due to cash flow problems, while businesses with negative profitability can exhibit excellent cash flow due to liquidation of resources. Thus, the manager must continually monitor the flow of funds through the business as well as through the household.

Now that we have made the necessary calculations, we can proceed to analyze the Frank Jones farm's financial performance for the past year. Remember, we need to look at several measures before we can make judgements with any high degree of confidence. But each measure helps to point us in a certain direction. The cumulative effect is what is most helpful.

Goals and Standards

Before going further we need to establish some realistic standards and/or goals for the profitability, liquidity, and solvency measures. These will vary, based on time, economic conditions, farm type, and farm location. You may want to develop, or may have already developed, similar measures for your situation and enterprise.

To analyze performance, you need to compare what happened with a standard—that is, what should have happened. There are three types of standards which may be used: (1) historical records—past performance of your business; (2) performance of others under similar circumstances—state or farm management association record summaries; and (3) realistic budgets or projections. In some cases you will want to use all three types of standards.

Profitability Analysis—Jones Farm

The profitability analysis asks the question, "Did I make any money last year?" It looks at the farm business from an accrual accounting system.

Jones's net farm earnings were reasonably high at $17,500.

When we subtract a return to his equity capital, there was a $1,000 per month return to the Jones family's unpaid labor and management, which is reasonably acceptable. The return to average farm investment of 6.2% is a bit low and should approach 8 to 10%. But Jones purchased his farm recently and paid top dollar for it in order to remain in his home community. Besides, it has all the things Jones wanted in the line of very fine buildings and machinery. But there is a cost to having everything just like a picture book. His average farm investment is $192,500, or over $4,800 per cow unit, which is a bit high. Overinvestment can cause lower returns to farm capital. Also, generally, money invested in an appreciating type of asset (such as land has been) will return less than market interest rates as investors also look at future capital appreciation as well as at a current cash income stream. The return to equity is also too low at 5.7%. As Jones is paying over 7% on all the borrowed capital and is making less (6.2%) on all capital, his capital (his net worth) is not doing as well. The asset turnover ratio of 28% is also a bit low—30 to 35% would be a good goal. As Jones had a productive herd, obtained top crop yields, and was fully utilizing his fixed facilities, the asset turnover points to the high investment problem. The net profit margin of 22.2% should be higher.

In summary, Jones had a moderately profitable dairy farm business with an adequate return to labor and management, but had a bit of an overinvestment problem which caused his return to capital to be lower than the current market rate of return and which also affected his asset turnover ratio and net profit margin.

Solvency Analysis—Jones Farm

Solvency analysis asks the long-run question, "Will I be able to stay in business in the future?" The Jones farm is excellent in this area. Jones owns 50% of his business with a good net worth, plus he has a very high equity in his non-farm assets. The current-intermediate ratio looks excellent. Based on these ratios, one could assume Jones is well financed with proper debt structure. His positive change in farm net worth indicates good profitability, adequate cost control, restrained but adequate family living expenses, and good tax strategies.

In summary, his long-run financial outlook is excellent.

Liquidity–Cash Flow Analysis—Jones Farm

This analysis asks the short-run question, "Could I pay my family living expenses, farm operating expenses, and debt service obligations in a timely fashion?" Jones has a current liability asset ratio of about 36%, which means he is 36% in debt for the short run, or his current liabilities are only 36% of his current assets. This is quite a strong position and would enable Jones to withstand some short-term adversity such as a drought, price decline, or cut in livestock production. The financial ratios of both solvency and liquidity also indicate that Jones has his debt quite well structured, with long-term debt financing long-term assets, and intermediate debt financing intermediate assets.

While the profitability analysis uses accrual accounting to examine the profit of the farm, cash accounting uses the cash method to look at the feasibility of the business, particularly in the short run.

Both ratios—ratio of cash operating expense to cash operating income, with and without interest—show that Jones has exercised excellent cost control in the business.

Jones's $21,000 net cash operating income is reduced by $7,500 (amount of capital purchases) for a net cash farm income of $13,500. When that $13,500 is reduced by $6,500 for debt repayment, only $7,000 remains for family living, income tax, and Social Security. Subtracting the $1,500 of income tax and Social Security, only $5,500 remains for family living. However, Mrs. Jones's off-farm income put $3,000 into the cash flow, enabling the Joneses to have $8,500 for family living.

In looking at his cash flow we do notice farm capital purchases of $7,500. As Jones is somewhat overinvested in capital items already, he needs to be particularly careful of making unwise long-term capital expenditures. Also note that some off-farm income helped the cash flow, which enabled the Jones family to keep a reasonable standard of living, while also increasing net worth. Jones also had some farm-raised food (garden, milk, and a beef animal) which helped in living expenses but did not show up in the financial analysis.

If things became a bit tight financially, some cuts could be made in capital expenses for the short run to see the business through.

In summary, Jones is doing quite well and certainly above average.

Jones also attempts to keep the farm financial records separate from the family records. Mrs. Jones keeps family account books. The family living money comes from a monthly transfer from the farm account to the family account. Separate household and farm business checking accounts are kept. The household and the business are budgeted separately.

Now let us look at another farm which has about the same bundle of resources as Jones's farm, and compare the two in Table 12-8.

Both of these farms were the same size, with the same soil type and similar buildings. What made the difference? A study of the records showed that Smith had fewer cows which produced at a low

Table 12-8. Comparison of Two Farms

	Jones	Smith
Profitability		
1. Net farm earnings	$ 17,500	$ 5,000
2. Return to unpaid labor and management	$+12,025	$– 6,000
3. Return to average farm investment	+6.2%	–3.7%
4. Return to farm net worth	+5.7%	–3.7%
5. Asset turnover	28.1%	20%
6. Net profit margin	22.2%	18%
Solvency		
7. Total farm liability asset ratio	50%	0%
8. Current plus intermediate liability asset ratio	31.8%	0%
9. Change in farm net worth	$+11,500	$– 8,000
Liquidity–Cash Flow Measures		
10. Current farm liability asset ratio	35.9%	0%
11. Ratio of cash operating expense .... to cash operating income		
a. Without interest	47%	80%
b. With interest	60%	80%
12. Net cash farm income	$ 13,500	$ 10,500

level, fair to poor crops, a lot of underutilized machinery, and high operating costs. He was late in doing his work, spent too much time away from the business, and did not adopt profitable technology.

But how could he stay in business when the records show he is losing money? How can Smith support his family? First of all, Smith inherited his farm and has no debts. There is no interest or debt retirement to pay. He made no capital purchases and he had fewer inventory items at the close of the year. So he is slowly consuming the farm capital and losing net worth. He was not profitable but was still able to generate cash flow. He received nothing for his unpaid labor management and equity capital. If he does not improve, he will soon be forced out of business. But in the meantime, he can live as well as Jones by using up his equity in the farm.

While all this gives us an overview of the farm business, there are several other areas we need to consider such as size, productivity (crop and livestock), efficiency, intensity of resource use, and organization of the business. The next chapter will discuss these factors.

Questions and Problems for Class Discussion

1. What are the 12 "key" measures of a farm's financial performance?

2. Why is income tax management important, and what are some tax management strategies to employ?

3. Compute the "vital" measures of your home farm or a case farm.

4. With the figures you calculated in Question 3, find the strengths and weaknesses of that farm business.

5. How would you capitalize on the strengths and improve the weaknesses of the business you analyzed?

CHAPTER 13

Analyzing the Parts of the Farm Business— Crops and Livestock

Highlights of Chapter

This chapter concentrates on the lower part of Fig. 12-2. The size, productivity (crop and livestock), efficiency, and organization characteristics of the farm business should be examined thoroughly. The several parts of the farm business must be evaluated separately. Strengths and weaknesses can then be identified, and the farm manager can capitalize on the strengths and take steps to correct the weaknesses. All these detailed analyses should be related to the vital signs discussed in Chapter 12.

In Chapter 12 we looked at the business objectives of (1) profitability, (2) solvency, and (3) liquidity–cash flow. We also looked at the "big three" business and financial reports: (1) Farm Earnings Statement, (2) Net Worth Statement, and (3) Cash Flow Statement. From this we generated 12 "vital signs" of the business.

The "vital signs" or "key" measures gave us an indication of the general health of the business. However, we did not examine the causes and effects which determine the performance levels of the "vital signs." To do this we must analyze the separate parts of the farm business. A look at Fig. 12-2 should give you a perspective of how this fits into the total business analysis procedure. We are moving from the general to the particular—each separate part of the business. We will take in turn those factors affecting profitability, solvency, and liquidity–cash flow.

Recognize the Problem

Unless one can see or recognize the problems and their relationship to one another, one cannot solve them. One must get a mental picture of the whole farm unit in order to understand the relationships of one enterprise to another. Many agricultural instructors, when studying farm management, take their class of students to a nearby farm to analyze the business. Sometimes a group of farmers on a tour will analyze a particular farm or enterprise for the purpose of determining the reasons for success. Much of the information on organization and management may be obtained from observation

Many times the first impression you get when driving by a farm, and even more when looking around the buildings, may show the size of the different enterprises. The presence or lack of adequate building space for hogs, chickens, and storage for grains and other crops will be evidence of factors controlling a combination of different enterprises. A yearly record of income and expenses will, if available, furnish valuable and reliable facts. Some of the most valuable information for analysis will come when you talk with the farm operator to learn about the methods and practices being followed.

Business firms, banks, and many other institutions employ an efficiency expert to analyze their businesses. They examine and question all phases of the organization to determine the efficiency of factors such as capital, machinery, equipment, labor, production, etc. An annual farm business analysis can do the same for the farm business.

A person trained in farm management, armed with a complete set of farm records plus a tour of the farm along with an in-depth interview with the farmer, can tell a great deal about the farm business. Strengths and weaknesses can be identified. Appropriate recommendations to capitalize on the strengths and to correct the weaknesses can be made. It will be up to the farm operator and manager to implement these recommendations.

It should be pointed out that no one number, or even several numbers, tells the whole story. Therefore, one must look at several measures and examine their interrelationships. Faulty analyses are made if one does not thoroughly examine all the various factors which affect the farm business performance.

I. PROFITABILITY

The main factors which affect profitability are (1) size, (2) productivity (crops and livestock), (3) efficiency, and (4) organization. One first looks at the total business, then at the crop and livestock sections of the business, and finally at each separate enterprise, for example, crops—cotton, corn, wheat, alfalfa, etc., and livestock—hog farrow, hog lot #1, dairy cows, dairy replacement stock, beef cow-calf operation, beef feeder lot #2, etc. This means that one keeps looking in greater and greater detail at each part of the farm business. This part of the analysis should be considered with a specific farm type or farm enterprise in mind.

A. SIZE

The size of a farm business is an important factor affecting profitability. Of course, low profits may be realized on a large farm business as well as on a small one, due to lack of efficient methods and practices. Those who have the largest farm business can often lose the most.

It is important to realize that size of business is not the only reason for differences in profitability. But remember, *price times volume equals gross income*! It is significant that the relationship between size of farm and profitability holds true regardless of the year considered or the area from which the records are obtained.

Records show that the operators on the largest farms not only take in more money than do those on the smallest farms, but their farms also generally have a higher profitability than the smaller ones. Costs per unit on the larger farms can be less than costs per unit on small farms due to spreading fixed costs over more units and having certain labor and other efficiencies.

But in one area, size has no relationship to obtaining more income. That area is types of technology which are easily divisible. These could include factors such as timeliness, better seed, proper pest control, fertilizer, higher quality livestock, etc. These inputs can be obtained in small divisible amounts as contrasted with a big piece of machinery such as a combine. These large inputs such as tractors or combines are sometimes referred to as "lumpy inputs." It is all or nothing. The other inputs can be applied to the business in

Fig. 13-1. A crop farm such as a wheat farm must be larger in size than a livestock farm to generate adequate income. (Courtesy, Allis Chalmers)

small increments. With these smaller items the smaller farms can compete favorably with the larger farms.

Size of Farm Measured in Various Ways

Size of a farm business is measured in many ways. No one method of measurement fits all farms. The most common ways of expressing size are (1) total acres, (2) crop acres, (3) productive adult work units, (4) livestock units kept, (5) capital invested, and (6) gross income. While the total acreage is usually the most common answer farmers give when asked how large a farm they operate, it is not a very satisfactory way of expressing the size of business. Total acres in farms differ widely in the United States and also within a state. The average dairy or livestock farm is generally smaller in number of acres than is a grain farm. Again, the grain farm is usually smaller than the beef or sheep grazing farm. However, even though a cattle or sheep farm has more total acres than a dairy farm, the volume of business may not be larger. Your instructor or county agent can give you appropriate size measures for your area and farm type.

Many farms have a large total acreage, but only a small part of the land is suitable for producing crops. Some farms have more hilly, stony, or swampy land than other farms, even in the same community. Because of this variation in land usable for cultivation, the number of crop acres is a much better measure of size than would be the total number of acres. That is the reason why the number of crop acres has become a common measure of the size of farm business. It is an easy measure to obtain.

It has always been important to have a large number of crop acres per farm, but it is even more important now than previously, because on a modern large-scale farm the machinery can be used more economically on a farm with a large number of crop acres. On farms of few crop acres, farm machinery is not used to capacity. It stands idle too much of the time, and idle machinery pays no return. The fixed costs are too high. Sometimes the use of custom work or exchange work can help the smaller farmer to compete better.

Productive Work Units

Another way of measuring the size of farm business is in terms of productive work units. Productive work units per farm are the number of 10-hour days of adult equivalent labor that would be required under average efficiency to do the productive work on crops and productive livestock. In states where cost-account records are kept year after year on a group of farms, the number of hours required to care for different crops and livestock is obtained. It is used as a means of arriving at the number of productive work units.

However, the use of work units also has its disadvantages, because work units differ considerably in different areas due to the differences in topography, soil type, etc. This will affect economical use of labor-saving machinery and equipment. For instance, it would take more productive work units to raise an acre of corn on rough, hilly land than on the level prairie soils where large-scale, labor-saving machines can be used effectively.

The productive work unit is considered a very good measure of size of farm business when comparing similar farms within an area. Several states have used this measure for many years.

Generally we arrive at about the same results in using productive work units as a measure of size of farm business as we do in using the number of acres. The conclusion in either case is that, as the size of the farm business is increased, the net farm earnings are also increased, assuming the farm is also productive, efficient, and well-organized.

Livestock Units as a Measure of Size. On a livestock farm the number of livestock kept is sometimes used as a method of measuring the size of the farm business. A livestock unit is considered as 1 dairy cow, 2 head dairy young stock, 1,500 pounds pork produced, 1,200 pounds beef produced, 2 beef cows, 4 head beef young stock, 7 sheep, 14 lambs, or 100 laying hens.

More Efficiency Possible on Large Farms. It takes less time per acre to care for a 20-acre cotton field than a 5-acre field. It is very seldom that one will find a 20-acre field on a small farm. The average person on a large farm does much more productive work than one on a small farm because usually there is not full time use of labor and equipment at productive work on the small farm. A greater percentage of the larger farms have power equipment which speeds up the work. The workers on small farms are at a disadvantage due to lack of efficient machinery, even though they usually have a larger machinery investment per crop acre.

Usually the family sized farm is the most profitable, but in many areas, with the opportunity to use modern labor-saving machinery, it should be larger than the present average farm. Of course, the advantage of size diminishes after reaching a certain point. The ideal size will vary with different regions and types of farming. As size increases above a certain limit, there is a duplication of machinery and buildings. Labor efficiency may likewise cease to increase. Management problems increase markedly on larger farms. Some smaller farms are so organized that the net profit is greater than on some of the larger farms. This is due to the ability of the farm manager rather than the small size of the farm.

The efficient use of labor is important on every farm, large or small, but the larger farm provides an opportunity to use it with the highest degree of efficiency. On any farm, much of the repair work on equipment can be done during slack time, rainy days, and winter months, instead of waiting until the day it is to be used. Planning the work ahead should also bring about more uniform distribution of labor throughout the year. This may avoid an excess of labor at one time of the year and a shortage at another.

The large farm gives more opportunity to have more than one adequate sized enterprise than does a small farm. Dairy and other livestock and poultry enterprises furnish productive work every morning and evening. Crop work alone does not make the best use of labor during the winter months.

The higher labor efficiency on the larger farms makes for lower production costs per unit of the crops raised. This, together with other economies due to size of farm, commonly results in a higher gross income and a net income proportionally even higher than those obtained on the smaller farms.

Size of Farm—How It Affects Equipment Costs. Larger farms have larger total investments in equipment than smaller farms, but not as much per acre. Also, the operating expense per acre is less for large farms than for small farms, as they generally can buy their inputs in larger quantities and at lower prices.

Machinery and buildings should fit the needs of the farm. There is a tendency to over-equip a farm rather than under-equip it. In many areas, farmers own the more expensive machinery cooperatively. Hay balers, corn pickers and shellers, forage harvesters, and combines are commonly owned in this manner. When a farmer owns one of these machines alone there may be opportunity to do custom work which will reduce the overhead.

The capital investment in equipment and buildings and the expense of repairs and maintenance are important costs on any farm. They need watching. Do not succumb to "iron and paint"

Fig. 13-2. Large equipment such as this can result in low equipment costs per acre only if the farm is large enough. (Courtesy, Steiger Company)

disease! But, you must have adequate machinery to get the job done in a timely fashion. *Timeliness of an operation increases production, reduces labor, and increases profits.*

Building Costs Lower on Larger Farms. Larger farms generally require less investment in buildings and improvements per crop acre. Also, the costs of maintenance and repair of buildings on farms which are overbuilt are more than the farm earnings will justify. The cost of a building should not be excessive. All space should be used fully and to the best advantage.

Many Small Farms. In almost every county it is quite common to find many small, inefficient farm units. There is not a full time job at productive work with the existing labor-saving equipment available. Some of these smaller units are over-equipped with such equipment. It saves labor, but the farm operator makes no profitable use of the labor saved. This still leaves high operating costs per unit. A larger business is needed if costs are to be reduced or even recovered.

How to Increase Size of Business

1. Use more land—rent, buy, clear, or drain.
2. Intensify crop production—obtain higher yields, add a cash crop, or change kind of crops.
3. Intensify livestock production—add another kind, increase the amount kept, substitute more intensive kind, use better feeding and care, or purchase feed.
4. Develop special markets—set up a roadside stand, begin a retail route, or process products at home.
5. Obtain outside work—trucking, road work, tractor work, custom work, or work in a nearby town or city.

Use More Land. Even when one owns a small farm, there are opportunities to increase the size of the business. If one cannot buy more acres, it may be possible to rent additional land, even at some distance, to improve the efficiency and increase the labor income by farming more acres. These additional acres can usually be farmed with little or no additional equipment. A few miles' travel to and from a rented farm is not as much of a handicap as it was before we had the auto, the trailer, the truck, and the rubber-tired tractor. Another way to increase the size on some farms is to clear or drain more land.

This will provide an opportunity to use more labor and will produce more feed for livestock or a cash crop which will add to the farm income.

Intensify Crop Production. The size of farm business can be increased by growing intensive crops. One can shift part of the cropland which is growing extensive crops such as grains and hay to intensive crops such as small fruits and vegetables, cabbage, potatoes, beans, peas, cucumbers, and berries. One should not try to grow crops which are not adapted to the area. Also, markets must be available. Crop yields can be increased by using commercial fertilizers to a greater extent, planting varieties of high yielding crops, and following better cultural practices even without increasing crop acres. Another alternative is to shift from common grains and crops to certified seeds for sale.

Intensify Livestock Production. A farmer can keep more livestock on a small farm by buying most of the feed except perhaps the roughage. Some successful farmers on small acreage even buy part of the roughage. When they follow this practice, the production per animal unit must be much above the average if the profits are to be satisfactory. Production per livestock unit can be increased on most farms through better feeding, culling, and management.

Fig. 13-3. Planting specialty crops such as potatoes can intensify crop production with a good cash crop. (Courtesy, Case Company)

Develop Special Markets. Another practice followed on some farms near cities is to retail many of the products, such as fruits and vegetables, dairy products, and poultry products, thereby obtaining higher prices than if the products are sold at wholesale. A few miles' travel does not make much difference today with the car and the truck. The person on the small farm usually has time to do some of this retail business.

Work Off the Farm. Many operators of small farms work off the farm at different jobs. They may drive trucks on a custom basis, drive school buses, or do custom work for neighbors with their farm equipment. It is significant that over 50% of the income to farm families comes from off-farm sources. Part time farming is a good alternative for many farm families.

B. PRODUCTIVITY—CROPS

It seldom pays to grow poor crops. As production is increased the cost usually decreases up to a point, as was illustrated in Chapter 5.

Some farm crops are used mainly for feeding livestock, as in the case of corn, oats, and hay. Some are sold as cash crops, such as wheat, soybeans, corn, potatoes, fruits, and vegetables. No matter how the crops are used, high yields are important.

Fig. 13-4. Improved varieties can help increase crop productivity economically.

Ways of Measuring the Importance of Crop Production. There are different ways of measuring crop production and its influence on profitability. One way of measuring the importance of crop production is by computing the total value of the crops grown on the farm and then dividing by the number of acres in those crops. This gives the average value of crops per acre. Such a measure includes both yields per acre and the choice of high or low value crops grown in the rotation.

A farmer with a large percentage of cropland in high value crops, such as corn, cotton, soybeans, or alfalfa hay, will generally show a higher crop value per acre even with only average yields. In contrast, a farmer who has a large percentage of cropland in low value crops will show a low average crop value per acre even with higher than average yields. As the value of crops grown per acre is increased, the labor income generally increases.

Why High Crop Values May Bring About Higher Labor Income. It takes no more labor to plow, harrow, and plant a field which returns a high crop yield than it does one which returns a low yield. Ownership costs of the land are the same as are the rental costs of the land no matter what the yield. Whether the crops are sold or fed to livestock, the result is the same. In either case, the higher the crop value, the greater the farm income (that is, within the limits of diminishing returns). The amount of livestock, and livestock products, a farm produces is closely associated with the amount and quality of feed grown on that farm.

Soil Type and Fertility Influence Crop Production. The soil is one of the basic factors to consider in obtaining economical crop yields. Crop yields and choice of crops are influenced by the kind of soil and its level of fertility. Some soils are so low in fertility that profitable crop yields are almost impossible. The soil type may be such that poor crop yields are more common than good crop yields. A light, sandy soil may be so deficient in moisture and fertility that whole fields and even large areas have been abandoned due to uneconomical production. On the other hand, a heavy clay soil may lack drainage, hence producing low crop yields because it cannot be planted early in the season. Irrigation or drainage may be profitable under these conditions.

Climate and Crop Production. Climatic conditions also affect the type of crops which can be profitably grown. The amount of rainfall during the growing season will affect crop yields and choice of crops. Either too much or too little moisture is bad. Some areas have greater rainfall than others. Maps showing distribution of rainfall are available for your state and should be studied when discussing crop production. The choice of crops grown on any farm should be determined by the expected rainfall for that area. Likewise, the length of growing season is an important factor in determining the kind of crops to grow.

How to Obtain Higher Crop Values per Acre

One should try to maintain crop yields at 25% or more above the county average. This is accomplished (1) by putting the different kinds of land on the farm to their best uses, (2) by following an appropriate crop rotation compatible with soil type and climate, (3) by using lime and fertilizer when needed, (4) by planting improved varieties of disease-free seed, and (5) by controlling weed, disease, and insect damage. Most of the practices and methods of obtaining higher crop yields are simple and easily understood. The difficulty comes in not doing them or in doing them at the wrong time, usually too late. Many farmers know how and what they should do to increase production but only practice part of these methods.

Usually there are limits to increased yields. Some of the reasons for these limits are that (1) farmers are dealing with living things, (2) they cannot control all factors influencing production, (3) the principle of diminishing returns (discussed in Chapter 5) applies, and (4) they cannot increase one item of cost without increasing some of the others.

Some of the important practices which successful farmers have found profitable to watch for and plan to do are:

1. *Fit a Cropping System to the Soil and Climatic Conditions.* Any crop will yield better if the soil and climate are favorable. A hay crop needs a wet, cool season early in the spring but relatively dry weather for hay harvest. Corn requires hot days and nights during the summer months. Oats requires a cooler climate than corn. Cotton requires warm weather. Some of the less productive cropland should be kept in hay as much as possible and the least productive area used for pasture. Crop only the good land. It does not pay to crop poor land or land that is too dry. In some areas it pays to summer fallow in order to build up or retain soil moisture. It is

advisable to follow soil conservation practices. One should also fully utilize all the available crop acres.

2. *Plan Good Rotation.* Where livestock are kept, it is desirable to raise about the same amount of the right kind of feed each year. A definite rotation with a certain acreage of each crop can be planned. Successful crop rotations should have a systematic succession of crops. The rotation should fit the soil type, climate, and topography. Generally, in the livestock and dairy regions, a good rotation should provide for a legume hay crop for one or more years. The cropping system followed will depend upon the kind of soil and amount of pasture land, the number and kind of livestock kept, and whether or not there is an opportunity to grow some cash crops profitably. On hilly, rolling land a longer rotation with hay and pasture is desirable. (Your local S.C.S. conservationist can help you in developing a cropping plan.) If hay seedings fail, or there is winter kill, then some emergency hay crop will need to be grown that year in order to maintain the rotation and provide feed for the livestock.

In summary, a good rotation of crops provides for (a) a maximum acreage of the most profitable crops, (b) livestock feed, (c) soil conservation, (d) a crop sequence, and (e) seasonal distribution in the use of labor and equipment.

The crop selected in the rotation will depend upon other factors, such as markets; size of the farm; available buildings, equipment and labor; and profitability of the enterprise.

3. *Choose High Profit Crops.* Livestock farmers are concerned with producing feed crops which provide the most feed nutrients. It is fortunate that corn and legume crops are valuable and also furnish the many feed nutrients. The soil and climate are also favorable for these crops in most of the main dairy and hog regions. Even in some parts of the dairy region where corn will not mature for grain, it is an important roughage crop grown for silage.

Besides growing feed crops on the well-organized farm, there is usually an opportunity to grow some cash crops. Market, soil, and climatic conditions determine what these will be. Some of the high profit cash crops, such as tobacco, cabbage, truck crops, sugar beets, and fruits, are confined to small areas. Canning crops are quite generally grown as cash crops over a wide area. The acreage of cash crops varies on different farms according to the type and fertility of the soil, the available labor and equipment, the market outlets, and the personal likes and dislikes of the farm operator.

Over a period of years the returns per hour of labor spent on some of these cash crops may be greater than on some livestock.

4. Include Legumes in the Rotation. Legume hay is a cheap source of important proteins and essential vitamins.

Grassland agriculture is now becoming quite generally accepted by some farmers. This does not mean that all the land is in hay. On some farms 30 to 50% is sufficient to prevent erosion, while on other farms over half of the cropland should be growing hay, preferably legumes, most of the time. On level farms most of the cropland can be in row crops.

The cropping system should not deplete the productivity of the soil. Deep-rooted legumes to build up and maintain soil structure should be included in some rotations. A large acreage of cultivated crops, such as corn, cabbage, potatoes, tobacco, and small grains, may have soil-depleting effects on the land. Hay crops, especially legumes, may leave the soil in an improved physical condition and increase the yields of other crops grown in the rotation following the hay crops. A combination of soil-building practices which pays best may include using both commercial fertilizer and livestock manure as well as turning under crop residues to build up and maintain soil fertility.

Fig. 13-5. A good crop of forage can help build a top livestock ration and can help conserve the soil. (Courtesy, Gehl Company)

5. *Test Soil.* Every three to five years a complete farm soil test should be taken to show the phosphorus, potassium, and organic matter content and pH of the soil. In some cases tests for boron, manganese, magnesium, and calcium can be taken. Further, tissue tests can be made of growing crops to determine nutrient levels in the plants themselves. Many farmers waste seed and money by planting crops on fields low in fertility. These tests can be made at a state laboratory or at a state approved commercial laboratory for a nominal charge. There are some areas where the condition of the soil is such that certain crops will not do well regardless of the application of lime and fertilizer. Your S.C.S. soil map and farm plan can help you spot these trouble areas.

Fig. 13-6. By testing the soil, farmers can determine whether it needs lime or fertilizer. Note the difference where lime was applied.

6. *Use Fertilizer.* When soil tests indicate a lack of certain elements in the soil, the recommended amount of fertilizer and lime should be applied. When capital is available, enough fertilizer should be applied to reach the maximum profit point. (See Chapter 5.)

Fig. 13-7. Proper manure handling is important if the maximum amount of plant nutrients is to be returned to the soil. (Courtesy, Patz Company)

7. *Handle Manure Wisely*. The proper handling of manure is important. Economical methods should be used to return the maximum plant nutrients to the soil and to prevent excessive run-off to avoid pollution. Manure handling methods and regulations are changing rapidly. Your instructor or county agricultural agent can keep you up-to-date on the best methods to use.

8. *Use Good Seeds*. Only good seeds should be used. Before sowing any seeds, you should know the germination and purity. Use nitrogen inoculation for legume seeds. Use only high yielding strains of grains. The experiment stations and commercial companies are continually improving crop yields by making new strains and varieties available through certified seed growers. Seed is such a small cost item in growing a crop and adds so much to the yield that it pays to use the best.

9. *Prepare a Good Seedbed*. In some areas the preparation of a good seedbed starts with fall plowing, followed by good tillage the next spring. On some soils in some areas, conservation tillage is a good practice. Crops make better yields when the soil is prepared and seeded at the right time. Some farmers are always a little behind in the work and as a result are too much in a hurry to fit the soil properly for the crops. Such practices pay off in low yields.

A good seedbed helps to control weeds. The main reason for cultivating a crop is to control weeds. If the corn can get a start before the weeds, it is much easier to control them. However, new chemicals are now being used which make control easier. Watch for the new tested remedies.

10. *Control Crop Diseases and Insects.* Most crops are subject to disease and are infested with some kind of insects. Some of the crop diseases can be controlled by treating the seed before planting. Other diseases which affect the growing plants are controlled by rotation, by thorough cultural practices, or by dusting or spraying.

Fig. 13-8. This machine can be equipped with different booms for the timely application of pesticides throughout the season. (Courtesy, John Deere)

11. *Store Seeds and Grains Properly.* Many bushels of grain, which were of high quality when harvested, have spoiled in the storage bin. It is very important to store the seed grain in a dry, well-ventilated place. Some fields are badly infested with weed seed which, if not cleaned out of the grain when stored in large, deep bins, will cause the grain to heat. Unless this grain is dried or at least exposed to the air enough to give it ventilation, it will mold and be spoiled for either seed or feed. Further, insects in stored grain can be a problem unless proper precautions in storage are taken.

Fig. 13-9. Special handling, drying, and storage facilities are needed for farm crops such as rice.

Some of our corn cribs are too wide for best storage, especially when we have a year with soft, immature corn. Many farms have gone either to field shelling of corn and drying, or to ensiling high moisture corn grain as ground ear corn or as shelled corn. It is excellent livestock feed but is difficult to market in some cases.

12. Use the Crop Index as a Way of Measuring Crop Production. The crop index of a farm, as commonly used, is expressed as a percentage of the county or state average, or of the average of a group of farmers. This average becomes the standard for calculating your crop index. The index might, for example, be 85%, 110%, or 140% of this standard.

A crop index is obtained by dividing the total production of each crop on your farm by the average (or standard) yield per acre of those crops for the area selected—state, county, or group of farms selected. This will show how many acres with average yield per acre it would require to obtain your farm crop production. The computed acreages of all crops are added and the sum divided by the total acres of crops grown on the farm. This gives your crop index and shows in percentage the relationship of crop yields on your farm with that of the average, which is 100%. To illustrate, suppose your farm had the following:

(1) Crop	(2) Yield	(3) Acres	(4) Col. 2 × Col. 3: Production	(5) Standard Average Yield in Area	(6) (Col. 2 ÷ Col. 5) × Col. 3: Average Acres Required
Corn for silage	17 tons	20	340 tons	15 tons	22.66
Corn for grain	100 bu.	30	3,000 bu.	90 bu.	33.33
Oats	75 bu.	25	1,875 bu.	60 bu.	31.25
Alfalfa hay	4 tons	75	300 tons	3 tons	100.00
Crop acres	—	150	—	—	187.24

The figure 187.24 is 124.83% of 150. This means that the crops grown on this farm were 24.8% better than average for the area. Thus, the crop index of this farm would be 124.8.

General

Look for symptoms and causes of unprofitable receipts or costs in the cropping section and in each crop enterprise in the farm business. Then take proper steps to improve the weak points. Also, keep sight of the strengths and then capitalize on them. Your county agricultural agent or instructor can furnish up-to-date technological information on profitable crop production practices.

C. PRODUCTIVITY—LIVESTOCK

On livestock farms much of the cash income is from the sale of livestock and livestock products. Livestock make a market for feed crops; hence, if the production of livestock is not efficient, it would be better to sell the crops. Some farmers work all summer growing crops and then make a low yearly income when they feed the crops to low-producing or inefficient animals.

On a dairy farm, pounds of milk sold per cow has a large influence on the farm's profitability. On poultry farms, eggs laid per hen will also affect profitability. On other farms where hogs account for a large source of income, the number of pigs raised per litter, rate of gain, and feed efficiency will influence profitability. The same

Fig. 13-10. Diagnosing crop disease problems is the first step in taking corrective action. Here a university specialist examines corn leaf tissue under a microscope.

principle holds for other classes of livestock and poultry as well. High production per animal is an important goal toward which a farm manager should strive, because it can reduce the cost of each unit produced and therefore can increase farm income. In many instances, farmers with low-producing herds make only one-half or less as much labor income as the average. The ones with high-producing herds generally make more than the average. This variation in production per cow is not due to the size of the herd kept. It is usually the result of a combination of things, such as the way the cows are fed and cared for and the methods of breeding the cows.

There is little or no assurance that the person growing good crops will feed them to high-producing animals. When both high livestock production and high crop yields are obtained, then labor income can be increased still more.

It usually costs more to obtain high production, but generally not enough more to offset the higher value of the product unless carried to the extreme.

The capital invested in buildings and equipment is usually no more where high-producing animals are kept than where lower production is obtained. Likewise, and of greater importance, the time spent in care and management, such as feeding the animals and cleaning the buildings, is only a little more for high-producing livestock than for lower-producing livestock.

When all costs are considered, several times as much net profit generally can be made with high-producing livestock and poultry as with low-producers. No farmer can expect to be successful without reasonably high production per animal.

Of course, full utilization of existing fixed livestock facilities and equipment is important.

To obtain higher livestock production one should:

1. *Coordinate the Livestock and Cropping System.* The kind and number of livestock kept should be chosen with a view of using the permanent pasture and the feed crops adapted to the farm to best advantage. Ruminant animals will use pasture and roughage; therefore, they fit well in areas where hay and pasture do well. Nonruminant animals will use large amounts of grain, so they fit well where a large acreage of corn or other feed grains are grown. Farmers have more opportunity to change their livestock enterprises than their crops, and they have more chances to increase the net farm income through a wise choice of livestock kept.

The supply of feed and the kinds grown will tend to determine the kind of livestock kept. But purchasing feed may be an excellent idea. If the farm produces mainly roughage of good quality, a major portion of the grain may be purchased. The price of purchased feed, price of livestock, available markets, and available buildings, equipment, and labor should also be considered when choosing the number and kind of livestock to be kept.

Even in a cash grain region there is usually some non-cropland which livestock could use for pasture to produce cash income. The low value products on a farm, such as cornstalks, straw, low-grade hay, soft corn, and damaged grain, can be converted into salable livestock products.

The final balance between feed required and feed produced may demand some shift in livestock numbers and in crops for feed or for sale. Some feed will need to be purchased to make up the best rations for any class of livestock.

2. *Keep High-producing Livestock.* The cost of producing 100

Fig. 13-11. These hogs have been marked so that their carcasses can be evaluated for consumer preference. (Courtesy, University of Wisconsin Department of Agricultural Journalism)

pounds of milk, a dozen eggs, or 100 pounds of pork, beef, or lamb varies on different farms, but within limits decreases as the production per animal increases. Rate of milk production per cow is one of the most important factors in determining profits on the dairy farm. High egg production per hen is essential for a profitable poultry enterprise. Livestock farmers have increased production through using better breeding stock and selecting high quality replacement stock and raising them well.

3. *Control Livestock Diseases.* As numbers of livestock increase in any area, diseases and parasites tend to increase. At such a time, there is greater need for sanitation for preventing and controlling diseases and parasites. One way to do this is to raise young pigs and poultry in a sanitary environment. Other ways of controlling dis-

eases are giving treatment for worms and mange mites, testing for infectious diseases, maintaining proper disposal of infected animals, and vaccinating. Prevention is better than cure!

4. *Feed Least Cost Balanced Rations.* An economically balanced ration for livestock can be made up mostly of home grown grains and roughage, supplemented with proteins and minerals. The use of such rations is one of the reasons for success with different livestock enterprises. If high production is to be maintained, it is necessary to feed properly.

There are several substitutions between the home grown grains. The animal science departments at the various state colleges of agriculture have set up simple standard feed requirements which may serve as guides for balancing rations. Also, new computer technology helps farmers quickly select least cost balanced rations for their livestock.

5. *Produce to Meet Market Demands.* The consumer is king of the marketplace. Thus, farmers and food processors must market foods which consumers demand. Low fat dairy products; meatier, leaner cuts of meat; and ready-to-eat or cooked foods continue to gain in popularity. Further, consumers demand an even flow of high-quality, economical food throughout the year.

6. *Test for Production.* Performance testing programs are available for poultry, pork, beef, dairy, and lamb producers. These testing programs can improve quality and profitability of the livestock enterprises. For example, to enable dairy farm managers to cull out low-producers intelligently, it is essential that they enroll their herds in one of the dairy herd improvement associations. Milk is weighed one day each month and tested. Feeding and selection recommendations are made on modern computerized printouts to give farmers fast, accurate data upon which to base feeding, breeding, and selection decisions. Members of dairy herd improvement associations average more production per cow than the state average, yet only a relatively small percentage of dairy farmers test their cows. Dairy farmers belonging to such associations find that it pays.

Some characteristics of various livestock enterprises are:

Dairy Cattle: Dairying requires much labor and furnishes steady employment throughout the year. Dairy cattle use large amounts of high-quality, home grown roughage and make use of

Fig. 13-12. Performance testing for livestock is increasing year by year. This results in more efficient livestock production. This photo shows ultrasonic measurement of fat thickness. (Courtesy, Carl Hirschinger)

rough pasture land. Capital needed for the cattle is moderate; whereas, capital needed for buildings and equipment is fairly high. Dairying is very labor intensive and fits smaller farms with a good labor supply and cropland suited for roughage production.

Beef Cattle. The breeding herd requires very little labor. Beef cattle use low-quality roughage and little grain, but returns per dollar of feed used are generally low. There is low overhead in buildings and equipment. Income per head is low as it is limited to one calf per year. Best adapted to large farms with lots of cheap pasture, this is a labor extensive enterprise which can fit in with part time farming, or it can be a good supplementary enterprise on some farms.

Fig. 13-13. Range land put to its best use with a herd of beef cattle. (Courtesy, Soil Conservation Service, USDA)

Feeder Steers. Steer feeding requires a large amount of grain but very little labor. Profits are highly dependent upon the spread of the purchase price and the selling price. Steer feeding is a rather risky business.

Hogs. This enterprise requires large amounts of grain but very little labor. Farrowing uses more labor relative to feed than the feeding operation.

Hens. This enterprise requires a large amount of feed and moderate labor. Like dairying, family labor can be used daily throughout the year. It is most successful where grain is plentiful with good markets available.

Sheep—Breeding Ewes. This enterprise requires much pasture and roughage but very little labor. It will make a profitable minor enterprise on some farms or a profitable major enterprise in the range area.

Feeder Lambs. Lamb feeding requires large amounts of grain and roughage in proportion to labor. It requires a great deal of capital for short periods. Profits depend upon gain in the sale price per pound over the purchase price. Lamb feeding is a high risk business.

Each farming type area has certain conditions which favor the choice of different classes of livestock.

Fig. 13-14. Sheep are a profitable source of income on thousands of farms. This flock of 95 ewes produced 145 lambs. The lambs were sold at four months of age, averaging 91.5 pounds. This shows efficient management of the flock.

Classes of Livestock Which May Be Kept

1. *Cattle*

   Dairy

      Raise replacements

      Buy replacements

   Beef

   Breeding herd

      Finish for market

      Sell feeders

   Feeders

      Finish for market

      Sell off pasture

2. *Hogs*

   Brood sows

      Raise one litter per year

      Raise two litters
         per year

      Sell feeders

      Finish hogs for market

   Feeders

3. *Chickens*

   Produce pullets for replacements

   Buy grown pullets for egg production

   Produce broilers

4. *Sheep*

   Breeding ewes

      Raise hothouse lambs

      Finish lambs

      Sell lambs as feeders

   Feeder lambs

General

Closely evaluate the livestock section as well as each livestock enterprise in your farm business. Look for symptoms and causes of unprofitable receipts. Then take appropriate steps to correct the weaknesses and capitalize on the strengths. Your county agent or agricultural instructor can furnish up-to-date technological information on profitable livestock practices.

D. EFFICIENCY

Efficiency is a measure which uses a comparison of outputs (production) to inputs (cost). The inputs and outputs can be measured in physical units, for example, 1 pound of gain for 2.75 pounds of feed, or in monetary units, $200 of livestock production for each $100 of feed fed.

Obviously, the productivity (output per unit) of each of the farm enterprises affects efficiency. But that is only one side of the equation. High productivity, while important, comes at a cost—the inputs. In some cases the cost may be too high. Efficiency measures can help determine this relationship.

Measures of Efficiency

Production efficiency may be measured on a per crop acre, per livestock unit, per adult labor equivalent, per hen (or other type of poultry), per cow (or other type of livestock), or per dollar of feed basis. As every farm type and locality is different, specific goals cannot be outlined here. Therefore, you should contact your county agent or agricultural instructor for goals and standards appropriate for your farm type and locality.

Feed Efficiency. The average livestock returns per $100 of feed used on a group of dairy farms were $204. This is called feed efficiency. It means that $2.04 was received from livestock, livestock products, and changes in livestock inventory for every dollar's worth of feed used. The operators of the farms on which the returns were low ($1.83) received nearly $11,790 per year less for their labor and management than those where the returns were average ($2.04) for each dollar of feed used. Such a difference has been found

Fig. 13-15. This livestock feeder is interested in feeding a least cost balanced ration to obtain high feed efficiency. (Courtesy, Gehl Company)

through farm records for many years. The high income farms returned $2.39 for each $1.00 of feed fed and had a labor income of about $11,000 more than the average. Of course, not all of the difference can be attributed to feed efficiency. Some of the reasons feed efficiency was higher are: (1) better balanced rations, (2) sufficient feed furnished according to the ability of the animals to produce, (3) improved genetic capabilities of livestock, and (4) better than average prices received for the livestock and livestock products.

Feed is the largest item of expense for any livestock enterprise. Cost account records over a period of years show that feed represents roughly 70% of costs for hogs and fattening cattle, 65% for beef breeding herds, poultry, and sheep, and 50% for dairy cattle. Livestock in the hands of an inefficient feeder may return less income for the feed than if the crops were sold.

It is vital to measure the value added to the feed input by each livestock type or enterprise. Also, one needs to measure the feed cost per pound of gain or per hundredweight of milk equivalent, sales per livestock unit or units of a specific livestock enterprise, etc. The number of feed crop acres per livestock unit in relation to purchased feed is another efficiency measure.

Production Efficiency per Crop Acre

Several factors should be examined to determine the production efficiency per crop acre. One can look at this as intensity of use. These factors can include total capital invested per crop acre, labor use per crop acre, and operating income and expense per crop acre. The cost of fertilizer and lime, seed and plants purchased, and the other crop expenses per crop acre are also important factors.

Fig. 13-16. Timely cultivation, along with herbicides and timely operations, combined with an adequate amount of other inputs, can help make for production efficiency in the cropping enterprise. (Courtesy, International Harvester)

Production Efficiency
per Adult Labor Equivalent

Effective year-round use of the available labor supply is important. This can be measured in several ways. The adjusted gross receipts (A.G.R.), capital invested, crop acres, and livestock units (or units of a specific livestock enterprise) per adult equivalent basis can tell one something about labor productivity and efficiency.

General

Each separate part of the business should be examined for efficiency factors appropriate for that specific part. Efficiency can be increased in two ways: (1) by reducing costs more than income and (2) by increasing income more than costs. Efficiency measures force one to critically examine the relationship of production to income by looking not only at physical measures but also at dollar values and relationships.

E. ORGANIZATON

Every person operating a farm is interested in the returns received from it. Naturally one operates the farm to make money. In order to get the highest possible net return, farm operators have to decide how best to use their labor, the labor of their family, and hired labor. How much labor should be used on the farm? How much and what kind of machinery should be purchased? How large and how expensive should buildings be? How much should be done to improve the land by adding fertilizer or lime or by investing money on soil-conserving methods? In general, this amounts to the question of how farm operators should combine their land, labor, and capital to get the best return.

Organizing the Factors of Production

We generally call each of these—land, labor, and capital—a "factor of production." In farm management terms we ask, "How shall we combine the factors of production—land, labor, and capital—to get the best net returns?" (These factors were defined in Chapter 5.)

The well-organized large farms generally make more money than the well-organized small farms. On the other hand, the poorly-organized and -operated large farms lose more than the poorly-organized and -operated small farms. The advantages of size can be easily lost when things such as crop and livestock productivity are below average or when efficiency is low.

Most results of farm studies in different states show no relationship between size of farm and rates of production. Higher rates of production (yields) are caused by following efficient methods and practices, not by the size of the enterprise. In other words, the yields of grain, hay, cotton, and other crops generally average no higher on small farms than on large ones. The production of milk per cow or eggs per hen generally averages no higher in the small herds and flocks than in the larger ones. It is true that the small livestock farms are sometimes more heavily stocked per crop acre than the larger farms. On a larger farm it is easier to diversify income. Each of the enterprises can be of sufficient size to be of economic importance. On a small farm it is more important to have one good-sized efficient enterprise than several small ones. A little bit of everything and not much of anything is the downfall of many small farm operators.

We have talked about the three factors of production—capital, labor, and land, but we have made no attempt to show how to combine the three in order to get the best return. Farmers, to be successful, will need to balance these factors. We suggest that capital on a farm can be classified in three general ways: (1) highly productive capital, such as livestock, fertilizer, etc., (2) capital which is only indirectly productive, such as machinery, buildings, and supplies, and (3) capital which is invested mainly for "show," for a large house, a barn built more for show than for usefulness, and a costly automobile, to mention only a few items. This is largely unproductive capital.

Likewise, labor can be grouped into three classes: (1) labor which is highly productive, (2) labor which is indirectly productive, and (3) labor which is unproductive—just "piddling around."

Land may also be divided into three classes: (1) highly improved land, (2) unimproved land, and (3) waste land.

Now suppose we apply highly productive capital with highly productive labor and highly improved land. That would result in a high return to the farm operator. To illustrate, if farmers used efficient labor operating good machinery directly on producing crops from the top grade land, they would get a high return. On the

Fig. 13-17. This modern machinery used on a high profit crop (corn), coupled with good crop practices on a productive soil, results in higher incomes. (Courtesy, International Harvester)

other hand, suppose they used a kind of machinery that is poorly adapted to its use on waste land. They would then get a very low return. The successful farmer attempts to put in as much available labor as possible with highly improved capital on highly improved land.

Separate Business from Pleasure. In balancing the factors of production, the farmer ordinarily considers purely the business aspects and not the question of personal pleasure. For example, many farmers maintain some wooded land mainly because they want a place for various kinds of wild game. That land is kept mainly for their enjoyment. But they will want to realize that they are spending certain money and doing certain things not because they pay dividends in the form of cash income, but because they pay dividends in the form of pleasure.

If success is to be attained on a farm, it is very important to first organize the farm properly. The setup or relationship among the available land for crops and pasture, the labor supply, and the capital for equipment, livestock, and buildings must be well balanced. Many farmers are doomed to financial failure right from the start when they have the wrong setup. It is possible many times to substitute more of one factor for a shortage in one of the others.

If one is short of labor, it pays to buy more labor-saving equipment. *Farmers adjust to get the best combination.* When cropland is limited, more labor can be used to grow intensive crops which give greater returns per acre. The combination which fits together best will use each factor in its best relationship to the others.

Many farmers seem to have a satisfactory farm organization, that is, a good balance of these production factors, but still fail, due primarily to the absence of the successful factors of production. To illustrate, a farmer keeps the most desirable class of livestock for that particular farm, but they are low-producers due to methods and practices being followed. Farmers could grow the crops best suited to their soil, but obtain very low yields because of poor seed, lateness in planting, and poor care during the growing season. The right setup on a farm is no assurance that a certain operator will be successful. The factors which bring about economical production of crops and livestock must be followed to insure success.

Thus, it is clear that farming is a business, and the principles of business management will apply to farming the same as they do to any non-farm business. Farm management as a subject is rather new, when compared with subjects such as soil, livestock, and crop management. The problems of farm management differ from those of agronomy, animal husbandry, and other agricultural subjects.

Farm management deals with the business side of farming. It is concerned with what crops to produce and how many acres to grow, what livestock to handle, and how many. It is the aim in studying farm management to fit together the important principles of crop and livestock production into one working unit on the individual farm.

The problems of balancing rations, feeding, breeding, and caring for animals are animal husbandry problems, but the decisions of whether to keep dairy cattle, beef cattle, hogs, or poultry, and how many of each are farm management problems.

The questions with regard to methods of growing the different crops, methods of fertilizing, varieties of seeds, and requirements of fertility are agronomy problems. What kinds of crops and how many acres to devote to them on any particular farm and whether they shall be fed to livestock or sold are farm management problems.

Have One Main Source of Income

Diversity does not mean a little bit of everything and not much of anything. There should be one main source of income on most farms which would account for nearly 40 to 60%, and in many cases more, of the total farm income. The rest of the income could come from one or two other sources. It is more important to have each of the minor enterprises large enough to use labor, equipment, knowledge, and capital effectively than it is to add more enterprises.

It is more difficult for small farms to gain as much by a diversified income as large farms, especially when some enterprises are not large enough to be efficient. Some farms appear to be highly specialized, but they may not truly be. Dairy farmers producing the roughage, farm grains, and replacement livestock are really quite diversified. They are in milk production, replacement heifer production, roughage production, and grain production. Dairy farmers who buy all their feed and replacements and only milk cows are very highly specialized.

Some enterprises require a nearby market, while others can ship products a long way. Before preparing to add any source of income to those already being produced, be sure of the market. Where there is a choice of several enterprises, farmers will usually make most by choosing the ones they like best. Some farm operators do not wish to milk cows; others dislike hens on the farm; still others prefer not to grow cash crops. Where cash crops can be grown, it usually pays to use part of the labor force in growing some of the more profitable ones. The most fertile parts of the farm should be used for such cash crops. It may even require large amounts of certain kinds of commercial fertilizer, and in some places irrigation must be supplied.

If a farm is particularly well suited to only one or two enterprises and not to others, it may be best to specialize. It should always be recognized that with some specialized enterprises, it often requires less land, labor, and capital to get started than a large diversified business. Such specialties require expert knowledge and above average ability of the farm operator. There are some areas very favorable for crop specialties, such as potatoes, cranberries, other fruits, etc. Much of the acreage in such regions may be in the hands of commercial growers on a large-scale production basis.

General

The six "vital signs" of profitability aid the manager in determining what to look for in causes and effects of the profitability analysis. The profitability analysis should be specific for various farm types and enterprises. One needs to closely examine the size, productivity, efficiency, and organizational factors appropriate to the specific farm type and location. County agents and agricultural instructors can furnish current information about these factors.

II. SOLVENCY

As outlined in Chapter 12, the "vital signs" of solvency are the total liability asset ratio, the current plus intermediate liability asset ratio, and the change in net worth.

If any of these "vital signs" of business health is weak, there are four areas to examine: (1) profitability of the business, (2) income tax strategies employed, (3) form of farm business organization selected, and (4) level of family spending.

The profitability analysis (causes and effects) was discussed earlier in this chapter; income tax management was discussed in Chapter 12; and the various forms of farm business organization were examined in Chapter 7.

The level of family spending affects solvency. Money used for consumption is not available for debt retirement. Rapid debt retirement improves the solvency of the business. But, this objective of rapid debt retirement may conflict with the use of funds for current family living. Thus, the level of family consumption may be sacrificed to meet the solvency objective. However, increasing profitability may be another strategy to employ.

All these factors work together. So there will be some trade-offs to most closely meet the objectives of the family and the business. Compromises must be made.

If the business has strong solvency characteristics, it can withstand some short-run setbacks. Therefore, one should put a high priority on moving toward a relatively strong solvency position compatible with other realistic goals.

Continual study of the net worth statement and changes in that statement can help monitor changes in the solvency situation.

III. LIQUIDITY–CASH FLOW

The liquidity–cash flow characteristics of the business are meas-

Fig. 13-18. Financing long-term and intermediate assets such as land and machinery with short-term debts can lead to cash flow problems.

ured by the vital signs of the current liability asset ratio, net cash farm income, and the ratio of operating income to operating expenses (with and without interest). There are eight areas affecting the liquidity–cash flow characteristics of the business to examine: (profitability; (2) debt structure; (3) family living expense, family savings, or labor cost (in case of a corporation where family members are paid a wage); (4) non-farm income; (5) debt repayment policies; (6) income tax strategies; (7) form of farm business organizaton; and (8) sales policy of farm products, inventory items, an capital gains.

Number 1 was discussed in the profitability section of this chapter and in Chapter 12. Numbers 6 and 7 were covered in the solvenc section of this chapter and in Chapter 12.

Debt Repayment and Structure

One of the most important factors in putting pressure on cas flow is accelerated debt repayment. This may be caused by having the objective of "getting out of debt" as soon as possible. But many farm families are realizing that this objective, while it may have popular appeal, is not realistic. It surely does not entirely fit with the objectives of having good profitability and providing for adequate family living.

The main problem in the debt repayment area appears to be in debt structure. That is, managers have a tendency to finance intermediate assets (such as machinery) with current liabilities or to finance long-term assets (such as land) with current or intermediate liabilities. Perhaps one should view the Net Worth Statement as a Balance Sheet and attempt to balance current assets with current liabilities, intermediate assets with intermediate liabilities, and long-term assets with long-term liabilities.

In many problem financing cases, if the solvency characteristics are adequate, refinancing can provide the solution. Repayment schedules are lengthened, and more debt is placed on the long-term assets and is financed over a longer period of time.

You will want to carefully examine your present debt structure. In some cases refinancing will be in order. In other situations you will do well to avoid the problem by arranging for proper balanced financing at the outset.

Family and Non-farm Cash Flows

The amount of money spent on family living affects liquidity–cash flow. Every act of consumption means that an act of investment or debt repayment cannot be made. Family savings and investment outside the farm business, while contributing to the overall family financial health, do not contribute to the farm net worth. On corporation farms, the dollars paid for labor are dollars which go for family living, savings, and investments. Thus, the family cash outflows may not be available for farm business use. Of course, adequate cash must be generated for decent, adequate family living conditions.

In many cases family members work off the farm or have other non-farm sources of income. While these income sources do not contribute to the profitability of the farm business, they can have an impact on the cash flow. This added cash flow can help beginning farmers develop a stronger liquidity position and eventually strengthen their solvency position.

But caution should be exercised. It is easy to mask farm business financial problems by depending on outside sources of cash to carry the business. Too often farm families only look at cash in and cash out. If adequate cash is available they feel content. If cash is short they feel as if the farming business is not desirable or successful.

Sales Policy

Economic conditions and marketing strategies might persuade a farmer to keep and store certain farm products, inventory items, or capital items. Keeping an additional 20,000 bushels of corn from one accounting period to another will show up in inventory change. This will show up as a credit on the farm earnings statement. But it will *not* show up in the wallet. Thus, the cash flow position for that year would be low.

General

These liquidity–cash flow measures speak to the feasibility of the continuation or survival of the business. Even those businesses which may exhibit moderate to excellent profitability may find themselves in a difficult position due to cash flow problems. On the other hand, some businesses with low profitability can show a good cash flow due to liquidation of resources. The manager must continually monitor the flow of funds through the business as well as through the household and be alert to the fact that adequate cash flow is not always a very good indicator of business success. It is only one important factor but is too often used as the only factor.

Cash accounting with consideration of inventory and capital change will lead to better conclusions than just cash in and cash out or cash left at the end of the year.

A Final Word

Analyzing the business is not a quick and simple task. It takes good records properly arranged into an analytical format. No one number or set of numbers tells the whole story. It is a matter of interrelationships. The various analysis factors have a cumulative effect—they reinforce each other.

All the material in Chapters 11 and 12 fit all farm types. So does the solvency and liquidity–cash flow analysis in this chapter. Only the causes and effects of the profitability analysis have to be designed for specific farm types and situations.

Fig. 12-2 should assist you in seeing how all this ties together.

Questions and Problems for Class Discussion

1. What four factors affect the "vital signs" of profitability?

2. How does your farm or an example farm measure up in these four main areas?

3. What are some measures used to evaluate the four main factors affecting profitability?

4. What four factors affect the "vital signs" of solvency?

5. How does your farm or an example farm measure up in this area?

6. What eight factors affect the "vital signs" of liquidity–cash flow?

7. How does your farm or an example farm measure up in this area?

8. Discuss the strengths and weaknesses of your farm or an example farm. How would you capitalize on the strengths? How would you correct the weaknesses?

CHAPTER 14

Credit

Highlights of Chapter

Credit is becoming more and more an important tool in modern agriculture. But if mistakes are made in using it, credit can end up in a financial loss instead of a gain.

This chapter will center attention on how to use credit to the best advantage and what mistakes to watch for. It is obvious that one must consider the chances of a financial loss as well as a possible gain by using credit to build up a farm operation.

The three types of credit—current, intermediate, and long-term—must be properly balanced with the type of asset financed. Debt repayment schedules should be flexible to cope with possible variations in the farm's production. In addition, the terms of the credit and interest rates need to be carefully considered, along with the ability of the business to meet the debt payment when it is due. Because credit is a tool, one will gain by shopping for credit like any other tool. There are many credit institutions with well-trained loan officers serving agriculture. As with all business matters, properly written credit documents should be used.

Credit in the farm business is becoming an ever increasingly important resource on nearly all commercial farms. Agriculture has changed from a labor intensive to a capital intensive industry. Most commercial farms use both their own capital and borrowed capital. But, they have to compete for credit in the money market as do other businesses.

Borrowed capital, properly used, can contribute to the farm's net income in several ways. Credit can (1) help establish and maintain a farm business of adequate size; (2) assist in making the needed changes in the farm business to meet changing conditions; (3) improve the efficiency of the farm business, such as substituting machinery for labor; (4) keep the business moving through times of income fluctuation due to variations in income and expenses and the uncertainties of price, weather, disease, etc.; and (5) provide for the transfer of a profitable farm business to another operator.

The Three Rs of Credit

Credit is another tool in the farm business which must be used properly and effectively just like a tractor, fertilizer, or any other input. It is important that credit be used properly and that farm managers plan for wise credit use. In using credit wisely, remember the three Rs of credit: *returns, repayment capacity*, and *risk*.

Generally when a farmer wishes to make some change in the farm business, added capital is needed to make that change. One must ask, "Will this proposed change pay off for me?" or "Will I get sufficient returns from the change to make it profitable?" Because credit and capital are limited, one must also ask, "Is this the most profitable use of capital?" To make the use of credit pay, it must provide adequate *returns*.

Farm managers must also look at the *repayment capacity*. Some loans are self-liquidating; that is, they pay for themselves by producing returns large enough to pay for principal and interest. An example of this is fertilizer or feed short-term loans. Intermediate loans are at least partially self-liquidating, such as loans on breeding animals and machinery. This will depend on the term of loan and the rate of depreciation or obsolescence. Non-self-liquidating loans are those used either for consumption items or for non-depreciable assets, such as farm land. Farm managers must carefully budget to see that they can pay the loan obligation after family living and operation expenses, capital item replacement costs, and taxes are paid.

Risk-bearing ability is the ability or capacity to stand unexpected low income and unexpected expenses and still remain in business. It is made up of the ability to make and save money, stability and reliability of income, and owner equity. Farmers face many risks and must plan their borrowing to take this into consideration.

Successful Use of Credit

To use credit successfully, you must see that it adds to the net income of the business and to the repayment capacity of the total business. Here are some ways you can help strengthen the repayment capacity of the business: (1) build your equity in the business; (2) organize and operate the business to maximize net income; (3) adjust the business so that production methods will make the maximum use of self-liquidating loans when resources are limited; (4) use the total capital structure of the business when financing; and (5) plan your repayment schedule to fit your income by using a cash flow budget. For maximum repayment capacity, the length of the loan should correspond to the length of time needed to recover the investment on a self-liquidating loan. On non-self-liquidating loans, use the net income-producing capacity as a guide.

Many farmers get into serious trouble using credit. Here are some major reasons why: (1) inadequate size or not enough volume of business; (2) failure to use profitable modern technology; (3) lack of experience, knowledge, or ambition; and (4) inability to control costs and to determine timeliness. Problems may also arise if budgets are poorly prepared, if a poor analysis is made of the situation, if a realistic look at the cash flow situation is not taken, or if the costs of family living and taxes are not analyzed. Trying to pay off too much too soon, or having too many credit sources with a rapid repayment schedule, may also cause serious problems.

Farmers should not spread their credit among too many creditors. Generally, two or three lenders can adequately serve their legitimate credit needs. One or two short-term and intermediate credit suppliers can team up with a long-term creditor to serve the normal credit needs of a borrower adequately. In some cases, more may be desirable, but not very often.

Balancing Types of Credit

As discussed in Chapters 11, 12, and 13, there are three types of assets and liabilities—current, intermediate, and long-term.

It is important to balance the repayment schedule with the type of asset financed. That is, one should finance current assets with current liabilities, intermediate assets with intermediate liabilities, and long-term assets with long-term liabilities. In other words, fertilizer, which is financed and used to raise corn, should be financed with short-term credit. The fertilizer loan should be paid by the time the corn is converted to cash. Machinery purchases which are financed should be paid for before the machinery is worn out or

Fig. 14-1. This cotton crop required a large amount of capital for production costs (short-term), machinery and equipment (intermediate-term), and land (long-term). (Courtesy, John Deere)

becomes obsolete. Land purchases should be financed with long-term liabilities.

Many people get into serious financial problems by not properly balancing their repayment schedules with the type of asset purchased. It takes an extremely profitable business and/or a much lower standard of living to pay off long-term assets with short-term liabilities.

Flexibility

Because of the income variability in farming, it is important to have the debt so structured that adjustments may be made to meet unexpected circumstances.

In good times a prepayment privilege is desirable. When surplus funds are available, the debt can be paid off ahead of time without a prepayment penalty. In bad times, provisions should be made for additional time or a credit extension.

More and more creditors are developing the "line of credit" concept. In this case, the borrower and lender set up either a sinking or a replenishing (or level) line of credit. The *sinking* line of credit is set up at a maximum amount of dollars. The borrower can borrow up to this amount and then has to pay it back according to the terms and conditions of the loan. The *level* line of credit is a revolving line of credit. It is the most common type. With this type of credit line, the borrower and lender set up a maximum amount of available credit. The borrower can then borrow against this credit line and pay off at any time, and then reborrow without applying for a new loan each time.

The line of credit enables the borrower to get a capital commitment from the lender. The lender knows how much capital will have to be supplied. It is simple but flexible. It makes borrowers plan ahead. There are fewer unpleasant surprises. The borrower can borrow when needed and pay off when funds are no longer needed. The cost of capital can be lower. The planning involved often results in better credit conditions for both borrower and lender.

Interest Rates

Interest rates will vary with general economic conditions, type of loan, purpose of loan, degree of risk, demand for credit, type of business, and personal characteristics of the owner.

An increasing number of lenders are making loans with a variable interest rate. This means the interest rate will go up or down, depending upon the cost of money in the money market.

The "prime rate" is generally referred to as the lowest rate charged by commercial banks for short-term loans to the lowest risk borrowers. The "prime rate" typically applies to only a small portion of the total number of borrowers.

Simple interest is interest paid only on the unpaid loan balance. Therefore, if you borrow $1,000 at 8% for one year, you will repay $1,080 ($1,000 + $80) at the end of the year. We will continue to use this 8%, $1,000 annual loan in the next examples.

A front end loan is one in which you receive $920 ($1,000 − $80) and pay back $1,000 at the end of the year. This sometimes is called a discount loan.

Another loan type is the add-on interest loan. Here the interest is figured on the full value of the loan and added to the loan. This total ($1,000 + $80 = $1,080) is divided by the number of payments to be made (12, or 1 per month) for a monthly payment of $90. Both the discount loan and the add-on loan result in higher interest rates than the 8% simple interest loan.

The amortized loan is another type of loan which is becoming more common. Some amortized loans are referred to as "interest on the unpaid balance" loans. Another term used for these is the "decreasing payment plan." The interest is paid only on the unpaid balance and therefore declines over the life of the loan. But the principal remains the same for each payment. Payments are higher early in the life of the loan.

A more common amortized loan is the "equal payment" loan. The periodic payments are equal. At first a large part of the payment is interest. The equal payment amortized loan can help farmers with a large debt by having the debt service obligation lower in the early years of the loan than with the decreasing payment plan.

Some loans are "interest only" loans. The loans do not call for any principal payments for the early years of the loan—generally one to five years. Then interest and principal payments are made over the remaining life of the loan.

"Balloon" loans fall into two categories. In the case of the "interest only" loans, the principal may become due in a lump sum after the initial years of interest only. More commonly, a regular repayment schedule will be set up on an amortized basis for a long period of time, such as 20 to 40 years. But at the end of 5 to 10 years the total principal amount becomes due in a lump sum, or a balloon payment. Many times, retiring individuals selling a farm will finance a beginning farmer with this type of loan. This gives the beginning farmer a chance to get established, create a record of performance, and gain some equity. The balloon payment will then be financed by an institutional-type creditor.

Some special loan conditions do affect the cost of credit. These would be things such as compensating balances and required stock purchases. Many financial institutions require borrowers to keep a certain minimum balance in their checking or savings accounts during the life of the loan. These are called compensating balances. The Production Credit Associations (P.C.A.'s) and Federal Land Banks (F.L.B.'s) require stock purchases in proportion to the amount of money borrowed.

The interest rate and other terms and conditions of the loan determine the true cost of borrowed capital. (See Appendix A-3e for the formula for computing the true cost of interest.)

How Much Debt?

One frequently hears the questions, "How much money can I or should I borrow?" or "How much is safe to borrow?" The answer to the first question is: "As much as you can *profitably* borrow *and* meet *debt service* (principal and interest payments) obligations in a timely fashion."

If you can borrow money for fertilizer at 9% and earn 15% on it, you will be gaining 6%. On the 6% gain, you generally will have to pay taxes and the rest will be available for other purposes such as additional debt repayment, family living, or business expansion. This set of conditions makes it profitable. But what about servicing the debt in a timely fashion?

Too often, rapid debt repayment causes a severe cash flow bind. So repayment schedules must be carefully budgeted to coincide with expected income. In the fertilizer example, the fertilizer loan should be repaid when the corn is converted to cash. The information in the chapters on budgeting (Chapters 15, 16, and 17) can help you determine how much money will be available annually for debt service.

The question relating to safety is more difficult to answer. Farming is a risky business. There is potentially great variation between incomes from one year to another. If you figure you will have $6,000 annually for debt repayment on the average, you must realize that half of the years will probably be below $6,000. Therefore, you need to allow for these variations.

For those with large debts in relation to assets, the matter of risk is even more important. If you are strong financially, you can accept and deal with larger risks. So careful study of the risk-bearing abilities of both the farm business and farm operator is required before the safety question can be adequately answered.

Will the borrowed funds have a high return? If so, it is a safer type of loan. Loans for assets which have a high and quick payoff should have a high priority. One should put additional funds into enterprises which have had a history of high payoffs. Loans which enable farmers to fully utilize existing fixed facilities, to make use of economies of size, and to do a better job of marketing also have a high priority.

There should be a high margin to service the debt. A high-margin between cash expenses and what is left for family living, fixed cost, and debt service will make for safer loans.

Calculating Amount of Debt You Can Handle

The process of calculating debt service capacity is quite easy if you have done an adequate job of budgeting. The computation goes this way:

Item	Example
Cash farm income	$ 40,000
Cash farm expense (less interest)	$−22,000
Subtotal	$ 18,000
Cash needed for capital goods replacement or expansion	$− 3,000
Subtotal	$ 15,000
Family living, income tax, Social Security	$ 10,000
Subtotal	$ 5,000
Net non-farm income available	$+ 1,000
Amount available annually for debt service (principal plus interest)	$ 6,000

Based on this budget, $6,000 would be available annually for debt service—that is, interest and principal.

The next step is to determine the rate of interest which must be paid and the length of the loan. Then, with the help of an amortization table (Appendix A-3c) and the following equation, one can determine the size of loan which may be serviced by an equal payment amortized loan.

Annual amount available for debt service ÷ amortization factor = amount of total debt which can be serviced

If we have an interest rate of 8% and a 20-year loan to service annually with our $6,000, about a $59,000 debt can be serviced. $6,000 ÷ 0.1018 = $58,939. The 0.1018 factor was taken from the amortization table in the column under 8% and the 20-year line.

A 40-year loan at 8% with a $6,000 annual payment could service over $71,500 of debt ($6,000 ÷ 0.0838 = $71,599).

Absolute vs. Relative Size of Debt

An equity position of 60%—that is, for every $1,000 of total assets there are $400 of liabilities with an owner's equity of $600—is generally thought of as a strong financial situation. In this situation, only $400 of principal has to be paid off. If all the assets became worthless overnight, it would not be impossible to pay off the $400. Both the absolute ($400) and the relative (40%) amounts of debt are low.

But, what if your equity position is still 60% but the total assets are $1,000,000? Then the 40% of debt is $400,000. The risk to both the lender and the borrower is greater. In some cases there will be legal or financial limitations which would make it difficult, if not impossible, for an individual lender to work with one farmer with a high absolute debt.

In these cases, the credit line may be split among a long-term lender, an intermediate-term lender, and a short-term lender.

With larger loans or low-equity loans, both borrower and lender need to feel comfortable about the loan. Some individuals cannot cope with large or high risk loans from either a psychological or a business managerial standpoint.

Shopping for Credit

Credit is a tool in the farm business as is a tractor. You certainly would shop for the best buy and top performance in a new tractor. Similarly, you should shop for the best buy and terms of a loan.

Fig. 14-2. You should shop for credit just as carefully as you shop for land, buildings, and machinery. (Courtesy, International Harvester)

Some questions to ask are: What are the lending policies of the lender? Are the credit conditions and terms suitable for my farming type? What about length of loan? How is the repayment schedule structured? How much and what kind of collateral must I have? Do I have a line of credit? What happens if I have a bad year or two bad years in succession? What is the true interest rate? Does the lender have an agricultural specialist on the staff? If so, will that person be able to give me some financial management advice?

The lender is not doing you a favor by lending money! It is the lender's business, and the success of that business depends on you. So ask hard questions and demand solid answers.

But, credit shopping is a two-way street. The lender is lending depositors' funds and must exercise reasonable caution. So you must also be able to answer some hard questions. Good farm business managers can and will have the necessary information.

This would include having a reasonable amount of farm production, business, and financial management skills. Some record of past performance, or at least some obvious signs of being able to perform well, good financial records, and a carefully prepared budget are also required.

Fig. 14-3. Vegetable crop production requires a great deal of knowledge as well as capital. Irrigation equipment represents a large capital investment. Many times, the capital must be borrowed.

Lenders look for the three Cs of credit: *character*, *capacity*, and *collateral*. Do you have the strength of *character* to perform well as a farmer and repay debts? You need to have certain personal characteristics to become a successful farm manager. Does the business have the repayment *capacity*? The business must be profitable and have adequate cash flow characteristics to handle debt. Is there enough *collateral*? It is very risky to make 100% loans. The borrower needs to have some of his or her own money to put into the business.

Borrowers and lenders must be able to communicate with each other. A problem such as not being able to make a payment should be discussed as soon as the problem is discovered, rather than waiting until the last minute. Frank discussion will create a climate of respect and trust.

Lenders do not make money by, nor do they enjoy, foreclosing on loans. It is not profitable, and it certainly is not pleasurable. Therefore, lenders in a way shop for good borrowers just as borrowers shop for good lenders. Good lenders plus good borrowers equals successful farmers and lending institutions.

Sources of Credit

There are many sources of credit to qualified farm borrowers. These would include the following:

A.S.C.S., or the Agricultural Stabilization and Conservation Service, makes intermediate-term (up to seven years) loans to farmers for grain storage structures at reasonable interest rates. Currently the interest rate is 7%.

Banks are among the major suppliers of short- and intermediate-term credit to farmers. More and more banks are employing farm representatives to assist their farm customers. Many banks provide auxiliary services, such as professional farm management, estate planning, trusts, and tax consultation, to their customers. Most small country banks will have correspondent relationships with large city banks to provide overline credit.

C.C.C., or the Commodity Credit Corporation, provides loans to farmers on eligible commodities. The C.C.C. is a wholly owned government corporation. Sometimes the loans are contingent on participation in government programs. Your local A.S.C.S. office can give you current information on these loans.

Credit unions in rural areas provide not only personal loans but also farm loans. Most of these loans are of a short-term or intermediate nature, while some are long-term loans. Credit unions are not major agricultural lenders nationally, but are major lenders in some local areas.

Dealers and merchants furnish a significant amount of credit generally of a very short-term nature—usually less than 30 days. Interest is usually not charged unless the accounts exceed a certain time limit, such as 30 to 60 days. Of course, this service is built into the price of the goods and services sold. But this short-term credit is granted in a somewhat more liberal manner, without any extensive paper work. In some cases dealers have their own credit organizations for the conditional sales contracts they make to farmers. Others have working relationships with local credit institutions for these longer-term credit needs.

Finance companies in rural areas lend on a short-term and intermediate credit basis. They are somewhat like the banks and credit unions, but in some cases have higher interest and service charges. Some cater to higher risk loans which are more costly to service.

Fm.H.A., or the Farmers Home Administration, is a government lending agency which operates in the U.S. Department of Agriculture. It is a supervised credit program providing operating loans, ownership loans, and emergency loans. Its field staff is specifically trained to help low equity farmers get financing. The character and capacity of the borrower, rather than collateral, are considered. When farmers have enough equity to get financing elsewhere, they are required to do so.

F.L.B.'s, or the Federal Land Banks, make long-term loans on real estate. These loans cannot exceed 85% of the appraised value of the real estate. There are 12 Federal Land Banks in the United States—one in each of the 12 Farm Credit Districts. The loans are made through the F.L.B. Associations scattered throughout each district. Those on the field staff are trained specialists in agricultural credit. Details on their loan programs and procedures are available from the F.L.B. Association officers.

Individuals are major suppliers of agricultural credit. A high percentage of farm real estate sales are financed by the seller. In many cases the buyer and seller are related. It is important that these loans be carried out in a businesslike fashion, with appropriate legal documentation.

Insurance companies provide a significant amount of long-term credit for farm real estate. The insurance companies will generally concentrate on top farming areas to make larger, relatively low risk loans. These loans must provide a competitive return with low servicing costs. Insurance company farm loan officers have a broad background in agricultural lending.

P.C.A.'s, or Production Credit Associations, are major suppliers of short-term and intermediate credit for farmers. They loan for production items such as fertilizer, livestock, machinery, etc. The F.I.C.B., or Federal Intermediate Credit Bank, in each of the 12 Farm Credit Districts is the chief source of funds for the P.C.A.'s. The F.I.C.B. also supervises the local P.C.A. Field representatives for the local P.C.A.'s are well trained in agricultural lending. Some P.C.A.'s are providing other services such as farm record keeping, estate planning, and income tax services in addition to supplying credit.

S.B.A.'s, or Small Business Administrations, are fairly recent additions to the list of suppliers of agricultural credit. They are not a major source of agricultural credit as yet. Your local S.B.A. can give you the most recent information on their farm loans.

Loan brokers—In some areas of the United States, people well acquainted with agricultural lending and having broad contacts in the lending community arrange for loans. The people work for a fee—usually a one-time flat percentage of the total loan. The fee is sometimes added to the loan. The broker will arrange for current, intermediate, or long-term financing needs of the borrower through the various loan agencies.

Loan Documents or Credit Instruments

About all loans, except the 30-day dealer or merchant charge accounts, are supported by some type of written record or document. These are commonly called credit instruments. There are several kinds of credit instruments.

The most common one is the check. A check is just an order in writing to the bank to pay a specified amount of money to the person or organization named on the check. The check is signed by the party ordering the bank to make the payment. Another instrument much like a check is a draft, except the order the bank pays is not charged to the signer but to a specified third party.

A promissory note is a written instrument which is signed by the maker of the note. The maker of the note makes a promise to pay under conditions a fixed sum of money to the payee named on the note. There may be one or more makers. It is important that all the terms and conditions of the note, including the interest, be clearly specified. Some notes are "signature only" notes, with no collateral, but most are secured notes designating some form of collateral. An example of this would be a mortgage note on a farm real estate loan. The real estate would be the security or collateral for the loan which is documented by a promissory note.

Another common instrument is the warehouse receipt. This is simply a written document or receipt stating that the warehouse operator has received a specified quantity and quality of a commodity and has it in storage. The warehouse receipt is then used as collateral for a loan. The commodity can later be sold or redeemed and the loan paid off.

Almost all debt instruments are recorded in the county courthouse. Therefore, when the loan is paid, a proper release or loan satisfaction document should be obtained and recorded. It is vital that all the appropriate paper work regarding loans be done on a timely basis.

Questions and Problems for Class Discussion

1. What are the three Rs of credit?
2. What is meant by balancing types of credit?
3. How can you use, or how have you used, credit successfully?
4. Why is flexibility important to credit?
5. What are the sources of farm credit?
6. What is an amortized loan?
7. Calculate the debt carrying capacity of your home farm or a case farm.

PART FOUR

Planning for the Future

In Part Three we discussed farm records, income tax management, financial and business analysis, financial management, and credit. This helps you answer the question, "Where has the business been, and where is it now?"

In Part Four we will present methods to help you answer the questions, "Where do I want the business to be in the future?" and "How can I get the business adjusted to the future plan?" This involves some general budgeting information and the use of partial, total, and transitional farm budgets.

CHAPTER 15

The Budgeting Process

Highlights of Chapter

Forward planning or budgeting takes much thought on the part of the farm manager. The manager has to estimate what the prices may be of the crops and livestock expected to be produced and compare each one with each of the others. This will give the manager a sort of overall picture. Having done that, the manager needs to estimate the yield of the crops and the cost of producing the various kinds of livestock (hogs and cattle, for example), and make a comparison as was done with prices. These amounts are commonly referred to as the "coefficients of production." Comparisons are made between different related items or factors.

When this has been done, it is a good idea to estimate the length of time it will take to get the plan into normal operation, which is referred to as the "time frame" of the adjustment period.

Next the manager should attempt to get information on the potential market for the products for sale. With this information the manager will have a rather clear idea of how profitable the operation may be. The *enterprise budget* will be exceedingly valuable in the planning procedure. We grant that it means considerable work, but it will pay out well even if it is not perfect.

A farm plan can be to the farmer what the architect's specifications are to the building contractor. Farming has become so commercialized that the ability of a farm operator to adopt improved methods and practices and to combine the different farm enterprises into a profitable working unit is one of the most important factors for successful farming. A good plan combines land, labor, capital, and management into an efficient, productive, and profitable unit, which has adequate solvency and liquidity–cash flow characteristics.

Most farm businesses can be improved if one makes a careful study of the complete farm organization. Farm planning is the process of selecting methods and practices to make improvements. A successful farmer has to look further ahead and has to plan carefully. A sound plan, if followed, should result in a larger farm income, conservation of land and other resources, and better living for the family.

When you are making a total farm plan or budget, consider the whole farm business as a unit. The overall plan should include:

1. An inventory of resources.

2. A cropping system which maintains or improves productivity, prevents erosion, and gives maximum income. An up-to-date soil map should be used.

3. A livestock setup, adapted to available markets, which will fit the cropping system, make efficient use of feed crops, and give proper balance to the business.

4. An adequate volume of business that will provide full use of productive resources and maintain a good balance between enterprises.

5. Ample supply and efficient use of labor, machinery, power, buildings, and working capital.

6. Products for home use if they can be produced economically.

7. The use of a map of the present fields and building arrangement and the making of a revised farm map showing an improved arrangement which will be desirable.

8. A financial budget tied to the aforementioned items which examines the profitability, liquidity–cash flow, and solvency characteristics of the proposed business changes.

Budgeting enables you to test quickly and economically on paper before committing a great deal of time and money to a project. *Test before you invest!*

Who Should Make the Farm Plan

A farm plan should be made by the farmer and the family. They are in a better position to do it and will be more apt to carry it out if it is their own. However, many times professional and technical help can be most valuable to the farm operator. The first plan may not be the best, but by working at it, a good one can be developed. There are many factors which are outside the control of the farm operator, such as those affected by weather, prices, and institutional factors. Some others difficult to predict are outbreaks of disease and insect infestation of crops and animals. These uncertainties make it difficult to plan with a high degree of assurance that the outcome will be exactly as expected. But, this is no reason for not planning! In fact, the budget can be constructed using different price and productivity assumptions to test the sensitivity of the plan to these various uncertain factors. This enables one to test before investing.

In making any plan of crops to be grown and livestock to be kept, one should use those which are adapted to the natural resources of the farm and to the liking and ability of the farm operator. It is always a problem to combine all the resources in such a way that each will be used in the most productive manner. One factor may be limited, thus affecting the combination that will best fit all other resources. One sometimes uses more of one factor and less of another to balance the situations.

Soil and Planning

The soil is the foundation for successful farming and it should be put to its most profitable use, consistent with good soil conservation practices. Some soil types are more productive than others. Areas with good soil are capable of producing large acreages of cultivated crops, such as corn, tobacco, potatoes, cotton, soybeans, etc. Other areas are hilly and subject to erosion, making it necessary to keep such land in hay and pasture as much as possible. The climate will affect the kind of crops that will be best suited to different areas. Whole areas are known as hay and pasture regions, and others as grain, livestock, cotton, and range regions.

A farm may not have a uniform soil type or topography, which makes it necessary to follow different rotations on different fields. A three-year rotation of corn, oats, and hay will permit one-third of the cropland in corn, but a four-year rotation of corn, oats, and hay (two years) will allow only one-fourth of the land in corn or other row crops. It is advisable on some fields to exclude row crops altogether and produce permanent hay, using small grains primarily as a nurse crop or using chemicals when seeding back to hay. The permanent

Fig. 15-1. The soil is the foundation for successful farming. Profitable crop production is tied to good solid conservation practices. (Courtesy, Soil Conservation Service, USDA)

pasture land will determine to a great extent the amount and kind of livestock kept. In the wheat areas the producing wheat fields may be rotated with fallow fields.

Getting the Work Done

To make the crop and livestock plans succeed, it is necessary to get the work done on time. The plan should provide productive work well distributed throughout the year, making good use of the land, buildings, equipment, and capital.

The power and equipment to be used will be determined by the size of the farm, type of farming, and labor and capital available.

Type and Size of Equipment

The type and size of equipment should be determined by the type of work to be done, the size of the job, and the number of days in which the job must be done. Many new types of farm equipment which will replace other types are now coming on the market. Many livestock producers are using more equipment around the farmstead to save daily chores. The need for capital in other parts of the farm business may slow up the installation of some of this new

Fig. 15-2. Big equipment such as this can best be used on large farms with adequate-sized fields. (Courtesy, Melroe Company)

equipment. When purchasing any labor-saving equipment, one should be certain that there is some productive work which can be done with the labor saved, or else the cost may not be justified.

Some tasks, such as cleaning barns and feeding silage, can be done by hand if the number of animals is relatively small, if capital is scarce, and if family labor is available. Other jobs may be done by hiring custom operators of combines, pickers, forage harvesters, feed grinders, sprayers, etc. Some of these machines can be owned jointly with neighbors.

The maximum amount of power needed to operate a farm will be that amount which is required to do the work satisfactorily at the time of year when the most power will be needed to carry out the crop and livestock plan. Be sure the farm and need of the machine justify its purchase. Any machine should reduce the labor, increase the size of business, make the operations more timely, increase the yields, or decrease the costs.

Labor Use

Farm management experts have assembled data on the average amount of production work done in a 10-hour day for crop and livestock production. Each farmer will vary from the average in the amount of labor required for crop work as the size of fields, arrangement, shape, and distance from farmstead change. Few farmers, except those who have kept records, realize the number of hours

Fig. 15-3. This traveling gun irrigation system is sprinkling liquid manure. (Courtesy, *Wisconsin Agriculturist*)

required to care for crops and the different classes of livestock. Some farmers require more time than others to do chores, due to skill and to building arrangement for feeding, watering, and cleaning.

Besides required labor on crops and livestock, on every farm there is much necessary work on maintenance of buildings, equipment, and fences, on hauling manure, and the like. Also, time must be allocated to keeping records and managing the business.

It is difficult and probably impossible to work out a farm organization which requires a uniform amount of labor each day, week, or month throughout the year. There will be peak loads and slack periods, but one should aim to have reasonably uniform distribution. The total amount and distribution of labor needed, and at what time, will depend upon the size of business and the kind and amount of crops grown and livestock kept. It is wise in planning the work program to do the maintenance work on buildings, equipment, fences, etc., at slack time and on rainy days.

Labor distribution on different crops and livestock has been plotted from farm records in several states and differs somewhat even in different parts of a state. Extra hours of labor can be eliminated by efficient arrangement of fields and buildings. By spending this time in care of crops and livestock one can increase production. More lime and fertilizer, better seeds, and improved practices and methods can be used to increase production. While this may require a little extra time, it is almost certain to bring about higher yields. As an example, one can grow a small acreage of some intensive crop or keep more intensive livestock to make better use of the labor force. Information on crop and livestock labor requirements and their distribution is generally available for your state from your county agent or instructor.

Time Period of Budget or Plan

Planning the farm business may take different time frames into consideration. Short-run planning will deal with one production planning period, while long-run planning covers several production planning periods. Variable costs are more crucial to the short-run plan, while fixed costs become more crucial to the long-run plan. Also, in long-run planning the manager needs to do transitional planning. This involves a series of short-run plans to arrive at the long-run plan.

Prices and Coefficients of Production

The selection of appropriate prices to use in making out the budget is of utmost importance. Two types of prices need to be considered. They are *absolute prices*, the actual price level to be used, and *relative prices*, the relationship among the various absolute prices selected.

Do not be too optimistic in selecting your absolute price levels! Be reasonable and realistic. You will only fool yourself by using prices which are too high or too low. If you are doing short-run planning, use prices appropriate for that time period. In long-run planning, use the *average* expected price for the several production planning periods under consideration.

Absolute prices pay the bills and provide the income. But to select the right combination of enterprises, the price relationships need to be considered. Thus, if you use $2.40 as a long-range planning price for corn, an appropriate relative price for hogs must be

used if the optimum combination of enterprises is to be selected. If
you believe the long-range corn/hog ratio to be in the 17 range, then
a $40 per hundredweight price for hogs is appropriate (40 ÷ $2.40 =
16.7). A $30 price for hogs results in a 12.5 corn/hog ratio, while the
ratio at $60 for hogs is 25, both of which are out of a normal or
average range. Appropriate absolute and relative prices are extremely important items to consider when budgeting.

The next step is to determine the physical amounts of inputs
needed in the business. The price selected times the physical
amount of input required equals the cost. Some inputs may not have
a cash cost associated with them. These could include items such as
unpaid family and operator labor, unpaid management, equity capital and depreciation, etc. For proper accrual budgeting you need to
assign a value to the quantity being used. In cash flow or feasibility
budgeting only cash costs are considered.

On the output side, you need to estimate carefully what level of
productivity might be reasonably expected during the planning period under consideration. Past records on the crop and livestock
sections of the business would be most helpful. If you have been
weaning an average of 8.1 pigs per litter, selling 13,000 pounds of
milk per cow, producing a 90% beef calf crop, or having a 120%
lambing percentage in the recent past, these would be good coefficients of production to start from. Or if you can *realistically* assume
that your proposed changes in the business will make these kinds of
coefficients appropriate, you should use them. A crop production
history over a three- to five-year period can give you an excellent
feel for realistic crop production expectations.

In the absence of such a history, either because you lack needed
records or because you are approaching a new venture, your county
agent or agricultural teacher has information about realistic livestock and crop coefficients of production for your area.

The selection of appropriate prices and coefficients of production is the most difficult and important part of the budgeting process.
A great deal of time, thought, and research must be given to obtain
the best available information about these items. If these are wrong,
your budget will be wrong.

We now have to ask and answer some questions about the
proposed change.

Can It Be Done? This vital question looks at the *technical* feasibility of the plan. Are the soil type and topography, as well as the

Fig. 15-4. In budgeting the appropriate technology of crop selection, you must consider seed-bed preparation, pest control, planting, harvesting, and marketing for a profitable enterprise. (Courtesy, International Harvester)

climate, suited for the crop under consideration? Is irrigation water available if you are planning to irrigate? Is the type of livestock you are considering adapted to the area? Does the technology available enable you to control pests for the crop or livestock species in that area? These and other technical questions must be answered with the help of various production or technical specialists. Further, you need to obtain information about the various production systems or alternatives in executing the plan.

Technical feasibility and the production system to be used must be clearly outlined in detail before budgeting begins. Then the inputs can be priced. The coefficients of production associated with the system can be integrated with the prices and put into the budget.

Is There a Market? Before starting a production process, all producers—farm and non-farm—have to ask this question. This needs to be considered when deciding on prices. (See Part Five of this book for a further discussion on marketing.)

Is It Profitable? The next question to be answered relates to the expected profitability of the plan. This is done using accrual accounting methods. We will discuss this further and outline methods of determining profitability in Chapters 16 and 17.

Is It Feasible? Even if the plan meets all of the prior require-ments we have outlined, the answer to this question still must be "yes." This question is answered using cash accounting. Sometimes a budget shows profitability but may not be feasible because of liquidity–cash flow problems. But if the budget is not profitable, it should not be implemented even if it is feasible.

The cash flow budget will show if family living, operating ex-penses, and debt service can be paid on a timely basis. This will be discussed in Chapters 16 and 17.

Enterprise Budgets

An enterprise is a single separate project or undertaking for the purpose of making a profit. A beef feed lot of 100 steers is an example of a livestock enterprise, while 100 acres of corn for grain is an example of a crop enterprise. The total farm business is made up of several enterprises integrated into a complete business.

Enterprise budgets can be most helpful in developing a total farm plan. They can be put together by following these steps. An example has been provided to help your understanding.

1. Develop a description of the enterprise—for example, 100 acres of corn for grain; 40 dairy cows (including raised replace-ments) producing 14,000 pounds of milk for sale per year, 30% of the herd replaced annually, etc. We will just follow through with the corn example.

2. Select appropriate coefficients of production—soil type, to-pography, and climatic conditions which provide for a 120-bushel per acre long-term average yield of No. 2 yellow shelled corn.

3. Select appropriate input and output prices. (See Table 15-1.)

4. Develop the receipt or income part of the budget. (See Table 15-1.)

5. Develop the cost part of the budget (variable and fixed costs). (See Table 15-1.)

6. Calculate the returns to the enterprise. (See Table 15-1.)

7. Make appropriate notes as to assumptions used in the bud-get. (See Table 15-1.)

8. Utilize the budget for forward planning, decision making, and evaluation.

Table 15-1. Grain Corn Enterprise Budget[1]

Receipts (annual)	
Yield per acre	120 bu.
Price per bushel	$ 2.25
Gross receipts per acre	$270.00
Variable Costs (annual)	
Fertilizer	$ 47.80
Seed	$ 15.00
Pesticides	$ 17.50
Machinery operation and drying	$ 29.65
Interest on operating capital (9% for 6 months)	$ 4.95
Total Variable Costs	$114.90
Fixed Costs (annual)	
Machinery, equipment, and storage	$ 36.00
Land charge	$ 90.00
Labor ($16/A)	$ 16.00
Management (5% of value of production)	$ 13.20
Total Fixed Costs	$155.20
Total Costs	$270.10
Returns	
Gross receipts per acre	$270.00
Variable costs	114.90
Returns over variable costs	$155.10
Total fixed costs	155.20
Return over fixed and variable costs (Total Costs)	$−0.10
Labor and management charge ($16.00 + $13.20)	$ 29.20
Return over fixed and variable costs	−0.10
Return to labor and management	$ 29.10
Land charge	$ 90.00
Return over fixed and variable costs	−0.10
Return to land	$ 89.90
Management charge	$ 13.20
Return over fixed and variable costs	−0.10
Return to management	$ 13.10

[1]This budget assumes a single crop annually, 100 acres of grain corn with the operator supplying all the crop inputs, labor, management, machinery, capital, and storage. Typical technology for the area is used. The budget is done on the accrual basis and reflects profitability. The manager would also want to test the feasibility of the budget by doing a cash flow analysis.

Your state and county University Extension farm management specialists can give you enterprise budgets appropriate to your area.

Business Objectives of Budgeting

The budget looks at the farm business in future planning periods, while the farm business analysis looks at past business performance. However, the same analysis procedure can be used to evaluate expected or planned performance. Thus, at the end of the budgeting procedure the manager looks at the profitability, solvency, and liquidity–cash flow characteristics of the plan.

Profitability

The forward plan should improve or at least maintain present profitability of the business. The plan can utilize several strategies for business improvement.

Some strategies to consider involve improving the use of resources presently controlled. This could include fully using the existing resources. One should not add resources unless existing resources are fully utilized. Specifically, one does not add buildings, livestock, or acres unless those in the business are being used to capacity. Another strategy to consider is the change of enterprises or the mix of enterprises. An example would be shifting to different combinations of crops grown or changing livestock species, such as going from cattle to hogs. Further, the productivity and efficiency of the enterprises need to be examined for potential improvement. In some cases one needs to look at the fixed or capital assets used in the business. Should they be replaced, discarded, expanded, shared with others, or sold? The procedures for purchase of inputs and sale of outputs need to be evaluated and improved. In some cases expansion is *not* the answer. In other cases contraction of the business can improve profitability.

All the factors which have a bearing on the profitability characteristics of the business need to be carefully considered.

Solvency

Good solvency characteristics are vital to the long-term survival of the business. One needs to consider carefully how the plan or budget will affect these measures. How can capital costs be cut? How can assets grow faster than liabilities? What is the leverage position of the business? Will an increased leverage position improve the business? What risks are associated with it? Can one profitably use risk reducing techniques such as irrigation, crop drying, pest control, improved marketing, hedging, forward contracts, etc.? Will another form of business organization help? Should one lease? Should the business refinance? All these factors will affect solvency. The manager needs to answer carefully these questions in the budgeting procedure.

Liquidity and Cash Flow

Often a business has profitability and solvency, but lacks liquidity and cash flow. One needs to look at methods of increasing cash inflows and reducing cash outflows. The structure of the debt is most important. Many times, managers put a high premium on fast debt repayment. But this may put them in a severe cash flow bind. Keeping relatively large cash reserves can help in solving liquidity and cash flow problems. But this may have an adverse effect on profitability. This trade-off needs to be evaluated in light of the characteristics of the business and the goals and objectives of the manager.

How Many Alternatives? Most farmers have rather limited options for employing their resources. Therefore, it will not be difficult for them to narrow the reasonable choices down to two or three alternatives. These alternatives can then be budgeted alongside one another with a projection of the present operation to determine which most closely meets the business and personal objectives of the farm family. Also, the farm families need to consider their past and expected production and their business and financial management abilities, as well as the question of whether the proposed change would help improve the business based on past performance.

Finally, the business should always be budgeted in detail each year for the following year so it can be used as a control or monitoring device to measure actual performance with planned performance. A long-range budget should also be prepared and periodically updated to give the manager long-run direction in the management of the business.

The budgetary process can help managers select the best combination of enterprises to put into their farm businesses and can help them evaluate the profitability, liquidity–cash flow, and solvency characteristics of the farm plan.

Tools to Help Make Budgeting Easier

Electronic hardware is a rapidly developing and improving type of technology. It is easily adapted for use in farming and can help handle complex calculations in an extremely accurate and easy fashion. There are basically two types of hardware farm managers should consider—calculators and computers. Each of these types has several variations.

With the low price of simple electronic calculators, no farm manager can afford to be without at least one. Some are small enough to fit easily into a pocket, wallet, or purse. Others are hand held, and some are larger desk models. One of each would be ideal.

Many of the desk-type and hand held calculators have at least one memory function. Newer, programmable calculators have ap-

Fig. 15-5. The electronic technology of calculators and computers is being used more and more by the better farm managers to quickly compute information for better decision making.

peared on the market. These may have a library of programs with them as well as the capability of allowing the manager to do the programming. This can be done quickly, economically, and easily. Many farm managers can afford to own one of these more sophisticated instruments.

Computers are not particularly new and have already been adapted to many farming uses. These would include farm business record keeping, farm business and financial analysis, forward planning, soil test recommendations, livestock production testing, and least cost ration balancing. A few farmers have already installed computer hardware on their own farms and have adapted them to their specific uses. Interactive teletype units are available which can call into a central computer and get hard (printed) copy of input and output immediately.

Some of the less complicated programs are now available for the programmable calculator. So, farm managers can do their own computations at their own desks. These could include various partial budget routines, enterprise budget generators, financial management calculations, ration balancing, crop buying and selling guides, break even analyses, crop moisture adjustments, livestock schedulings, and many other computations.

Being able to use this new technology effectively in farm decision making has perhaps more profit potential than being able to run any other machine on the farm. Farm managers and agricultural professionals serving farmers will do well to adopt this technology as rapidly as possible.

Questions and Problems for Class Discussion

1. Why must soil type, topography, and climate be considered in budgeting?

2. What sources of information would you look for in selecting appropriate prices and coefficients of production?

3. Why are absolute and relative prices important? What is the difference between absolute and relative prices? Give an example.

4. Develop a crop and livestock enterprise budget to fit your farm situation.

5. What are the business objectives of budgeting? How can they help the manager?

CHAPTER 16

Partial Budgeting

Highlights of Chapter

Partial budgeting is a rapid technique for testing the profitability, repayment capacity, and financial impact of alternative adjustments in the farm business. It should only be used to analyze relatively minor adjustments in the farm business which can be conveniently analyzed without affecting the total business. A break even analysis can also be of help in analyzing alternatives.

Many changes in the farm business do not involve a complete or major revision of the total farm business. When just one segment of the business is to be adjusted, the partial budget saves the work of the total budget. The partial budget is a shortcut method for testing the profitability repayment capacity and financial impact of this type of decision. The partial budget method should only be used for decisions such as adding an enterprise, purchasing a new machine, and deciding the better alternative between two courses of action, such as custom hiring vs. owning your own equipment. For major changes in the business, the total budget should be used. (See Chapter 17.) But the partial budget is a simple, powerful tool to use in farm management decision making. By mastering its technique, you will have an effective, useful tool.

What Is a Partial Budget? A partial budget is a formal or informal device for examining two alternatives and deciding which one is more profitable. (See Table 16-1.) The partial budget deals only with the costs and returns which change as a result of changes in one part of the business. Look at the partial budget as a scale where you

Table 16-1. Partial Budget for Purchase of Corn Harvesting Equipment and Discontinuation of Hiring Custom Work for 200 Acres of Corn for Grain (Proposed Plan)

Credit			Debit		
Added Return and/or Reduced Cost			Added Cost and/or Reduced Return		
Added Return	Profitability	Repayment Capacity	**Added Cost**	Profitability	Repayment Capacity
Added income from proposed plan			New investment and added annual investment costs from proposed plan		
Reduced field loss, 2 bu./A @ $2/bu.	$ 800	$ 800	Annual fixed costs, $10,000 @ 18%	$1,800	$ 900
	$ —	$ —		$ —	$ —
Total Annual Added Returns	(1a) $ 800	(1b) $ 800	Total Added Annual Investment Costs	(4a) $1,800	(4b) $ 900
Reduced Cost			Added annual operating costs from proposed change		
Reduced costs from proposed plan			Cash operating costs	$ 700	$ 700
Custom work, 200 A @ $12/A	$2,400	$2,400	Value of extra operator labor	$ 600	$ —
	$ —	$ —			
Total Annual Reduced Costs	(2a) $2,400	(2b) $2,400	Total Added Annual Operating Costs	(5a) $1,300	(5b) $ 700
TOTAL CREDITS (1 + 2)	(3a) $3,200	(3b) $3,200			

(Continued)

Table 16-1 (Continued)

Credit	Debit		
Added Return and/or Reduced Cost	Added Cost and/or Reduced Return		
	Reduced Return	**Profitability**	**Repayment Capacity**
	Reduced income from proposed plan		
		$ _____	$ _____
		$ _____	$ _____
	Total Annual Reduced Return .... (6a) None	(6a) None	(6b) None
	TOTAL DEBITS (4 + 5 + 6) .... (7a) $3,100	(7a) $3,100	(7b) $1,600
$3,200 (3a) Total Credits	△ $3,100 (7a) Total Debits	(7a)	
(8a) **CHANGE IN NET INCOME—ACCRUAL** (3a − 7a)	$ 100		
$3,200 (3b) Total Credits	△ $1,600 (7b)	(7b)	
(8b) **CHANGE IN NET INCOME—CASH** (3b − 7b)	$1,600		

FINANCIAL ANALYSIS

(9) Total added investment $10,000
(10) Return/$ added investment (8a ÷ 9) 1%
(11) Years required to pay back (9 ÷ 8b) 6.25

balance the dollar weights of the credits and debits of a proposed change against each other. Credits can be added returns and/or reduced costs. Debits can be added costs and/or reduced returns.

Partial budgeting does not show if the proposed change is the *most* profitable use of resources, but a series of partial budgets can help evaluate several alternative uses of the resources. Thus, the budgets can be used to approximate the most profitable use of the resources.

The profitability analysis of the partial budget looks at the income-generating ability of the proposed change on the accrual basis. The repayment capacity analysis looks only at the cash-generating ability of the change. The financial analysis shows the returns per dollar of *added* investment and the years required for the change to generate enough cash to equal the added investment.

How to Use a Partial Budget

An example might best illustrate how to use a partial budget. (See Table 16-1.) Suppose you want to evaluate the purchase of corn harvesting equipment and discontinue hiring custom work. The first thing to consider is the profitability analysis using accrual accounting. If the adjustment appears profitable, then the repayment capacity analysis is made using cash accounting. If the repayment and cash flow analysis is positive, then the financial analysis is made. At this point you decide to implement the plan or to run additional budgets to see if there are other alternative uses of the resources which might be more profitable. As we discussed in Chapter 15, appropriate prices and coefficients of production must be used. As much information as possible should be used from your own farm records.

Profitability Analysis

Using our example, let us see how the partial budget form might be used for the profitability analysis. The added returns in this example fall into two categories—added income and reduced costs. The manager in this case felt the custom operator was not doing a satisfactory job. This could be due to poor equipment, carelessness, or lack of timeliness. It was felt that an additional 2 bushels of corn per acre valued at $2 per bushel would be obtained. This would add returns amounting to $800 per year.

Of course, the custom operator cost would be eliminated. $12 per acre on 200 acres amounts to $2,400. The total added returns are $3,200 ($800 + $2,400).

But there is an added cost to this added return! The manager estimates the annual fixed costs to be 18% of the purchase cost of the equipment. The 18% is divided in this way: depreciation, 9% ($9,000 with $1,000 salvage value); interest, 4.95% (9% × [(10,000 + 1,000) ÷ 2] the average investment); maintenance, 3%; insurance and housing, 1.05%. 18% of $10,000 is $1,800. There are also added cash operating costs which are estimated to be $700 annually. Another cost the manager must consider is the value of the extra labor supplied. While this is not a cash cost, it should have a dollar value associated with it. In a livestock budget, the value of home grown feeds must be considered as well as labor. The extra labor is valued in our budget at $600. The total extra operating costs are $1,300, making total debits of $3,100 ($1,800 + $1,300).

There are no reduced returns in this example. However, if one is considering dropping an enterprise, or if more field losses are expected, there would be reduced returns.

The added profitability returns are $3,200, with $3,100 of costs leaving an extra $100 per year. This is marginally profitable, so we will continue with the repayment capacity analysis.

Repayment Capacity Analysis

In this analysis we switch to *cash* accounting. In our example all added returns are cash returns, so no difference exists. Thus, we have $3,200 added returns.

On the cost side some differences exist. Depreciation is not a cash cost. Therefore, the $900 annual depreciation is subtracted. As all the money will be borrowed, interest is a cash cost. We have figured the average annual interest cost. It will be larger in the first years and smaller in the last years. This becomes crucial in the early years if the cash flow analysis is tight. The average annual cash costs are $900.

The cash operating costs are the same for the profitability analysis as they are for the repayment capacity analysis. But the additional operator labor input that was valued at $600 is not a cash cost *unless* the operator plans to use the money earned for family living or saving or some purpose other than debt retirement. The total cash costs are $1,600 ($900 + $700). This leaves $1,600 ($3,200 − $1,600) for debt retirement.

We end up with a $10,000 investment which yields an annual "profit" of $100 and an additional cash flow of $1,600 for replacement of the capital asset or debt retirement.

Financial Analysis

In the financial analysis we want to calculate the returns to the *added* investment. We have already charged 9% to the added capital used. As we have been charged appropriate rates for all resources used, we can assume that the $100 residual in the profitability analysis can be credited as a return to capital. $100 divided by $10,000 yields an *additional* 1% return to capital for a total return of 10% (9% + 1%).

The next question is how fast the debt can be repaid. With $1,600 available annually for principal payments, it will take 6.25 ($10,000 ÷ $1,600) years to repay the debt. If a five-year note is

Fig. 16-1. A partial budget can help you decide if it is more profitable to own a machine or to hire the work done on a custom basis. (Courtesy, John Deere)

signed for the machine, the manager will have to generate $400 income from other sources to make the payment. $10,000 divided by five years equals $2,000 per year ($2,000 − $1,600 = $400).

Other Considerations

The managers might consider some changes in the assumptions used. Could they persuade the custom operator to do a better job by offering to pay an additional $2 per acre? If losses are eliminated, this saves $4 per acre. Also, if average corn acreage falls, this move would not be profitable but might still exhibit a positive cash flow. Larger acreage could make it somewhat more profitable. Further, does the manager actually have the extra labor available at the crucial harvest period, or will extra labor have to be hired after all? Also, could the borrowed capital be used more effectively in some other part of the business?

In the partial budget process, one also needs to consider the use of unused facilities, risk factors, effective capital utilization, time preference for money (discounting), markets, and strong personal preferences, as well as any effects the proposed change may have on other segments of the business.

Once the decision is made it must be implemented, monitored, and evaluated. Remember, the budget applies only to the specific situation with its unique price and production coefficients.

The partial budget can provide managers a quick and relatively simple method of testing a proposed change in their business before committing a major amount of time and money.

Break Even Analysis

Once a partial budget has been developed it is relatively simple to find the break even point. The break even point is the amount of use needed for one method to break even with (or be equal to) another method. Returning to our owning corn harvesting equipment vs. hiring a custom operator, we can calculate the break even acreage when it would be best to stay with custom harvest. Here is the formula:

$$\text{Break even acreage} = \frac{\text{annual fixed cost}}{\text{custom rate} - \text{variable cost per unit}}$$

Our annual fixed cost is $1,800 (18% × $10,000). The variable cost per unit is $6.50 per acre ($1,300 ÷ 200 A). The custom rate is $12 per acre. But, how will we handle the added income from the reduced field loss? Simple! Just add the $4 per acre saved in field loss to the custom rate of $12. This gives us $16 ($12 + $4). Putting these numbers into the formula we come up with this:

$$\text{Break even acreage} = \frac{18\% \times \$10,000}{(\$12 + \$4) - (\$6.50)} = \frac{\$1,800}{\$9.50} = 189 \text{ acres}$$

That is, if annual harvested acreage is 189, you are indifferent to the method used. Both are the same. With less than 189 acres, custom work is better. With over 189 acres, ownership is better. The 189 acres is close to our budgeted 200 acres. But we would expect the break even acres to be close, as our accrual or profitability change in net income was small.

If the field losses were not a factor—that is, if there was no difference between hiring and owning—the break even acreage would be 327 acres.

$$\frac{18\% \times \$10,000}{\$12 - \$6.50} = \frac{\$1,800}{\$5.50} = 327.27 \text{ acres}$$

The field loss estimate was a crucial factor in shifting from a 189-acre break even to a 327-acre break even. This is a 138-acre difference.

Table 16-2. Break Even Analysis

(1) No. Acres	(2) Variable Cost ($6.50/A)	(3) Fixed Cost (18% × $10,000)	(4) Total Cost (Col. 2 + Col. 3)	(5) Cost per Acre (Col. 4 ÷ Col. 1)
25	$ 162.50	$1,800	$1,962.50	$78.50
50	$ 325.00	$1,800	$2,125.00	$42.50
100	$ 650.00	$1,800	$2,450.00	$24.50
150	$ 975.00	$1,800	$2,775.00	$18.50
200	$1,300.00	$1,800	$3,100.00	$15.50
250	$1,625.00	$1,800	$3,425.00	$13.70
300	$1,950.00	$1,800	$3,750.00	$12.50
327	$2,125.50	$1,800	$3,925.50	$12.00
350	$2,275.00	$1,800	$4,075.00	$11.64
400	$2,600.00	$1,800	$4,400.00	$11.00

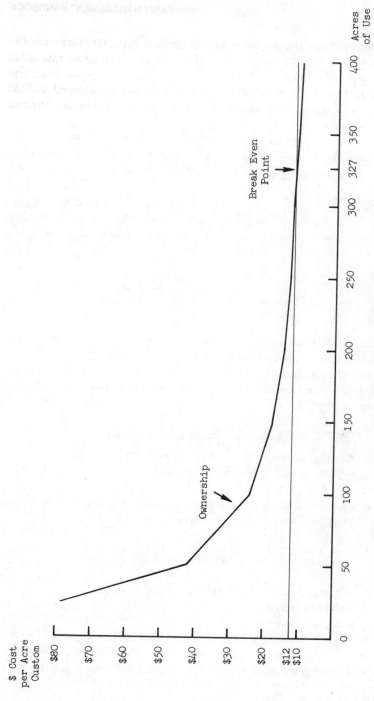

Fig. 16-2. Break even analysis.

So we can see it is very important to use the correct or appropriate assumptions in building a budget of this type.

This is illustrated in Table 16-2 and in Fig. 16-2.

The break even point with a $12 custom rate is between 300 acres and 350 acres (327 acres). (See Fig. 16-2 for a graphic presentation.)

As you can see, it is possible to use a table, a graph, or a formula. The formula is easiest and quickest, but the graph helps to understand the process. The table gives the numbers needed for the graph.

Another way to use break even is in the comparison of two alternative machines. In other words, when will one machine have the same total costs per unit as another machine, or what is the break even acreage? Here is the formula:

$$\frac{(\text{Annual total fixed cost for Alt. 2}) - (\text{Annual total fixed cost for Alt. 1})}{(\text{Variable cost per acre for Alt. 1}) - (\text{Variable cost per acre for Alt. 2})}$$

Let us use an example. Suppose Alternative 1 has an annual fixed cost of $300 and a variable cost per acre of $8, while Alternative 2 has an annual fixed cost of $600 and a variable cost per acre of $5. Putting those numbers in the formula, we come up with 100 acres as the break even.

$$\frac{(\$600) - (\$300)}{(\$8) - (\$5)} = \frac{300}{3} = 100 \text{ acres}$$

For over 100 acres, Alternative 2 is best. For under 100 acres, Alternative 1 is best.

Break even analysis and partial budgeting are powerful but simple tools for farm management decision making.

Questions and Problems for Class Discussion

1. What is a partial budget? How would you use it?

2. Differentiate between the profitability and repayment capacity analyses.

3. What is the financial analysis in the partial budget, and how is it used?

4. Develop a partial budget for a situation on your own farm.

CHAPTER 17

Total Farm Budgeting

Highlights of Chapter

Total farm budgeting is recommended for major changes in the business. It involves a detailed look at all parts of the business. Total farm budgeting integrates all parts of the business into one unit. The budgeting can be done by hand, through the methods outlined in this chapter, or with computer technology. The total budget enables the manager to test the profitability, solvency, liquidity, and cash flow characteristics of the business on paper and to examine alternative ways of operating the business.

The total budget can be done on a long-run basis or on an annual basis. The annual budgets can be viewed as transitional budgets to help managers work their way to the long-run budget. The budget can be used as a control tool and monitoring device. Farmers will be spending more of their time in the budgeting process in the future.

For any major change in the farm business, a total farm budget is the most appropriate method of testing the technical and economic feasibility of the change.

Several factors should be considered when determining the best combination of crops and livestock for any farm plan. These could include:

1. Climatic conditions of the area.
2. Topography of the farm land.
3. Number of acres of tillable land as compared with untillable.
4. Productivity of the soil.
5. Size of the farm.
6. Amount of capital required and amount available.

7. Amount of labor required and amount available.

8. Amount of building space required and amount available.

9. Distribution of labor throughout the year.

10. Relative returns of different enterprises and extent to which they can be developed economically.

11. Crop rotations to maintain soil fertility.

12. Available markets.

13. Use of by-products.

14. Distribution of income throughout the year.

15. Risks involved.

16. Personal preferences and goals.

17. Input and output prices.

18. Production coefficients.

19. Business goals.

The combination best suited to one farm may be wrong for another, even in the same community.

When one has the information listed above, he or she is ready to begin the total budgeting process.

Long-Run Budgeting

To provide a decision benchmark, it is a good idea to project the present farm operation and organization into the future. By doing this, the manager can see if the proposed changes in the farm business will be an improvement over the projected present farm plan. It will provide a comparison budget and can help the manager make the most appropriate decision.

The projected present farm budget is done in the same way as the proposed farm budget(s). Simply it boils down to this.

	Present Farm Budget Projected	Alternative 1	Alternative 2
All farm income	$+_____	$_____	$_____
All farm expense	$-_____	$_____	$_____
Net farm income	$ _____	$_____	$_____

But to arrive at these totals, a great deal of thought and effort must be given. Let us go through the steps required to arrive at the final figures. As we have assembled all the necessary information (as outlined earlier in this chapter and in Chapters 15 and 16), we now need only to look at the budgeting methodology.

With your base information, you first need to determine your initial goals or limits of the farm plan alternatives to be considered. With those established, we are ready to begin the actual budgeting process.

Most agricultural colleges and Extension Agents, as well as agricultural instructors, have detailed budget forms you can use. Thus, we will deal with somewhat generalized headings. You may want to use these to develop your own more detailed forms.

Budgeting the Crops

Generally it is simpler to start with the crops. (See Table 17-1.) The crop rotation is first determined with the number of acres of each crop to be produced annually. These are placed in Col. 1 and 2. The estimated annual yields are put in Col. 3. Col. 4 is Col. 2 times Col. 3. For convenience in figuring feed requirements, the forage is reduced to dry matter hay equivalents, and the grain is reduced to No. 2 shelled corn equivalents. One ton of air dry hay is 0.9 hay

Fig. 17-1. Here agronomists discuss the relative merits of corn and soybeans. Farm managers must decide what crop is the most profitable for their farm. (Courtesy, University of Wisconsin Department of Agricultural Journalism)

Table 17-1. Generalized Crop Budget (Example)

(1) Type of Crop	(2) Annual Acres	(3) Est. Yield per Acre	(4) Total Prod.	(5) Feed		(6) Sales			(7) Variable Costs		(8) Labor	
				(5a) Bu. Corn Equiv.	(5b) Ton D.M. Hay Equiv.	(6a) Units	(6b) Price	(6c) Total Value	(7a) Per Acre	(7b) Total	(8a) Hours of Labor	(8b) Total Hours
Corn-Grain	40	120	4,800	4,800		400	$2.10	$ 840	$105	$ 4,200	4.5	180
Corn-Silage	30	20	600		200				$115	$ 3,450	10.0	300
Hay	70	5	350		315				$ 50	$ 3,500	7.0	490
Oats	20	80	1,600	800					$ 35	$ 700	4.0	80
Soybeans	20	40	800			800	$5.00	$4,000	$ 55	$ 1,100	4.5	90
Total	180	—	—	5,600	515	—	—	$4,840	—	$12,950	—	1,140

Fig. 17-2. A vegetable crop can be a profitable cash crop on certain farms.

equivalent (H.E.), 1 ton of forage dry matter (D.M.) is 1.0 hay equivalent (H.E.), 2 tons of 50% D.M. low moisture silage is 1 ton H.E., 3 tons of 33% D.M. corn silage is 1 ton H.E., and 5 tons of 20% D.M. green chop is 1 ton H.E. One bushel of No. 2 shelled corn is 1 corn equivalent (C.E.), and 2 bushels of oats is 1 C.E. Therefore, in Col. 5a feed grains are put in as corn equivalents and in Col. 5b forage is put in as hay equivalents. Cash crops, specialty crops, and feed crops for sale are put in Col. 6. The units (Col. 6a) times price (Col. 6b) equals value (Col. 6c). Col. 7 enables you to identify any or all of the variable costs per acre for each crop. Your prior cost information and enterprise budgets will be most helpful in making these estimates. Col. 2 times Col. 7a equals Col. 7b. Finally, the labor requirements must be estimated. The required hours per acre are listed in Col. 8a. Col. 8a times Col. 2 equals Col. 8b, the total labor required. The columns are then totaled, and we have completed the crop section. Unallocated expenses related to the crops and total farm will be dealt with in another section.

Budgeting the Livestock

The next step is to budget the livestock section of the business. This is done in a similar fashion to the crop budgeting. (See Table

Table 17-2. Generalized Livestock Budget (Example)

(1)	(2)	(3)	(4)	(5) Feed		(6) Sales			(7) Variable Costs		(8) Labor	
Type of Livestock	Number of Units	Prod. per Unit	Total Prod.	(5a) Bu. Corn Equiv.	(5b) Ton D.M. Hay Equiv.	(6a) Units	(6b) Price	(6c) Total Value	(7a) Per Unit	(7b) Total	(8a) Hours per Unit	(8b) Total Hours
Dairy cows 30% replacement rate	65	140 cwt.	9,100 cwt.	5,200	514	Milk 9,100 cwt.	$ 9.00	$81,900	$300	$19,500	70	4,550
Calves and cull cow sales						Cattle 65	$140.00	$9,100				
Total	—	—	—	5,200	514	—	—	$91,000	—	$19,500	70	4,550

17-2.) In Col. 1 the type of livestock is identified, followed by the number of units in Col. 2. Col. 2 times the production per unit in Col. 3 equals total production in Col. 4. Col. 5 shows the feed requirements in hay and corn equivalents. Enterprise budgets are most helpful in arriving at these requirements. Col. 6 contains sales information. Col. 6a, number of units, times Col. 6b, price per unit, equals Col. 6c, total value. Col. 7 lists the variable costs. Col. 7a times Col. 2 equals the total variable costs in Col. 7b. Again, enterprise budgets or your own past records can help you arrive at appropriate variable costs. In Col. 8, labor requirements are computed by multiplying Col. 8a by Col. 2 to get the total labor requirements for Col. 8b. These are only total labor requirements on an annual basis and say nothing about labor distribution. The columns are then totaled.

Table 17-3 shows if there is a feed surplus or deficit. Surplus feeds are sold in Col. 6a, 6b, and 6c of Table 17-1. As the forage surplus was so small in the example, it was ignored.

Fig. 17-3. Livestock are an important part of many farm operations. This young person is getting involved early in feeding replacement heifers. Family labor can help fill in the gaps at peak labor periods on the farm. (Courtesy, *Wisconsin Agriculturist*)

Table 17-3. Feed and Livestock Resolution

	Feed Type	
Item	Corn Equivalent	D.M. Hay Equivalent
Feed produced	5,600	515
Feed required	5,200	514
Feed balance (±)	+400 bu.	+1.0 T.

Budgeting Cash Operating Expenses

Our next task is to identify and quantify all the other cash operating costs for the farm plan. (See Table 17-4.) The same care in selecting the type and quantity of inputs and their appropriate prices must be used in this table. Your past farm records and enterprise accounts can help in furnishing some guidelines.

Table 17-4. Other Cash Operating Expenses

Crop variable costs (From crop budget)	$12,950
Livestock variable costs (From livestock budget)	$19,500
Hired labor	$10,000
Machinery repair	$ 1,250
Building and fence repair	$ 500
Rent	None
Machine hire	None
Gas, fuel, oil	$ 1,450
Storage and warehousing	None
Taxes—real estate, personal property	$ 1,750
Insurance	$ 500
Utilities	$ 2,250
Freight, trucking, etc.	$ 2,000
Auto expense	$ 350
Held-for-sale items (feeder livestock)	None
Miscellaneous	$ 500
Total	$53,000

Budgeting Interest and Depreciation

The fixed costs of interest and depreciation also need to be considered. These are outlined in Table 17-5. Your depreciation record can give you the depreciation cost, or you may wish to use a higher or lower figure if you think that is appropriate. In inflationary times perhaps a greater depreciation allowance should be used so that adequate cash reserves can be allocated for higher replacement costs. The interest figures should be available from the farm records or from estimates of the costs of additional borrowed capital.

Table 17-6 shows a brief summary of the present total assets, total liabilities, and net worth of the business.

Table 17-5. Interest and Depreciation

Interest on real estate	$ 7,200
Interest on non-real estate	$ 2,700
Interest on operating expenses	None
Total Farm Interest	$ 9,900
Depreciation or Replacement Allowance	$10,000

Table 17-6. Farm Assets, Liabilities, and Net Worth

Farm assets	$275,000
Farm liabilities	$120,000
Farm net worth	$155,000

Budgeting Labor Distribution

To help determine the effective use of fixed labor, a labor distribution table should be constructed. In the example (see Table 17-7), two full time men were available during the year with some additional family help in the summer months. Perhaps some way should be considered to utilize the surplus labor in January, February, March, and December. The surplus in April and November can guard against abnormally early or late field work, while the July and August surplus could provide for vacation periods.

Table 17-7. Labor Distribution

Monthly Enterprise	Total	Jan.	Feb.	Mar.	Apr.	May	June	July	Aug.	Sept.	Oct.	Nov.	Dec.
Corn-Grain	180	0	0	0	10	75	25	0	0	0	50	20	0
Corn-Silage	300	0	0	0	5	45	15	0	5	185	45	0	0
Hay	490	0	0	0	5	30	200	125	90	30	10	0	0
Oats	80	0	0	0	30	5	0	5	25	0	5	10	0
Soybeans	90	0	0	0	0	40	10	0	0	0	40	0	0
Dairy	4,550	400	400	400	400	350	350	350	350	375	375	400	400
Overhead	115	20	15	15	10	5	5	5	5	5	5	10	15
Total Required	5,805	420	415	415	460	550	605	485	475	595	530	440	415
Total Available	6,350	500	500	500	500	525	600	600	600	525	500	500	500
Surplus or Deficit	+545	+80	+85	+85	+40	-25	-5	+115	+125	-70	-30	+60	+85

Overhead labor considers time for record keeping, budgeting, business analysis, attendance at educational and business meetings, and other activities directly related to a productive part of the farm business.

Calculating Profitability, Liquidity–Cash Flow, and Solvency

We now can calculate the profitability characteristics of the extended plan. Table 17-8 shows the profitability analysis along with the calculation procedure. It is essentially the same as the profitability analysis used in looking at historical records.

The liquidity–cash flow–debt servicing characteristics of the plan are shown in Table 17-9. Again, this is essentially the same as

Table 17-8. Profitability Analysis

1. Farm receipts ($91,000 + $4,840)	$95,840	
2. Farm expenses ($53,000 + $9,900)	$62,900	
3. Net cash (1 − 2)		$32,940
4. Depreciation or replacement allowance	$10,000	
5. Net farm earnings (3 − 4)		$22,940
6. Interest on present net worth (6% × $155,000)	$ 9,300	
7. Return to unpaid labor & management (5 − 6)		$13,640
8. Net farm earnings (Line 5)	$22,940	
9. Farm interest paid	$ 9,900	
10. Subtotal (8 + 9) (Return to unpaid labor, management, and all capital)		$32,840
11. Value of unpaid labor management (est.)	$15,000	
12. Return to farm capital (10 − 11)		$17,840
13. Farm interest paid (Line 9)	$ 9,900	
14. Return to farm net worth (12 − 13)		$ 7,940
15. Return to farm capital (Line 12 ÷ $275,000)	6.5%	
16. Return to farm net worth (Line 14 ÷ $120,000)	6.6%	
(For proposed budget eliminate lines 13, 14, and 16 and con-tinue)		
17. Added return to added capital	$_____	
18. Added capital invested	$_____	
19. Return to added capital (17 ÷ 18)	_____%	

the analysis of historical records of the business. A detailed cash flow is shown in Table 17-10.

Table 17-11 computes the solvency characteristics of the business by looking at the total liability asset ratio of the projected business.

Table 17-9. Debt Servicing–Liquidity–Cash Flow

1. Net cash (Line 3, Table 17-8)	$32,940	
2. Net non-farm income	None	
3. Net cash available		$32,940
4. Family living	$10,000	
5. Income tax and Social Security[1]	$ 3,000	
6. Annual real estate principal payment	$ 3,000	
7. Subtotal (4 + 5 + 6)		$16,000
8. Cash available for non-real estate principal (3 − 7)		$16,940
9. Non-real estate principal payments		$ 5,000
10. Additional cash available for debt (8 − 9)		$11,940
11. Depreciation or replacement allowance		$10,000
12. Cash available after replacement allowance (10 − 11) .		$ 1,940
(For proposed plan add these lines)		
13. Added debt to be paid	$_____	
14. Added annual debt principal payment	$_____	
15. Cash surplus or deficit (10 − 14)	$_____	
16. Years required to pay additional debt (13 ÷ 15)	_____	
17. Years required to pay added debt with no replacement $\left[13 \div (15 + 11)\right]$	_____	

[1]Use current income tax table and regulations to compute this.

Budgeting the Alternative Plans

In budgeting the alternatives which deviate from the extension of the present plan, one needs to budget investment changes first. The format in Table 17-12 shows this. Investment changes can be either increases (purchases) or decreases (sales). These figures can provide the basis for computing increased costs such as depreciation, interest, debt repayment, changes in operating costs, etc., or decreased costs.

Table 17-10. Cash Flow (Generalized Scheme)

Items	Jan. Proj.	Jan. Act.	Feb. Proj.	Feb. Act.	Mar. Proj.	Mar. Act.	Apr. Proj.	Apr. Act.	May Proj.	May Act.	June Proj.	June Act.	July Proj.	July Act.	Aug. Proj.	Aug. Act.	Sept. Proj.	Sept. Act.	Oct. Proj.	Oct. Act.	Nov. Proj.	Nov. Act.	Dec. Proj.	Dec. Act.
Beginning bank balance																								
Capital sales																								
Farm operating income																								
New money borrowed																								
Other inflows																								
Total cash inflows																								
End bank balance																								

(Continued)

Table 17-10 (Continued)

Items	Jan. Proj.	Jan. Act.	Feb. Proj.	Feb. Act.	Mar. Proj.	Mar. Act.	Apr. Proj.	Apr. Act.	May Proj.	May Act.	June Proj.	June Act.	July Proj.	July Act.	Aug. Proj.	Aug. Act.	Sept. Proj.	Sept. Act.	Oct. Proj.	Oct. Act.	Nov. Proj.	Nov. Act.	Dec. Proj.	Dec. Act.
Capital purchases																								
Farm operating expense																								
Family living																								
Income tax and Social Security . . .																								
Principal payments																								
Total Cash outflows																								
Surplus or deficit[1]																								

[1]Total cash inflows minus total cash outflows.

Table 17-11. Solvency

1. Added investment	$_____
2. Cash available	$_____
3. Added debt (1 − 2)	$_____
4. Existing liabilities	$_____
5. Total liabilities (3 + 4)	$_____
6. Total assets	$_____
7. Total liability asset ratio (5 ÷ 6)	_____%

Fig. 17-4. One-story barns with silos are becoming more common. (Courtesy, Wick Buildings)

When all the computations are made for the extension of the present farm plan and the desired number of alternatives, they should be placed side by side for easy comparison. (See Table 17-13.)

The manager now needs to compare the probable outcomes of all the plans and see how they fit with the goals, values, and objectives of the family and the business. The profitability, solvency, and

Table 17-12. Changes in Investment

	Purchased	Sold
Land and improvements	$_____	$_____
Buildings and improvements	$_____	$_____
Machinery and equipment	$_____	$_____
Breeding and dairy livestock	$_____	$_____
Total	$_____	$_____
Net change	$_____	

Table 17-13. Summary and Comparison

	Present Plan Extended	Alterna- tive 1	Alterna- tive 2
Plan description	_____	_____	_____
Profitability analysis	_____	_____	_____
Debt service–liquidity–cash flow	_____	_____	_____
Solvency	_____	_____	_____

liquidity–cash flow characteristics need to be evaluated. Then a decision needs to be made and the plan implemented, monitored, and evaluated.

"What If" Questions

At this point the manager may also want to ask some "What if"–type questions. What if the price is higher or lower than I expect?; What if the coefficients of production are higher or lower than I expect?; etc. One can go back through the budgets and change the assumptions and work through the figures again.

Use of the Computer in Budgeting

But this sounds laborious, and it is. Enter the computer—that powerful but stupid tool. It is powerful because it can do complex arithmetic functions rapidly, easily, and accurately. It is stupid because first a highly trained farm management person needs to develop a detailed, sound methodology of budgeting the farm. Then a highly trained computer programmer needs to develop a computer program telling the computer how to make each detailed step in the calculations. The farm management person needs to know what numbers to enter and how to enter them. And finally, he or she needs the ability to interpret the output.

Once you have mastered the hand technique of budgeting you will know which numbers need to be fed to our powerful but stupid friend, the computer. You also will be in a far better position to interpret the output. But remember the old computer saying *GIGO*—garbage in, garbage out.

Approach computer budgeting as you would a friend. Give the right information to the appropriate computer program and you will be pleased with the results. It will enable you to do the arithmetic quickly and accurately, and you can spend your managerial time as a data interpreter rather than as a data creator. Remember, you are a manager, not a key punch operator.

The computer will be used more and more in forward planning the farm business.

Use of Discounting Procedures

It is out of the scope of this book to discuss the discounting approach to budgeting. This procedure will be used more frequently in the future as the use of computer budgeting becomes more common and as programs are written.

We have taken a relatively simple approach by looking at profitability using the average return to investments. As we explained in Chapter 5, discounting involves the time value of money. We use discounting because money or capital is limited and has alternative uses.

This procedure of discounting in budgeting uses one of two approaches—net present values or the internal rate of return. In both cases, one looks at the expenditures in cash flows and then evaluates these cash flows in terms of their time values.

Alternatives which are very close in their outcomes, but different in the timing and length of income and investments, are good candidates for this type of analysis.

Transitional Budgeting

Our prior discussion involved the long-run plan. But most plans cannot be implemented in their entirety immediately. Further, some start-up time is needed to get the manager and the operation fully integrated into their new roles.

While many plans work out in the long run, there are some early growing pains. New skills need to be learned. Expenses are sometimes higher than planned at the start. Productivity may, and generally does, suffer during the growing process. Therefore, transitional budgeting should be done to account for these conditions.

Transitional planning or budgeting is simply using the same general tools we used in long-range planning. The difference is that these plans and budgets are made in more detail and are done on an annual basis. It is generally a good idea to make an annual projection for each of the first three years, particularly if the long-range budget is for five years ahead.

A detailed cropping plan is integrated with a detailed livestock plan for each of the years involved. A livestock feed requirement and supply balance can be determined.

An annual investment estimate can be made showing the timing and description of added capital investments. This can be integrated with an investment summary.

All other associated cash operating costs, cash incomes, family living, and non-farm income can be estimated and put in the annual budget.

Debt service projections also need to be made, as well as income and Social Security tax projections.

The first year cash flow also should be mapped out on a monthly basis. Then at the beginning of each accounting period, another annual cash flow projection can be made. (See Table 17-10.) This can be used as a control and monitoring tool.

The cash flow can point out the sources and uses of funds. It also can show where surplus and deficits occur. Thus, better plans can be made for debt service.

Finally, a pro forma (projected) Farm Earnings Statement and Net Worth Statement should be made for each of the years. These are the same as the historical Farm Earnings and Net Worth statements, only looking into the future.

You can view your farm business records of the past years as the "rear view mirror" approach to the business. The long-range budget is the road map to show the way to your long-run destination, while the transitional budget serves as the road signs along the way to measure your present state of progress toward the long-run goal.

The annual projection of the business can serve as a monitoring and control device. Actual performance is compared to planned performance. If all goes as planned, then you are in good condition. If things are not going as planned, you are aware of this early. Then corrective measures may be taken before obvious and disastrous results take place.

Budgeting provides an organized method of planning the business in future time periods. It gives the manager the opportunity to plan the business and then to monitor and control it. Farmers will be spending increasing amounts of time in this budgeting and managing function in the future.

Questions and Problems for Class Discussion

1. What information do you need to have before starting to construct a total farm budget?
2. How do you go about budgeting crops? Livestock?
3. Why is it important to budget labor distribution?
4. What is transitional budgeting?
5. How can long-run budgets be used?
6. Develop a long-run budget for your home farm.
7. Develop an annual budget for the next year on your home farm.

PART FIVE

Adjusting the Farm
to Price
and Market Conditions

The production of crops and livestock is just part of the task of farm managers. In Part Five we will discuss the successful marketing strategies which have a great impact on the profitability of their businesses. The concepts of price and of supply and demand which enable producers to make better marketing decisions are also discussed.

CHAPTER 18

Marketing the Farm Products

Highlights of Chapter

Successful farm managers need to know how their products are marketed so they can best adjust to market situations. In many instances, they can adjust their production so as to market their products during the season of the year when prices are the most favorable, and they can produce the quality of a product that will bring the highest price.

The marketing system performs many tasks: (1) it moves farm products from where they are produced to where consumers want them; (2) it stores the products until they are needed; (3) it processes and packages them so they are attractive for consumers. In brief, it makes the raw farm products ready for consumers in the *form* at the *place* and at the *time* the consumers want them.

Management Adjustments to Get the Best Markets

Several years ago a prominent farm paper presented a cartoon showing, at the left side, a farmer selling a bushel basket of potatoes to a buyer. For that bushel of potatoes the farmer is paid $1. On the right side of this picture is a city consumer buying a similar bushel basket of potatoes from a retail store merchant. The consumer is paying $2. The area in the middle of the cartoon, between these two pictures, is just a large blotch of ink—a blackout. The title of the cartoon is "What Happens in the Dark?" According to this cartoon, the farmer is getting only half as much for the potatoes from the local buyer as the final consumer pays to the retailer in the city. (See Fig. 18-1.)

Fig. 18-1. What happens in the dark?

It is only natural that people will ask why there is so great a difference between what the farmer gets and what the consumer pays. Why is it so expensive to market our farm products? What happens in our marketing or distribution system—this system operated by middlemen? In this book, mainly on farm management, we will devote only this chapter to marketing. With some understanding of how the marketing system works, farmers will have *a better idea of where and when to sell their products and what kind or quality of products to produce.* As a result farmers will make better returns from their farms.

The Marketing System—What It Does

The marketing or distribution system performs many important jobs.

1. It transports the farm products from the farms where they are produced to the cities where they are consumed. This is usually carried on in two or more entirely separate steps. The first step is transportation from the farm to the place where the products are processed.

2. It manufactures—or processes—the farm products into such a form that they can be conveniently used. For example, wheat is ground into flour and the flour is made into bread; milk is made into butter, cheese, or ice cream; hogs are slaughtered and the meat is processed into bacon, ham, or sausage.

3. It packages the products into a kind and size of package that consumers prefer.

4. It stores the products until consumers are ready to use them.

Neither producers nor consumers know much about what is involved in the whole process of handling farm products as they pass through the marketing journey. Consumers are likely to blame the retailer or other so-called middlemen for high prices, or at least what to them seem to be high prices. When consumers learn that farmers get less than half of the dollar they pay for food, naturally they are disturbed. Some consumers insist that they are victims of high profits. Others insist that they are victims of a wasteful system of distribution.

Farmers may also wonder whether there is justification for so wide a spread between what they get per pound for the pig on the hoof and what their friends in the city pay for the finished bacon, ham, or sausage. Let us see if we can shed a gleam of light on this "area in the dark"—the area between producer and consumer of farm food products, that is, the marketing system. Here are examples of how two of our important farm products move through the marketing channels.

1. *Wheat*. Wheat is usually delivered by the farmers to the local grain elevator where it is run through cleaning machines which take out weed seeds and other foreign materials. From there the wheat is shipped to a terminal elevator where it is stored until a flour mill is ready to grind it into flour. Only about three-fourths of a bushel of wheat actually goes into flour for human food. The balance goes to bran and middlings and is used mainly as livestock feed, usually for dairy cattle.

The flour is sent on to wholesalers who sell it either to retail stores or to bakeries. The bakeries bake the bread and dispose of it to retail stores where it is purchased by the final consumers.

2. *Livestock*. Livestock are marketed in a similar manner, although the marketing system is slightly different. The livestock are sold to a local buyer or handled by a local cooperative livestock shipping association. From there the animals are shipped by truck or railroad to the central market or the nearby meat packing plant. If the animals which are shipped to the central market are ready for slaughter, they go directly to the meat packer, where they are slaughtered. If they do not carry enough fat—or finish, as we call it—they are likely to be shipped to feeders, that is, farmers who feed them until they are ready for the meat packer. In many cases livestock are shipped direct to packing plants, thus bypassing the

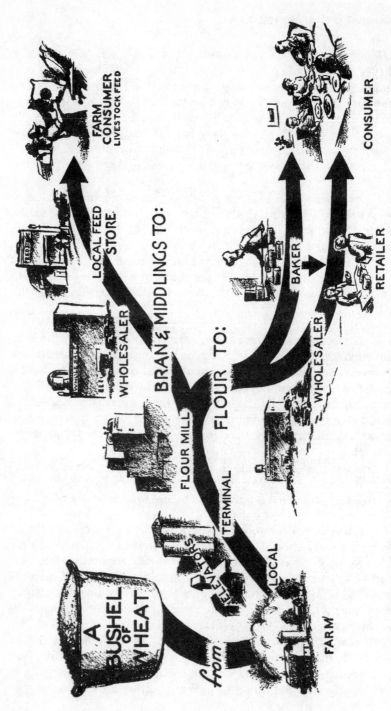

Fig. 18-2. Transporting a bushel of wheat, milling it to flour, and then moving the flour to the wholesaler and finally to the retailer are all parts of the marketing job. The job requires the investment of a large amount of capital and the labor of many people.

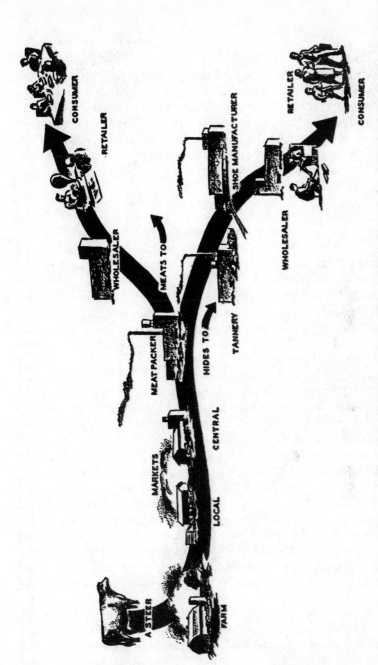

Fig. 18-3. Before a steer has any value as meat to consumer, it must be transported to the packing plant where it is slaughtered. From the packing plant it is moved through the marketing channel to the wholesaler and then to the retailer where the consumer can select the cut of meat desired.

central market. In fact, several years ago the large central livestock market in Chicago was closed.

This gives only a sketchy idea of how complex the modern marketing system has become. The reason that it is so complex is because of the great distance between the area where most of the farm products are produced and the cities where a large portion of them are consumed, and also because of the rapid growth of our cities. During the earlier period of this country, the marketing system was relatively simple. Farm managers had few problems in marketing their products.

Historical Development

Suppose we go back in history a little. When the settlers first moved in and started to eke out a living in America, they worried little about this so-called middleman or about the marketing system. In fact, there was no marketing system in those days. For the most part, producers consumed their own products or sold them in the local village. Generally they traded butter, eggs, meats, and the like at the store for groceries.

During that period, the families in the city or village produced some of their own foodstuffs at home. Many kept a small flock of chickens and a few pigs. They usually had a family cow, and most of them raised a garden. Abraham Lincoln sold his family cow when he became president of the United States.

As long as city people kept a family cow, they had no worries about the middleman in the milk business. They did not worry about milk delivery or marketing costs. In short, they were not concerned about the distribution system. The family cow supplied the milk, cream, and even butter. With the gradual concentration of population in the cities, the family cow gave way to factories, apartment houses, corner drugstores, gasoline stations, and supermarkets. With this change in our economic system, meat, milk, and grain products now have to go through the modern, complex marketing system.

It is easy to see that under those earlier conditions the cost of distributing milk, for example, would be low. It did not tend to bring about a wide margin between what the producer received and what the consumer paid. During that time there was no thought of pasteurizing, or even of bottling, milk. Consequently, there was no cost of pasteurizers, homogenizers, bottles, cartons, bottle washing, or filling machines. For the most part, the milk was delivered by family labor so there was very little labor cost and no serious labor problems. In general, milk delivery was simple and inexpensive, and the farmers obtained a large share of what the consumers paid. When they delivered their products directly to consumers, they got all of the consumers' dollar, but had the cost of delivering it.

Yet, under those methods of marketing farm products there were many drawbacks. Take the case of milk being sold by the farmer directly to the city consumer. There was no particular assurance of cleanliness. There was no testing of the cows for disease. There was no pasteurizing of the milk and often no adequate sterilizing of the utensils. In brief, there were no adequate safeguards against poor sanitation or even against disease.

Today those conditions have been changed entirely. The consumers of dairy products—as well as other food products—are assured that highly sanitary methods are being employed and that the foods are clean and wholesome. So, during these many years as the business of distribution has grown more and more complex, the margin between what the consumer pays and what the producer receives has widened. At the same time, better methods have been

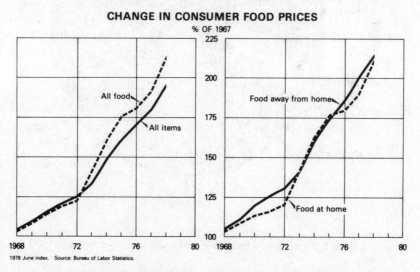

CHANGE IN CONSUMER FOOD PRICES
% OF 1967

1978 June index. Source: Bureau of Labor Statistics.

Fig. 18-4. After 1972 the price index of all food went up more rapidly than the price index of all items. From 1973 to 1975, food at home kept pace with food away from home but then increased less rapidly than did food away from home.

adopted to guard the health of consumers. Laws which require care in handling food have been passed. Also, consumers are demanding and receiving more of their foods in convenience packaging with more processing. More and more food products are table ready.

As one example, the business of distributing milk has become a complex—and rather costly—service. Over the years it has grown from an infant business to a large industry. Today, some of the milk

WHAT MAKES UP THE FARM-FOOD MARKETING BILL

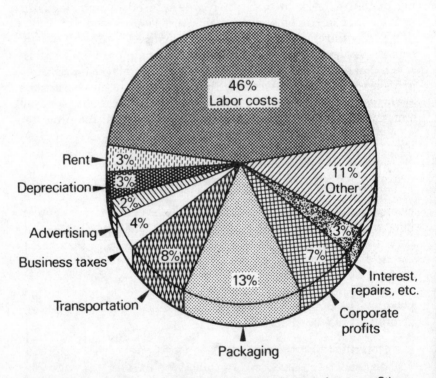

Transportation is intercity rail and truck. Corporate profits are before taxes. Other includes utilities, fuel, promotion, local hired transportation, insurance, etc. 1977 preliminary.

Fig. 18-5. Costs of marketing have risen over the past several years. Many items enter into these costs. Labor and packaging comprise about 60% of the total marketing costs.

distributing companies in our cities are large national organizations working side by side with local medium-sized or small independent companies.

Today, milk truck drivers stop at the farms, load the milk, and speed off to city markets. The milk itself is transformed into dairy products, or is pasteurized and put in bottles or cartons for delivery to doorsteps and retail stores. The major portion of dairy products is now marketed through supermarkets rather than through door-to-door delivery.

The changes that have taken place in the fluid milk business are used only as an example of what has happened to most of our distribution system handling other farm products.

Amount of Consumers' Dollar Going to Farmers

It will be noticed from Fig. 18-7 that since the 1960s about 40% of the consumers' dollar has gone to farmers, and 60% to the distribution system.

Now what about price spreads between farmers and consumers for individual products? How wide are they? How much do they vary from product to product? What items make up the costs?

Briefly, the job of the marketing system is *to make farm products available exactly when consumers want them, where they want them, and in such form as they want them.* A pig in the pen of an Iowa farm has no particular value to a consumer in New York or Chicago when the consumer wants pork chops for supper. But when the pig has gone through the transformation to become a pork chop or a link sausage and is placed in a show counter at the New York or Chicago grocery store where and when the consumer wants it, then it has value and can command a price. In other words, before a farm product can command a price from the consumer, three main adjustments must be made.

1. It must be put into *such form* that the consumer can use it. The pig must be changed from an animal on the farm to a pork chop or link sausage.

2. It must be kept until the consumer is *ready to use it.* The pig, after being transformed to a carcass, may have to be kept in a cool and sanitary place for six days, six weeks, or even six months.

3. It must be transported to the place *where it is wanted.*

MARKETING BILL, FARM VALUE, AND EXPENDITURES FOR FARM FOODS

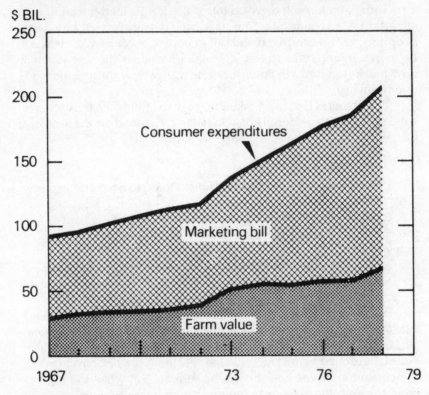

For domestic farm foods purchased by civilian consumers for consumption both at home and away from home. 1978 preliminary.

Fig. 18-6. Consumer expenditures for food have risen sharply since 1972 due to inflation, higher marketing costs, and a moderate increase in the farm value of foods.

This is essentially the job of the marketing system—to make a product available *when, where, and the way* it is wanted. This job, considering our entire economic system, requires about as many of the nation's workers and costs about as much as does the job of bringing the products into such form that they are ready for distribution.

WHERE THE FARM FOOD DOLLAR GOES

PERCENT OF RETAIL COST

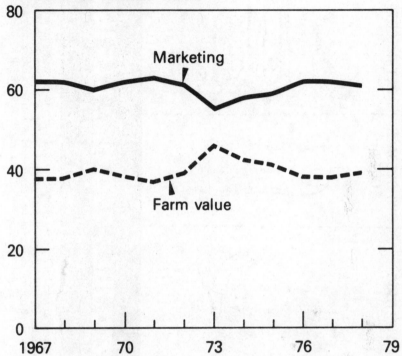

Share of dollar consumers spent in retail food stores for market basket of domestic farm-food products. 1978 preliminary.

Fig. 18-7. On the average, farmers receive only 40% of the consumers' dollar. The other 60% goes for marketing.

Increase of Efficiency in Production and Marketing

We have gone much further in the increase of efficiency in manufacturing goods than in distributing them. We have attacked problems in production with vigor and success. We have lowered production costs through mechanization and through careful and

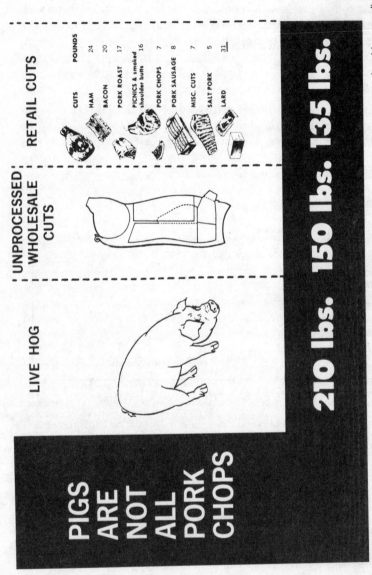

PIGS ARE NOT ALL PORK CHOPS

LIVE HOG

UNPROCESSED WHOLESALE CUTS

RETAIL CUTS

CUTS	POUNDS
HAM	24
BACON	20
PORK ROAST	17
PICNICS & smoked shoulder butts	16
PORK CHOPS	7
PORK SAUSAGE	8
MISC. CUTS	7
SALT PORK	5
LARD	31

210 lbs.   150 lbs.   135 lbs.

Fig. 18-8. Converting pigs into chops, ham, bacon, lard, and many other products ready for sale to the consumer is a big, complicated job. It involves packer services such as cutting up the meat, curing, smoking, slicing, wrapping, refrigerating, canning, transporting, etc. Less than two-thirds of the weight of a live hog is edible. From a 210-pound live animal, the meat packer gets 150 pounds of dressed hog. When it reaches the consumer, there is only 135 pounds of salable meat and lard. The 75 pounds of "lost weight" is worth but a few cents a pound, although it includes many important by-products.

scientific management. We have equipped our factories with automatic labor- and cost-saving machines. We have provided them with an assembly belt system so that one worker spends an entire day at a single operation which brings about the highest efficiency. In short, we have brought about the economies of mass production. On the other hand, scientific and organized effort to attack the mounting distribution costs is just beginning to take form.

Why Is Progress So Slow in Marketing? Manufacturing or processing lends itself to machine operation with little resistance or opposition from consumers or anyone else. In distribution, it is less easy to practice machine mass methods and cost reduction. For example, shoes—a product of hides from animals—can be manufactured on a large scale and hence on a low-cost basis. Improved and less costly machine methods are gradually replacing the more costly hand operations. Not so with sales of the shoes. Can you imagine a mechanical device replacing the shoe salesperson? Consumers insist on personal attention, courtesy, and service. The shoe factory *deals with things*; the shoe salesperson *deals with people*. Each situation is new and different. Each customer has his or her own ideas and whims. The shoe factory can mechanize the machine and the processes that make the shoes, but the shoe salesperson cannot mechanize the consumer. The same thing is true in the case of food products.

In summary, there are at least four important reasons why the cost of marketing—especially of retailing—is high.

1. Consumers demand their food purchases in small quantities. Purchases such as 5 pounds of potatoes, ¼ pound of butter, or 1 pound of meat are not uncommon.

2. They want their food carefully packaged. As an illustration, consumers demand, and get, soda crackers in a 1-pound package with three wrappers—(a) a cardboard box, (b) a paraffined paper inside, and (c) cellophane on the outside.

3. They are often slow in deciding what they want. Thus, they take a large amount of time from the store clerks.

4. Some want the privilege of returning the goods if for some reason they are not satisfied.

Margins in Marketing Livestock and Meats

In Fig. 18-7 we showed that about 40% of the dollar paid by

consumers for food products goes to the farmers who produce the food. The rest is paid to the marketing and distribution system.

According to recent figures, farmers received about 66% of the consumers' dollar for eggs, 60% for pork, 54% for beef, 30% for potatoes, 10% for bread, and 8% for corn flakes. The marketing bill is divided among labor, packaging, before tax profits, business taxes, depreciation, rent, advertising, repairs, bad debts, contributions, and interest.

The gross margin for meat packing may vary considerably among concerns, owing primarily to the extent to which the meat is processed. Processed meat is costly to prepare, chiefly because of the labor involved and the expenditures for supplies and containers.

At the retail level, as the size of the meat order diminishes, the selling cost per hundredweight generally increases. The selling and delivery costs are nearly the same per package regardless of the quantity delivered. This means that the cost per pound is higher when meat is sold in small packages.

It is important for farm managers to know where the consumers' meat dollar goes because then they are in a better position to know what, if anything, they can do to improve marketing systems to their advantage. It seems clear that if only 4 cents of the consumers' dollar goes for transporting the livestock from the farm to the slaughterhouse—or meat packing company—then, even if the farm managers were able to save one-fourth of that expense, they would save only 1 cent out of every dollar paid by consumers.

Charges for wholesaling, involving warehousing and local delivery to stores, range between 5 and 8% of the retail selling price for most food products. But wholesaling costs vary widely among foods. If these costs were cut by one-fourth—which would be very difficult—farmers would save only 1.25 to 2.0 cents of the dollar paid by the final buyers, the consumers.

There are, however, areas where farmers can make considerable savings. For example, they can feed and care for the animals in order to get low-cost gains. They can feed them to the proper finish, market them at the time when prices seem favorable, and choose the best market in which to sell their livestock. They can learn a good deal about the range in prices for livestock by observing conditions in their local market, and by keeping up-to-date on federal and state market reports. To be more specific, they can do things such as the following:

1. They can determine the differences in price among *different*

1000 lbs STEER	590 lbs BEEF	465 lbs RETAIL CUTS	
			Lbs
		Porterhouse, T-Bone & Club steak	35
		Sirloin steak	40
		Round steak	65
		Rib roast	45
		Boneless rump roast	25
		Chuck roast	100
		Hamburger	45
		Stew meat & misc. cuts	110
		Bones, Fat, Waste & Shrink	125

Cattle are not all beef . . . Beef is not all steak

Fig. 18-9. The value of by-products, such as hides, fats, hair, animal feeds, fertilizer, etc., about offsets packers' dressing, handling, and selling expenses, so that the beef from a steer normally sells at wholesale for less than the live animal cost. Retailer mark-up must cover costs such as rent, labor, depreciation on equipment and fixtures, etc., as well as shrinkage in weight of the beef carcass when converted into retail cuts. (Courtesy, American Meat Institute)

grades and quality of livestock, livestock products, and crops and then produce the quality of product that brings the most money. Here are a few examples:

    a. Livestock which are well finished will generally sell for more money per pound than those which are not well finished.

    b. Clean, fresh, uniform eggs will generally bring more money than eggs which are soiled. If enough poultry producers get together, they can find a market that will pay premium prices for top quality eggs.

    c. Many dairy farmers have an opportunity to sell milk to a market which pays premium prices. This may be a fluid milk market, a condensary, a milk drying plant, or a milk plant that sells fluid milk or cream to a distant market.

    d. Certain varieties of grain sometimes sell for more money than other varieties. An alert farm manager watches for these possibilities.

    e. High-quality potatoes will bring a much better price than potatoes of low or medium quality.

    f. Many fruits and vegetables will be of poor quality and hence bring a poor price unless they are properly sprayed and cared for.

2. They can determine the *price difference between the local market and a central market*, such as Minneapolis or Kansas City, and may be able to choose the one that pays the best price.

3. They can determine the *seasonal price changes* for various classes of livestock and adjust their farm programs so that their products will be ready for market when the price is the most favorable.

4. They can determine what is the *basis for paying locally*. Who are the local buyers? Are they private individuals who buy and sell at the best market they can get, or are they representatives of the local and central meat packing companies? Which buyers pay the most favorable price?

5. They can sometimes sell their farm products *directly to a retail store* or even directly to consumers. Many eggs are delivered by farmers directly to consumers in cities or villages.

6. They can form cooperatives. Where the privately operated system of marketing is not serving the farmers satisfactorily, it may be possible for them to band together as a group and form a *cooperative organization* to sell their products. There are many examples of farmer-owned and -controlled cooperatives which have been highly

successful. There may be a cooperative in your area which you can join so that a new cooperative does not have to be established.

Vertical Integration Important in Some Farm Operations. Another marketing trend is also taking place in some types of agriculture. This is called "vertical integration." By vertical integration we mean a linking together of two or more steps in production and marketing. As commonly used today, vertical integration involves several persons or firms working together, perhaps under contract, to unite their efforts in producing and marketing a product. Here the control and management decisions may be centered largely in one individual or firm. In some non-agricultural industries integration is quite complete from the producer to the consumer. In the gasoline and oil industry there has been almost complete vertical integration for many years. The same firm owns and controls every step in the production and marketing, from the oil well to the retail gasoline station.

Vertical integration in agriculture has become very common for a few commodities. The best illustration is in the production and marketing of chicken broilers, although it is also true for the production of turkeys and certain vegetables, and in some areas is beginning to show up in hog production.

In the more typical integrated broiler operation the feed supplier (generally the manufacturer) provides the feed on a credit basis, gives the grower advice on operations, determines to some extent the feeding and management program, and decides when and where the birds are to be sold. This is relatively complete vertical integration centered in one organization, the feed company, which is the integrator—the organization in control.

In producing broilers (and to a lesser extent in producing turkeys, vegetables, and hogs) there are five basic economic advantages of integration.

1. Integrators can determine the amount to produce so the production will be geared to the specific market outlets.
2. The income per unit for these products is low, so farmers have to carry on large operations in order to make an acceptable income. Very few farmers have enough funds to finance an operation large enough for economical production.
3. The integrators usually have quite complete control and can dictate the quality of the product to meet market demands.
4. They can provide "know-how" in management problems.

5. They usually work with many modern producers so they have a large enough volume to bypass certain middlemen in the market system, such as the wholesaler or jobber. In many instances, the products from these operations are sold directly to retail food chain stores. This saves part of the expense of handling through food wholesalers, jobbers, brokers, or other middlemen.

These five advantages can be summarized into a few words—(1) controlling supply, (2) financing, (3) maintaining quality control, (4) providing know-how, and (5) marketing directly to the retail chain store.

In the production of these products all these advantages of integration are very pronounced—much more so than in the production of most other products of agriculture.

Only Limited Advantages of Integration in Some Kinds of Farming. In some kinds of agriculture there is very little advantage in integration. For example, in dairying, in the raising of beef, or in the growing of grains, the advantages of integration are much less important. Integration could not be very effective in controlling supply in dairy, beef, or grain. Most of the beef, dairy, and grain farmers are able to provide their own financing and to maintain quality of their products. They are also quite well qualified in production and management abilities, so integration would not be very helpful on those points.

Questions and Problems for Class Discussion

1. More than 50 years ago, many farmers sold their products directly to consumers. Give the important reasons why this is not practical on our present commercial farms.

2. What products produced on your farm could you market directly to consumers? Would it pay you to do so? Give your reasons.

3. What services does the marketing system perform today that were not performed 50 years ago? List these services for specific products, such as meat, milk, flour, and a common vegetable.

4. What could be done on your farm to obtain a larger part of the consumers' dollar? (a) Could you improve the quality of some of your farm products? How? (b) Could you change your production seasonally so as to take better advantage of seasonal high prices? Discuss fully.

5. What is vertical integration?

CHAPTER 19

Adjusting the Farm Business to Prices

Highlights of Chapter

Years ago farmers sold their products on an open "free" market. There were no government price support programs. If supplies of any farm product were unusually large, prices would be forced down seriously. Also, in case of a depression or recession, city people could lose part of their buying power, so they would have less money to buy food (finished farm products). Prices of farm products varied much from year to year, and farmers found it difficult to adjust their operations so they could meet running expenses and gradually pay for their farms.

Out of this unsatisfactory situation grew a demand on the part of farmers for government aid to agriculture to stabilize prices of products and maintain them at a level so farmers would have a reasonable level of living. Even with this support from government, farmers still find it difficult to adjust their farm business to price changes of their products.

Farmers today plant their crops and raise their livestock with the idea of selling them at the best prices they can get. Hardly any farmers produce grain or livestock entirely for their own use. They sell their products in the market and buy the things needed to operate the farm and maintain the home. In fact, farming has continued to become more and more commercialized and is still moving rapidly in that direction. For that reason, the price farmers receive for their crops, livestock, and livestock products means much in determining prosperity. If they have some understanding of what makes farm prices move up and down, they are in a better position to know when and where to sell their products. They are also better able to adjust their farm operations to get the best return from their farms.

Everyone knows that prices of farm products are constantly changing. They change from day to day, month to month, and year to year. Still more important are the changes that continue in one direction—either up or down—more or less constantly over a period of several years. These are called cycles.

Prices in a "Free Market"

If there is no government control, and no strong element of monopoly among buyers or sellers, we say there is a "free market." This means that any person or business organization is always free to sell or buy anything at any price agreed upon between the seller and the buyer. Under these conditions the forces of supply and

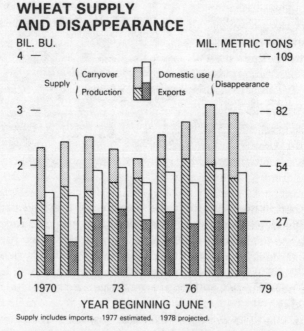

Fig. 19-1. Domestic use of wheat remains relatively constant. Production has risen somewhat, while carryover and exports have varied considerably.

demand establish the price. The so-called free market operates automatically something like this: *An increase in demand* for a farm product such as wheat raises its price. The rise in price tends to bring forth more production because it pays farmers to increase their output. In this way production will soon catch up with demand so the price again sags back to a lower level.

In the same fashion, *a decrease in demand* for wheat (or other product) will push the price down. When the price shrinks, farmers will produce less wheat so the price automatically moves upward again. This tendency for prices to adjust themselves automatically has been referred to as the operation of the "law of supply and demand."

Some Reasons Why Prices Change

We know that this so-called automatic price adjustment has not always been "automatic," nor has it been entirely satisfactory as a way of determining the prices of farm products—or of other products. Adjustments have been erratic and unpredictable, and at times have worked so poorly that farmers have insisted that a better system should be adopted.

Farmers find it difficult to adjust their farm operations to prices that are constantly changing, and they wonder what makes them change. There are many fundamental reasons for these changes, some of which we shall now explain.

1. Variation in Crop Yields. Even though farmers attempt to control the production of their crops in order to adjust supply to demand, it is almost impossible for them to do so. A farmer may plant the same number of acres of corn, wheat, or oats every year and yet have a much larger crop one year than the next. This is because the growing conditions may be favorable one year but very unfavorable the next year. Factors such as rainfall and temperature vary greatly from year to year. The result is that the yield per acre will be both unpredictable and uncontrollable. Farmers can adjust the acreage planted, but they have only limited control over the yield per acre. With the new technology available, farmers now have more control over yields.

Thus, the yield per acre determines much of the year-to-year variation in the total U.S. production of our leading crops. In recent years, yields have steadily worked upward.

Once farmers have adjusted their farm operations to produce a certain number of acres of a crop, it is difficult and costly to change their cropping systems noticeably. They can change their acreage some, but not much. Neither can they afford to leave many of their acres idle. The result is that they continue to produce about the same number of acres from year to year, whether prices are high or low.

The fact should be mentioned that, while yields vary for particular crops, or for several crops in an area of the country, the combined total production of all agricultural products over the country generally varies only slightly.

2. Livestock Production Slow to Respond. Many farmers *attempt to adjust their livestock numbers* to meet prices and crop conditions as they are *at the time* rather than taking a long-time view. They do not stop to realize how long it takes to increase the number of livestock on the farm, nor do they realize how prices may change between the time when a calf or pig is born and the time when its offspring are ready for market. This slowness of adjustment and the tendency of many farmers to adjust in a similar manner bring about a "price cycle" for some kinds of livestock, especially for hogs and cattle.

Let us take the case of farmers producing hogs and corn who ordinarily sell some of their corn. A large corn crop will force corn prices down so the farmers feed more of it to their hogs instead of selling it; that is, they feed them to heavier weights and thus produce more pork. They may even keep over more gilts for brood sows in order to feed up the corn. Many farmers respond in this way because of the high corn yield and low price that year. When the large hog numbers reach the market from six months to two years later, hog prices are forced down. In turn, those low hog prices force many farmers entirely, or partly, out of the hog business. Fewer pigs are raised, and a year or two after that, fewer hogs reach the market. The result is that hog prices rise to abnormally high levels.

This tendency on the part of many farmers to respond in a similar manner, that is, to market many hogs in certain years and only a few hogs in other years, sets up a price movement. This uniform change in price has become known as the "hog price cycle." The high points of the cycle are about four to six years apart.

A similar price cycle exists for cattle, although it is much longer. On an average, the complete cycle takes about 15 years. This is because it ordinarily takes farmers a longer time to increase or

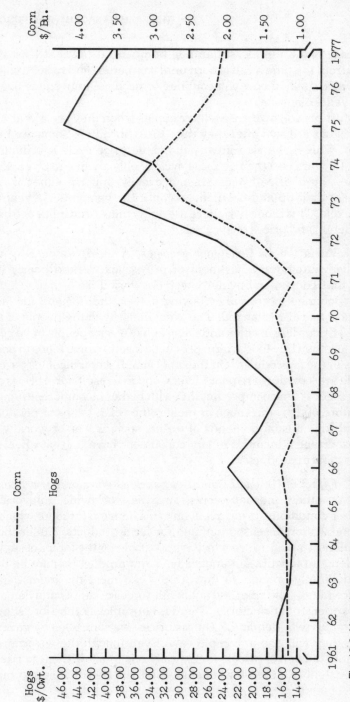

AVERAGE PRICES RECEIVED BY FARMERS FOR HOGS AND CORN, U.S.—1961 to 1977

Fig. 19-2. Hog prices generally move upward for two or three years and then downward for about the same length of time to make a complete hog cycle every four to six years. In recent years the hog cycle has been a bit more erratic. Both hog and corn prices increased dramatically after 1971. (Source: Agricultural Statistics, 1972, 1977; Agricultural Prices, Annual Summary, 1975, 1976, 1977; courtesy of Mr. Jack)

decrease cattle numbers than hog numbers. It takes at least two years from the time a calf is born until it is mature and raises a calf of its own. Usually a cow will continue to produce until she is five to eight years old.

Most brood sows raise a litter of pigs when they are a year old. Many sows are sold after they raise their first litter. Some are held longer. This is the reason why the cattle price cycle is ordinarily some 15 years and the hog price cycle is only about 4 to 6 years. Of course, these price cycles are not exactly uniform either in the extent of their up-and-down movement or in the number of years of each cycle. This is because there are many things that influence both production and prices of livestock.

3. Variation in Consumer Incomes. A third reason why the so-called automatic adjustment of prices has worked poorly has been that consumer buying power has varied from time to time. With a change in consumer buying power, the demand for farm products has also changed. The great majority of the people of the United States live in cities and villages. When city people have good incomes, they buy foods (farm products) freely, which tends to boost prices of these products. On the other hand, when incomes for city people are low, they are poor buyers, and as a result, farm prices are depressed. It is also important that with higher incomes, consumers buy more of a product such as meat rather than beans or potatoes. Except for unusual demands of events such as war or worldwide crop shortages, incomes of city consumers have a great effect on prices of farm products.

4. Effect of Unusual Conditions such as Wars on Farm Prices. Wars or other unusual events, such as worldwide unfavorable weather conditions, bring about an extra demand for food, which in turn means an increased demand for farm products. Under those conditions it is easy to see why it is impossible for the forces of supply and demand to work automatically. Farm products cannot be produced rapidly enough so that supply can meet the intense food requirements. The so-called automatic forces of supply and demand do not operate satisfactorily. There is not sufficient time for "supply to catch up with demand." Unless prices are controlled by government, they will rise at a rapid rate. Even though the government attempts to control prices, it generally has to allow them to rise to some extent in order that enough food will be produced to meet requirements.

Why does a war push the prices of farm products up, and why do they fall again after the war is over? During a war, the fighting nations need food, clothing, and all other farm products (as well as industrial products, of course). Prices of these products are bid up in order to encourage an increased production of them. The government buys food and other products freely in order to have the necessary supplies to carry on the war, and civilians are fully employed, usually at good wages, so they also buy food and other goods freely. The general result is a rapid upward movement of farm prices even though production is increased. Then, after the war is over, the large production of farm products is continued. It does not pay farmers to reduce production once their land has been put under cultivation and machinery has been purchased to farm the land.

The main reason for the difference between farming and industry is that in farming the largest expenses are for the land, machinery, and buildings. Once they have been purchased farmers cannot afford to leave them idle, because their expenses are almost

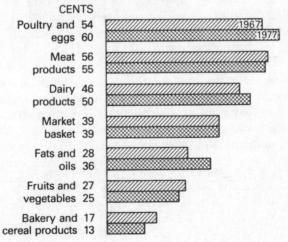

FARMER'S SHARE OF THE MARKET-BASKET DOLLAR

CENTS

	1967	1977
Poultry and eggs	54	60
Meat products	56	55
Dairy products	46	50
Market basket	39	39
Fats and oils	28	36
Fruits and vegetables	27	25
Bakery and cereal products	17	13

Foods from U.S. farms.

Fig. 19-3. The farmer's share of the market basket varies among products but on the average amounts to about 40¢ of the total dollar spent for food.

as high whether they keep their farms in full production or not. By keeping production up, they have more to sell and it costs them very little extra to produce the additional amounts. What we are saying is that farmers have high fixed costs.

In manufacturing, the items of cost are quite different from what they are in farming. In a factory the largest cost items are raw products and wages. Thus, a factory can reduce the largest cost items by reducing the amount of its output. Most of these costs are called variable costs.

It is easy to see that increased agricultural production to meet war demands and heavy purchases by civilian buyers create their own trouble. Once agriculture production is up it tends to stay up; that is, farmers continue producing heavily several years after the war ends.

With production of farm products continuing at a high level after a war, and with shrinking demands, naturally prices of farm products will be forced down.

5. *Variation in Exports of Farm Products.* When products are exported to foreign markets, the effect on demand is the same as if they were used by consumers in this country. It adds to the total demand. The amount of agricultural products exported to foreign countries has varied considerably through the years.

During the entire span of years from 1910 to 1978, production of agricultural products continued to increase gradually but consistently. Even during the years 1934 to 1936, when the country suffered from a serious drought, total U.S. agricultural production dropped only slightly and soon afterwards increased to new and higher levels. There is every evidence that the production will continue to increase, but at a slower rate, as the years unfold. Agricultural production in this country has increased at a more rapid rate than has population of the country.

6. *Day-to-Day and Seasonal Price Changes.* The five preceding reasons are the important ones as to why it is impossible for prices of farm products to adjust to an even keel under a so-called free market system. There are at least two more reasons, although they are somewhat less pronounced. They are (a) short-time (day-to-day) price changes and (b) seasonal price changes.

a. *Short-time or Day-to-Day Price Changes.* The things which change prices from day to day are usually not the same as those which bring about seasonal price changes or the longer-time price changes (which we have just discussed).

Suppose we take wheat as an example. News of a drought in the area where wheat is produced, especially if the drought covers a large area, will push the price of wheat up. The same thing would be true in case of an attack of grasshoppers or an epidemic of black rust which might seriously reduce the yield. This is because the drought, the grasshoppers, or the black rust will reduce the amount of wheat grown, and hence buyers will scramble harder to get the amount they need. A few days after the first report of the drought, the grasshoppers, or the rust, it may be discovered that the damage was not as great as had been first thought. Then prices would again slip back down.

Again there may be news of an increased demand for wheat in Europe because of bad crops there. This will call for more of our supplies, and prices may be pushed upward.

U.S. EXPORTS FROM HARVESTED ACRES

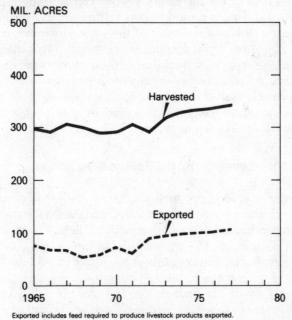

Exported includes feed required to produce livestock products exported.

Fig. 19-4. The total harvested acreage has increased since 1972. So has the number of acres used for exports. These exports have helped our balance of payments.

The price of hogs and other livestock usually does not change as much from day to day as do crop prices, because there are not many things that bring about quick changes in the amount of livestock on farms. Of course, an unusually early frost may reduce the corn crop seriously. With less corn for hog feed, hogs will be sold at lighter weights so there will be fewer pounds of pork available, and naturally the price of pork will go up and so will the price of hogs. These are only a few illustrations of the factors that influence the day-to-day changes in prices of wheat and other crops.

b. Seasonal Price Changes. If you observe the price changes of most farm products you will notice that during some months of the year prices are higher than during other months. These changes are common from one year to the next. The main reason for this variation from one season of the year to another is that farm products are produced mainly during certain months of the year.

As you know, wheat and other grains are harvested in the fall, so practically the entire year's crop is ready for sale and delivery during a period of two or three months, and none is harvested the other months of the year. However, consumers take about an equal amount every month. This means that a part of the crop must be stored until consumers are ready to use it. Storing a wheat crop—or any other product—costs money. If the grain is stored on the farm, bins must be built, which involves expense, and if it is stored in elevators or mills, the storage there costs money.

Leveling Out the Seasonal Variations

In order that food products will be available to consumers the year around, some farm products are stored during the period when there is no production or when production is light. Wheat is stored in elevators; flour is kept in warehouses in towns and cities; butter, cheese, eggs, fruits, and vegetables are stored in cold storage warehouses; and some cured meats are kept under refrigeration at meat packing and wholesale houses. Fresh meats are seldom stored for any great length of time. More frozen foods are being used.

Naturally, prices of farm products are higher during the season of low production than during the season of high production. In times of low production, prices are high, and the products that have been stored are taken out and moved into the wholesale or retail stores where they are sold to consumers.

The job of storing these products is done by middlemen— usually privately owned concerns, but sometimes by farmer-owned cooperatives. The charges for storing the products are generally not much above what it costs to operate the storage warehouse and handle the product. Those who buy the products for storage pay the market price for them and again sell them at the new and higher price when they are moved out of storage. The fact that prices are higher when farm products come out of storage than when they went in does not prove that middlemen are making an unreasonably high charge for storage, or that they "manipulate the price." In fact, most studies have shown that the charge for storage is not unreasonable when one considers the expense connected with the job of storing and the risk connected with the operations. Of course, if farmers want to do so, they can store their own wheat, corn, and other grains on the farm. In fact, many of them do. Farmers could also form a cooperative to store their own butter, cheese, eggs, and other products. Indeed, there are many such farmer cooperative organizations in the country.

We can summarize the answer to the question on seasonal variation of prices by a statement like this: Seasonal price changes are closely in line with the cost of storing the product and the loss due to shrinkage, as in the case of grains, or with the loss of quality, as in the case of eggs. Products such as grains are easy to store. They do not need refrigeration, and the loss or shrinkage is small. As a result, the cost of storing them is reasonably low, and the seasonal change in prices is also low. On the other hand, for products that are perishable, such as eggs and fruits, the cost of storage is high and the seasonal change in prices is also high. In the case of corn, the total cost of storage at a public storage elevator is about 1½ to 2 cents a bushel per month. Other costs for storage are (1) the interest on money invested in the corn, (2) "shrinkage" or loss of weight of the corn during the time it is stored, and (3) loss due to insects, rats, mice, etc. On the basis of 1½ to 2 cents per month this would mean that from the time the corn was stored, say December, until the following August, the price of the same quality of corn would increase about enough to pay for the above costs. The seasonal price variation in all farm products would change in line with the cost of storage together with the loss during the period it is stored.

Government Support of Farm Prices

As we said earlier, the free market price system has been only partly satisfactory. When the demand for foods is abnormally intense, prices of farm products rise to such high levels that many consumers are unable to buy the foods they need. Later, prices of all farm products generally fall drastically. If they are permitted to find their own level, as they would in a free market, then they might skid so low that many farmers would be in a serious financial condition and others might lose their farms entirely.

Price Support in World War II. During World War II, prices of all products—non-agricultural as well as agricultural—were controlled by government; that is, they were not permitted to move above a certain point. In order to hold down the general price level and yet encourage farmers to produce as much food as possible, the government paid the farmers a subsidy for certain farm products which were needed to carry on the war. These payments were in addition to the market prices of those farm products. This was clearly a kind of price support which largely replaced the system of a free market.

Parity Prices. During the period of depressed farm prices after World War I, the idea of *parity* prices was developed. The term "parity" essentially means *equality for agriculture*.

During the five-year period, 1910–1914, farm conditions were reasonably favorable. Many spokespersons for agriculture took the position that this was a period when there was equality for agriculture, and their aim was to maintain that equality. It was assumed that if prices of farm products were such that farmers would have a buying power equal to that of this five-year period, then farm prices would be at the *parity level*. They would be equal to, or on a parity with, the prices received in 1910–1914. That five-year period became known as the *base period* for agriculture. The prices of farm products, *in terms of prices of items bought by farmers*, for that period were used as a basis for comparisons with later years.

How Parity Is Determined. The parity idea is applied to prices of individual farm products as well as to an average of all farm products *treated as a group*. Let us first use as an example one product—cotton. The price of cotton averaged 12.4 cents per pound during 1910–1914, the base period. At a recent date it was 57.1 cents per pound. If we take 12.4 cents as 100, the 57.1 cents will be 460.5. This

PRICES RECEIVED AND PAID
BY FARMERS

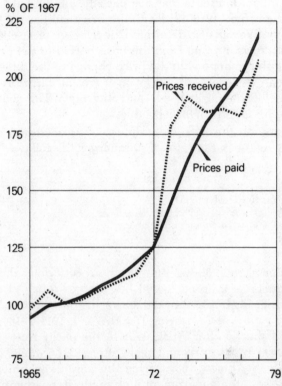

% OF 1967

Prices paid includes commodities and services, interest, taxes, and wage rates.
1977 forecasted.

Fig. 19-5. The index of prices paid by farmers has increased at a rapid rate, particularly since 1972. Prices received by farmers have also increased, but at a more irregular rate along with some downturns.

means that the price of cotton at this recent date was 460.5% of the price in the base period. But how about the things farmers buy?

In order to arrive at a figure of the increase in price of those things, we have to take an average of a large number of items commonly bought by farmers. The price of most of these items has risen since the base period, 1910–1914. As an average they are now 749.0% of the 1910–1914 level. With the price of cotton now at 460.5% of the base period level, you will see that cotton prices have not risen as much as the things bought by farmers. This is another way of saying that cotton prices are below parity. Specifically, the price is 61.5% (460.5 ÷ 749.0) of parity.

In a similar manner we can compare the increase in price of any farm product since 1910–1914 with the price increase of the things farmers buy. We can also determine the average price change of *all farm products as a group* from the base period to the present. By comparing this change with the price change of the things farmers buy, we can determine if, on an average, all farm products are above or below the parity level—and how much. This shows what is called the *parity ratio* of farm products.

Each month the U.S. Department of Agriculture publishes a table showing the parity ratio. A summary of this follows:

	1910–1914 = 100	*Recent Date*
Prices received by farmers		537
Prices paid by farmers (This includes interest, taxes, and wage rates for hired labor.)		749
Parity ratio		72

The parity ratio shows that, on the recent date, the prices of farm products as a group would buy 72% as much of the things farmers generally buy as they did during the base period, 1910–1914. The parity ratio was 72. During World War I, 1915–1918, and again during and shortly after World War II, the parity ratio was above 100. But from 1920 to 1942 and again after 1951, the parity ratio has been noticeably below 100. During the periods when agriculture was depressed, the government took many steps to improve farm prices in an attempt to hold them near the parity level.

Parity prices do not tell the whole story. The total *(gross) income* of a farmer is determined by the amount of products produced on a farm and the selling price per unit of each product. The *net income* is determined by the total production and the price, less the expense of producing those products.

New methods of controlling the weeds and insects, of cultivating the crops, and of fertilizing the land have increased yields per acre. Modern farm machinery has reduced the expense of production, so farmers are able to produce farm commodities at a lower unit cost now than they did in the base period. This is especially true of those farmers living on the larger and more productive farms. Many of these farmers have made a satisfactory income even when prices of farm products were below the parity level.

Recently the base period of 1910–1914 has been changed to a "moving average"; that is, when parity prices are being calculated, they are considered in relation to a period of years just preceding the calculation. However, the general concept of parity as equality remains the same. The parity ratio is a measure of price relationship—not a measure of farm income, of farmers' total purchasing power, or of farmers' welfare.

Free Market Yields to Government Control. To the extent that the government supports farm prices, the free market price will be pushed into the background and the government might be spending many millions (if not billions) of dollars a year to maintain prices of farm products at the 90% parity level or at some other level determined by Congress.

Rising and Falling Prices

It is a simple matter for farmers to adjust their operations to a rising price level, but it is quite difficult to adjust when prices are falling. When prices are moving upward over a period of years, grain farmers will get a high price for their grain at harvest time as compared with the price of the seed they planted and the fertilizer they applied in the spring. Likewise, livestock farmers will get a high price for their hogs or cattle compared with the price of the breeding stock with which they started.

Adjusting to a Falling Price Level. When prices fall, the price received for farm products is generally low compared with the prices paid for commodities used in their production, such as machinery, fertilizer, seed, labor, and perhaps land. This is just the reverse of what occurs when prices in general are rising.

In order to best meet the condition of falling prices, it is necessary for farmers to make adjustments such as the following:

1. Put off buying those things which seem out of line in price, unless they will pay for themselves quickly.

2. Place more emphasis than usual on the economy of production. This can be done by carefully selecting seed, maintaining good cultural practices, and culling the livestock and poultry in order to obtain maximum production and income for the amount of capital and labor invested.

3. Save labor where possible. When prices are falling, wages

will likely be relatively high. Farmers should therefore utilize labor for the most productive use, employ labor-saving equipment, and better arrange the farm and field layout.

4. Produce high-quality products. Even though prices are falling, as long as employment in the city is maintained and business conditions are good, the demand will be fair. Under these conditions it will pay farmers to turn out choice grades of agricultural products.

5. Sell direct to consumers where possible. Since retail prices will be high compared with farm prices due to the relative cost of distribution, direct sales carry an advantage.

6. Produce more of the home food supplies. Because of relatively high retail prices, this adjustment will be advantageous to farmers.

7. Exercise more careful planning and financial control of the farm business to keep expenses low.

8. Strive for higher production of crops and livestock through efficient methods.

9. Pay up any unsecured and mortgage debts as quickly as possible. As prices of farm products fall, debts incurred at high prices will be paid for by low-priced farm products. In a period of general declining prices, the longer one waits to pay debts, the more products it will take to pay up a given amount.

10. Be slow in buying land. Generally, it is difficult to pay for high-priced land with low-priced farm products.

11. Reduce the inventories of farm products. The longer they are kept on the farm, the lower the price is likely to be. Many farmers have made the serious mistake of holding their grains during the declining price period.

Questions and Problems for Class Discussion

1. It generally takes about 4 to 6 years to complete a "hog price cycle" and about 15 years to complete a "cattle price cycle." Explain fully the reasons for the difference in the length of time between the two.

2. Would it be practical to produce the same amount of milk, or the same number of hogs or eggs from month to month throughout the season?

3. Explain why it is difficult for farmers to adjust their operations to a period of long-time, gradually falling prices of farm products.

4. What is meant by "parity prices"? Show how parity prices are determined for an individual farm product such as wheat or cotton. How is it determined for "all farm products"? Explain fully.

CHAPTER 20

The Demand Side—
How Farm Prices Are Made

Highlights of Chapter

The food and other items made from farm products are finally purchased by consumers. But these same consumers also buy many items that are products of industry. Thus, farm products compete with many industrial products for the consumers' dollar. If food prices seem high to consumers compared with other things needed, then consumers will buy less food—or less expensive food items. The result will be that food supplies will increase and prices will drop.

The demand by consumers for food is reflected through the marketing system to the farm; therefore, under a free marketing system, the buying power of consumers, their intensity of demand for products of the farm, and the supply of farm products are the basic forces in establishing the prices of farm products. However, with a system of government support of farm prices, it is the type and extent of support that is partially responsible for establishing them, especially in the area of food grains and cotton.

In years past, we heard a great deal about the power of a few individuals or concerns to fix prices where they wanted them. People said that prices were "manipulated" by a few people for their own profit. More recent studies of the factors that determine prices show that the whole question of price changes is very complex. Those studies also show that today there is very little, if any, manipulation of prices of farm products.

Farm Products Compete with Other Products. No farm products—or any other products—could be sold *unless there was a de-*

mand for them. Two things are necessary to bring about a demand for any product. First, *people must want it* and second, *they must have buying power to buy it.*

People have wants or desires for farm products (or goods of any kind) for any one of several reasons. An individual may desire a certain product because it satisfies a physical want. For instance, food, a product of the farm, satisfies the appetite. Of course, it also builds and maintains health. Clothing protects the body against the cold, heat, or rain. Some types of clothes are worn almost entirely for protection. This is true of our more common work clothes. On the other hand, our more attractive and expensive clothing is worn for style which has grown into common usage.

Other goods, not products of the farm, such as furniture and automobiles, also satisfy fundamental, but perhaps less important and less intensive, wants than do food and clothing. However, *they compete with farm products for the consumers' dollar.* Since we are especially interested in prices of farm products, we shall talk mainly about consumer desires for those products and attempt to point out how their prices are determined.

Middlemen Bridge Gap Between
Producer and Consumer

In our modern complex economy, farmers seldom come in direct contact with city consumers. In Chapter 18 it was shown that middlemen bridge the gap between the producers of farm products and the city consumers. They provide the marketing machinery that handles the farm products from the farms to the city, town, or village homes where they are finally used. Middlemen do not necessarily use the products. We say that their demand is indirect. They resell them with the hope of making money by handling them. Middlemen not only move the products from the place where they are delivered by farmers, but they also manufacture, or as we say, process, them into the things farmers and consumers want. For example, they grind the wheat, bake the bread, slaughter the cattle and hogs, and cure the bacon and ham.

Consumers make their wants known through these middlemen; that is, they buy pork chops, beef, or bread from their local retail store—a middleman. So you can see why the middleman's demand is said to be indirect. As an example, consumer demand for beef roast, steak, and hamburger brings about the local buyer's indirect demand for beef steer from the farm. We say that consumer demand is reflected back to the farmer.

For the most part, farmers dispose of their products to middlemen known as local buyers. The local grain elevator is usually the local or initial buyer for wheat, oats, corn, and barley. The local milk plant buys the milk or cream. Local livestock buyers purchase cattle, hogs, and sheep. Some livestock are also shipped by individual farmers or through local farmer-owned and -controlled cooperative shipping associations to the stockyards. Many are trucked directly to meat packing plants. Regardless of who may be the initial buyer of these farm products, the price received by the farmer is known as the market price. Even if the farmers believe that the price offered is too low, they usually have no choice. They have to accept the price or keep their beef, hogs, milk, or wheat.

Middlemen's Prices Reflect Consumer Demand. Since buyers of farm products quote or indicate the prices they will pay, many farmers believe that the middlemen establish or fix the price. You have often heard this statement by farmers: "When I deliver my wheat to the elevator or ship my hogs to the stockyards, the buyer sets the price, but when I buy groceries from the store, the seller sets the price. I have no choice at either end. When I sell my product, I take the price the middleman sets, and when I buy anything, I have to pay the price the middleman asks."

While this statement may be correct, it is far from the whole story of price making. Few, if any, local buyers are able to *establish or fix the prices to be paid for farm products*. There may be conditions where local, or central, buyers may *influence the price*. To what extent, it is hard to determine, but they definitely do not fix or set it. To repeat, they merely reflect the price which becomes established by the final consumers. Middlemen are limited in what they can pay by what they are able to get for that product on resale. For example, the local creamery is limited in what it can pay for butterfat by what it can get in selling the butter to wholesalers or jobbers. Wholesalers, or jobbers, in turn are limited in what they can pay by the amount they can get from the retailers. Retailers name the price for which they will dispose of butter to the final consumers. Individual consumers have no choice but to take it at that price or leave it. That is exactly what consumers do—they take much or little butter depending upon whether they think the price is low or high. *It is clear that an individual consumer has no particular influence on retail butter prices, but if many consumers respond in a similar manner by buying less when prices are high and more when prices are low, they play an important part in determining the price at which butter will be sold at the retail store as well as at every other point in the marketing system.*

When Prices Are High, Consumers Buy Less. If consumers think that butter prices are too high, they will buy smaller amounts of it. The result is that more will be left in the retailers' refrigerators. Retailers, in turn, will buy less from the wholesalers. Wholesalers, likewise will become less active buyers; hence butter supplies will be left in the cold storage houses. The net result is either that butter prices will be forced down or that supplies will continue to increase until they can be consumed later, usually at lower retail and whole-sale prices. You can see that lower prices all along the market system will finally force down prices at the point of the first sale, that is, the farm price. It would seem clear then, that, on the demand side, the consumer is the one who finally determines the prices of farm products. In this case, butter is used as an illustration. The same principle would be true of other farm products. Because of the nature of the demand for farm products, a small percentage change in the quantity of a farm product offered in the marketplace will trigger a larger percentage change in its price.

The Middlemen's Margin. There is another part to the story. The farmers do not get as much as the final consumers pay for a product. The middlemen must have something for handling the butter, wheat, meat, or other products. We call that the middle-men's margin—a payment for work they perform and services they give. The amount of this margin depends upon how efficient middle-men are and how large their profits are. Some say that the middle-men's charges are too high because they have a monopoly control and make monopoly profits (that is, profits that are higher than are necessary or justified). Actual studies have shown, however, that there are few monopoly profits in the handling of farm products. In fact, we often find places where there are so many small dealers that they are inefficient. We find very few, if any, conditions where dealers are large enough in size, and few enough in number, that they could maintain monopoly control and so set a monopoly price. Generally, a large company middleman can operate at a higher efficiency and therefore at a lower cost than a smaller one can.

Consumers Want Other Items
Besides Farm Products

Before it is possible to understand the factors that determine the demand of the final consumers for farm products, you need to have some understanding of what other items are needed and wanted by consumers. In fact, you must understand something about the facts that make consumers decide what to buy, not only of food (farm products), but of all other things. Farm products make up only a small part of the total purchases of consumers. For you to understand the whole problem about consumer buying, you need to understand something about consumer habits.

Here are a few of the things you should know. How much importance do consumers place on the various kinds of goods they buy? For example, how much importance do they place on beef roast for supper, as compared with having a little extra money to buy other things? They might spend $8.50 for beef roast for dinner, or they might spend $2.50 for beans and have $6.00 left over for gasoline for the car or for some personal item. As a matter of fact, we must consider not only the consumers' willingness to spend their money for each of the various kinds of goods to be consumed in the immediate future but also must consider their desire to spend for consumer goods in general, over and against their desire to save for the future.

What are the various calls for the consumers' money? What about their necessary or desirable expenditures for educational and social purposes, housing, and many other purposes? Of course, there can be no single answer to any of these questions. There are variations from one consumer to another. The most important variations between one consumer and another—or between one group of consumers and another—will depend upon the amount of income available for purchases of consumer goods and for savings. We can be sure, however, consumers do not single out food and clothing (agricultural products) as being the only items that they need to buy. In some respects, food and clothing, beyond a point of bare necessity, may not even have the first claim to the family budget. Taxes, money for medical and dental care, and other expenses necessary to preserve life or health often come first.

Not All Purchases Are the Result of Careful Thought and Planning

So far in the discussion, it has been assumed that consumers buy things only after they have carefully determined how useful a particular item will be. We have assumed that consumers compare the use or satisfaction they will get out of each thing they buy. Some people buy something "on the spur of the moment" without deciding carefully how much satisfaction they will get out of that amount of money. Generally, however, people do decide rather carefully *how they will get the most for their money*. Let us take an example of a high school student.

Suppose, for example, a high school student—a consumer—decides to get along with a cheese sandwich for dinner and go to a movie theater, rather than order a full dinner—with meat—and not go to the movie. *In that case the student would consider the show more important than the full dinner. In a strict sense, the movie—a form of entertainment—becomes a direct competitor of meat—a product of the farm.*

Consumers are constantly making choices between the things they will purchase and those they will do without. Few people have incomes large enough to buy everything they want. The consumers' wants are not limited to *material things only*. They involve, for example, a new shirt today, a dance on Saturday night, or money to put into the church collection on Sunday.

With such a variety of calls upon the family budget, how do consumers go about deciding what to buy? How do they determine the way they will spend their money? It is clear they do not buy all the good food they would care to eat and go without other things, such as movies, dances, and other necessities and luxuries.

Regardless of the exact methods used by consumers in selecting food products, it is a fact that the selection in buying foods is often made with the idea of reducing the food budget as much as possible and still having reasonably good food. The expenditures for foods made by individuals have an influence on the farm income obtained by producers of these products. If they make large expenditures for foods, farm prices and therefore farm incomes will also be larger, providing that supplies do not increase faster than demand.

Consumers as a Group Determine Prices

Here is the way that consumers—as a group—determine or set prices. Suppose, for example, that the Joneses go to the store to buy pork chops. If chops are, say, $1.65 a pound, they may buy 3 pounds. But if chops are $2.20 a pound, they might take only 2 pounds. As members of only one family, they have no control over the price they pay. The price is already named, and they have to pay whatever the storekeeper asks or leave the pork chops. But what they do is to *buy more pork chops when the price is low and fewer when it is high.*

When many consumers do the same thing, that is, buy fewer when the price is high, then all the pork chops simply will not be sold. This means that storekeepers will not buy more from wholesalers until they have sold what they have on hand—unless they can buy it cheaper than they did before. If they do not buy from the wholesalers, then the wholesalers will not buy from the meat packers, and so the meat will be left in the packing houses. Then the only way meat packers can sell what they have on hand is to reduce their selling price. If they are operating on a narrow margin of profit, they cannot sell their pork for less money unless they can buy hogs for less. So they offer less money for the hogs they buy. All livestock buyers (meat packers) who have had difficulty in selling their pork are forced to reduce their paying price for hogs. This means, of course, that hog raisers (farmers) who ship hogs to packing plants or to local butchers will have to take less for their hogs if they are to sell them. Farmers do not need much pork for their own use, so they will sell their hogs, even if they have to take lower prices.

Actually then, the price that consumers *as a group* are willing to pay for pork chops, and other cuts of pork, determines what farmers can get for their hogs. As we said earlier, if a consumer will take 3 pounds of pork chops at $1.65 per pound, but only 2 pounds at $2.20, then that consumer, *together with all other consumers* who do the same thing, really determines the upper limit in price that farmers are able to get for hogs.

All that middlemen really do is handle the meat for a certain number of cents per pound; that is, they attempt to keep the margin wide enough for handling the meat so that they can make a little money by selling it. This margin of the meat packers is the difference between what they pay for hogs and what they get for the dressed meat. The retailers' margin is the difference between what they pay for the carcass and what they receive for the different cuts of pork.

In the last chapter we saw that, generally, farm prices are high when incomes of city workers are high. To apply that idea to this discussion we would say that, when the family has a *good income*, the consumers would buy, say, 3 pounds of pork chops even though they were $2.20 a pound. But if the family income is low, they would buy only, say, 2 pounds—or even 1 pound—at that price. Moreover, if their income is low, they will spend more of their food money on less expensive meats. Or perhaps they would buy some cheese and beans and only a little meat. Thus, consumers substitute one food for another depending on price variation.

In summary, it seems clear from this analysis that consumers as a group determine the price for food products. This price is reflected through the middleman system and determines the price farmers will get for the farm product. Middlemen are not able to set or fix prices at any level they wish. Of course, they do influence prices by the amount of the "margin" or "spread" they get for handling the products. If the middleman system handles wheat, pork, or any other farm product efficiently and at a low profit, then farmers get a larger share of what consumers pay than if the middleman system handles these products with low efficiency and high profit. Usually competition among different middlemen drives profits down to the point where some of the least efficient middlemen are barely making enough profit each year to stay in business. This does not mean that farmers are now getting as large a share of what consumers pay for those same products as might be hoped. The middleman system could be made more efficient, and probably will become so in the future. Increases in efficiency are constantly taking place. For example, supermarkets have reduced costs to a level considerably below what they were under the older system of handling foods. Competition among these highly efficient stores will tend to reduce the margin of handling still more.

However, there are two important changes taking place in the business of handling food products in the marketing system. One change involves the increase of wage rates paid to workers. The second change involves the entire system of processing, packaging, and retailing. Today, many foods are nearly completely processed and neatly packaged, ready for the consumers' kitchens or almost ready for their dining tables. The marketing system is carrying out many of the jobs that were formerly done by consumers. As long as that trend continues, a larger percentage of the consumers' food dollar will go to the functions of marketing them and a smaller percentage to the farmer who raises them.

Questions and Problems for Class Discussion

1. Suppose you were selling eggs (or any farm product) directly to a consumer. How would price be arrived at? Discuss fully the various factors that would be considered, such as retail store prices, quality, cost of production, and other price-making forces.

2. Do you think a middleman can fix the price of a farm product? Give reasons for and against. Call on local buyers of a product you sell from your home farm and get their ideas on what forces establish buying prices.

3. Discuss what is meant by the middleman bridging the gap between the producer and the final buyer—the consumer.

4. What is the process under which consumers as a group influence the price of a food (farm) product? Explain fully.

CHAPTER 21

The Supply Side—
Cost of Production and Prices

Highlights of Chapter

Some farmers are quite insistent that the cost of producing a farm product should determine its price. The real situation is that the cost of producing a product has an influence on future prices. Farmers will not continue to produce a product unless the price will cover its costs.

Middlemen, such as wholesalers and retailers, mark up their sales prices high enough to cover their costs plus a profit. But that does not mean they always cover their costs, because they may not be able to sell their products at the price at which they are marked. In order to get rid of all the goods on hand, they may have to reduce the selling price to their cost price or even below it. Every year many middlemen go bankrupt because they are unable to get prices high enough to cover their costs.

There are always farmers who are unable to cover their costs of production while their more efficient neighbors make a profit. This is due to a great variation in production costs.

Some farmers think that the cost of production should determine the price of farm products. They believe that merchants and manufacturers get the cost of production—plus a reasonable profit—for the things they sell. Comments from farmers such as the following are not uncommon: "When I buy goods from a merchant I pay what the goods cost plus a profit. Why shouldn't farmers get cost of production plus a reasonable profit just the same as the merchants?"

Prices based upon "cost" seem to many farmers to be associated with a sense of "fairness." Some people insist that they are fair to both farmers and consumers, since farmers should not be expected to suffer a loss in their efforts to supply products of food and clothing to American consumers.

Do the Retail or Wholesale Merchants or Manufacturers Get Cost of Production—Plus a Profit?

Retail Merchants. When retailers decide upon the price at which they will sell flour, tea, or pork chops, they first determine what the goods cost and then add a certain margin to this cost price. Clothing stores, dealers in farm merchandise, and others from whom farmers buy the things they need follow that same general practice of arriving at the sale price of their products. For example, when retail clothing merchants buy a dozen suits, they determine the cost of them. From this cost figure they determine the resale price by marking up the purchase price, say 20%, or perhaps 30 or 40%. This mark-up, they expect, will be sufficient to cover the expenses of selling the suits and still leave a reasonable profit. *However, if no one will buy the suits at that price, the retailer will be obliged to reduce the price or have them left on the racks.*

Wholesalers. Wholesalers who buy articles from their manufacturers establish their selling price in much the same manner as do retailers. This is true of all middlemen—the wholesalers, jobbers, and retailers. Indeed, it is equally true of manufacturers. You can see from this that it is not strange that many farmers get the idea that all prices of retailers, wholesalers, and even manufacturers are determined upon the basis of cost of production—plus a profit.

Manufacturers. Let us stop a moment and see if this is, in reality, the method by which prices of manufactured goods are established. An illustration from a manufacturer of men's suits may make the point clear. A certain manufacturer sets out to make men's suits. After he had finished designs of certain types of suits, he found that they would cost him $48 each to manufacture. He then surveyed the prospective territory to determine what prices were being charged for suits by competing manufacturers, and discovered that some suits were being sold to retailers at $35, others at $45, some at $47.50, and a few at $50. He also found that only a relatively small number of suits were being sold to retailers at $45 or more. From this he concluded that if he were to sell large numbers of suits, it would be necessary to sell them to the retailer at $45 or less.

He had already determined that the suits as designed would cost him $48 to manufacture. How then could those suits be sold for $45? If his cost were $48, was he entitled to the cost of production? Perhaps he was, but the fact remained that not very many retailers would buy suits at that price. Accordingly, it became necessary for him, if he were to sell suits in large numbers, to reduce his costs so that his price would be within reach of a large number of buyers. He did this by (1) more carefully buying cloth—or by buying cloth of a slightly lower grade, (2) more efficiently using his manufacturing plant, (3) reducing the amount of his hoped-for profit, and (4) reducing salaries and wage rates—or briefly by slashing all through the system and in all areas of cost. The resultant decreased prices stimulated the sales. The larger number of suits sold reduced the overhead cost per suit.

In that case the costs, as they were first calculated, certainly did not determine the selling price of the suits. *Rather the price which the manufacturer was able to get for his suits determined what his costs would be.* If he had been unable to reduce his costs below those originally calculated he might, in time, have been forced to close his factory. This is the manner in which prices are determined by most manufacturers. Those who are not able to keep their costs down in order to meet competition are forced out of the business.

The same thing is true of the wholesaler and retailer. If one retailer can reduce her costs of handling goods and thereby reduce her sales price, she will attract new customers and sell more goods to her regular customers. As she increases the amount of sales, the net income for her store may also be increased, even though the amount of margin on each item handled is actually decreased. *The total annual income of a business concern is determined by the margin of net profit on each unit multiplied by the number of units sold.*

Many merchants follow the policy of keeping their costs and their margins to an absolute minimum so as to lower the sales price and thereby increase the volume of sales. This policy, they believe, gives them the greatest net annual income. When one merchant reduces the selling price to consumers, others in the same area are forced to follow suit sooner or later. Therefore, the costs of the middlemen and their margins are influenced greatly by competitive conditions.

Every business firm has to sell its products in competition with other firms. Competition is generally extremely severe and is a powerful force in developing high efficiency and low cost of operation. There is little hope for a firm with low efficiency and high costs to stay in business for long. In the final analysis, it is thus more correct to say that *costs of manufacturing or of wholesaling or retailing* goods are determined by *prices* than it is to say that *prices* are determined by *costs*. It makes no difference how much the goods have cost the merchants; they can sell them for no more than a buyer or buyers are able and willing to pay. *Thus, no manufacturers, wholesalers, or retailers operating in an ordinary competitive business can be assured of their costs of production. The business world simply does not work that way. If merchants were assured of cost of production, why would thousands of them fail every year?*

Consideration in Arriving at the Cost of Production of Farm Products

Let us suppose that prices of farm products were to be arrived at on the basis of cost of production. How accurately could these costs be determined?

The total cost of production of any crop or kind of livestock would include these items:

1. Payment of all cash expenses, including interest and capital purchases.

2. A charge *or* credit for inventory and capital item change.

3. A reasonable and competitive return to the unpaid labor and management of the operator.

4. A reasonable and competitive return to equity capital.

5. A reasonable and competitive return for unpaid family labor.

Difficulties in Determining Labor Cost of the Farmer and Family. Much of the labor for the farm is furnished by the farmer and the family. How much is this labor worth? Some members of the family are able, at least at times, to find employment away from the farm. Where this is true, a wage rate could be arrived at on the basis of what they could obtain in those other forms of employment. Of course, some members of the farm family usually cannot be employed away from the farm; hence, there is little basis for establishing a wage rate as a return for their labor; that is, it cannot be calculated on the basis of money costs. Suppose that an operator and members of the family are employed a certain number of days during the year on the production of a certain product, such as wheat or milk. What wage rate shall be considered as reasonable payment for their time? Shall the rate be the same during the rush season of harvest as during the dull season in winter? Suppose the operator is unable to obtain employment away from the farm; does this labor have a market value? If it does not, what should be the basis of determining the rate of pay?

To take another case, what rate of pay should be assigned to family labor for doing chores or other farm work during the winter months when that family labor might otherwise be idle? There are sociologists and psychologists who argue that a certain amount of labor will contribute to the welfare of the adolescent child and that such work recommends itself even though it must be performed without pay. If that be true, then the task of doing useful work which contributes to well-being should be considered a benefit rather than a sacrifice. Hence, under the conditions stated, no one can say what rate of pay should be assigned to this age group. If they have no opportunity for employment away from the farm, it can hardly be said that their time has a market value.

Wage rates of employees in industry are determined, in part at least, by what those employees might obtain in positions other than the ones in which they are engaged, given their ability and present training. Should this also be applied as a measure in establishing the wage rate assigned to an operator and the family during the winter when employment is slack or probably unobtainable? Certainly, it would be difficult to find sound reasons for assigning a specific wage rate to either an operator or the family if their time could be used for nothing else.

Farm cost studies commonly calculate the rate of pay of family labor in terms of what it would cost to hire work done. The time required for a mature person to do the work is estimated, and this amount of time multiplied by the rate for hired labor is used as a figure to determine the value of the family labor. Under this method of determining costs, *labor may be assigned to work which would be unprofitable to have done by hired help.* It is done only because there is a surplus of family labor that can be used in no other way, or as we say, labor which has no alternative value.

Difficulties in Determining the Cost of Land. Turning from the farmer to the farm itself, what basis should be used in arriving at the valuation of the farm in order to calculate the amount of the interest charge? Should the market value of the farm be used as the basis of valuation? If this method were to be used and if no farms had changed hands in that vicinity during recent years, how would this market value be determined? Should the original cost, plus improvements put into the land, be used as a basis? If such a method were used, the person who bought a farm during a year when the general price of land was low would show a lower interest cost than a farmer who bought equally valuable land during a period when the land prices were high. Such difficulties would become especially significant if the figures so arrived at were to be used as a basis of establishing prices of these products.

Farm buildings and part of the equipment may be constructed or repaired by the farmer and the family during the seasons of the year when their time could otherwise not be employed with profit. Since that labor cannot be used for any other purpose that will return an income, what rate of return shall be charged for it? If we are unable to determine the cost of labor used to construct or repair buildings, it is impossible to arrive at inventory values of the buildings.

Variation in Production Costs. Even if it were possible to arrive at some satisfactory method of determining the cost of producing crops and livestock, there would still be the important question of whose costs—that is, what farmer's costs—should be used. The cost of producing a farm product varies greatly among farmers. Costs vary from farm to farm in the same area, and also from one area to another.

Whose Costs Should Be Covered? Considering the wide variation in costs among farmers, whose costs should be covered? Should prices be high enough to cover the costs of all producers whether their costs are high or low, or should prices be established at a level so that they would cover the cost of only the lowest-cost farmers? Should it be at some middle point—that is, an average cost?

If the cost of production is calculated on the basis of the lowest-cost producers, then the higher-cost farmers would lose money. On the other hand, if the costs are calculated on the basis of the highest-cost producers, then the lower-cost farmers would make so much income that they would be encouraged to increase their production as time went on, and thus farm surpluses would soon be developed.

Difficulties in a Cost of Production Plan. Under the ordinary free market system farmers may sell all the products they wish.

They sell them at the best prices they can get. They hope to cover the costs of producing them, but even if all their costs are not covered, they still sell their products. If a plan of cost of production were established, who would guarantee that prices would be high enough to cover cost of production? Would the federal government guarantee these prices? If the government did guarantee to maintain prices high enough to cover cost of production, funds would be necessary to maintain such prices, because chances are they would be above the market level.

Funds necessary to hold these prices above market level would probably have to come from the taxpayers of the country. Would the people be willing to pay taxes for this purpose?

The Effect of Cost of Production on Future Prices

Any cost of production plan which would be satisfactory to farmers would likely have to cover costs of the majority of the farmers. Prices of farm products would be higher than they would be under a free market. This would encourage more production. Farmers would be encouraged to buy more feed, machinery, fertilizer, and land. These purchases would stimulate prices.

Wages of farm laborers would gradually increase as more and more farmers found it worth their while to employ more labor. It therefore seems inevitable that costs would be gradually forced upward, and in turn, prices of farm products would move in the same direction. Suppose the cost of producing corn was established at $2.40 per bushel. With no change in the general price level it could easily be demonstrated, one or two years later, that the cost had by that time increased to $2.50. Farm land values might increase proportionately as much. If corn prices were established at $2.50 the cost would, the following year, probably be shown to have increased to $2.60, and so on. Thus, there might be set up a continuous spiral of higher costs and higher prices. Where would such a spiral end?

The conclusion should not be reached from what we have said that the cost of production has no influence on prices. Costs do influence prices.

Short-Run Periods. Let us suppose that farmers were producing melons as one of their important crops and marketing them directly to retail stores. Suppose further that during a certain marketing season the supplies of ripe melons ready for the market were unusu-

ally plentiful. Finding that the melons were not moving at the existing price, the farmers would likely choose to reduce prices in order
to dispose of a larger amount, because if they were not moved into
consumption rapidly, they would deteriorate.

In deciding upon the price to place upon them, they would base
their judgement largely upon what they could get, knowing they
must move them rapidly in order to avoid heavy spoilage. Even
though they might reckon that the expenses of growing the melons
had amounted to, say, $3 per crate, they might decide to sell them at
a price much lower than that amount if they could not be disposed of
otherwise. Since virtually all their melons not already marketed
were ripe, and ready for the market, they would have none to
dispose of in the days or weeks immediately following. Accordingly,
they would not worry about depressing future prices unduly, or to
use another expression, they would not worry about "spoiling" or
"breaking" the market. They would be more inclined to reduce the
price, if necessary, to a very low point in order to dispose of their
entire crop. Of course, they would not sell at a price so low that they
could not afford to devote their own time to the job of selling or to
cover the expenses of employing someone else to do so.

In summary, if farmers knew in advance the price they would
obtain for their products, they would go to the expense of delivering
them to the market if, and only if, their income from the sale of it
were greater than the expected expense of marketing. Rather than
sell at a price below that point they would let the melons spoil in the
garden.

If, on the other hand, they did not know in advance what the
product would bring, or what their expenses would be, they might
take the product to market hoping that the income from the sale of it
would more than cover the marketing expense. This principle applies not only to the marketing of a farm product but also to the
production of it.

Long-Run Periods. In producing melons the following year
farmers would use the same reasoning as they did in marketing,
except the calculations would be for a longer-run period. Let us
follow through their reasoning in this case.

The following spring, when these farmers decided upon their
planting operations for the season just ahead, they would plant
melons only if they had reason to believe that the returns for them
would cover those production and marketing expenses still to be met

from the time under consideration. These would include seed, fertilizer, hired help employed in the care of the crop, all actual expenditures of marketing, and any other outlay.

After calculating the expenses, the farmers would determine, the best they could, whether the prospective crop of melons would pay for the above outlay and still leave a greater net return for meeting taxes, interest, and other expenses than they could get by turning their attention to the production of some other crop. Here they would need to consider the adaptability of their land for other products and the use of any machinery for producing certain crops. In case the farmers had no alternative to which they could turn their land and their own labor capital, they would plant their acres in melons if, in their judgement, they could cover all expenditures which would be incurred in the production of the product from the *point of time under consideration* and leave themselves something in additon.

An Important Principle. This leads to a general and important economic principle similar to that just stated—namely, once a product is in the process of production and the *land, capital,* and *labor* which have been assigned to its use cannot be turned advantageously to some other purpose, the farmers will continue the steps in producing and preparing the product for sale if the prospective price is sufficiently high so that the expenses *still to be met in future steps of the production and marketing process* can be covered and some return will be left in addition, regardless of how small the amount. This would include some consideration, although not necessarily a going wage rate, for their own and family labor.

Those costs which have been incurred in the processes of production *prior to the point* at which the consideration is being made will not ordinarily enter in when farmers are deciding whether to continue the production or marketing processes of a product. Such costs are looked upon as having been "sunk" in the enterprise; hence they are left out of consideration in determining whether to continue the steps of producing or marketing the product in question. For instance, seed becomes a "sunk" cost when it is planted in the spring. Fertilizer becomes a "sunk" cost as soon as it has been applied to the land, unless the land is actually sold for a higher price because of the addition of it.

The cost of buildings and other improvements made on the farm become "sunk" during their entire span of existence except if they can be turned to uses other than those intended when built, or unless they can be disposed of (in which case the difference between the original cost and the price at which they were sold becomes a "sunk" cost). Money paid for a farm becomes a "sunk" cost to the owner until the farm is disposed of. If the resale price is less than the original price paid by the buyer in question, then the "sunk" cost to that buyer is the difference between the two amounts.

Stated in another way, the costs of production which have already been "sunk" at any point in time have no—or virtually no—effect upon future supplies and hence no effect upon prices. On the other hand, the costs which are still to be met from any point of time do have an influence upon supplies and therefore upon price. In general, the only relationship between costs and prices is that costs are instrumental in determining future supplies and thereby in influencing future prices.

Questions and Problems for Class Discussion

1. To what extent is it true that the retailers who sell you food products or clothing always cover their costs and in addition make a profit? Call on one or two retailers and ask them what factors determine their selling price.

2. How would manufacturers of men's clothing determine the price they should charge for their suits? Could they always be sure of their covering their costs and making a profit? Discuss in class.

3. What are the items you would consider in arriving at the costs of producing a farm product, such as wheat, corn, milk, hogs, or beef cattle? What cost items are the most difficult to determine?

4. How do production costs influence the supply of a product for (a) a short period of time, and (b) a longer period, such as a year or more?

PART SIX

Other Important Considerations

A successful farm business manager has to consider many factors in managing the farm. We have examined many of these factors in the preceding five parts. In Part Six we will deal with several other important areas the modern farm manager must contemplate.

CHAPTER 22

Protection from Accidents and Insurance Against Risks

Highlights of Chapter

A large number of accidents on farms could be avoided if proper precautions were taken. Most accidents are due to individuals being careless and not following some simple, sensible safety rules. Potential dangers include machinery, tools, fire, animals, and noise. Farming is a risky business. There are methods of coping with many of the risks. These methods are costly but can make farming somewhat less hazardous.

Recent figures available from the National Safety Council show there are over 5 fatal farm accidents per day and over 520 disabling injuries per day in the nation. This adds up to about 1,900 deaths and 190,000 injuries per year. Costs of farm fires run up to millions of dollars per year. The sad part is that most of these accidents and fires could be avoided if proper care were taken. You will want to protect yourself against accidents and fires. You will also want to protect the others who work with you from these hazards.

Farm accidents can be avoided. The hazards on the farm which may lead to accidents need to be checked, and what is more important, the hazards must be removed. Many farmers know that they have conditions on the farm that are unsafe—but they do nothing about them. That is plain carelessness, yet it happens every day. Many times it's the little things that kill. Perhaps 9 out of 10 accidents could be prevented by using intelligent foresight—followed by action.

Reducing Risks in Farming

In every business there are risks, but farming probably has more than its share. Heavy rains may drown out some or all of the crops; a severe drought may burn them up. Right up to the day of harvest, a hailstorm may destroy them. Insects or diseases of crops may reduce the crop yield seriously or wipe it out entirely; likewise, a disease of epidemic proportions may attack certain livestock and cause heavy losses. A livestock feeder buying steers or lambs for feeding may suffer heavy losses because of a slump in prices. The barn or house may burn, resulting in losses that will take years to make up. Then, of course, life itself is uncertain. Untimely death may take the life of the father, mother, or any other family member. A progressive farmer attempts to provide protection against risks.

Insurance Against Risks. It is possible to carry fire insurance which will enable a farmer to replace at least a part of the property lost. It is also possible to insure against loss from hail even though that may be expensive, especially in areas which have a bad record for hail losses. Life insurance may also be carried by the parents so that in case of death through accident or another cause the survivors will have some funds to carry on until they have been able to make adjustments. Reliable insurance agents can be of help in advising on the best type of insurance to carry. There is a danger, however, that agents, in their enthusiasm, may encourage prospects to take out more insurance than they can or should carry. Remember, insurance provides for a small sure loss, the premium, to avoid a large potential loss—the loss of property through fire, loss of crop, loss of ability to work through injury, loss of income, etc.

The increased use of complex farm machinery has resulted in many accidents, some of which have been fatal. Tractors and other machinery have done much to improve the efficiency and to reduce the costs of farming, but have also increased the hazards. These hazards may be covered, in part, at least, by accident insurance. While no amount of insurance can exactly compensate for the loss of an arm or a leg, insurance can help pay for someone else to carry on while the person who suffered the loss is unable to work. The kind and amount of insurance farmers should carry depend upon their particular circumstances.

It would seem that no farmer can afford to be without some fire insurance to compensate, at least in part, should the house or barn be destroyed by fire. Neither can farmers afford to be without automobile liability insurance. Farm liability insurance of an adequate amount should also be carried. The purchase of life insurance is a good deal like the purchase of anything else. One must decide how much of it to buy, recognizing that money spent for insurance is diverted from other uses. The same thing is true of accident insurance. Generally, it is desirable to carry a certain amount, but the kind needs to be chosen wisely.

The question is frequently raised as to how much life insurance one should carry. There is no one answer. It depends on each individual situation. Being overinsured is costly while one is living. Being underinsured is costly when a tragedy strikes.

Perhaps the best way to determine how much life insurance you need is to estimate how much money your survivors will need if you die. From that you subtract the amount of assets you have—Social Security, non-farm investments, farm investments, existing insurance, and other assets. The remainder may be covered by insurance. If you are interested in using insurance as a savings method, buy whole life insurance. If you want to buy the needed protection as economically as possible, use term insurance. And be sure to shop for the best deal. *There is a great variation in the cost of insurance policies which provide the same protection.*

As you grow older, generally your assets increase and your family financial responsibilities decrease. Thus, the need for life insurance will decrease. Your total insurance program should be flexible enough to adjust to changing needs.

Danger from Farm Tractors and Machinery

Our modern farm machinery saves labor and makes farm work more attractive, but it also carries more hazards. You need to be on the lookout to avoid those dangers which may lead to accidents. A tractor is generally built so that it is safe, but accidents happen because the operator is not alert or is careless.

Here are some rules that may save doctor and hospital bills and that may also save an arm or a leg:

1. Before you start the tractor engine—is the gearshift in neutral?

2. Before you start backing the tractor—is your hand or foot on the brake?

(*Left*)—He knew the support was shaky . . . but he took a chance.

★

(*Right*) — He knew the doll was there . . . but he took a chance.

Fig. 22-1. Do not take chances on having an accident.

3. Before you get off the tractor, or get in front of it—is the tractor standing still?

4. Before you reach through a belt or chain—is it moving? If it is, you may lose a hand.

5. Before you start the machine—are the covers and guards in place?

6. Before you handle gasoline around the engine—is the engine stopped? Are you smoking? What individuals want their hair scorched or their clothes burned off?

Of course, individuals should know enough to keep their hands and feet a safe distance from moving rolls, knives, sickles, chains, disks, or other dangerous moving parts. Yes, people know better—but they get careless, and carelessness may be costly.

Before letting anyone operate a machine, instruct that person thoroughly. Here are some suggestions for tractor operations:

1. Securely fasten your seat belt if the tractor has an ROPS (rollover protective structure).

2. Where possible, avoid operating the tractor near ditches, embankments, and holes.

3. Reduce speed when turning or crossing slopes, and when on rough, slick, or muddy surfaces.

4. Stay off slopes too steep for safe operation—or you may land under the tractor.

5. Watch where you are going, especially at row ends, on roads, and around trees.

6. Do not permit others to ride.

7. Operate the tractor smoothly—no jerky turns, starts, or stops.

Fig. 22-2. Many states require that the triangular slow-moving vehicle (SMV) sign be attached to farm equipment on the highway. This sign enables motorists to see a piece of equipment from a greater distance and to adjust their driving pattern. All farm equipment should have this sign. (Courtesy, International Harvester)

8. Hitch only to the drawbar and hitch points recommended by tractor manufacturers.

9. When tractor is stopped, set brakes securely and use park lock, if available.

Other Important Safety Suggestions

Here is another list of ways to eliminate potential hazards on your farm. How many of these are you practicing?

1. Study, understand, and practice provisions of present health and safety standards which apply to your farm.

2. Pick up all the junk, litter, and debris in and around buildings which could cause falls or other injuries.

3. Maintain ladders, stairways, power tools, and other equipment in safe working order.

Fig. 22-3. In this tractor tipping demonstration, the spectators can observe firsthand how improper hitching can cause a tractor to tip backwards. (Courtesy, University of Wisconsin Department of Agricultural Engineering)

4. Read the safety precautions and instructions in the operating manuals of all farm machinery used on your farm.

5. Establish a work policy that no machinery will be operated without all safety shields in place and operative.

6. Establish a work policy that there will be *no riders*, except drivers and operators, on any machinery.

7. Establish a work policy that every machine will be stopped before it can be unplugged, repaired, or adjusted.

8. Investigate the safety features and values of safety shoes, hearing protection devices, hard hats, safety glasses, respirators, and types of protective clothing.

9. Put up a stop sign at every driveway leading to a highway.

10. Employ an electrician to inspect wiring and electrical power units.

11. Make certain at least one member of your family or organization has completed first aid or medical self-help training.

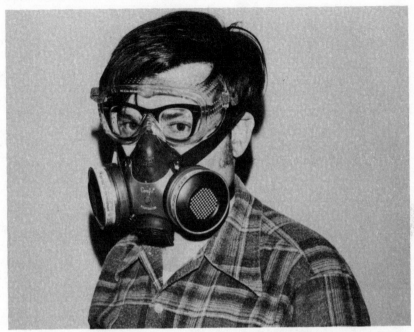

Fig. 22-4. Safety glasses protect the eyes, while a respirator protects the lungs. (Courtesy, Don Jensen)

12. Be sure that all family members and employees are instructed in, and understand, the safe uses of any equipment they operate.

Farm hand tools can also be a source of injury. Are you using them properly and taking sensible safety precautions?

1. *Wrenches*

    a. Select a wrench of the right size for the work to be done.

    b. Adjust the wrench so jaws fit snugly on the nut.

    c. Brace yourself and use a short, steady pull.

    d. Never attempt to tighten or loosen a nut on moving machinery.

    e. Do not use a wrench as a hammer.

    f. Be sure your footing is good before you pull.

2. *Screwdrivers*

    a. Never use a screwdriver as a chisel, gouge, or lever.

    b. Use the right-sized screwdriver to fit the screw.

3. *Axes*

    a. Check frequently for tightness on handle.

    b. Chop so that the axe handle is as nearly horizontal as possible when the axe strikes.

    c. Keep the area of swing clear of obstructions.

    d. Use a chopping block instead of your foot.

    e. Use a short stroke when chipping ice in water tanks.

    f. Never use the axe as a maul.

    g. Store the axe properly.

    h. Keep your eye on the point where you want the axe to strike.

4. *Rakes, Hoes, Forks, and Scythes*

    a. Do not leave rakes and hoes where they can be stepped on, for they may strike someone in the face, break a nose, or blacken an eye.

    b. Keep your foot clear when you are using the rake—rake teeth will puncture a foot.

    c. Do not throw a fork down from a mow, and then jump down—many permanent injuries have been caused this way.

    d. Hang up rakes, forks, and scythes when you are through with them.

Noise is also a potential hazard. You can avoid damage to your hearing. Try to reduce noise level in work situations by:

1. Shielding or enclosing the source.
2. Increasing the distance between the source and the ear.
3. Placing a shield between the source and the ear.

No one needs to suffer noise-induced hearing loss, at least while on the job, if available hearing protection is used. Have your hearing tested. If your work involves significant exposures to noise exceeding 85 db(A), use hearing protection devices.

Two basic types of ear protection are available: insert-type and muff-type. The insert-type, which is made of rubber, soft plastic, etc., is placed in the ear canal. It is very important that inserts be properly fitted to the user.

There are state and federal regulations governing safety practices on the farm. They are important. Check with Occupational Safety and Health Act (OSHA) officials and local officials for the latest regulations. You should also check on the Federal Child Labor

Fig. 22-5. Muff-type ear protection can help reduce hearing loss. (Courtesy, Don Jensen)

Law regulations and the Federal Minimum Wage Law. Your county agent will have current information regarding these important regulations.

Danger from Animals

Injuries from animals have dropped in the past several years. But the safety hazard still exists. No bull is safe, but the older he is, the more dangerous he becomes. The bull that always seems gentle may turn on you on a second's notice. The "gentle" bull kills more people than the real "ugly critter." If the bull is really ugly, owners are usually careful about keeping him in a safe bull pen. Experienced livestock people will tell you that the only really safe way to handle any bull is to keep him in a bull paddock. Your agricultural teacher or county agent can give directions on how to build a safe paddock.

A boar is never safe. Nor is a sow with newborn pigs. Goats and rams have injured many children as well as grownups. Why take chances? You feel so foolish to be butted under the manger by a ram, even if he doesn't break your leg!

The following are a few hints from practical livestock breeders to avoid the hospital—or the morgue:

1. Treat all livestock kindly, but always have the upper hand. Always be in control of the situation. Do not let them catch you off guard.

2. When an animal is in a stall, speak softly before you enter. Keep equipment in good condition. A break in a piece of equipment may cost a life—yours, a family member's, or a friend's. "Jack be nimble, Jack be quick" is not safe as a policy to avoid the hospital. It is smarter to play it safe.

3. If you must handle the bull, lead him with a staff hooked safely in the nose ring. A nose ring may not be comfortable for the bull, but neither is his horn in your ribs comfortable for you.

Fire Prevention[1]

The majority of farm fires are due to seven causes—all largely preventable. These are:

1. Defective chimneys and heating apparatus
2. Combustible roofs
3. Lightning
4. Spontaneous ignition or combustion
5. Misuse of electricity
6. Matches and smoking
7. Gasoline, kerosene, and other fuels

A large number of the farm fires are caused by carelessness.

Many of the old chimneys in the houses are unsafe, as they were built with no inner lining and the mortar has crumbled away. New chimneys have a tile flue around which the bricks are laid in cement.

Nearly one-fourth of all the fires are caused by lightning. Those can be reduced by the use of lightning rods. A well-rodded building is rarely struck. A barn covered with a galvanized roof is well-

---

[1]You can get more safety information free by writing the National Safety Council, 444 North Michigan Avenue, Chicago, IL 60611.

Fig. 22-6. Many farmers are risking their lives, families, and property investments by letting fire hazards exist around farms. A ton of ashes is worth less than an ounce of fire prevention.

protected against lightning if at opposite corners a copper or galvanized wire is soldered firmly to the roof and well grounded.

Faulty wiring or overloading of an electric wire invites trouble.

Many smokers are careless as to where they throw matches. "No Smoking" signs may help to prevent some fires. Proper facilities for the storage and handling of gasoline and kerosene should be provided. It is too risky to use gasoline for home dry cleaning or kerosene for starting fires.

Some losses are caused by spontaneous combustion. These can be reduced by having all hay and grain thoroughly dry and well cured before putting them into the barn. If there is danger of spontaneous combustion, the hay may be scattered around the barn in different mows or, in some cases, removed.

Hay or other forage-type materials having a moisture content of over 30% can be a potential fire hazard. If the material cools as fast as heat is produced, it will turn brown or mold. If the heat cannot escape and air can get in, a fire may result.

Even silos have been known to burn. Material stored in a silo at less than 40% moisture can ignite. Careful checking of moisture of hay, silage, and grains is important to avoid spoiled crops and the possibility of fire.

Having a few fire extinguishers strategically placed around the farm buildings and farm home, as well as mounted on farm machines, can help you put out a fire or control it until help arrives. The extinguishers should be of a proper type and serviced regularly. All persons should be instructed in their use.

Methods Used by Livestock Feeders to Reduce Risks. Many farmers buy feeder lambs or feeder beef and feed them until they are ready for slaughter. If prices should rise during the feeding period, then the feeder not only gets paid for the gains but also gets paid for the price increase. That is a very fortunate situation!

On the other hand, if prices slip rapidly during the feeding period, a heavy loss may be incurred. Some people have lost everything because they struck two or three bad years. In order to avoid such losses, some feeders contract with the owner of the livestock to be paid a certain amount for each pound of gain which is made by the feeder. This arrangement generally pays a little less. But the

Fig. 22-7. The correct type of fire extinguisher can help fight small fires before they become large fires. (Courtesy, Don Jensen)

system has an advantage in that the feeder takes no risks from price declines. Of course, one does not get the advantage of price increases either. It is a safe, conservative method. Other arrangements to spread price risks are the use of the futures market, forward prices, and other contractual arrangements. One must be careful to select the arrangement that is best for his or her own set of circumstances.

We should not conclude that the risks of farming are so great that one is helpless to meet them. Nor should we conclude that the outlook is a discouraging one. We need to remember that farmers, like other business persons, take risks; they always have and always will, so long as they assume the responsibilities of running a business or a farm. The problem of the individual farmer is that of planning how to meet the risks in such a way that one can keep a farm and family going from year to year and maintain a reasonably high standard of living and a happy livelihood.

Coping with Risk

We talked about risk and uncertainty briefly in Chapter 5. A few more comments about risk are in order. Every manager sees risk in a different way and reacts accordingly. Certainly, some variability keeps things interesting and challenging. But too much can be disastrous. For some, a high degree of risk is difficult to cope with psychologically. For others, their financial condition cannot tolerate it.

Farmers are always subject to price and yield risk. Other risks are changes in technology, personal misfortunes, legal risks, government policy changes, and government regulations.

To effectively deal with risk, we need to know the alternative ways of reducing risk. With this information the most appropriate strategies for an individual situation can be taken. But there is a cost to transfer risk.

One method is to transfer the risk to some other party. We already have discussed insurance. For a fee—the premium—the risk is transferred to the insurance company. With a share rent the risk is shared by the tenant and the landlord. By participating in government programs, a farmer can transfer some risk to the government.

For some, diversification of enterprises spreads risk but may result in higher production costs and lower profits. Selling products throughout the year reduces market price risk, but the profit potential of a more reasoned marketing program is lost. Some may hold larger cash reserves, or inventory reserves, but the more effective use of these resources is lost. These may not be the most efficient risk minimization methods.

For some farmers the selection of more stable enterprises is a satisfactory method of risk reduction. However, the more stable enterprises are generally lower return enterprises. Others like to be flexible in their operations and change with changing conditions, but they have the danger of being in when they should be out. Some will select low-cost fixed assets or lease assets, while some will use custom operators. Potential profit opportunities could be lost.

Appropriate marketing strategies can help overcome price risk. Hedging and forward contracting can lock in prices and reduce risk. The opportunity to cash in on a significant price rise is also reduced.

Individual farm managers have to select which risk minimizing strategy fits their own personality, farm situation, and risk bearing ability. Each has a cost. But many times the reward may be worth it.

Questions and Problems for Class Discussion

1. Check your house and barns to determine if there are fire hazards that could be removed.

2. How about the electric wiring? Is it adequate for the load it is carrying?

3. What are some serious types of accidents with farm machinery? How can they be avoided?

4. There are seven common causes of fires on farms. Name and discuss what you think are the four most serious ones in your area.

5. What types of insurance should be carried by a farmer to give protection against fire and accidents? Are those types carried in adequate amounts on your home farm? What about liability insurance?

6. What are some of the methods you use on your farm to avoid the risk of large price changes?

7. How much life insurance do you need? Are you overinsured or underinsured? Why? What action should you take?

8. What are some ways to cope with risk? List five and discuss their advantages and disadvantages. Which will fit your farming situation?

CHAPTER 23

Soil Conservation, Water Management, and Field Arrangement

Highlights of Chapter

Practically every farm is subject to either water or wind erosion. On many farms soil losses are so severe that a large part of the productive capacity is lost. Practical methods of conserving the soil have become rather well established, and the latest practices are discussed in the pages that follow.

On many farms irrigation will increase crop yields enough so that it will pay to irrigate if proper methods are followed.

The field arrangement on many farms is determined largely by things such as the slope of land, hills, swamps, and creeks running through the place. On many farms the present field arrangement is the result of changes over the years, so any further worthwhile changes may be a long, slow process.

It is more expensive to farm small fields than large ones. This is especially true when large-scale farm machines are used.

In arranging fields one needs to have in mind that soil erosion should be prevented and a long-time crop rotation system should be planned. The main reason for replanning the field layout is to increase the efficiency of labor and equipment and soil conservation.

Conserve the Soil on Your Farm

The top 6 to 8 inches of soil on your farm largely determines its value. If the topsoil is washed away by rains or blown away by winds, your farm is as good as lost.

Successful farmers are always on the lookout for ways to conserve the topsoil and build up its fertility. Farmers who conserve their soil are the ones who make the money over the long pull. Some farmers do not farm their land. They mine it! Many farms have been handled so carelessly that much of the topsoil has been wasted. However, more and more of the better farmers everywhere have come to realize that if their farms are to continue to produce and give them a profit, the soil must be conserved and built up to make it more productive.

The Soil Feeds Plants. Plants reach down into the soil through their root system to absorb nutrients from the soil. The nutrients used by plants consist mainly of those nutrients called "primary elements"—nitrogen, phosphorus, and potassium. Secondary materials are sulphur, calcium, and magnesium. Others, called micronutrients, are in the soil, usually in small amounts. All crops, if they produce good yields, must be able to obtain these nutrients in the proper amounts. If some of the nutrients are lacking, they will have to be supplied by adding barnyard manure or commercial fertilizer, or the crops will be poor.

Soil samples should be taken at least once every rotation or every three years. The soil samples are then chemically analyzed and fertilizer recommendations are given, based on the test for the various crops on different soil types.

Put Land to Its Best Use. On many farms there is some land that is suitable for crops and some that is usable only for grazing or for woodland, brush, and other forms of cover for wildlife. The first job of a farm manager is to determine what land should be used for each of these purposes. When the manager has decided upon the land that is satisfactory for crops, then the next step is to determine what crops to produce on that land and what kind of soil conservation practices to follow to keep the soil from eroding.

For the land that is not suitable for crops the farmer has to decide what portions to use for grazing and what to use for woodland and cover for wildlife.

The greatest loss of soil is the result of erosion. The word "erosion" comes from the word "erode" which means to gnaw out, to eat away, or to destroy slowly. When we say the soil is eroded, we mean that it has gradually been eaten away or destroyed.

Loss in plant food from the growing of crops can, of course, be replaced by adding manure and commercial fertilizer. But the loss of soil that is carried away by water or blown away by wind cannot be replaced. When we talk about erosion of soils we usually refer to losses by these methods.

Erosion Starts Slowly. In some ways erosion is like creeping paralysis, or perhaps even more like cancer. It takes place so slowly that you scarcely realize that a change is going on. If you look at a corn or potato field right after a heavy rain, you may notice many small, narrow furrows, waterwashes, or rills where the water has been running and has carried the soil along with it. This is the beginning of water erosion.

If the land is not handled in a way to stop the erosion, the little rills grow wider and deeper. They become trenches which carry away more and more surface water and along with it more surface soil. In time the trenches may grow into gullies.

If the soil is not protected against further erosion, the land may finally be literally cut to pieces by water run-off. Thus, this last stage, "the cancer," which first appeared innocent and unnoticed, finally takes its victim.

Fig. 23-1. Small rills soon become trenches like these. Fertile soil goes off in car-load lots.

Eight Basic Practices to Reduce Erosion

1. Fit the crop to the class of land.
2. Farm on the contour.
3. Establish a system of strip cropping or contour strip cropping.
4. Use terraces where needed.
5. Build grassed waterways.
6. Plant cover crops.
7. Use conservation tillage.
8. Increase soil efficiency.

Fig. 23-2. Manhandled soil! Once fertile acres are now a complete waste.

Countless worn-out farms remind us
We must farm these soils to stay,
And, departing, leave behind us
Farms that have not washed away;
For when our sons assume the mortgage
On these farms that had our toil,
They'll not ask the question:
Here's the farm, but where's the soil?

(Courtesy, Soil Conservation Service, USDA)

1. Fit the Crop to the Class of Land

Most farms have at least three or four classes of land, and some may have as many as eight classes. These are known as capability classes.

These different classes of land must be handled differently.

Class I land is excellent land from every point of view. It is level or nearly so and will not wash or blow under ordinary conditions. It has water-holding capacity and good fertility and can be cultivated with almost no risk of erosion.

Class II land is good land but not quite as good as Class I land. It may have enough slope to cause danger of slight erosion. It may be slightly wet and not drain well, or it may be slightly dry and not have as good water-holding capacity as Class I land. Because of these limitations, Class II land requires special attention and may be limited in its uses.

The slope may be great enough to require contouring. Attention must be given to fertilizer, crop rotation, and water management. This attention also has to be given to the other land classes.

Class III land is only moderately good compared with Classes I and II. However, it may be cultivated and seeded to crops every year, but the Class III land which is sloping will require some kind of conservation practices, or erosion is almost sure to occur. The Class III land which is poorly drained may require drainage to obtain satisfactory crop yields.

Class IV land is good enough for cultivation if a careful cropping system is followed. It is not suited for the production of cultivated crops—at least not every year. On much of the Class IV land the slope is so steep that regular cultivation is likely to cause soil erosion. Generally speaking, Class IV land is more suitable for pasture than for crops.

It is not very safe to seed it to cultivated crops such as corn, except perhaps for one year out of every five or six, and even then, if heavy rains come, erosion may be rather serious.

Class V land usually includes land that is quite level and not subject to erosion but that is too wet or has too many permanent obstructions, such as stones and boulders, to be suited for cultivation. This land is commonly used for grazing or forestry.

Class VI land and Class VII land are most safely used for some kind of permanent cover. These classes of land are usually characterized by steep slopes, banks, and cutting, so much so that it cannot be used for crops. These kinds of land are usually made up of shallow soils that are not very productive.

Class VIII land is not suitable for economical crops. It is used mainly for wildlife, watershed protection, or recreation.

Table 23-1 gives a summary of the various land classes and their uses.

The Problems of Soil Conservation and Even of Farm Management Are Entirely Different with Each Class of Land. The more

Table 23-1. Land Use Capability Chart[1]

Major Land Use Suitability	Land Capability Class (Degree of Limitations)		Practices That May Be Applicable (by Subclass)
	I Few limitations. Very good land from every standpoint.		Normal good soil and crop management.
	II Moderate limitations or risks of damage when used for crops.	c	Contour strip cropping, terraces, waterways.
		w	Protection from flooding, drainage.
		s	Maintaining good soil structure.
Suited for Cultivation	III Moderate to severe risk of damage, or limitations. Regular cultivation possible if limitations are observed.	c	Contouring, contour strip cropping, terraces, diversions.
		w	Surface and/or tile drainage, diversions.
		s	Wind erosion control, irrigation, moisture conserving practices.
	IV Severe limitations. Can be cultivated with special management.	e	Contour strip cropping, diversions, renovation or top-dressing, woodland.
		w	Protection from flooding, surface drainage.
		s	Moisture conserving practices, wind erosion control.

(Continued)

Table 23-1 (Continued)

Major Land Use Suitability	Land Capability Class (Degree of Limitations)	Practices That May Be Applicable (by Subclass)
Not Suited for Cultivation	V Not suited for cultivation because of wetness, stones, overflows, etc.	*Adapted to:* Grazing, forestry, recreation.
	VI Too steep, stony, wet, or droughty for cultivation. Moderate limitations for grazing or forestry.	Grazing, forestry, recreation.
	VII Very steep, rough, wet, or sandy. Severe limitations for grazing or forestry.	Grazing, forestry, recreation.
	VIII Extremely rough, swampy, etc.	Wildlife, watershed protection, recreation.

[1]Land classes are shown in Roman numerals I through VIII. The classes are divided into subclasses and units. Subclasses are designated by letters. The letter "e" stands for an erosion hazard, "w" for a wetness hazard, "s" for a permanent soil limitation such as shallow depth and/or droughtiness, and "c" for a climatic hazard such as a short growing season.

classes of land on a single farm, the more varied and difficult is the problem of soil conservation.

Manage Each Class Differently. Farmers cannot hope to be successful if they follow the same soil management and conservation practices on Classes III, IV, or V land as on Class I or II. Each class has to have its own system of management, cultivation, and conservation practices. This is a basic problem for all farm managers. (See Table 23-1.)

The Conservation Farm Plan. The heart of a conservation farming program is the S.C.S. Farm Plan. The first step is to make a soil map of the farm. This is really a detailed soil inventory which shows the soil type, percent of slope, and degree of erosion. All these factors are noted on an aerial photo of the farm.

The final product is a detailed land capability map of the total farm. Brief descriptions which go with the map tell something about

Fig. 23-3. Eight classes of land—each class must be farmed differently from every other class. (Courtesy, Soil Conservation Service, USDA)

each different kind of land. They describe the texture and depth of the soil, the steepness of slope, and the degree of erosion. From this detailed information recommendations can be made for cropping practices, erosion control methods, water control measures, and other conservation features of land management.

After the land capability inventory is done, the conservation farm plan can be laid out. It will show which conservation practices should be adopted and where they should be installed. A suggested crop rotation can be outlined. Plans can then be made for the implementation of a long-range farm conservation plan.

Soil conservation farm plans are designed with both the farm and the farmer in mind. Appropriate adjustments in the plan must be made to accommodate modern technology.

A conservation plan properly designed and implemented means sense and cents (or dollars) for farmers and for the nation.

2. Farm on the Contour

By contour farming we mean a layout of the fields so the edge of each field is at a constant level even though the land is sloping. By laying out the fields in this way the rows of the crops will also be on a level.

Fig. 23-4. Rows follow the contour and help to retain the water where it falls. (Courtesy, John Deere)

Ask the Farm. Perhaps the best way to determine whether contour farming would be better than "straight line" farming is to ask the farm! If the soil is eroding, then serious consideration should be given to farming on the contour. Farming under this system has proven to be less costly in the use of labor, tractor power, and farm machinery than "straight line" farming.

"Contour farming" is a general term. You can follow a system of contour farming by merely arranging the fields on the contour under a regular rotation system or no rotation system at all. The more common system, however, is to maintain a rotation system. An even more effective method of conserving the soil by contour farming is to use a system of strip cropping.

3. Establish Strip Cropping

Strip cropping is one of the less expensive methods of soil conservation and will do much to stop or reduce soil erosion on land where the slope is not too steep or too long. If the slope on the land is more than 12 to 15% and continues more than 250 to 300 feet, then strip cropping alone may not stop erosion. Other methods may also be necessary.

Select the Most Desirable Method for Your Farm. There are two kinds of strip cropping in common use—contour strip cropping and field strip cropping. A less common method is wind strip cropping.

Contour strip cropping is an arrangement where the land is

Fig. 23-5. Strip cropping on the contour offers protection against erosion if slopes are not too steep. On the steeper slopes, terraces are necessary to hold the water or to divert it from the field without soil erosion. (Courtesy, John Deere)

farmed in strips or bands on the contour at right angles to the natural slope of the land. As the water from rains runs down the hillside, it will run across these strips. Each strip will vary from 70 to 100 feet in width, depending upon the amount of slope and the kind of soil. The real value of strip cropping is that different crops are grown on adjoining strips. A good practice is to have a hay crop on every other strip and a cultivated crop, such as corn or another grain crop, on the strips between the strips seeded to hay. Crops are generally grown on these strips in a definite rotation. For example, a rotation of two years of hay, one year of corn, and one year of grain might work well on a livestock farm. The strip with the hay would stop water run-off that comes from the field above. By keeping the rows of corn on rather narrow strips at right angles to the natural slope of the land, you can prevent water erosion or, at least, greatly reduce it.

Vary Width of Strip. Both the upper and the lower edges of the strips are generally laid out on the contour. It is very seldom that the slope along a hillside is uniform. Where it is not, the width of the strips will not be the same over its entire length. This makes the job of farming the strips a little more difficult than if they were the same width throughout their entire length. However, this is not a serious handicap when one considers the advantage of preventing water run-off from the land.

Fig. 23-6. Where wind erosion is severe, the practice of planting rows of evergreens at right angles to the prevailing winds prevents the soil from blowing. (Courtesy, Soil Conservation Service, USDA)

Where the fields slope uniformly in one or two directions, contour strip farming is very satisfactory. But it is not so practical where the land differs greatly in slope and is irregular in topography. If strip cropping is to be the most effective, both the upper and lower edges of the strips must follow the contour. The job of laying out the contour in this manner requires some experience and should be done by someone who understands how to do it. The Soil Conservation Service in your area will help lay out the fields. Your agricultural instructor or county agricultural agent will be able to tell you how to obtain whatever help you need.

Field strip cropping is similar to contour strip cropping, but the strips are the same width throughout and are run on a straight line, not along the contour of the land. If the lay of the land on your farm is so irregular that contour strip farming is not practical, then field strip cropping may be workable. The purpose of both contour and field strip cropping is to prevent or reduce water run-off, and the better of the two should be chosen.

The purpose of *wind strip cropping* is to prevent soil blowing. Here the strips are usually straight and of uniform width, and they run at right angles to the prevailing winds. Wind strip cropping is recommended where the land is reasonably level and where wind erosion is a problem.

Fig. 23-7. This dairy-hog farm has a complete conservation plan in operation. Note the contour strips, grass waterways, and farm pond located behind the modern farmstead. (Courtesy, Ken Allen)

4. Use Terraces Where Needed

Divert the Water by Terraces. The best way to prevent water erosion is to hold the water where it falls! If it cannot be held, the next best thing is to get the water to "walk off the fields—not run off." Terraces are surface drainage channels built along the level of rolling land. The purpose is to hold the water on the field or to conduct it from the field in a way so as to keep down water erosion. A terrace will break the long slope of a field by providing a way that will stop the water from continuing to run down the slope and erode the soil.

There Are Several Types of Terraces. One type of terrace makes water walk—or at least run slowly. Used in connection with contour farming, it is an excellent combination method. Another type of terrace holds the water until it has soaked into the soil.

Terracing is practical where crop rotation, strip cropping, and contour farming will not control erosion. Two general types of terraces are the "graded channel type" (a drainage terrace) and the

Fig. 23-8. The result of wind erosion—soil piled up to the top of the fence. This type of erosion could be stopped or at least reduced by proper cultural practices and tree planting. (Courtesy, Soil Conservation Service, USDA)

"level type" (a terrace that absorbs the water). Both types have a channel, or shallow ditch, with a ridge at the lower edge. Several terraces may be built across the same slope with considerable distance between them. The distance or space between two terraces will depend upon the type of soil, the amount of erosion that has already taken place, the steepness of slope, the general topography, the amount of rainfall, and the kinds of crops grown.

The graded channel terrace that carries the water away slowly is constructed with a slight grade—a few inches of fall per 100 feet of terrace. This kind of terrace is used in areas where the rainfall is heavy enough so that without it the water carries away the topsoil. Such a terrace will stop straight downhill run-off and will give the soil a chance to absorb the water and to carry the excess away slowly into a natural drainage outlet that is protected from erosion.

The level terrace has no grade at all. It holds the water until it has soaked into the soil. This kind of terrace is generally satisfactory in the drier regions where the rainfall is not so heavy that the water has to be carried away. Other types of terraces are the broad base

Fig. 23-9. Here water is being diverted by a terrace and spread over a level area where it is causing no damage. This shows good soil management. (Courtesy, Soil Conservation Service, USDA)

terrace and the grass back terrace. The terrace is really an "eave trough" that catches the run-off water from the land like the eave trough on your house.

Field crops are not the only ones which are protected by terraces. Orchard crops may also be.

5. Build Grassed Waterways

After a heavy rainfall some water will pass over the land as run-off. An important job in soil conservation is to divert this run-off so it will not cause soil erosion. Even if a farm manager follows a good crop rotation or a system of strip cropping, contour farming, or terracing, there may still be water run-off.

Remove Water Safely. Water will collect in draws in the fields, or even in the pastures. This water must be removed without causing

Fig. 23-10. A grass waterway is maintained in a plowed field to divert the water so that erosion will be avoided. The job of maintaining such a strip is an inexpensive and very effective way of preventing the formation of gullies. (Courtesy, Allis Chalmers)

erosion and damage to the land. A waterway planted to grass forms one of the best ways to divert this water. Such grassed waterways should be located where the water drains naturally.

If they are wide enough and have the right shape, the water can be drained off the draws with no erosion. From these the water is diverted to a place where it will do no damage. In order that the waterways will have grass with a good root system and good growth, it is important to keep them well fertilized and seeded with hardy grasses.

6. Plant Cover Crops

Cover crops are planted to provide protection to the soil between regular cropping intervals. They protect the soil surface from the impact of raindrops, add organic matter, and minimize leaching. Water is absorbed more readily because the pore space on the surface of the soil is kept open. Several crops can be used as cover crops. Some are small grains, domestic rye grass, hairy vetch, and sweet clover.

7. Use Conservation Tillage

Conservation tillage is defined as the least amount of tillage necessary to provide a good seedbed, resulting in quick germination and a good stand. Here one restricts cultural operations to those that are properly timed and essential to producing a crop and those in which crop residues are properly managed. The herbicides and tillage equipment available today make this possible. Check with your county agent to see which methods of conservation tillage are working best in your area.

8. Increase Soil Efficiency[1]

The more efficient your soil, the greater the income you can expect from your farm. Consider these points in order to increase the soil efficiency:

a. Crop yields are basic factors in determining farm income. Soil management is therefore very important. Good management of medium or poor soils will often produce higher yields than will poor management of good soils.

b. Secure the help of your local soil technician in laying out a long-time soil and water conservation plan.

c. Do something each year to complete the conservation plan.

d. Test the soil to determine the lime and fertilizer needs of each field.

e. Each year use as much lime and fertilizer as is profitable.

f. Handle stable manure and apply it so you get the most out of it.

Water Management

Many areas are farmed where the water supply is too limited to produce a satisfactory crop yield. In parts of the United States,

---

[1]For an excellent discussion on the methods and practices of soil conservation, see *Our Soils and Their Management* by Roy L. Donahue, Roy H. Follett, and Rodney W. Tulloch, published by The Interstate Printers & Publishers, Inc., Danville, Illinois.

Fig. 23-11. The new pattern of soil conservation. This covers many adjoining farms and shows the results of cooperative effort. (Courtesy, Case Company)

especially in the western states, the total rainfall (including water from the snow) may be as low as 8 to 20 inches per year. In those areas, irrigation is common as a way of getting enough water to produce good crops.

For profitable crop production there should be ample moisture in the soil for steady plant growth from the time of planting until the time when the crop reaches maturity. The total amount of water needed to produce a crop and the time of the year when it is required depend on the kind and amount of crop grown, its stage of growth, the soil, and climatic conditions.

More water is required in the hot, dry climates and longer growing seasons of the plains than in regions where the climate is more temperate and the growing season shorter. Irrigation is rather costly, so one must plan on maximum crop production. It is the extra bushels, pounds, and tons of crops above the extra expenses that are necessary for profitable farming. The costs and returns from irrigation should be carefully budgeted.

Fig. 23-12. A man-made dust storm! Dust storms like this would not exist if the land had been put to proper use. In some areas, land that should have been left in grass has been plowed up. In these areas, the farming practices will have to be adjusted to reduce or stop these serious dust storms. This is not a job that can be done by one individual farmer. Rather, it is a problem that must be faced by large numbers of farmers working with the U.S. Congress to obtain a workable program to fit the area. (Courtesy, Soil Conservation Service, USDA)

Capacity of the Soil to Store Water

Perhaps the greatest single factor influencing irrigation on any farm is the soil. The soil acts as a reservoir in which water is stored between irrigations for the use of the plants. While soils on different farms vary in their capacity to store water for plant use, the soil on any individual field or farm has rather fixed irrigation properties. Once these properties are determined, they may be used indefinitely as a guide in irrigation practices, regardless of changes in crops and irrigation methods. These properties are:

1. Size of soil particles—texture.
2. Depth of surface soil to subsoil or water table.
3. Character of subsoil, whether hardpan or porous sand and gravel.

The moisture storing capacity depends upon the texture of the soil, its depth, and the presence of hardpan, porous subsoils, or a

Fig. 23-13. Irrigation is becoming more common and important. This aerial view shows irrigation on test plots on an experimental farm. (Courtesy, University of Wisconsin Department of Agricultural Journalism)

high water table within reach of plant roots. Information on these points may be obtained by the use of a soil auger. Your S.C.S. soil map and conservation plan can help here.

Fit the Irrigation System to Your Farm

Each farm layout for irrigation will be an individual unit designed for particular crops, soil, and operators' preferences. No two farms will be set up identically and give equal results.

The first problem in setting up an irrigation system is to determine the amount of water available for irrigation. The second is to find out whether this water contains anything that is harmful to crops. Have the water analyzed for concentration of various salts contained in it. Your college of agriculture will make the analysis. Do not use water that the college does not recommend for irrigation. Your soil conservation technician and county agent can help you in planning a profitable irrigation system.

Caution. Modern farming methods with chemical pest control measures call for some cautions. Weed control chemicals, especially those which control grassy weeds, present a particular hazard. Spraying close to or over grass waterways calls for accurate application. Also, remember that water-soluble chemicals can wash into adjacent waterways, terrace bottoms, and fields. Years of effort in developing conservation practices can be destroyed or their effectiveness diminished by careless application of pest control measures. Also, tillage too close to conservation practices can cut their effectiveness and possibly destroy them.

Field Arrangement

Modern machines cannot be used efficiently on an extremely small farm, or even on a large farm which has small, irregular shaped fields.

The farmstead and the buildings which will make efficient use of labor and farm equipment will be discussed in the next chapter. Our present-day farms have been settled a long time. The buildings, the farmstead, and the field arrangements have become rather definitely established as the farms have developed. One who buys a farm can change the field arrangement in two or three years' time, but it is a slower process to change the arrangement of the farmstead or of the larger and more important farm buildings. Indeed, that is a very slow process.

Early Settlers Gave Little Thought to Field Arrangement. The field arrangement or layout, especially in the originally wooded area, is the result of many years of work. Usually the first settlers were more concerned about making a home than about any definite field arrangement. Many of them worked in nearby lumber camps in the winter months. They came home in the summer to clear their land and grow their crops. Most of the clearing was done without machinery. Stones and stumps had to be dug out by hand. They were hauled short distances and in many areas made a fence for a field. There is still evidence in parts of the United States where the stones and stumps are being used for fences. Many times the cleared areas of such fields are small and irregular.

Fields Are More Regular in Prairie Areas. In the area of prairie soils where few, if any, trees and stones interfere with field layout, the fields are more regular in shape and larger than in the wooded area. This makes it possible from the beginning to use more labor-saving equipment to a greater advantage. It reduces the time and cost of seeding and harvesting an acre of land.

Fig. 23-14. Large, well-arranged fields make for more economical use of modern labor-saving machinery.

On many farms, especially outside the prairie area, the field layout still needs rearranging into larger and more regular fields. While the present-day smaller tractors can be used on small fields, they will operate at a lower cost per acre on the larger fields. For that reason the farmers who have small, irregular shaped fields are at a disadvantage, at least until they can rearrange their field layout.

It is usually too expensive to change fences, remove stones and trees, and drain wet spots all at one time. It is best to sketch a plan of arranged field layout, then, when fences have to be rebuilt, put them where the new plan indicates. Stones and trees can be removed and drainage done at the season when time will permit.

Essentials of a Good Field Layout. When planning the field arrangement, give consideration to:

1. Topography of cropland.
2. Length of crop rotation.
3. Size and shape of fields for most efficient use of labor and equipment.
4. Economy of fencing.
5. Efficiency of livestock production.

Topography and soil condition may be such that it will be difficult to make large and regular shaped fields.

If possible, obtain the help of the Soil Conservation Service through your local S.C.S. District Office in making the field layout, as this service will determine the soil capability of each field and the length of rotation which is best suited for the different fields. If contour or strip cropping is needed, it is best to know it and to lay out field boundaries on the contour lines and have them conform with the natural waterways.

The Soil Conservation Service, in determining the land capabilities, takes into account soil type, degree of erosion, slope, and any other factor that will affect the long-time use of the soil. The land is classified as (1) land suitable for cultivation with a short rotation, (2) land which must be in hay and pasture for a longer rotation, or (3) land not suitable for cropping but used for either pasture or woodland.

After you have decided which fields are to be cropped and which are to be in permanent pasture and woods, the next thing to do is to develop a long-time cropping sequence.

Length of Rotation. If possible, it is desirable to have the same number or a multiple of the same number of nearly equal-sized fields as there are years in the rotation. A four-year rotation of corn, small grains, and hay (two years) would require four fields of nearly equal size. Where it is impossible to do this, it is advisable to combine the acreage of two or more fields by planting them to the same kind of crop.

Size and Shape of Fields. In the early days when farm work was largely done with hand tools and with a team of oxen or horses, the size and shape of fields did not limit efficiency as seriously as they do today. If a tractor and tractor equipment are to be used efficiently, the fields must be fairly large and regular in shape. The farms on the open prairie were the first to use large units of farm equipment.

Farmers located in the cutover region find it difficult to compete with them in the prairie region in crop and livestock production.

Studies at many universities have shown that the time spent in crop production is less in large fields than it is in small ones. This time saving is just as important in reducing cost per unit of production as it is in increasing yields per acre.

Economy in Fencing. An oblong field is the most efficient for use of labor and equipment, but a square one is most economical to fence. With the use of the electric fence as well as confinement feeding, it is hardly necessary to have each field bounded with a permanent fence. The farm boundary line, permanent pasture, and some roadside are usually all that need to have permanent fencing. When needed for rotation pasture, the crop fields could be fenced with electric wire.

Field Layout and Livestock Production. In planning the field arrangement it is very important that consideration be given to the ease of reaching the pasture land. Where pasture land does not join the farmstead, a lane should be provided.

Rearranging the Field Layout

The first step in rearranging the field layout is to make a diagram of the present layout. Here is a good chance to use the aerial photo maps available at the S.C.S. or A.S.C.S. office.

The main reason for replanning the field layout is to make more efficient use of labor and equipment. Another reason is to have more uniform acreage of crops to provide feed for the livestock. The revised plan can provide a more uniform sequence of crops year after year.

It is possible, however, that some crop damage through winter injury, summer drought, or another cause may make it necessary in any particular year to change the long-time plan in order to make best use of the land. It is advisable to plan seed and fertilizer requirements each year for each field or combination of fields.

There are many farms on which the present field arrangement requires careful planning and several years to change over to an economical field layout.

The many small and irregular shaped fields on some farms make for inefficient use of labor and equipment. Feed requirements for livestock make it necessary to produce as nearly as possible the same amount of feed crops each year. Of course, the plan must be flexible enough to allow for changes in technology and economic conditions.

Questions and Problems for Class Discussion

1. Name the basic steps in conserving the soil on a farm. Why are these so important?

2. Give reasons why you believe you are doing a good job of fitting the crops to the land on your farm.

3. How many and what particular classes of land are on your farm?

4. How would you distinguish between a level-type and a graded-type terrace?

5. What are the important factors which determine the capacity of the soil to store water for plant use?

6. If you were to irrigate any part of your farm, what would be the source of the water supply?

7. How many and what kind of important changes in the field arrangement have been made on your home farm during the past three years?

8. What were the reasons for making those changes? Will you be making other changes?

9. Draw up a plan of your present field arrangement and show what changes should be made. Show the changes to be made each year until the plan has been completed.

10. Estimate how many days in the use of labor and farm equipment would be saved by the new plan.

CHAPTER 24

Farmstead Arrangement, Farm Buildings, and Farm Machinery

Highlights of Chapter

The farmstead includes the area occupied by all the farm buildings, the service yard, and the livestock lots. On practically all our farms the farmstead arrangement has already been established. Changes and improvements will take good planning and time. One needs to consider the farm home, farmstead utilities, crop storage, machinery storage, and livestock housing. Building investments and design must be properly and thoroughly thought out and budgeted. Machinery is a major investment and cost item. Several questions must be answered before the appropriate machinery complement is selected.

We usually think of the farmstead as the entire area occupied by the farm buildings. It includes the house, lawn, garden, walks and drives, trees and shrubbery, and other features that contribute to the convenience and appearance of the place.

Very few people who go into farming have a chance to plan their own farmstead. Usually it is already there when they take over the farm and is the accumulated effort of the past owners. The most they can do is to reorganize some major features of it. The amount that any starting farmer can do depends upon how many permanent buildings are already there. It is generally possible to rearrange at least some of the yards, driveways, gardens, and shrubbery quite easily. Some of the buildings may also be remodeled to improve the appearance of the place and increase the efficiency of doing the chores and other farm work around the buildings. On livestock farms about one-half of all labor is spent in and around the buildings. With farm consolidation and expansion, owners of many larger farms will have a good chance to guide their farmstead development.

When buying a farm it is important that one takes into account the arrangement and condition of the buildings. On farms where permanent farm buildings have already been constructed it would be very expensive to reorganize the farmstead quickly. It is costly to move buildings; therefore, some minor adjustments are usually made which will make the best use of them in their present location. As new buildings are constructed—when the old ones are no longer usable—they can be conveniently arranged.

Planning the Farmstead

Planning, or rearranging, the farmstead is a much bigger job

Fig. 24-1. This young farmer and his family are studying the scale drawing of their present farmstead to enable them to turn it into a long-range building plan. (Courtesy, *Wisconsin Agriculturist*)

than planning a barn or some other farm building. Rearranging or reorganizing the farmstead involves three steps:

1. Analyzing the site. The site should be carefully and thoroughly analyzed by taking into consideration its relation to fields and highways, water supply and sewage disposal, topography, prevailing winds, orientation, and view.

2. Examining the present farmstead arrangement. Here you would consider the type of farm operation, use and condition of existing buildings, natural influences, and chore route. It would be a good idea to prepare a scale map of the existing farmstead arrangement. The map should show buildings, yards, wells, sewage disposal, fences, lanes, trees, drainage, channels, and slope.

3. Planning for a better arrangement. Things such as efficiency, good traffic circulation, flexibility, and fire safety must be considered. It is a good idea to put all projected building plans on paper before building a new structure. This way you can see how the whole farmstead plan looks before you build. You may even want to project building plans into the future of your farmstead plan. This way you will reduce the chance of putting up a building that might be in the way of future expansion. You should always look at the different possibilities of present and future farmstead mechanization.

Good farmstead planning can reduce costs, increase efficiency, and make farm work more pleasant.

Farmstead Planning Considerations

The farmstead should be planned with a long-range view in mind. That way each step can be taken to accomplish the long-range objectives gradually. Do not let small, partially depreciated, inefficient buildings influence your long-range thinking. Removing some building which may be structurally sound can prove to be the best decision. Remember, depreciation measures not only wear and tear but also economic and functional obsolescence.

Some short-run, low-cost measures can be taken immediately. They have a quick payoff. These could include changing the use of a building, relocating a building, removing a building, or relocating fences, gates, lanes, and yards.

Efficient use and placement of buildings is the key. You can use your farmstead scale map to develop a flow chart. This shows how farm crops, livestock, machinery, people, and outside units servicing the business move around the farmstead. Good traffic circulation must be provided. All-weather types of surfacing should be used in important heavy traffic areas. Of course, safety must be considered along with convenience and efficiency.

With constantly changing technology and economic conditions, the matter of flexibility of design is important. Can buildings be converted to other uses, expanded, contracted, or moved? Can additions be made to the farmstead?

Fire safety is becoming an increasing concern as investments go up and farmsteads contain larger, more sophisticated buildings located close together. Some construction design and layout principles long used in off-farm industries are finding their way to the farm.

Of course, a major consideration is having an attractive farmyard. While farming is a business and must be treated as one, the livability of the farmstead can contribute much. It is just as easy and requires no more time to place shrubs, flower beds, gardens, and driveways in a pleasing arrangement in relation to the house than to put them in the wrong place.

Some types of trees and shrubs, when properly set, seem to "tie" the house to the ground. On the other hand, there are plantings and arrangements which give one the feeling that the house is ready to fly away.

Does your farmstead look attractive and invite attention? Look at it as others see it. Farmers should think of the farm as their home, and the surroundings should create pride of ownership. The young folks can do much to make this home a place where they will feel proud to bring their friends. It is the place where they will spend the best years of their lives. Many of us have cherished memories of those early years on the home farm. Let's make it as attractive as possible.

We all like to do business with firms that have their merchandise arranged in a neat and orderly fashion. No doubt city people who drive over the country roads admire an attractive, well-kept farmstead. They, too, may wish to buy eggs, milk, meat, and other foods from such farms rather than from one with run-down, unkempt buildings and premises. A well laid out farmstead can reduce labor and increase efficiency while being attractive.

Fig. 24-2. This well-engineered building fits in with the total farmstead plan. Along with the landscaping and all-weather surface, it makes an efficient, pleasant place to work. (Courtesy, Wick Buildings)

The part of the yard between the house and the barn and other buildings is sometimes called the service yard. It is used by the farmer every day; therefore, it should be as dry and clean as possible. It is used as the place to get equipment ready for field use. When machinery is brought in from the field, it should be put in its place instead of left standing in the yard for several weeks. Sometimes several pieces of equipment are left there for months. Perhaps the reason for this is that the machine shed may not be in a location convenient to the crop fields. It is important to have a convenient equipment storage shed which is large enough to house the equipment.

The Farm Home

The house is part of the physical plant of the farm; it must not be ignored when the other buildings are being planned. The farmer may want to ask whether the house being planned is within the earning capacity of the farm. There are so many different demands on the farm income that farmers choose what they think is the best use of their money. Investment of capital where it will make for most efficient use should gain preference. A house need not necessarily be large to be comfortable, but it should be "livable."

Fig. 24-3. This modern solar farm home is designed with energy conservation and pleasant farm living in mind.

When building a farm house, one needs to consider the following:

1. Better living conditions will encourage some ambitious farm youths to stay on the farm and to take over where their parents leave off.

2. There is a close relationship between a convenient building arrangement and labor efficiency.

3. The plan should be such that it will not be unduly expensive to make changes in the future.

4. In addition to space to carry on the regular housework, there is a need for room for people to clean up when they come in from work.

5. There should be office space for the farm manager to do the bookkeeping and to keep the farm records.

Farmstead Utilities

Electrical, water, communication, and fuel services are important factors in modern farming. Adequate electrical service should be available to serve present and anticipated needs. A wiring diagram of the farmstead can help locate trouble spots and help in future additions.

An adequate water supply is vital to serve the home, livestock, and other farm activities, such as spraying. A well should meet or exceed local, state, and federal codes for personal safety and for the production of wholesome food products.

Waste water disposal is a problem for the dairy farm and for the farm home. Adequate sanitary disposal of waste water must be provided for.

Communication is an important part of an efficient operation. A main phone is essential. In many situations extension phones in the shop, barn, and other locations can save time and money. Many farmers are using citizens' band radios. These are especially helpful in emergencies and are a convenience, particularly when the farm fields or buildings are spread over a large area.

Adequate fuel storage space must be provided so delays in the busy season can be avoided. Fuel storage should be designed so it is safe and convenient for the farm operation and the place of use.

Farm Buildings

As farmers begin to see more clearly that their buildings have been put up with no planning and that the arrangement is inefficient, they ask for help from specialists, including those from state agricultural colleges. Alert farmers realize that well-planned buildings will save labor and reduce the cost of doing the farm work. Here are some of the ways in which buildings will make a return on investment:

1. By saving crops, both in quantity and quality.
2. By contributing to increased production.
3. By reducing livestock mortality losses, veterinary fees, etc.
4. By saving labor with convenient arrangement.
5. By furnishing partial insurance against loss from severe storms.
6. By making a better land use program with storage space provided.
7. By reducing the difficulty encountered in hiring help if good buildings are provided.
8. By making it possible to secure better tenants.

9. By increasing the effectiveness of operators in buying and selling their products.

10. By increasing safety in farm work.

11. By making the farm a more desirable place to live and work.

12. By adding to the real estate value of the farm.

Economy in use of labor is of great importance in all farm operations. Before constructing a new building or rearranging an old one, the farmer should make floor plans and trace the lines of travel which will have to be covered in doing work. Once a building is built, it lasts for many years. For this reason a great deal of thought and study should be given to it. A wrong location of feed room, stairs, silo, and other parts about the building may cause many miles of useless travel in a year. The arrangement of most livestock facilities could be changed so as to save much labor. The reason why many farmers do not eliminate some of the inconveniences is that it takes less time to do any one operation than to make the change, and they go on, year after year, covering many extra miles and consuming much valuable time.

Mistakes in purchasing a cow can be easily rectified. Mistakes in planting a particular crop affect the farmer for that year only. A mistake made in building arrangement is more serious, because the building lasts so long and is not easily changed. The dimensions

Fig. 24-4. This modern farrowing facility can save labor as well as prevent pig losses.

commonly found in many livestock facilities are not satisfactory. They are difficult to change and therefore remain as they are.

Successful farmers have found that it pays to "build on paper first." Instead of just starting to build or remodel with little or no thought given to efficient arrangements, one should make a complete plan.

After the first plan has been drawn on paper, changes can be made before the building is started. It is cheaper to change a paper drawing than to rebuild a building after it is completed or to continue to do work in one that is poorly planned.

Does the plan you have worked out on paper permit additions to the building at minimum expense? You may want to expand your operations in the future. Can the building be converted to other uses if economic and technological changes warrant it? Flexibility of building use is extremely important.

Remodeling or Enlarging a Building

There are many occasions when one must remodel an old building rather than build a new one. Many of the barns in use today have been remodeled. Many more are in need of a thorough overhauling. Some have outlived their useful life and should be removed.

The rearrangement of an old barn is a more difficult problem than the building of a new one, because each old barn is an individual problem and, in many cases, determines the procedure to be taken. Considering the labor cost involved in tearing down a barn and using the materials again, the cost of the remodeled building on many farms is more than the cost of a new one.

The greatest trouble with our early farm buildings is that they were made too small. It was a common practice to build a small barn and to add others to the sides and ends of this barn as more room was needed. After a number of years there would be a group of inconvenient buildings.

It is more economical to have as few buildings as possible, arranged conveniently to save labor. It is preferable to have one large barn located reasonably near the house, rather than many small buildings scattered over too much ground.

Many persons think that the fire risk is too great when all the stock and the produce are under one roof. There is real truth to that statement. On the other hand, where there are so many small, scattered buildings, the time involved in doing chores is also a disadvantage because of the high cost involved. Several hundreds of miles of travel would be saved each year with well-arranged, concentrated buildings.

Repairs Pay Out

Frequent repairs to buildings are necessary to preserve them. Unless these repairs are made in time, the expense of repairing will be greatly increased, and permanent damage to the buildings will often be the result. A small leak in the roof of a building will cause much damage unless it is stopped immediately. Much of the necessity of repairs to buildings is due to neglect. Roofs and foundations are important.

Crop Storage

Adequate space should be provided for crop storage. This can be for crops which will be either sold or used for feed. The buildings must have adequate capacity for peak loads, be strong enough to hold the heavy farm crop, be weather tight, be conveniently located for filling and unloading, be safe, and provide protection from birds, rodents, and thieves. Check with agricultural engineers specializing in building design for plans for buildings adapted to your farming situation which meet these requirements. New and better designs and building materials are constantly being developed.

Machinery Storage

With proper housing of farm tools, the life of these can be extended many years. Much time is lost in the field in repairing broken parts due to improper housing.

There has been a marked increase in the number and size of machines, resulting in the need of more and more space for storage. Due to the increased expense of machinery and repairs, it is becoming more important to furnish some kind of economical storage space.

The machine shed should be located where convenient access can be made to the fields. It should be placed in the farmstead

Fig. 24-5. This grain bin can be equipped with aeration and drying equipment. (Courtesy, Brock Company)

Fig. 24-6. The silos provide for crop storage, while the pole shed can be used for machine storage as well as crop storage. (Courtesy, Wick Buildings)

arrangement so that any piece of equipment standing out would be shielded from constant view—especially from the house.

In planning for adequate machine storage, one first has to figure the number of square feet required to house the present machinery complement and any expected additions. Machinery used at the same time of the year should be stored together. Machines which are frequently used should be stored so that they are easy to get in and out of the machine shed.

Measure all your machines and make scale cutouts of them. Then draw up a floor plan of the shed. The machine cutouts can be easily moved around to determine the most convenient and efficient way to store them. Anticipated changes in machine size or numbers should be considered. A few extra square feet of space is much cheaper when building than when it has to be added later.

Fig. 24-7. Valuable machinery such as this forage harvester should not be stored in the open. (Courtesy, Fox Division of Koehring)

Many machine sheds are designed with a shop area. If this is paved, insulated, and heated, it can be a great convenience. Repairs and maintenance can be done out of the weather and during the off season.

Livestock Housing

Proper livestock and poultry housing can do much to increase livestock efficiency and productivity. The same can be said for labor used in livestock production.

Crowded housing conditions are a problem on many livestock farms. On dairy farms the housing of replacement heifers is neglected many times. The important factors in the housing of livestock are keeping it dry and draft free and providing adequate space.

Many livestock and poultry facilities lack adequate ventilation. There is a close correlation between ventilation and insulation. Rapid and extreme variations in temperature and humidity must be guarded against. Livestock and poultry efficiency go down in extreme heat and cold and in high humidities.

Your county agent and agricultural instructor can provide modern plans for livestock and poultry housing appropriate for your area.

Building Investments

With all the important demands for building space on a farm, it is necessary to hold the cost of all buildings down as low as possible and still have them efficient. It is easy to overinvest in buildings as well as in land and machinery.

Before erecting or remodeling any building, a farmer should keep in mind the different ways in which the new building, or the remodeled one, will bring a return on the investment.

If the farm is overbuilt the farmer faces a much higher fixed cost structure. This cuts down profitability. In the event of a sale, the buildings may not contribute much to the sale value of the farm. The same can be said for poorly designed buildings.

In some cases, small, poorly designed buildings without any alternative uses may have a negative value. That is, they are worth less than nothing. In order to get them off the tax rolls and off the insurance policy listing, they must be removed from the farm. Their value then is a negative one—the cost of removing them. This has become a common problem with farm consolidation and new, more efficient building design.

Budgeting for building investments follows the same general budgeting procedure outlined in Part Four, "Planning for the Future."

Machinery Management

The trend to larger, more specialized, and highly sophisticated machinery suggests that increasing consideration should be given to machinery management. Because machinery is such an important part of the farm business, managers have a great opportunity to improve efficiency and/or increase productivity through wise machinery management decisions.

Some questions to consider are:

1. What benefits can be achieved by increasing or changing the machinery complement?

2. What machinery complement is appropriate for the farm type and farm size?

3. Should the machinery be new or used?

4. What about machinery leasing?

Fig. 24-8. Big tillage equipment works well on large, level fields. (Courtesy, Glencoe)

5. Does hiring custom or contract farming have a place in the operation?

6. Does doing custom work have a place in the operation?

7. What about exchange work with others?

8. What are your machinery costs—ownership (fixed) and operating (variable)? Can they be changed?

Machinery costs money to own and operate. But it is necessary for the operation of a modern farm. It can save time and labor and make labor more productive as well as more efficient. Better timeliness in operations can increase yields, make for better quality, and reduce field losses. Livestock and livestock products can be cared for in a better fashion. Yes, machinery can be helpful in making farming more profitable and pleasant. But the costs have to be weighed against the benefits.

The appropriate machinery complement must be selected to fit the farm and to fit together. A large, fancy set of hay making machinery is useless to a cotton farmer. A four-wheel drive tractor does not fit well with a three-bottom plow or an 8-foot disc. Machines must be matched to each other and to the farm. Frequently one machinery decision will trigger other machinery decisions. The addition of a larger power take-off–driven machine will call for investment in a larger tractor. Careful budgeting is important in making the right decisions.

In many cases, used machinery will be the most economical alternative. While the investment will be lower, the repair costs will be higher. There is a trade-off here. Reliability may be lower with used equipment. But the savings can be well worth it. If acreages are small, if the machine will only have a few hours' use, if there have been no major technological breakthroughs in design, if the machine will perform the job in a timely fashion, and if repair parts and service are available, the used machine can be an attractive alternative.

Machinery leasing, custom farming, and contract farming have increased in popularity in recent years. These methods can fill the need for many farmers. Trading machinery use with neighbors works very well in many situations. One farmer may own a baler while the other has a forage harvester. They can work together in forage harvesting activities and charge each other custom rates. This helps spread fixed costs over more acres and puts together a bigger crew for these jobs. If extra time and labor is available

Fig. 24-9. On smaller farms, used, smaller equipment may be the most economical alternative. (Courtesy, International Harvester)

without sacrificing taking proper care of the home operation, doing custom work for others can earn extra income from a machine.

To compare with projected costs of machinery or to evaluate the present machinery situation, one must know his or her present costs of machinery operation. These would be both fixed and variable costs. Individual machine records would also be of help. It would also be a good idea to separate the field machinery costs from the livestock machinery costs.

Each state has useful publications about machinery costs. Up-to-date information on expected use life of machines, purchase cost, repair cost, and operating cost can help you budget for more effective and efficient machine selection and use.

Questions and Problems for Class Discussion

1. If you were to rebuild the important buildings on your home farm, show the arrangement you would recommend. Make a scale farmstead map. Submit your new arrangement to the instructor and class for evaluation and discussion.

2. Develop a budget for one of the following: crop storage, livestock facility, machinery storage.

3. What are some considerations you should think about in farmstead planning?

4. What questions should you ask about machinery management?

5. Develop a budget for machines on your farm.

6. What are the machinery costs on your farm?

CHAPTER 25

Government Assistance
Available to Farmers

Highlights of Chapter

For well over 100 years, federal and state governments have given certain indirect or direct assistance to farmers. The first form of assistance was to carry on experiments to control plant and animal diseases and to develop improved varieties of crops and the like.

The second type of aid took the form of lending farmers money for emergency purposes and developing a farm credit system.

The third form has been more direct and also much more costly. This has centered attention mainly on controlling the output of farm products and improving their prices.

The federal government has helped farmers for many years, or perhaps it would be more correct to say that farmers have helped themselves through their own government. This help can be divided into three different kinds. At first the government helped by showing farmers how to improve their soil and how to grow better crops and livestock. We might call that first aid. It showed how to select seed which would produce better crops, how to till and fertilize the land, how to kill weeds and insect pests, how to feed and care for the livestock, how to test the soil, how to manage their business better, and a dozen other things. Later on, it loaned them money to buy seed grain and to market their grain and livestock. The third kind of help was more direct; in fact, it was an outright government payment to farmers so that they would produce the kind of crops that were most needed by the country and also the crops that would protect their soil from being blown away by wind or washed away by water.

Help First Given Through Agricultural
Experiment Stations

Abraham Lincoln was one of the first presidents of the United States to give real aid to American farmers. He signed a bill, passed by Congress, that started a college of agriculture with an agricultural experiment station in every state in the Union. Money to operate these colleges was paid in part by the federal government.

The federal government has, of course, also given help to businesspersons and manufacturers, but in many ways, the amount of

Fig. 25-1. This research agronomist is yield checking this trial corn plot. (Courtesy, University of Wisconsin Department of Agricultural Journalism)

help made available to farmers has been more direct and perhaps greater in amount than to other groups. This is partly because there are so many things that cause trouble for farmers which they as individuals cannot remedy. For example, there are many insects which attack crops and many different kinds of crop and animal diseases that farmers do not know how to control. The income of farmers is too small to enable them to hire a specialist to find ways of overcoming these troubles. The amount of income of an individual farm is very small compared with the income of a large business concern.

Big Factories Have Their Own Specialists. The Ford Motor Company manufactures millions of cars in a year with sales in the billions of dollars. Only three automobile companies manufacture most of the automobiles made in this country. This means that they are big business concerns. Most big manufacturers, such as Ford, hire engineers and other specialists, who spend their full time in finding out how to improve their product and how to reduce the cost of making it. The Ford Motor Company knows that people will buy more Ford automobiles if they are good cars than if they are poor. They also know that if they can find ways of lowering the cost of producing their automobiles there will be more money left as profit for the company.

The Ford Motor Company is used here only as an illustration. What we have said about it is true also for the other large automobile companies. In fact, it is true also for most large business concerns. Large companies, such as manufacturers of automobiles or radios, can afford to hire specialists, because when they make many cars or radios and have a large gross income, the cost of hiring these specialists is small for each car or radio.

In farming, it is quite different. Farming is fully as complex as manufacturing, but there are less than 3 million farms in the United States, each one making only a relatively small income a year. If farmers are to produce good crops, such as wheat, corn, potatoes, or cotton, or good livestock, such as cattle, sheep, or hogs, they have to know the "tricks of the trade." They need specialists just the same as an automobile manufacturer does, but farmers who produce only $20,000 to $30,000 worth of crops and livestock a year cannot always afford to hire their own specialists. About the only way most farmers can get help from specialists is by many farmers using *the same specialists*, each farmer using only a small amount of the specialist's time. One of the best ways for many farmers to get together in the employment of such specialists is through their own government. We might say that the government helps the farmer, but what we really mean is that the people of the United States agree to pay enough taxes so that some money from these taxes can be used to hire specialists to work on problems that trouble the farmers.

Many larger farms are now hiring some agricultural consultants on a fee basis for short-term consulting work, especially in the area of farm management. Other farmers belong to farm management associations which provide records, tax, and management services. These services are paid for by the farmer and are given on a continuing basis. Some farmers hire specialists for pest control, building design and layout, livestock production testing, and other purposes. This type of private consulting will grow as farms become larger and farming becomes more technical and specialized.

These government programs have helped not only farmers, but city and village people as well. For instance, foods, such as meats and dairy products, were inspected so they would be free from disease germs that might be harmful to those who ate them. The government scientists also tried to improve crops, such as fruits and vegetables, so they would satisfy consumers. A great deal of work was done to help farmers grow potatoes, apples, and other fruits and vegetables that were smooth and clean in appearance so they would have more "consumer appeal." To use an example, most of you have no doubt seen potatoes with a rough scurf called "scab." Consumers do not like scabby potatoes any more than they like automobiles with part of the paint chipped off. As another kind of experiment, tests were made regarding how to kill insects and plant diseases that were harmful to wheat, corn, potatoes, and other crops.

The college experiment stations hired many men and women who were specialists. Some of them started experiments in which different kinds of wheat, corn, cotton, and other crops were grown to determine which kind would give the largest yield. Fields were divided up into small plots, and different kinds of grain were seeded in each plot so that the different kinds could be compared side by side to determine which were the best. Seed grain was also shipped in from European countries and other countries and grown in these plots. New kinds of wheat, corn, and cotton were developed by scientific methods of plant breeding, and experiments were carried on to find out how much commercial fertilizer and lime could be used to get the best crop yields. In general, this work was done at the college experiment stations—not on farms.

County Agricultural Agents. A few years after that, about 1914–1916, county agents, also well-trained specialists, were hired jointly by the county, state, and federal governments to work directly with farmers on their own farms. The county agents studied the new things developed at the experiment stations and carried the information to the farms. They helped the farmers in their jobs of controlling diseases and insects and improving the quality of the crops and livestock that were grown on their farms. These county agents really were specialists like those in the Ford factory, but the county agents worked for many farmers—not just for one. Without this help given by the government it would have been impossible for farmers to improve their crops and livestock as much as they did. Better crops and livestock, of course, meant higher farm incomes and lower costs for consumers.

Out of the work of the U.S. Department of Agriculture and the state colleges grew the work with youth known as 4-H Club work,

Fig. 25-2. The county agricultural agent works with farmers as a group or on an individual basis right out on the farm. Here the agent and dairyman are shown in a newly constructed free stall dairy barn for 125 dairy cows. University specialists are constantly researching better housing methods for livestock.

carrying on various kinds of projects. A little later, teaching of agriculture in high schools came to be under the Smith-Hughes Act. From this grew the organization known as the Future Farmers of America (FFA).

The Government Supplied Information on Crop Production. The help given to farmers during this period of first aid was almost entirely with crop and livestock production problems. Gradually, farming developed more and more into a commercial system, and the farmers sold their crops and livestock to a marketing system or to middlemen. These middlemen in turn sold the products to people in cities and villages. The marketing of farm products became more

Fig. 25-3. These two agronomists are doing field research on plant diseases. (Courtesy, University of Wisconsin Department of Agricultural Journalism)

important, and some farmers thought that the middlemen's charges were too high. They thought that middlemen had "secret information." In order that farmers would be able to obtain as good information as was available to some businesspersons, laws were passed giving the federal government the job of making information available on the supply of and demand for farm products. This information gave farmers a chance to find out how many acres of wheat, corn, and potatoes were being grown. Forecasts were made of crop production. This information would help farmers to know whether it would be best to sell their crops in the fall or wait until winter or spring; that is, it gave farmers just as much information on market conditions as millers, large elevator operators, and meat packers were able to get through their own information agencies.

The Second Kind of Help

The help given to farmers as was just discussed was largely of an indirect nature. In a real sense it was primarily helpful along educational lines.

In the second phase, one of the most important government services was to provide farmers with loans at low interest rates which could be used to purchase land and seed grain and to finance their production operations and the operations of their farmer cooperatives. Loans to purchase land were made by the Federal Land Banks which were established in 1916 and grew rapidly, especially during the 1920s. The Federal Land Banks laid the groundwork for the Farm Credit Administration (F.C.A.) which was then developed. The work of the F.C.A. was enlarged to include four agencies in the Farm Credit System:

1. The Federal Land Banks which made long-term loans on farm land.

The Banks for Cooperatives which made loans to farmer cooperatives.

3. The Production Credit Administration which made short-term loans to farmers for production purposes.

4. The Federal Intermediate Credit Bank which served as a "go-between." It arranged to dispose of the securities of the three operating banks to the financial agencies of the country.

All the money furnished by the government has now been

Fig. 25-4. Credit assistance is necessary to supply capital for investments in new technology, such as irrigation. (Courtesy, University of Wisconsin Department of Agricultural Journalism)

repaid. The Federal Farm Credit System is now a quasi-government system which operates on its own and is farmer-owned and -controlled.

A Third Type of Help

Since the 1930s the federal government has had various types of programs designed to assist farmers in getting better prices for their products and in stabilizing their output to meet actual market demands better. These programs change frequently, and alert farm managers must keep up with new programs to decide if they may benefit from them.

Questions and Problems for Class Discussion

1. For many years, federal and state governments have provided information to farmers on control of plant and animal diseases, weed control, and improvements in methods of producing crops and livestock. This has been a program of indirect aid to farmers. Similar help has not been given to manufacturers of industrial products. Why has such farm assistance been necessary?

2. How else might such aid to farmers be carried on?

3. In addition to the indirect aid to farmers, they have also had an opportunity to borrow money through agencies sponsored by the government. Describe those programs.

4. Discuss the role of private agricultural consultants in the future. Could this provide you a career opportunity?

Appendices

APPENDIX A

General Farm Management Information

1. FARM BUSINESS AGREEMENTS

Essentials of a Farm Lease

The purpose of a farm lease is to specify in detail the agreement between the landlord and the tenant.

The agreement should be as fair as possible to the landlord, the tenant, and the soil. The soil is a third party to this contract. The tenant and landlord should share in the income in the same proportion as the contribution which each has made to the business.

A good farm lease should provide for profitable farming and allow for a system of farming that will maintain or increase the productivity of the farm. It should give as much assurance as possible to the tenant that if a good job is done the lease will continue.

The Lease Should Be in Writing. Farm leases should be written. A written lease may be no more binding than an oral lease, but taking the time to discuss the different items and to write them out may avoid many misunderstandings between landlord and tenant.

The written lease gets the landlord and tenant together on different items before, rather than after, the farm is leased.

Legal Requirements. There are certain points that are common in all states to make a lease legal. It need not be written on a complicated form to be legal. It should state the names of the parties involved and have their signatures. It should describe the property to be leased. It must state the terms of the rental agreed upon, the date, and the period of time which the lease is to run.

The body of the lease can go into detail concerning contributions furnished by the landlord and the tenant and the division of income between the landlord and the tenant. It is essential to state what goes with the farm and what does not. If some land and buildings or other property on the farm is not included, it is best to state it in the lease.

Long-Term Leases. One of the unfortunate features about renting farms is that too many tenants move every year. The fault may be in the way the lease is written. Frequent moving is difficult for both the tenant and the land. Provisions can be made for automatic renewal from year to year.

To terminate such a lease, one party must give notice in writing to the other, usually three to six months before the beginning of the next year's lease. Landlords will benefit by having the same tenant for several years, as it enables them to carry out many crop and livestock practices which add to the productivity of the soil.

Tenants should be assured of enough security of tenure to protect them from financial loss and to permit them to operate the farm most efficiently.

The farm lease may need to be changed considerably to meet some of the recent changes in markets, increased use of fertilizer, and use of pesticides. It is best to spell out what each, the landlord and the tenant, will do when new practices are followed on the farm.

Certain dairy markets require special cooling equipment and more exacting methods in handling the milk. The amount of application per acre of commercial fertilizer is increasing on most farms. Will the tenant and the landlord still share equally in this expense?

Some kinds of noxious weeds are controlled by using pre-emergence sprays and by spraying weeds in the corn row. Should the landlord pay for part of this cost if done by custom machine? The landlord may feel this is the best way to control the weeds and may be willing to pay for spraying. In the past, control of weeds and insects has been done with the tenant's labor supply. Some agreement should be made in the lease on items such as the minimum number of livestock to be kept, the number of acres seeded to legumes, and the number of acres of grassland, etc. It is also advisable to designate the analysis and amount of commercial fertilizer to be applied to the different crops. Modern drying, storage, and crop harvesting technology must be considered.

Divison of Income. The division of income is the most important part of the lease. The best way to divide income is to share in proportion to the contribution of each party in the expense items. This method will compensate both parties for their efforts. The trouble with many tenant and landlord agreements is that they follow too closely some lease form that is community custom without regard to the contribution of each.

Farms that have highly productive soil and good buildings should return to the landlords more than those which are run-down in soil fertility and poor buildings. Tenants are at a handicap on poor farms. Unless they receive a larger than usual percentage of the income, they will be ready to move at the end of the year. If good renters are to remain on farms, they must receive fair returns for their time.

The type of farming followed should also determine the division of income. It requires much more of the tenants' time to care for certain crops and livestock than for others. Tenants should realize this at the time the lease is made rather than find it out later. How and when settlement of income is to be made should be stated.

a. Sample Lease Forms—Cash and Share
(Crop and Livestock)

Sample cash and share lease forms appear on pages 438 through 457.

CASH FARM LEASE: form

The following Cash Lease is an example. *The parties to a lease should consult their attorneys before entering into a lease agreement.*

SECTION I. DATE, CONTRACTING PARTIES, DESCRIPTION OF PROPERTY, TERMS, AND EXTENT OF THE LEASE

1. This lease is made this _____ day of _____, 19_____, between _____ herein called the *Lessor*, and _____ herein called the *Lessee*.

2. The Lessor, in consideration of the agreements with the Lessee hereinafter set forth, hereby leases to the Lessee, to occupy and to use for agricultural purposes only, the _____
(name of farm)

farm, containing _____ acres (more or less), located in _____, _____, legally described as
(county)   (state)

_____ , _____ , _____ ,
(township)   (section)   (range)

with all fixed improvements thereon except _____
_____.

3. This lease shall become effective on the _____ day of _____, 19_____, and shall continue in force until the _____ day of _____, 19_____, and from year to year thereafter unless written notice of termination is given by either party to the other on or before the _____ day of _____.

4. The terms of this lease shall be binding on the heirs, personal representatives, successors, and assigns of both Lessor and Lessee, in the same manner as upon the original parties.

5. The Lessee shall neither assign this lease to any person or persons, nor sublet any part of the real estate for any purpose without written consent of the Lessor.

6. No partnership is established. The terms of this lease shall not be construed as establishing a partnership relation between the Lessor and the Lessee, and neither party is to be held liable for any debts or obligations incurred by the other without written consent except as permitted in Section _____ Clause _____.

SECTION II. LAND USE AND CROPPING PROGRAM

1. Approximately _____ acres of the farm are to be cultivated, _____ acres are to remain in permanent pasture, _____ acres in woods, pasture and _____ acres in woods not to be grazed. The tracts that are to be included in the respective classes shall be designated in writing by the Lessor at the beginning of the lease.

2. The combined annual acreage of cultivated crops shall not exceed _____ acres. Each field and the crops to be grown or rotation to be followed are listed as follows:

	Crops to Be Grown or
Field	*Rotation to Be Followed*
_____	_____
_____	_____
_____	_____
_____	_____

3. During each year that this lease is effective, sufficient legume or legume-grass shall be seeded or maintained to provide for approximately _____ acres. Seed required for such crops shall be furnished by _____. If any legume, or legume-grass seedings fail, the substitute crop or crops shall be mutually agreed upon.

4. No permanent pasture shall be plowed without the written consent of the Lessor.

5. **Other Provisions:** _____
_____.

NOTE: SECTION III IS IN FOUR PARTS TO ACCOMMODATE THE REGULAR CASH RENT AND THE THREE VARIABLE CASH RENTS. (Strike out the three section III's which do *not* apply.)

SECTION III-A. RENTAL PAYMENTS AND SECURITY—CASH RENT (Regular)

1. **Amount of Rent and Time of Payment:** The annual cash rent for this farm to be paid by the Lessee to the Lessor is $_____ and is to be paid in _____ installment(s) of $_____ each. The first installment is to be paid on _____, 19____. The other installments are to be paid as follows: ___
_____.

2. **Other Provisions:** _____
_____.

3. Overdue rental payments shall bear interest at the effective annual rate of _____%.

SECTION III-B. RENTAL PAYMENTS AND SECURITY—VARIABLE CASH RENT (Price Risk)

1. **Amount of Rent and Time of Payment:** The annual rent for this farm to be paid by the Lessee to the Lessor is the dollar value of

_____
(total amount of physical quantity, i.e., bu., tons, lbs.)

based on _____, _____,
(specific grade or quality measure)   (crop type or kind)

priced as follows:

a. The price location point will be _____.
(market or place)

b. The price will be based on the crop and grade as stated above. The price used will be an average of _____
(months, dates, times)

quoted in _____
(market news sources)

at the close of the market days for the dates, months, and times stipulated above.

c. The following adjustments shall be made to the unit price:

(1) Grade _____
(2) Location _____
(3) Time _____

2. The first payment shall be made on _____ _____,
(month)   (date)

19_____, and shall be computed by taking the agreed upon expected yield and grade, times an agreed upon expected price, times _____% of the agreed upon physical amount.

The other installment(s) to be paid as follows: _____
_____.

3. Upon mutual agreement, the Lessor can take the agreed upon physical amount of the crop in kind. If this option is selected, it must be stated by the Lessor in writing 60 days before the first installment is due. The Lessor will then receive the rent in kind at the harvest of the crop.

4. **Other Provisions:** (such as arrangements for hauling, storing, and marketing of Lessor's crop) _____
_____.

5. Overdue rental payments shall bear interest at the effective annual rate of _____%.

SECTION III-C. RENTAL PAYMENTS AND SECURITY—VARIABLE CASH RENT (Price and Yield Risk)

1. **Amount of Rent and Time of Payment:** The annual rent for this farm to be paid by the Lessee to the Lessor is the dollar value of _____% of the total physical amount of _____, priced as follows:

(crop type or kind)

    a. The price location point will be _____.

(market or place)

    b. The price will be based on the crop as stated above.
The price used will be an average of _____

(months, dates, times)

quoted in _____

(market news sources)

at the close of the market days for the dates, months, and times stipulated above for the kind and grade of crop produced, the grade of crop to be determined by generally accepted grading procedures *or* as follows: _____

_____.

    c. The following adjustments (if any) shall be made to the unit price:
        (1) Grade _____
        (2) Location _____
        (3) Time _____

2. The first payment shall be made on _____ _____,

(month)   (date)

19_____, and shall be computed by taking the agreed upon expected price times _____% of the agreed upon expected physical amount.

    The other installment(s) to be paid as follows: _____

_____.

3. Upon mutual agreement, the Lessor can take the agreed upon physical amount of the crop in kind. If this option is selected, it must be stated by the Lessor in writing 60 days before the first installment is due. The Lessor will then receive the rent in kind at the harvest of the crop.

4. **Other Provisions:** (such as arrangements for hauling, storing, and marketing of Lessor's crop) _____

_____.

5. Overdue rental payments shall bear interest at the effective annual rate of _____%.

SECTION III-D. RENTAL PAYMENTS AND SECURITY—VARIABLE CASH RENT (Sliding Scale)

1. **Amount of Rent and Time of Payment:** The annual rent for this farm to be paid by the Lessee to the Lessor is the dollar value as stipulated in the sliding scale "Cash Rent Table" at the time of division or disposition of crop.

CASH RENT TABLE

$ Value of Crop Production	Lessor's Share of Crop Percent	
$_____	$_____	Base Amount
$_____	_____%	
$_____	_____%	
$_____	_____%	
$_____	_____%	

2. The "$ Value of Crop Production" used is to be determined at the time of the division or disposition of the crop. The price and physical measurement method is to be mutually agreed upon at the beginning of this lease or in the event of sale to market the proceeds are to be divided as in paragraph 1.

3. Upon mutual agreement, the Lessor can take the agreed upon physical amount of the crop in kind. If this option is selected, it must be stated by the Lessor in writing 30 days before the division or disposition of the crop.

4. **Other Provisions:** (such as arrangements for hauling, storing, and marketing of Lessor's crop) _____
_____.

5. Overdue rental payments shall bear interest at the effective annual rate of _____%.

SECTION IV. THE LESSOR AGREES AS FOLLOWS: (Strike out items or parts of items not desired.)

1. **Taxes and Insurance:** To pay all the taxes and the assessments against the real estate, all taxes on the Lessor's personal property on the farm, and premiums for the insurance carried on the farm buildings.

2. **Buildings, Fences, and Water Supply:** To furnish materials for maintenance and repairs and for such improvements to buildings, fences, and wells as may be added; also labor for new fences and major repairs and improvements on buildings, fences, tile drains, and wells.

3. **Limestone:** To furnish all limestone used on the farm, together with all costs of hauling and spreading. If the Lessee hauls and/or spreads the limestone, furnished by the Lessor, the Lessor shall pay the Lessee the customary rate per ton for such work done. The rates for such work shall be mutually agreed upon before the work is done. The Lessor agrees to apply limestone in an amount sufficient to bring the pH to a _____ pH level.

4. **Repairs and Improvements:** To make the following repairs or improvements on the farm by the dates specified or as near as practicable thereto:

Repair or Improvement	*To Be Completed By:*
_____ Date:	_____
_____ Date:	_____
_____ Date:	_____

5. **Additional Items:** To furnish the following additional items (for example: this might include items such as silo unloader, barn cleaner, bulk milk tank, irrigaton equipment, grass and legume seed, pesticides for use on existing unusual pest infestations, corrective fertilizer to correct existing low fertility levels, etc.): _____
_____.

6. **Other Provisions:** _____
_____.

SECTION V. THE LESSEE AGREES AS FOLLOWS:

1. **Soil Conservation:** To follow the Soil Conservation Plan for the farm. When the farm does not have a conservation plan, then to follow farming practices that are generally recommended and best adapted to this type of farm and for this locality unless other practices are agreed upon.

2. **Maintenance of Conservation Practices:** To preserve established water courses, tile drains, tile outlets, grass waterways and terraces and to refrain from any operation that will injure them. Land subject to serious erosion is not to be fall plowed. The numbers or descriptions of such fields are as follows: _____
_____.

3. **Labor:** To furnish all labor for the *minor* repair and the *minor* improvements of buildings, fences, and drains, the material to be furnished by the Lessor. The buildings, fences, and other improvements on the farm are to be kept in as good repair and condition as they are at the beginning of the lease, or in as good repair and condition as they may be put in by the Lessor during the term of the lease; ordinary wear, depreciation, or unavoidable destruction excepted.

4. **Hauling Material:** To haul to the farm, except when other arrangements are agreed to with the Lessor, any material provided by the Lessor for the *minor* repair or *minor* improvement of buildings, fences, and drains; and to do all the necessary hauling on the farm at no expense to the Lessor.

5. **Manure Hauling:** To keep the manure hauled out and spread. Manure is not to be removed from the farm. If, at the end of the lease period, the Lessee does not have the manure hauled out and spread, Lessee agrees to pay the Lessor at the rate of $_____ a load (a load is defined as _____ cubic feet of solid manure *or* _____ gallons of liquid manure) for such manure for the purpose of enabling the Lessor to hire such work done.

6. **Grazing:** To keep livestock out of the fields when the soil is soft and to protect sod crops, especially new seedings, from too close grazing that might impair the following year's crop. To refrain from grazing or taking a crop from legume seedings during the crucial regrowth period until growth terminates.

7. **Weed Control:** To cut, spray, or otherwise control noxious weeds before they go to seed. To cut or control weeds in lots, around buildings, or along roadsides whenever necessary to prevent re-seeding. Noxious weeds to be defined as: _____

_____.

8. **Insurance Restrictions:** Not to house automobiles, motor trucks, or tractors in barns or otherwise violate restrictions of the Lessor's insurance contract and local ordinances, if any.

9. **Other Restrictions:** Not to add electrical wiring, plumbing, or heating to any buildings without the consent of the Lessor. If consent is given, such additions must meet standards and requirements of power and insurance companies and local ordinances, if any.

10. **Relinquishing Possession:** To yield peaceable possession of the farm at the termination of this lease.

11. **Other Provisions:** _____

_____.

SECTION VI. REIMBURSEMENT FOR UNEXHAUSTED APPLI-CATIONS OF FERTILIZER

At the termination of this lease, the Lessor agrees to compensate the Lessee for (check one— None ____ ⅓ ____ ½ ____ ⅔ ____ Other _____) of the Les-
(specify)
see's cost of commercial fertilizer applied the last year of the lease, except for nitrogen applied alone or fertilizer applied in the row for cultivated crops.

SECTION VII. RIGHTS AND PRIVILEGES

1. The Lessor or anyone designated by him shall have the right of entry at any reasonable time to inspect his property and/or the farming methods being used.

2. The Lessee shall have the right to use dead or fallen timber for fuel, but he shall neither cut live trees nor market timber, gravel, or any other part of the real estate without the written consent of the Lessor. The Lessee shall not have any above or below ground mineral rights.

3. The Lessee shall have the right to erect, maintain, and remove at his expense, temporary fences and movable buildings on the farm, provided that such fences or buildings or their removal does not damage the Lessor's property in any way.

4. If this lease is terminated before the end of the normal production year the Lessee shall have the right of entry for the purpose of the annual harvesting of crops seeded before the termination of the lease in accordance with normal farm practices, or to sell his interest in such annual crops either to the Lessor or to the succeeding Lessee provided the Lessee does not interfere with normal field operations of the succeeding season. If the Lessee, in view of the approaching termination of the lease, fails to plant crops in a timely manner and in accordance with accepted farming practices, the Lessor or his designated agent shall have right of entry to plant crops.

5. If this lease is terminated before the Lessee shall have obtained the benefits from any labor or formerly agreed upon expense he incurred in operating the farm, according to contract or agreement with the Lessor during the current lease year, the Lessor shall reimburse the Lessee for such labor or expense. The Lessee shall present, in writing to the Lessor, his claim for such reimbursement at least _____ days before the termination of this lease.

6. **Other Provisions:** _____
_____.

SECTION VIII. ENFORCEMENT OF AGREEMENTS AND ARBITRATION

1. Failure of either the Lessor or the Lessee to comply with the agreements set forth in this lease shall make him liable for damages to the other party. Any claim by either party for such damages shall be presented in writing to the other party, at least _____ days after the termination of this lease.

2. Matters which are not specified in this lease, but which may arise, shall be settled by agreement between Lessor and Lessee.

3. In the event the Lessor and Lessee cannot reach an agreement on any matter connected with the lease or its application, the matter shall be referred to a committee of three arbitrators, one chosen by the Lessor, one by the Lessee, and the third by the two thus chosen. None of said arbitrators shall be related to either party or have any interest, directly or indirectly, personally or otherwise, in the questions decided. The decision of this committee shall be accepted as final by both Lessor and Lessee. The cost of arbitration shall be borne equally by both parties.

4. **Other Provisions:** _____

_____.

SECTION IX. TERMINATION OF AGREEMENT

1. Either Lessor or Lessee may terminate this lease by giving written notice of termination at least _____ days prior to the end of the lease period.

2. Failure on the part of either party to perform any of the terms, covenants, or conditions covered by this agreement shall constitue grounds for termination thereof, at the option of the other party.

Failure on the part of the Lessee to perform any of the terms, covenants, or conditions covered by this agreement shall give the Lessor the right to enter into possession of the premises, and to perform, or have performed, any of the terms, covenants, or conditions remaining undone by Lessee and to sell or retain sufficient of the current year's crop to cover all costs incurred in fulfilling the contract. In case of dispute, the decisions as to the violation of the agreement shall rest with the committee of arbitration herein provided for.

SECTION X. OTHER AGREEMENTS

_____

_____

_____

_____.

SECTION XI. SIGNATURES

_____   _____
(Date)   (Lessor)

_____   _____
(Date)   (Lessee)

SHARE FARM LEASE: form[1]

[For the Share Leases, delete Sections III, IV, and V from the Cash Farm Lease and add the following to Section VII—Rights and Privileges.]

7. The Lessee shall have the right to use as a garden or a truck patch not more than _____ acres of the farm and orchard without charge.

8. Neither party shall have the right to bind the other, without his consent, by any contract or agreement that is not provided for in this lease. Any purchase or sales of jointly-owned property involving more than $_____ shall be made by mutual agreement.

9. The Lessee shall have the right to use eggs, poultry, and dairy products produced from jointly-owned livestock, as needed for his family and for hired help. Settlement between Lessor and Lessee for meat animals slaughtered for home use shall be made on the basis of their live-weight market value at the time of slaughter.

[Then, add the following sections to the Share Lease.]

RECORDS AND FINANCIAL SETTLEMENTS

1. The Lessee Lessor (cross out one) shall keep a full account of all transactions in the matter agreed upon by both parties in this lease.

2. Record system used shall be either an electronically computed system or a hand-computed record book adapted for this type of farming.

3. A duplicate copy of records showing full information on income and expenses shall be provided the Lessor Lessee (cross out one) each month.

4. A financial settlement shall be made by the Lessor and Lessee by the _____ day of each month, or at intervals mutually agreed upon.
Specify: _____
_____.

5. All joint receipts shall be handled as follows: _____
_____.

6. All joint disbursements shall be handled as follows: _____
_____.

---

[1]Adapted from Cash Farm Lease A2850-1, Livestock Share Lease A2851-1, and Crop Share Lease A2852-1, by L. F. Huber, R. A. Luening, A. R. Allen, University of Wisconsin–Madison.

FARM MANAGEMENT AND OPERATION

1. All matters involving the operating and management of this farm shall be mutually agreed upon. In the event the two parties cannot agree, then the provisions of the section on Enforcements of Agreements and Arbitration shall prevail. Policy for off-farm work by the Lessee should be agreed upon.

THE LESSEE AGREES AS FOLLOWS: (Strike out items or parts of items not desired.)

1. **Soil Conservation:** To follow the Soil Conservation Plan for the farm. When the farm does not have a conservation plan, then to follow farming practices that are generally recommended and best adapted to this type of farm and for this locality unless other practices are agreed upon.

2. **Power and Machinery:** To furnish all power, machinery, and movable equipment and all operation and maintenance expenses on same to operate the farm properly, except as otherwise provided for.

3. **Labor:** To provide all labor required to operate the farm except as otherwise provided for.

4. **Taxes and Insurance:** To pay all taxes and insurance on property owned solely by him.

5. **Fuel, Oil, Grease:** To furnish fuel, oil, and grease for all farm machinery unless otherwise shared.

6. **Labor:** To furnish all labor for the *minor* repairs and the *minor* improvements of buildings, fences, and drains, the material to be furnished by the Lessor. The buildings, fences, and other improvements on the farm are to be kept in as good repair and condition as they are at the beginning of the lease, or in as good repair and condition as they may be put in by the Lessor during the term of the lease; ordinary wear, depreciation, or unavoidable destruction excepted.

7. **Hauling Crops:** To haul the Lessor's share of the crops produced to a mutually agreed upon elevator at harvest without expense to the Lessor. At the Lessor's option, the Lessee shall store the Lessor's share of the crops in space provided.

8. **Hauling Material:** To haul to the farm, except when other arrangements are agreed to with the Lessor, any material provided by the Lessor for the *minor* repairs or *minor* improvements of buildings, fences, and drains; and to do all the necessary hauling on the farm at no expense to the Lessor.

9. **Hauling Manure:** To keep the manure hauled out and spread. Manure is not to be removed from the farm. If, at the end of the lease period, the Lessee does not have the manure hauled out and spread, the Lessee agrees to pay the Lessor at the rate of $_____ a load (a load is defined as _____ cubic feet of solid manure *or* _____ gallons of liquid manure) for such manure for the purpose of enabling the Lessor to hire such work done.

10. **Grazing:** To keep livestock out of the fields when the soil is soft and to protect sod crops, especially new seedings, from too close grazing that might impair the following year's crop. To refrain from grazing or taking a crop from legume seedings during the crucial regrowth period until growth terminates.

11. **Maintenance and Conservation Practices:** To preserve established water courses, tile drains, tile outlets, grass waterways, and terraces and to refrain from any operation that will injure them. Land subject to serious erosion is not to be fall plowed. The numbers or descriptions of such fields are as follows: _____

_____ .

12. **Weed Control:** To cut, spray, or otherwise control noxious weeds before they go to seed. To cut or control weeds in lots, around buildings, or along roadsides whenever necessary to prevent re-seeding. Noxious weeds to be defined as: _____

_____ .

13. **Insurance Restrictions:** Not to house automobiles, motor trucks, or tractors in barns or otherwise violate restrictions of the Lessor's insurance contract and local ordinances, if any.

14. **Other Restrictions:** Not to add electrical wiring, plumbing, or heating to any buildings without the consent of the Lessor. If consent is given, such additions must meet standards and requirements of power and insurance companies and local ordinances, if any.

15. **Relinquishing Possession:** To yield peaceable possession of the farm at the termination of this lease.

16. **Residence of Lessee:** To personally reside on the farm for the full period of the lease unless Lessor agrees to some other locality.

17. **Other Provisions:** _____

_____ .

DIVISION OF FARM INCOME

1. The Lessor and the Lessee shall share at the following agreed upon percentage, _____ Lessor _____ Lessee (excluding sale of non-jointly-

owned items), all gross farm income, except the items listed which shall be shared by the two parties as follows:

Gross Receipts From:	Lessor's Share	Lessee's Share

DIVISION OF CROPS

1. All harvested crops produced shall be divided _____ percent to the Lessor and _____ percent to the Lessee. Exceptions are listed below and shall be shared as follows:

Crop	Lessor's Share	Lessee's Share

LESSOR AGREES AS FOLLOWS: (strike out items or parts of items not desired.)

1. **Land and Fixed Improvements:** To furnish the land and the fixed improvements previously referred to.

2. **Taxes, Assessments, and Insurance:** To pay all taxes, assessments, and insurance on property owned solely by him.

3. **Materials for Repairs and Improvements:** To furnish all materials necessary for the repair, improvement, and construction of buildings, wells, drains, and fences on the farm.

4. **Labor for Repairs and Improvements:** To pay the labor for making all *major* improvements or *major* repairs on buildings, drains, and fences on the farm.

5. **Limestone:** To furnish all limestone used on the farm, together with all costs of hauling and spreading. If the Lessee hauls and/or spreads the limestone, furnished by the Lessor, the Lessor shall pay the Lessee the customary rate per ton for such work done. The rates for such work shall be mutually agreed upon before the work is done. The Lessor agrees to apply limestone in an amount sufficient to bring the pH to a _____ pH level.

6. **Repairs and Improvements:** To make the following repairs or improvements on the farm by the dates specified or as near as practicable thereto:

Repair or Improvement	*To Be Completed By:*
_____ Date:	_____
_____ Date:	_____
_____ Date:	_____

7. **Additional Items:** To furnish the following additional items (for example: this might include items such as silo unloader, barn cleaner, bulk milk tank, irrigation equipment, grass and legume seed, pesticides for use on existing unusual pest infestations, corrective fertilizer to correct existing low fertility levels, etc.): _____
_____.

8. **Other Provisions:** _____
_____.

TERMINATION OF AGREEMENT

1. Either Lessor or Lessee may terminate this lease by giving written notice of termination at least _____ days prior to the end of the lease period.

2. Failure on the part of either party to perform any of the terms, covenants, or conditions covered by this agreement shall constitute grounds for termination thereof, at the option of the other party.

Failure on the part of the Lessee to perform any of the terms, covenants, or conditions covered by this agreement shall give the Lessor the right to enter into possession of the premises, and to perform, or have performed, any of the terms, covenants, or conditions remaining undone by the Lessee and to sell or retain sufficient of the current year's crop to cover all costs incurred in fulfilling the contract. In case of dispute, the decisions as to the violation of the agreement shall rest with the committee of arbitration herein provided for.

3. At the termination of the lease, the co-owned property shall be divided as follows (strike out items or parts of items not desirable or applicable):

a. All hay, grain, silage, and other feeds and all supplies co-owned, including straw and other bedding materials, shall be divided by measure or value, whichever is more equitable, with the Lessor and Lessee each receiving title to his respective share.

b. If in connection with any of the co-owned classes of property, the parties mutually agree to set aside the described plan of division, it is agreed that the Lessee shall set a value on the entire amount of the respective co-owned classes of property on the basis of which he will either sell his undivided one-half interest or buy that of the Lessor, at the option of the Lessor.

    c. If the parties mutually agree, the co-owned property may be disposed of by private or public sale arranged for that purpose at a reasonable time and place.

[Add the following sections to the Crop Share Lease.]

THE LESSOR AND LESSEE AGREE:

To furnish or pay for all direct crop production expenses not listed in other sections on a _____ percent by Lessor and _____ percent by Lessee division.

    1. Exceptions to the above division of expenses are listed below and will be shared as follows:

		Percent of Expenses to Be Paid by:	
Expenses for:	*Crop*	*Lessor*	*Lessee*
_____	_____	_____	_____
_____	_____	_____	_____

    2. Ownership of power, machinery, and movable equipment and maintenance and repairs on same not provided for in other sections and to be jointly owned shall be furnished as follows:

	Percent to Be Furnished by:	
Item	*Lessor*	*Lessee*
_____	_____	_____
_____	_____	_____

    3. **Additional Items:** _____
_____.

PRIVILEGE RENT PAYMENTS (for use of resources where the returns are *not* shared)

    1. The Lessee shall pay to the Lessor $_____ annually for the use of the permanent pasture and $_____ annually for the use of the buildings and lots on the farm. The privilege rent is to be paid in _____ installments of $_____ each. The first installment is to be paid on _____, 19_____. The other installments are to be paid as follows: _____
_____.

Other Provisions: _____

_____.

    2. Overdue privilege rental payments shall bear interest at the effective annual rate of _____ percent.

[Add the following sections to the Livestock Share Lease.]

THE LESSOR AND LESSEE AGREE:

Jointly to furnish the following items in equal shares (or _____ percent by Lessor and _____ percent by Lessee).

    1. All livestock, except for livestock listed in item 10 of this section.

    2. All crop expenses such as seeds and plants, inoculation, disease treatment materials, spray materials for control of weeds and insects in crops and in fence rows, soil testing, all fertilizers, twine, and other supplies used in the normal production of crops and livestock.

    3. Ownership of the following machinery and livestock equipment, and materials and skilled labor for repairs on same:

_____   _____   _____

_____   _____   _____

_____   _____   _____

    4. All feed, bedding, salt, and minerals for jointly-owned livestock including trucking, processing, and storage costs of farm produced grains to be fed and delivery costs of all feed to the farm.

    5. All veterinary expenses, breeding fees, livestock testing, D.H.I., registration fees, marketing costs, and other incidental livestock expenses for jointly-owned livestock.

    6. All the farm share of electricity; or _____.

    7. All fuel for tractors; or _____.

    8. All insurance and taxes on jointly-owned personal property.

    9. Harvesting costs and contributions to livestock production will be shared as follows:

Operation	Lessor's Share of Machinery Hire (Percent)		Lessor's Payment to Lessee for Use of Lessee's Machinery ($)
Combining	_____	Or	_____
Corn shelling	_____	Or	_____
Hay baling	_____	Or	_____
Trucking stock	_____	Or	_____

10. **Ownership of Livestock, Feed, and Supplies:** All livestock (except) _____
shall be owned jointly by Lessor and Lessee. Except as otherwise agreed in writing, no other livestock shall be kept on the farm. All feed and other supplies on hand at the beginning and during the terms of the lease shall likewise be owned jointly. The co-ownership shall be arranged by appraisal, prior to the beginning of the lease term of the property contributed by each party. The party furnishing property of higher value shall be compensated by the other party to an amount sufficient to give co-ownership as agreed upon.

11. **Additional Items:** _____
_____ .

INVENTORY SECTION

I. Feeds and Supplies

	Lessor		Lessee	
	Quantity	Value	Quantity	Value
Hay	_____	$_____	_____	$_____
Corn silage	_____	_____	_____	_____
Low moisture hay silage	_____	_____	_____	_____
Other silage	_____	_____	_____	_____
Straw	_____	_____	_____	_____
Ear corn	_____	_____	_____	_____
Dried shell corn	_____	_____	_____	_____
High moisture corn	_____	_____	_____	_____
Oats	_____	_____	_____	_____
Barley	_____	_____	_____	_____
Other grain	_____	_____	_____	_____
Concentrates	_____	_____	_____	_____
Other feeds	_____	_____	_____	_____
Grass seed	_____	_____	_____	_____
Fertilizer	_____	_____	_____	_____
Gas	_____	_____	_____	_____
Oil	_____	_____	_____	_____
Chemicals	_____	_____	_____	_____
Other supplies	_____	_____	_____	_____
Total Value		$_____		$_____

II. Livestock

	Lessor		Lessee	
	Quantity	Value	Quantity	Value
Dairy				
Milk cows	_____	$_____	_____	$_____
Bred heifers	_____	_____	_____	_____
Open heifers	_____	_____	_____	_____
Calves (under 6 mos.) ...	_____	_____	_____	_____
Dairy steers	_____	_____	_____	_____
Dairy bulls	_____	_____	_____	_____
Hogs				
Brood sows	_____	_____	_____	_____
Boars	_____	_____	_____	_____
Gilts	_____	_____	_____	_____
Butchers	_____	_____	_____	_____
Feeder pigs	_____	_____	_____	_____
Beef				
Brood cows	_____	$_____	_____	$_____
Replacement heifers	_____	_____	_____	_____
Calves	_____	_____	_____	_____
Feeders	_____	_____	_____	_____
Poultry				
Laying hens	_____	_____	_____	_____
Others	_____	_____	_____	_____
Other livestock				
_____	_____	_____	_____	_____
_____	_____	_____	_____	_____
Total Value		$_____		$_____

[*Add the following to the section: Termination of Agreement.*]

    d. The Lessee shall divide each class of livestock, as cows, steers, calves, hogs, and poultry, etc., into two groups and the Lessor shall take his choice of the two groups of each. In case the groupings cannot be made of nearly equal value, the difference in monetary value shall be stated before the choice is made and that amount paid to the one choosing the grouping of lesser value.

b. Sample Father-Son-Type Agreement[2]

THIS AGREEMENT is made between _____,
father and _____, son.

1. **PURPOSE:** The purpose of this agreement is to make possible the joint operation of a farm business on the land owned or rented by the father or by the father and son. The land included in this agreement consists of _____ acres and is in Section _____, Twp. _____, Range _____ in _____ County, State of _____.

2. **PERIOD COVERED:** This agreement shall start on the _____ day of _____, 19_____, and shall continue from year to year thereafter until written notice of termination is given by either party to the other at least _____ months before expiration of this agreement or renewal date.

3. **CONTRIBUTIONS:** Contributions to the business are made as follows:

a. It is assumed that the father owns the real estate.

b. **Personal Property:** At the beginning of this agreement, the father and the son shall make a complete inventory of the father's farm personal property. This inventory shall set forth the quantities and values of all livestock, machinery, movable equipment, feed, seed, and supplies furnished by each.

c. **Labor and Management:** Unless other arrangements are mutually agreeable, both the father and the son shall devote their full time to the labor and management required to operate the farm. The father and the son each shall receive the amount shown in the table for his labor on the farm during the year:

	Father or _____			Son or _____		
Contribution	Value ($)	Rate (%)	Value of Annual Contribution ($)	Value ($)	Rate (%)	Value of Annual Contribution ($)
Land						
Interest						
Taxes						
(Total Value)	$_____	_____%	$_____	$_____	_____%	$_____

(Continued)

_____
[2]Also for agreements between father and daughter, father and son-in-law, etc. An attorney should be consulted in drawing up any legal arrangement.

Contribution	Father or _____			Son or _____		
	Value ($)	Rate (%)	Value of Annual Contribution ($)	Value ($)	Rate (%)	Value of Annual Contribution ($)
Buildings						
Depreciation						
Interest						
Repair						
Taxes						
Insurance						
(Total Value)	$_____	_____%	$_____	$_____	_____%	$_____
Machinery and Equipment						
Depreciation						
Interest						
Repair						
Taxes						
Insurance						
(Total Value)	$_____	_____%	$_____	$_____	_____%	$_____
Livestock (Breeding and Dairy)						
Depreciation						
Interest						
Taxes						
Insurance						
(Total Value)	$_____	_____%	$_____	$_____	_____%	$_____
Labor and Management			$_____			$_____
Other Contributions	$_____	_____%	$_____	$_____	_____%	$_____

TOTAL ANNUAL CONTRIBUTION $		TOTAL ANNUAL CONTRIBUTION $
PERCENT TOTAL CONTRIBUTION %		PERCENT TOTAL CONTRIBUTION %

TOTAL ANNUAL CONTRIBUTION BY ALL PARTIES $

4. **FARM ACCOUNTS:** The father or son, with the assistance and cooperation of the other, shall keep the following farm records in a farm account book:

    a. A record of farm receipts from all sources.

    b. A record of all farm expenses paid or incurred during the year.

    c. An annual inventory of all livestock, grains, feeds, seeds, fertilizer, and all other kinds of working capital on the farm on the first and last day of this agreement.

    d. Depreciation records on permanent improvements and equipment.

5. **FARM RECEIPTS AND EXPENSES:**

    a. **When the son furnishes only labor:** The father shall receive all the income and pay all the farm expenses. The son shares in the net farm profits in proportion to his contribution.
Net farm profits shall be calculated as follows:

Total sales and income	$_____	
Inventory at the end of the year (includes livestock, feeds, seeds, and supplies)	$_____	
Total		(a) $_____
Inventory at the beginning of the year	$_____	
Livestock purchases	$_____	
Total		(b) $_____
Gross farm profits (a − b)		$_____
Cash operating expenses (not including new buildings or equipment or allowances to son)	$_____	
Depreciation on buildings and equipment	$_____	
Total expenses		$_____
Net farm profit		$_____

    b. **When the son buys one-half interest in livestock, equipment, and feeds:**
    Division of Farm Receipts:
       (1) The father shall receive the customary or calculated landowner's share of the gross farm receipts under the customary or calculated livestock-share contract.
       (2) The father and the son, as the co-operators, shall receive and share the customary or calculated renter's share of the gross

farm receipts under the customary or calculated livestock-share contract.

Farm Operating Expenses:

(1) The father shall pay all expenses associated with his real estate, including principal and interest paid on his real estate mortgages; taxes and insurance on his real estate; assessments against his real estate; materials for the repair of buildings, drains, and other fixed improvements; and the cost (including spreading) of all limestone and rock phosphate used on his land.

(2) As the landowner the father shall pay the share of the other farm operating expenses that is customarily paid or calculated in the community by a landowner who rents his farm on a livestock-share basis.

6. **ADVANCE PAYMENTS:** Each shall receive advance payments against his share of the net income of $_____ each month. It is agreed that the son shall not be required to make any refund in case the advance payments exceed the son's share of the net farm profit.

7. **HOUSING, ETC.:** (Strike out clauses or words which do not apply.) The father is to provide the son, without charge, the following:

    a. Room, board, and laundry.

    b. Separate living quarters for himself and his family.

    c. Garden space of not more than one acre.

    d. Not more than _____ pounds of dressed pork and _____ pounds of dressed beef raised on the farm.

    e. Dairy products, poultry, and eggs produced on the farm needed to supply his family table.

The father is to receive a reasonable quantity of products raised for home use.

8. **COMPENSATION FOR IMPROVEMENTS:** The father and son shall agree on what permanent improvements shall be made. The original cost for permanent improvements shall be paid according to the ownership of the property on which the improvement is made. This cash outlay shall not be included as a farm expense for computing net farm profit. Such items are terraces, drainage systems, buildings, water systems, etc. Costs of upkeep and repairs shall be a part of the farm expenses.

9. **MANAGEMENT:** Decisions in regard to the operation of the farm shall ordinarily be made by mutual agreement between the father and the son, but in recognition of the major contribution, final decisions shall rest with the father. At the time of inventory any failure to agree on values shall be arbitrated by a third party selected jointly by the father and the son.

10. **SETTLEMENT**: At the end of the year, the inventory shall be taken and the net farm income computed. The son's share of the net farm income shall be calculated and any and all amounts over and above the total of the advance payments already made shall be paid within _____ days after the end of the year by the father to the son in complete settlement for the year.

11. **OTHER PROVISIONS**:

    a. Neither party to this agreement shall have the right to bind the other party by any contract or agreement not herein provided without the consent of the other party.

    b. Neither party to this agreement shall be held responsible for debts and/or obligations incurred by the other party that are not herein provided for without the consent of the other party.

12. **ENFORCEMENT OF AGREEMENTS AND ARBITRATION**:

    a. The failure of either the father or the son to comply with the agreements herein set forth shall make him liable for damages to the other party. Any claim by either party for such damage shall be presented in writing to the other party at least _____ days before the termination of this agreement.

    b. In case either or both parties to this agreement die during the period of the agreement, the terms of the agreement shall be binding on the heirs, executors, administrators, and assigns of the party or parties involved.

Both parties to this agreement hereby agree to submit to arbitration all matters of disagreement which may arise under this agreement and which they themselves are unable to settle. Such arbitration shall be made by a board of three disinterested persons, one appointed by the father, one by the son, and the third by the other two members. The decision of the three shall be binding upon both parties to this agreement.

Date _____, 19_____

          Signed:

_____

_____

c. Wage Incentive Guide

This is just a guide. Any plan should be adjusted to fit your particular situation. For example, payment rates on large, more productive, highly mechanized farms employing several people should be different from those on small, less productive, poorly mechanized farms. Incentive payments should be tied to work responsibilities carried out by the employees and those over which they have some control. Select the most appropriate incentive for your farm type and employee-employer relationship.

TOTAL FARM BUSINESS

Percent of Gross Income

1. 0.5 to 2.0% of all gross receipts (adjust to size and type of farm)

Percent of Profits

2. 10 to 40% of profits derived by subtracting from the total farm operating income (including sales of breeding and dairy livestock) a labor and management charge for the operator, and a return on the operator's equity in the business. Adjust this amount by the inventory change that took place in the farm's personal property and buildings during the last taxable year.

Wage Adjustments and Bonuses

3. End of year bonus of 2 to 10% of cash wages
4. Paid vacation of 2 to 4 weeks per year during the low labor load periods
5. An annual increase in cash wages of 3 to 10% (depending on the inflation rate) if the employee stays

LIVESTOCK

Hogs

Feeder pigs purchased and fed out

6. 30 to 60¢/feeder pig bought and fed out
7. 0.25 to 1% of hog sales less cost of feeder pigs

8. If death losses are less than 4%, the employee receives 25 to 40% of the market value of these market hogs saved.

Feeder pigs produced (for sale or fed out on the farm)

9. $.50 to $1/pig weaned
10. $2 to $3/pig weaned above eight/litter
11. $4 to $6/sow that weans more than eight pigs/litter
12. 0.5 to 2% of gross income from hogs, including inventory changes

Complete hog program

13. 50 to 75¢/hog marketed during the year if employee stays until end of year
14. $3 to $6/sow that weans more than eight pigs/litter
15. 0.25 to 1% of gross income from hogs including inventory changes

Dairy

16. 0.5 to 2% of milk sales, paid monthly
17. Start at 0.5% of milk check and increase pay by gradually moving up to 2% of milk check
18. 10¢/cwt. milk sold, and rate is increased by 2¢/yr. employee stays, up to a maximum of 25¢
19. 25 to 50¢/cwt. milk sold over 12,500 lbs./cow
20. 50 to 75¢/cwt. milk sold over 15,000 lbs./cow
21. $5 to $10 for each calf saved over a 90% calf crop at the end of the year
22. 15 to 25% for each 1,000 lbs. over 450,000 lbs. of milk sold per worker

Beef

Cow herds (calves sold at weaning)

23. $2 to $3 for each beef calf weaned
24. 10% of gross income over $175/cow
25. $15 to $20 for each calf weaned over a 90% calf crop

Feeder cattle purchased

26. $.25 to $1/head of fed cattle marketed
27. 0.5 to 1.5% of beef sales less cost of purchased feeders

CROPS

28. 0.5 to 1% of small grain produced, including grain equivalent in silage

29. 5 to 7¢/bu. corn produced over 100 bu./A   These yields should be

30. 10 to 12¢/bu. soybeans produced over 30   adjusted for soil type,
bu./A   climate, and techno-

31. $1 to $3/ton alfalfa that yields over 3.5   logical changes.
ton/A

32. 0.25 to 1% of gross crop sales

33. $1 to $2/A bonus if corn and soybeans are planted without a single row missed. Employees receive the bonus if they catch and replant missed rows on their own.

d. Would You Be a Good Partner?[3]

Partnerships more often stumble over human relationships than over business arrangements.

Here is a farm partnership test that will tell you your chances of success and happiness in a father-son partnership.

After scoring yourself, see how you rate.

If you find that you don't score as high as you thought you might, don't despair. The couples who helped set up the test say that a good partnership doesn't just happen—it is developed by people who "put themselves out" to make it work.

If you decide after the test that a farm partnership isn't for you, there's nothing wrong with that. After all, not everyone is cut out to be a business partner. Many successful farmers would be unhappy in a partnership.

Rating Scale	
If your answer to the question is:	*Give yourself these points:*
A firm "yes"	10
Yes	9
Yes, but barely	8
Maybe, with "conditions"	7
Could live with it	6
Possibly	5
Very difficult	4
Isn't likely	3
Highly improbable	2
A firm "no"	1

---

[3] By Claude W. Gifford. Reprinted by special permission from *Farm Journal.* Copyright © by Farm Journal, Inc.

Partnership test for fathers:

Points: (See Rating Scale.)

_____ Are you willing to work up a partnership agreement with your son, or son-in-law—now—and put it in writing?

_____ Can you usually "suggest" advice to your son, or son-in-law, as a business partner—rather than giving him commands or correcting him as a son?

_____ Can you willingly "give in" to your son's, or son-in-law's, wishes when you see that it means a great deal to him, his wife and family? Even though it might cost you money?

_____ Are you willing to turn over definite areas of important responsibility to your son, or son-in-law, for him to make the management decisions? And then live by his decisions without grumbling?

_____ Can you discuss family and business affairs with your son, or son-in-law, without getting emotional, angry, or upset?

_____ Are you willing to cut down on your personal spending a bit, or even go deeper into debt to expand your farm, or livestock operation, to provide money for two families?

_____ If your son, or son-in-law, makes a mistake that you might honestly have made at the same age, can you mark it up as a "useful experience" in helping him grow—rather than scold him about it, or brood over it yourself?

_____ Are you willing to have a heart-to-heart talk with your son, or son-in-law, so that he knows fully now what his future is on the farm?

_____ Are you willing to accept the fact that your son's wife and his family—and his future—are rightfully his No. 1 concern?

_____ Are you willing to make a contract now that protects your son's, or son-in-law's investment of time and money in the farm in case of an untimely death for you?

====== **Your total score**

For mothers:

Points:

_____ Can you accept the fact that your son or daughter has married a person of his or her choice and that this partner and their future together is his or her No. 1 concern?

_____ Can you willingly accept the fact that it may be necessary for you and your husband to go deeper into debt in order to provide more income for two families?

_____ Are you willing to go along with your husband now in giving your son, or son-in-law, and his family, a clear picture of their future on the farm?

_____ Can you take pride in your daughter's, or daughter-in-law's, clothes and her home furnishings for the pleasure they bring her and her family— rather than comparing them with what you have or being upset when yours are not as new?

_____ Can you refrain from giving advice to your daughter, or daughter-in-law, about raising her children—yet enjoy them as your grandchildren?

_____ Can you accept the fact that young couples are likely to be more carefree, spend money more lavishly and be more irresponsible than couples of your age?

_____ Can you willingly compliment your son or daughter about his or her married partner's good qualities once in a while—and refrain from dwelling on his or her shortcomings?

_____ Can you let your young "in-laws" have their own life—with couples their own age—and be free to come and go without comment while you stay a reserved distance away, even though they live on the same farm (or even in the same house)?

_____ Do you believe that a farm partnership is a business arrangement with advantages to both families—rather than a favor for the young family?

_____ As you strive to get along in the partnership would other people say that you are kind and considerate; that you are discreet about what you say; and that you are a person who controls her anger?

_____ **Your total score**

For sons and sons-in-law:

Points:

_____ Can you accept advice from your father, or father-in-law, with an open mind—believing that it might have merit? Are you willing to "give it a try" when it is important to him, even when you think the advice might not work?

_____ Are you patient enough to take time to "grow into" the farm business that your father, or father-in-law, has spent a lifetime building up?

_____ Since you have the advantage of youth, strength and stamina, are you willing to do more than your share of the physical work on the farm without complaining or feeling resentment?

_____ Can you appreciate with understanding that your father, or father-in-law, may have spent many years running the farm, making the decisions, perhaps even dealing with you as a boy—and that it will take some time for him to get used to your coming in as a decision-making business partner?

_____ Can you feel that you may be getting a much faster start in life, with much more certainty, as a result of the partnership—and that this "debt" is something you owe to the partnership?

_____ In return for the advantages that the partnership offers you, are you willing to take on the prospect that maybe you will be primarily responsible for caring for your parents or "in-laws" in later years?

_____ Can you refrain from pressing your advice on your parents or "in-laws" regarding their personal or family affairs—keeping in mind that they may enjoy things that you wouldn't?

_____ Can you willingly reserve for your father, or father-in-law, an important area of responsibility in the farm business, even in his advancing years? Can you avoid imposing your will on him, in this area, even though he may "hold back" the farm business some?

_____ Are you willing to keep a good set of record books of partnership expenses and income so that you and your father, or father-in-law, can see what is making money and what isn't?

(Continued)

_____ In situations that call for judgment affecting the partnership and your father, or father-in-law, can you willing lean over backward so that others would judge you as being calm, fair, and considerate?

===== **Your total score**

For daughters and daughters-in-law:

Points:

_____ Can you accept without resentment the fact that your mother, or mother-in-law, has spent a lifetime raising a family and making the farm go, and that she is entitled to rest, travel, good furniture— things that you may not be able to afford at this stage of life?

_____ Can you appreciate the faster start in life that you may be getting as a result of the partnership; and be truly thankful without resenting your dependence on the older couple?

_____ Can you "make do" with the house you have, the furniture, the car, the conveniences—without complaining that the older couple is responsible?

_____ Can you accept the fact that married "spats" are normal and then keep them to yourself without burdening the older couple or expecting them to take your side; and without blaming them or "taking it out" on them because of the partnership?

_____ Can you use good judgment in not imposing too much on your mother, or mother-in-law, to take care of the children, prepare meals, baby-sit, and the like?

_____ Can you teach your children to enjoy the grandparents' attention and their home when the grandparents want the children; but otherwise keep the children from "having the run" of the grandparents' house?

_____ Can you be discreet around your children so they aren't "carrying stories" between the two homes?

(Continued)

_____ Are you willing to make and keep a budget of household expenses that will help you plan and get along on what may be "short funds" due to two families living on the same farm?

_____ Can you refrain from "egging" on your husband to get him to make more of the farm decisions, ask for a bigger share of money, or do less of the work or chores—when this makes the partnership more difficult and your husband more uncomfortable?

_____ If you're a daughter-in-law of the older farm couple, are you willing to take time to "grow into" your husband's family? If you are a daughter of the older farm couple, can you make your husband the "confidant" of your thoughts; work out your "troubles" with him; and not lean on your daughter-family relationships so that your husband feels like an outsider?

===== **Your total score**

Your chances for success as a good farming partner

Total points

91 – 100	You're a fine partner
81 – 90	You should make it go
71 – 80	It may be rough
61 – 70	Barely "passable"
51 – 60	Think of another setup
41 – 50	You'll be very unhappy
31 – 50	You couldn't stand it
21 – 30	Please don't do it
10 – 20	Not a chance in the world

If the combined total points reach 320 or more for the four people (two couples) in the partnership, it should be a success. If the combined total is 240 or less, the partnership will have major troubles.

2. FARM RECORDS

The Net Worth Statement (a), Farm Earnings Statement (b), and Cash Flow Statement (c) are the "big three" financial management and business analysis tools. They are fully coordinated statements which complement and supplement each other. Before the statements can be used for analysis purposes, their accuracy should be checked. The Accuracy Check (d) can be used for this. Minor differences and discrepancies ($500 or less) may be ignored. But major ones need to be corrected before a valid analysis can be made.

The valuation scheme used in the Net Worth Statement should be noted at the top. The type of valuation scheme used will affect interpretation of the data. Valuation choices generally break into four types—cost, adjusted tax basis, fair market value less selling costs including income taxes due, and fair market value. Cost basis is the actual acquisition cost. Adjusted tax basis is original acquisition cost, plus improvements made, minus depreciation allowed or allowable. Fair market value is what a willing buyer would give a willing seller in terms of money, given adequate time and knowledge. In some cases the selling costs (legal fees, commissions, broker fees, etc.) and income tax liability are subtracted from the fair market value to arrive at the net figure the seller would receive. See the chapters on farm records and business analysis, Chapters 7 and 8, for more detailed discussion.

a. NET WORTH STATEMENT* AS OF _____, 19___
(Balance Sheet or Financial Statement)

Valuation Scheme Used:

Land and Improvements _____

Name _____

Building and Improvements _____

Address _____

Machinery and Equipment _____

Phone _____

Breeding and Dairy Livestock _____

Major Enterprise _____

Current Assets _____

ASSETS		LIABILITIES	
Current		**Current**	
1. Cash on hand	$_____	25. Principal payments due in next 12 months	$_____
2. Accounts receivable	$_____	a. Intermediate debt	$_____
3. Livestock held for sale	$_____	b. Long-term debt	$_____
4. Crops held for sale, or growing crops	$_____	26. Farm accounts payable	$_____
5. Feed, seed, supplies, and prepaid expenses	$_____	27. Rent, taxes, interest due and unpaid	$_____
6. Other current farm assets	$_____	28. Other current farm liabilities	$_____
7. Subtotal farm (1 + 2+ 3 + 4 +5 + 6)	$_____	29. Subtotal farm (25 +26 + 27 + 28)	$_____
8. Non-farm current assets	$_____	30. Non-farm current liabilities	$_____
9. Total Current Assets (7 + 8)	$_____	31. Total Current Liabilities (29 +30)	$_____
Intermediate		**Intermediate**	
10. Machinery and equipment	$_____	32. Deferred principal payments over 1 year—Less than 10 Years. Not due this year.	
11. Breeding and dairy livestock	$_____	a. _____ (specify)	$_____
12. Other intermediate farm assets	$_____	b. _____ (specify)	$_____
13. Subtotal farm (10 + 11+12)	$_____	c. _____ (specify)	$_____
		d. _____ (specify)	$_____
		33. Subtotal farm (32a + b + c + d)	$_____

(Continued)

a. NET WORTH STATEMENT (Continued)

14. Non-farm intermediate
    assets $_____

34. Non-farm intermediate
    liabilities $_____

15. Total Intermediate Assets
    (13 + 14) $_____

35. Total Intermediate Liabilities
    (33 + 34) $_____

16. Total Current Plus
    Intermediate Assets
    (9 + 15) $_____

36. Total Current Plus
    Intermediate Liabilities
    (31 + 35) $_____

Long-Term

Long-Term

17. Land and non-depreciable
    improvements $_____

18. Buildings and
    improvements $_____

19. Other long-term farm
    assets $_____

20. Subtotal farm
    (17 + 18 + 19) $_____

21. Non-farm long-term
    assets $_____

22. Total Long-Term Assets
    (20 + 21) $_____

37. Deferred principal payments
    over 10 years.
    Not due this year.

    a. _____ $_____
          (specify)

    b. _____ $_____
          (specify)

    c. _____ $_____
          (specify)

    d. _____ $_____
          (specify)

38. Subtotal farm
    (37a + b + c + d) $_____

39. Non-farm long-term
    liabilities $_____

40. Total Long-term Liabilities
    (38 + 39) $_____

Total Assets

23. Total Farm Assets
    (7 + 13 + 20) $_____

24. Total Assets
    (9 + 15 + 22) $_____

Total Liabilities

41. Total Farm Liabilities
    (29 + 33 + 38) $_____

42. Total Liabilities
    (31 + 35 + 40) $_____

Net Worth Analysis

43. Farm Net Worth
    (23 − 41) $_____

44. Total Net Worth
    (24 − 42) $_____

45. Change in Farm Net Worth
    (This year 43 −
    last year 43) $_____

46. Change in Total Net Worth
    (This year 44 −
    last year 44) $_____

(Continued)

a. NET WORTH STATEMENT (Continued)

Ratio Analysis

Ratio	Farm	Total
Current ratio	(29 ÷ 7) _____%	(31 ÷ 9) _____%
Intermediate ratio	(33 ÷ 13) _____%	(35 ÷ 15) _____%
Current and intermediate ratio	(29 + 33) ÷ (7 + 13) _____%	(36 ÷ 16) _____%
Long-term ratio	(38 ÷ 20) _____%	(40 ÷ 22) _____%
Total Ratio	(41 ÷ 23) _____%	(42 ÷ 24) _____%

*Adapted from University of Wisconsin and University of Minnesota Farm Records Project, by R. A. Luening, A. J. Brannstrom, D. B. Welsch, R. O. Hawkins, K. H. Thomas, and from the North Central Regional Bulletin 34-2, "Managing Your Financial Future, Where Am I? Analyzing Your Farm Financial Performance."

b. FARM EARNINGS STATEMENT*
(Profit and Loss Statement or Operating Statement)

CASH OPERATING STATEMENT

INCOME

Livestock and Livestock Products

1. Milk $_____
2. Dairy cattle $_____
3. Hogs $_____
4. Beef cattle $_____
5. Sheep and wool $_____
6. Poultry and eggs $_____
7. Other livestock income $_____

Crops

8. Hay and other forage $_____
9. Grain $_____
10. Specialty crops $_____
11. Other crops $_____

Other Farm Income

12. Machine work income $_____
13. Miscellaneous income $_____
14. Total Cash Farm
    Operating Income
    (Sum of 1–13) $_____

EXPENSES

15. Hired labor $_____
16. Machinery repair—field $_____
17. Machinery repair—livestock $_____
18. Building and fence
    repair $_____
19. Interest—farm share $_____
20. Rent—farm share $_____
21. Feed $_____
22. Seeds and plants $_____
23. Fertilizer and lime $_____
24. Other crop expenses $_____
25. Machine hire $_____
26. Breeding fees $_____
27. Veterinary medicines $_____
28. Other livestock expenses $_____
29. Gasoline, fuel, oil—
    farm share $_____
30. Storage, warehousing $_____
31. Taxes, real estate, personal
    property—farm share $_____
32. Insurance—farm share $_____
33. Utilities—farm share $_____
34. Freight and trucking $_____
35. Auto expense—farm share $_____
36. Resale items purchased this
    year $_____
37. Miscellaneous expenses $_____
38. Total Cash Farm
    Operating Expenses
    (Sum of 15–37) $_____

39. NET CASH FARM
    OPERATING INCOME
    (14 − 38) $_____

(Continued)

b. FARM EARNINGS STATEMENT (Continued)

ADJUSTMENTS FOR INVENTORY ITEMS

	a. Feed and Grain	b. Livestock Held for Sale	c. Supplies and Prepaid Expenses	d. Accounts Receivable	e. Accounts Payable
40. Ending inventory	$_____	$_____	$_____	$_____	$_____ (begin.)
41. Beginning inventory	$_____	$_____	$_____	$_____	$_____ (end.)
42. Net adjustment (40 − 41)	$_____	$_____	$_____	$_____	$_____

43. ADJUSTED NET FARM EARNINGS
$[39 + (42a + b + c + d + e)]$ $_____

ADJUSTMENTS FOR CAPITAL ITEMS

	a. Dairy and Breeding Livestock	b. Machinery and Equipment	c. Buildings and Improvements	d. Land and Improvements
44. Ending inventory	$_____	$_____	$_____	$_____
45. Sales	$_____	$_____	$_____	$_____
46. Subtotal (44 + 45)	$_____	$_____	$_____	$_____
47. Beginning inventory	$_____	$_____	$_____	$_____
48. Purchases (boot)	$_____	$_____	$_____	$_____
49. Subtotal (47 + 48)	$_____	$_____	$_____	$_____
50. Net Adjustment (46 − 49)	$_____	$_____	$_____	$_____

51. **NET FARM EARNINGS** (Return to
unpaid labor, unpaid management,
and equity capital
$[43 + (50a + b + c + d)]$) $_____

*Adapted from University of Wisconsin and University of Minnesota Farm Records Project, by R. A. Luening, A. J. Brannstrom, D. B. Welsch, R. O. Hawkins, K. H. Thomas, and from the North Central Regional Bulletin 34-2, "Managing Your Financial Future, Where Am I? Analyzing Your Farm Financial Performance."

c. CASH FLOW STATEMENT*
(Sources and Uses of Funds—
Projected and Actual)

Item / Month	January Proj.	Jan. Act.	February Proj.	Feb. Act.	*(Mar–Nov)*	December Proj.	Dec. Act.	Total Proj.	Total Act.
1. Beginning cash balance									
2. Farm capital sales									
3. Non-farm inflows									
4. (specify)									
5. (specify)									
6. (specify)									
7. (specify)									
8. (specify)									
9. TOTAL CASH INFLOWS (Sum of 1–8)									
10. Hired labor									
11. Machinery repair									
12. Building repair									
13. Interest—farm share									
14. Rent—farm share									
15. Feed									
16. Seeds and plants									
17. Fertilizer and lime									
18. Other crop expenses									
19. Machine hire									
20. Breeding fees									
21. Veterinary medicine									

March through November—same as January, February, and December

(Continued)

c. CASH FLOW STATEMENT (Continued)

Month / Item	January Proj.	Act.	February Proj.	Act.		December Proj.	Act.	Total Proj.	Act.
22. Other livestock expenses									
23. Gasoline, fuel, oil— farm share									
24. Storage, warehousing									
25. Taxes, real estate, personal property— farm share									
26. Insurance—farm share									
27. Utilities—farm share									
28. Freight and trucking									
29. Auto expense— farm share									
30. Miscellaneous expenses									
31. Resale items purchased this year									
32. Capital purchases (boot)									
33. Family living and savings									
34. Income tax and Social Security									
35. Non-farm outflows									
36. Payment to primary creditor									
37. Payment to other creditors									

March through November—same as January, February, and December

(Continued)

c. CASH FLOW STATEMENT (Continued)

Month	January		February			December		Total	
Item	Proj.	Act.	Proj.	Act.		Proj.	Act.	Proj.	Act.
38. Desired ending balance									
39. TOTAL CASH OUTFLOWS (Sum of 10–38)									
40. SURPLUS OR DEFICIT (9 − 39)									
41. New Borrowing									
42. Ending Balance (40 + 41)									

*Adapted from University of Wisconsin and University of Minnesota Farm Records Project, by R. A. Luening, A. J. Brannstrom, D. B. Welsch, R. O. Hawkins, K. H. Thomas, and from the North Central Regional Bulletin 34-2, "Managing Your Financial Future, Where Am I? Analyzing Your Farm Financial Performance."

d. ACCURACY CHECK*

CASH FLOW

Item	Amount	Source of Information
1. Cash on hand (beginning)	$_____	Beginning Net Worth Statement
2. Cash farm operating income	$_____	Farm Earnings Statement
3. Farm capital sales	$_____	Farm Earnings Statement
4. New money borrowed this year	$_____	Cash Flow Statement
5. Other inflows (non-farm)	$_____	Cash Flow Statement
6. Total inflows (1 + 2 + 3 + 4 + 5)	$_____	—
7. Cash on hand (ending)	$_____	Ending Net Worth Statement
8. Farm operating expenses	$_____	Farm Earnings Statement
9. Capital purchases (boot)	$_____	Farm Earnings Statement
10. Principal payments on debt	$_____	Cash Flow Statement
11. Other outflows (non-farm)	$_____	Cash Flow Statement
12. Income tax and Social Security	$_____	Cash Flow Statement
13. Subtotal (7 + 8 + 9 +10 +11 + 12)	$_____	—
14. Calculated family living and savings (6 − 13)	$_____	—
15. Reported family living and savings ..	$_____	Cash Flow Statement
16. Unaccounted for difference (14 − 15)	$_____	—

PROFITABILITY

Item	Amount	Source of Information
17. Net farm earnings	$_____	Farm Earnings Statement
18. Net non-farm income (5 − 11)	$_____	—
19. Total net earnings (17 + 18)	$_____	—
20. Apparent family living and savings, income tax, and Social Security (12 + 14 + 16)	$_____	—
21. Net worth change calculated (19 − 20)	$_____	—
22. Net worth change reported	$_____	Ending Net Worth Statement
23. Difference (21 − 22)	$_____	—

d. ACCURACY CHECK (Continued)

LIABILITIES

24. Beginning liabilities .... $_____ Beginning Net Worth Statement
25. New money borrowed .... $_____ Line 4
26. Total to account for (24 + 25) ...... $_____ —
27. Principal payments on debt .... $_____ Line 10
28. Subtotal (26 − 27) .... $_____ —
29. Change in accounts payable .... $_____ Farm Earnings Statement
30. Ending liabilities calculated
    (28 ± 29) .... $_____ —
31. Ending liabilities reported .... $_____ Ending Net Worth Statement
32. Discrepancy (30 − 31) .... $_____ —

*Adapted from University of Wisconsin and University of Minnesota Farm Records Project, by R. A. Luening, A. J. Brannstrom, D. B. Welsch, R. O. Hawkins, K. H. Thomas, and from the North Central Regional Bulletin 34-2, "Managing Your Financial Future, Where Am I? Analyzing Your Farm Financial Performance."

Inventory Resolution or Check

If you remember the equation "BIPP minus EIS" you can easily make an inventory resolution or check. The Beginning Inventory plus Production plus Purchases is the total to account for. The Ending Inventory plus Sales subtracted from BIPP equals disappearance. The accounted for disappearance, subtracted from disappearance, equals the unaccounted for disappearance. This can be done for either physical or dollar amounts, or both. Any time frame (days, weeks, months, years, etc.) can be used.

e. INVENTORY RESOLUTION OR CHECK

Line No.	Item	Physical Amount	Unit Value	Total Value
1.	Beginning inventory		$	$
2.	Production		$	$
3.	Purchases		$	$
4.	Total to account for (1 + 2 + 3)		$	$
5.	Ending inventory		$	$
6.	Sales		$	$
7.	Total accounted for (5 + 6)		$	$
8.	Disappearance (4 − 7)		$	$
9.	Accounted for disappearance		$	$
10.	Unaccounted for disappearance (8 − 9)		$	$

Hundredweight of Livestock Produced

Many times it is useful to compute the physical amount of livestock produced in hundredweight (cwt.). By following the computational procedure outlined in the "Hundredweight of Livestock Produced" form you can easily compute this amount. Other physical amount (pounds, kilograms, tons, etc.) measures may be used. Various time frames (days, months, years) may also be used.

f. HUNDREDWEIGHT OF LIVESTOCK PRODUCED

Line No.	Item / Specify Livestock Class	Livestock Class (Cwt.)		
		(Specify)	(Specify)	(Specify)
1.	Ending inventory			
2.	Sales			
3.	Home use			
4.	Subtotal (1 + 2 + 3)			
5.	Beginning inventory			
6.	Purchases			
7.	Subtotal (5 + 6)			
8.	Production (4 − 7)			

g. ANNUAL* LIVESTOCK NUMBER CHECK

Line No.	Livestock _____ (specify)				Livestock _____ (specify)				Livestock _____ (specify)			
	Item In	No.	Item Out	No.	Item In	No.	Item Out	No.	Item In	No.	Item Out	No.
1.	Beginning inventory		Ending inventory		Beginning inventory		Ending inventory		Beginning inventory		Ending inventory	
2.	Purchases		Sold		Purchases		Sold		Purchases		Sold	
3.	Transferred in		Transferred out		Transferred in		Transferred out		Transferred in		Transferred out	
4.	Born		Died		Born		Died		Born		Died	
5.	Total in** (1+2+3+4)		Total out** (1+2+3+4)		Total in** (1+2+3+4)		Total out** (1+2+3+4)		Total in** (1+2+3+4)		Total out** (1+2+3+4)	

*This format can also be used for a weekly, monthly, quarterly, and semiannual livestock number check.

**The total "in" should equal the total "out" to balance.

3. FINANCIAL INFORMATION[4]

a. Discounting Factors* for Various Interest Rates and Time Periods
(Present Value of Future Amount)

Years	\multicolumn{12}{c}{Interest Rates (%)}

Years	4	5	6	7	8	9	10	11	12	13	14	15
1	.962	.952	.943	.935	.926	.917	.909	.901	.893	.885	.877	.870
2	.925	.907	.890	.873	.857	.842	.826	.812	.797	.783	.769	.756
3	.889	.864	.840	.816	.794	.772	.751	.731	.712	.693	.675	.658
4	.855	.823	.792	.763	.735	.708	.683	.659	.636	.613	.592	.572
5	.822	.784	.747	.713	.681	.650	.621	.593	.567	.543	.519	.497
6	.790	.746	.705	.666	.630	.596	.564	.535	.507	.480	.456	.432
7	.760	.711	.665	.623	.583	.547	.513	.482	.452	.425	.400	.376
8	.731	.677	.627	.582	.540	.502	.467	.434	.404	.376	.351	.327
9	.703	.645	.592	.544	.500	.460	.424	.391	.361	.333	.308	.284
10	.676	.614	.558	.508	.463	.422	.386	.352	.322	.295	.270	.247
15	.555	.481	.417	.362	.315	.275	.239	.209	.183	.160	.140	.123
20	.456	.377	.312	.258	.215	.178	.149	.124	.104	.087	.073	.061
25	.375	.295	.233	.184	.146	.116	.092	.074	.059	.047	.038	.030
30	.308	.231	.174	.131	.099	.075	.057	.044	.033	.026	.020	.015
35	.253	.181	.130	.094	.068	.049	.036	.026	.019	.014	.010	.008
40	.208	.142	.097	.067	.046	.032	.022	.015	.011	.008	.005	.004

*$X = \dfrac{1}{(1+I)^n}$

X = Factor

I = Interest rate

n = Years

Example: 8%, 5 years

$$X = \frac{1}{(1+.08)^5} = \frac{1}{1.469} = 0.681$$

Thus, the present value of $1.00 five years from now is $0.681 at an 8 % interest rate.

[4]Discounting, Compounding, and Amortization Factor tables generated by A. J. Brannstrom, University of Wisconsin–Madison.

b. Compounding Factors*
for Various Interest Rates and Time Periods
(Future Value of Present Amount)

Years	4	5	6	7	8	9	10	11	12	13	14	15
					Interest Rates (%)							
1	1.04	1.05	1.06	1.07	1.08	1.09	1.10	1.11	1.12	1.13	1.14	1.15
2	1.08	1.10	1.12	1.14	1.17	1.19	1.21	1.23	1.25	1.28	1.30	1.32
3	1.12	1.16	1.19	1.23	1.26	1.30	1.33	1.37	1.40	1.44	1.48	1.52
4	1.17	1.22	1.26	1.31	1.36	1.41	1.46	1.52	1.57	1.63	1.69	1.75
5	1.22	1.28	1.34	1.40	1.47	1.54	1.61	1.69	1.76	1.84	1.93	2.01
6	1.27	1.34	1.42	1.50	1.59	1.68	1.77	1.87	1.97	2.08	2.19	2.31
7	1.32	1.41	1.50	1.61	1.71	1.83	1.95	2.08	2.21	2.35	2.50	2.66
8	1.37	1.48	1.59	1.72	1.85	1.99	2.14	2.30	2.48	2.66	2.85	3.06
9	1.42	1.55	1.69	1.84	2.00	2.17	2.36	2.56	2.77	3.00	3.25	3.52
10	1.48	1.63	1.79	1.97	2.16	2.37	2.59	2.84	3.11	3.39	3.71	4.05
15	1.80	2.08	2.40	2.76	3.17	3.64	4.18	4.78	5.47	6.25	7.14	8.14
20	2.19	2.65	3.21	3.87	4.66	5.60	6.73	8.06	9.65	11.52	13.74	16.37
25	2.67	3.39	4.29	5.43	6.85	8.62	10.83	13.59	17.00	21.23	26.46	32.92
30	3.24	4.32	5.74	7.61	10.06	13.27	17.45	22.89	29.96	39.12	50.95	66.21
35	3.95	5.52	7.69	10.68	14.79	20.41	28.10	38.57	52.80	72.07	98.10	133.18
40	4.80	7.04	10.29	14.97	21.72	31.41	45.26	65.00	93.05	132.78	188.88	267.86

*X $= (1 + I)^n$

X = Factor

I = Interest rate

n = Years

Example: 8%, 5 years

$X = (1 + .08)^5 = 1.47$

Thus, the future value of $1.00 five years from now is $1.47 at an 8% interest rate.

c. Amortization Factors*
for Various Interest Rates and Time Periods
(Annual Payment per $1.00 of Loan)

Years	Interest Rates (%)											
	4	5	6	7	8	9	10	11	12	13	14	15
2	.5302	.5378	.5454	.5531	.5608	.5685	.5762	.5839	.5917	.5995	.6073	.6151
3	.3603	.3672	.3741	.3811	.3880	.3951	.4021	.4092	.4163	.4235	.4307	.4380
4	.2755	.2820	.2886	.2952	.3019	.3087	.3155	.3223	.3292	.3362	.3432	.3503
5	.2246	.2310	.2374	.2439	.2505	.2571	.2638	.2706	.2774	.2843	.2913	.2983
6	.1908	.1970	.2034	.2098	.2163	.2229	.2296	.2364	.2432	.2502	.2572	.2642
7	.1666	.1728	.1791	.1856	.1921	.1987	.2054	.2122	.2191	.2261	.2332	.2404
8	.1485	.1547	.1610	.1675	.1740	.1807	.1874	.1943	.2013	.2084	.2156	.2229
9	.1345	.1407	.1470	.1535	.1601	.1668	.1736	.1806	.1877	.1949	.2022	.2096
10	.1233	.1295	.1359	.1424	.1490	.1558	.1627	.1698	.1770	.1843	.1917	.1993
15	.0899	.0963	.1030	.1098	.1168	.1241	.1315	.1391	.1468	.1547	.1628	.1710
20	.0736	.0802	.0872	.0944	.1019	.1095	.1175	.1256	.1339	.1424	.1510	.1598
25	.0640	.0710	.0782	.0858	.0937	.1018	.1102	.1187	.1275	.1364	.1455	.1547
30	.0578	.0651	.0726	.0806	.0888	.0973	.1061	.1150	.1241	.1334	.1428	.1523
35	.0536	.0611	.0690	.0772	.0858	.0946	.1037	.1129	.1223	.1318	.1414	.1511
40	.0505	.0583	.0665	.0750	.0839	.0930	.1023	.1117	.1213	.1310	.1407	.1506

$$^*X = \frac{R(1 + R)^N}{(1 + R)^N - 1}$$

X = Factor
R = Interest rate/period
N = Total number of periods

Example: 8%, 5 years

$$X = \frac{.08(1 + .08)^5}{(1 + .08)^5 - 1} = \frac{.08(1.4693)}{1.4693 - 1}$$

$$= \frac{.117546}{.4693} = .2505$$

Thus, a $100.00 loan at 8% for five years would require five annual payments of $25.05 to cover principal and interest.

d. Interest Quickly Computed

The following will be found to be excellent rules for finding the interest on any principal for any number of days. When the principal contains cents, point off four places from the right of the result to express the interest in dollars and cents. When the principal contains dollars only, point off two places.

4%—Multiply the principal by number of days to run and divide by 90.
5%—Multiply by number of days and divide by 72.
6%—Multiply by number of days and divide by 60.
7%—Multiply by number of days and divide by 52.
8%—Multiply by number of days and divide by 45.
9%—Multiply by number of days and divide by 40.
10%—Multiply by number of days and divide by 36.
12%—Multiply by number of days and divide by 30.
15%—Multiply by number of days and divide by 24.

e. True Cost of Interest

True annual interest rate = $\dfrac{2IN}{B_t(n+1)}$ where:

I = Interest paid (or the amount paid back minus the amount received).

N = Number of payment periods in *one year*. Examples: Monthly = 12, Semimonthly = 24, Weekly = 52.

B_t = Balance or amount received in a loan.

n = Number of *actual* payments.

Example:

Mr. Edward Xavier Ample (Mr. E. X. Ample) borrows $100 for six months. The bank has a discount rate of 8% per year. For the six months' interest the bank deducts 8% times $100 minus one-half year, or $4, and gives Mr. E. X. Ample $96.

The true annual interest rate is as follows:

N = 2, since the loan is due in six months: there are 2 six-month periods in a year.

$$\text{Annual interest rate} = \frac{2 \times \$4 \times 2}{\$96 \times (1+1)} = \frac{\$16}{\$96 \times 2} = \frac{\$16}{\$192} = 8.33\%$$

Another Example:

> Mr. E. X. Ample purchased a piece of equipment for $2,200 with $200 down and the balance in 10 monthly payments of $200 per month.
>
> N = 12, since there are 12 one-month periods in a year.
>
> I   = $200 down payment + (10 × $200) − ($2,000) = ($200 + $2,000) − ($2,000) = ($2,200 − $2,000) = $200
>
> $$\text{Annual interest rate} = \frac{2 \times \$200 \times 12}{\$2,000 \times (12 + 1)} = \frac{\$400 \times 12}{\$2,000 \times 13}$$
>
> $$= \frac{\$4,800}{\$26,000} = 18.5\%$$

4. COST OF CUSTOM WORK

Your county agent or state crop reporting service can supply you with an up-to-date schedule of custom rates charged in your state or area. From time to time, several of the agricultural papers carry lists of rates, which would be helpful when kept as references.

APPENDIX B

Miscellaneous Information

1. LAND MEASURE

An Acre contains:
43,560 square feet
4,840 square yards
160 square rods

To find the number of acres in a rectangular field, multiply the length by the width in feet and divide by 43,560; or multiply the length by the width in yards and divide by 4,840; or multiply the length by the width in rods and divide by 160.

To find the number of acres in a tract of land, divide the number of square rods by 160, or the number of square chains by 10.

How many acres in a field 80 rods long and 62½ rods wide?

80 × 62½ = 5,000 sq. rods; 5,000 ÷ 160 = 41¼ acres (ans.)

How many acres in a tract 79 chains, 84 links (79.84 ch.) long and 41 chains, 25 links (41.25 ch.) wide?

79.84 × 41.25 = 3,293.4 sq. ch.; 3,293.4 ÷ 10 = 329.34 acres (ans.).

One Side of a Square Tract of Land Containing:

1	acre is 208.7 ft.	= 43,560 sq. ft.	$1/10$ acre is 66.0 ft.	= 4,356 sq. ft.
1½	acres is 255.6 ft.	= 65,340 sq. ft.	$1/8$ acre is 73.8 ft.	= 5,445 sq. ft.
2	acres is 295.2 ft.	= 87,120 sq. ft.	$1/6$ acre is 85.2 ft.	= 7,260 sq. ft.
2½	acres is 330.0 ft.	= 108,900 sq. ft.	$1/4$ acre is 104.4 ft.	= 10,890 sq. ft.
3	acres is 361.5 ft.	= 130,680 sq. ft.	$1/3$ acre is 120.5 ft.	= 14,520 sq. ft.
5	acres is 466.7 ft.	= 217,800 sq. ft.	$1/2$ acre is 147.6 ft.	= 21,780 sq. ft.
10	acres is 666.0 ft.	= 435,600 sq. ft.	$3/4$ acre is 180.8 ft.	= 32,670 sq. ft.

A lot 25 by 125 ft. contains nearly $1/14$ of an acre; 50 by 218 ft., $1/4$ of an acre.

To find the length of one of the two equal sides of a rectangular field when the length of the other two equal sides is known, divide the area by the length of one of the known sides. Thus, for a lot containing $^1/_{10}$ of an acre (4,356 sq. ft.) and having two sides of 25 ft. each, the other two sides measure $17^1/_4$ ft. each (4,356 ÷ 25).

2. U.S. GOVERNMENT LAND MEASURE

A township—36 sections, each a mile square.

A section—640 acres.

A quarter section, a half mile square—160 acres.

An eighth section, a half mile long, north and south, and a quarter mile wide—80 acres.

A sixteenth section, a quarter mile square—40 acres.

The sections are numbered 1 to 36, commencing at the northeast corner.

The sections are divided into quarters, which are named by the cardinal points. The quarters are divided in the same way. The description of a 40-acre lot would read: The south half of the west half of the southwest quarter of section 1 in township 24, north of range 7 west, or as the case might be, it sometimes will fall short and sometimes overrun the number of acres it is supposed to contain.

3. SURVEYOR'S MEASURE

7.92 inches	1 link
25 links	1 rod
4 rods	1 chain
10 sq. chains, or 160 sq. rods	1 acre
640 acres	1 sq. mile
36 sq. miles (6 miles sq.)	1 township

4. CUBIC MEASURE

1,728 cu. in.	1 cu. ft.
27 cu. ft.	1 cu. yd.
2,150.42 cu. in.	1 standard bu.
231 cu. in.	1 standard gal. (liquid)
1 cu. ft.	about $^4/_5$ bu.
128 cu. ft.	1 cord (wood)
40 cu. ft.	1 ton (shipping)

5. METRIC CONVERSION FACTORS

To Metric	From Metric
Linear Measure	*Linear Measure*
1 inch = 25.4 millimeters	1 millimeter = 0.0393701 inch
1 inch = 2.54 centimeters	1 centimeter = 0.393701 inch
1 foot = 0.3048 meter	1 meter = 3.28084 feet
1 yard = 0.9144 meter	1 meter = 1.09361 yards
1 mile = 1.609344 kilometers	1 kilometer = 0.621371 mile
Square Measure	*Square Measure*
1 acre = 0.404686 hectacre	1 hectacre = 2.47105 acres
1 sq. mile = 2.58999 sq. kilometers	1 sq. kilometer = 0.386102 sq. mile
Liquid Measure	*Liquid Measure*
1 fluid ounce = 29.5735 milliliters	1 milliliter = 0.033814 fluid ounce
1 pint = 0.473176 liter	1 liter = 2.11338 pints
1 gallon = 3.78541 liters	1 liter = 0.264172 gallon
Dry Measure	*Dry Measure*
1 pint = 0.550610 liter	1 liter = 1.81617 pints
1 bushel = 35.2391 liters	1 liter = 0.0283776 bushel
Weight	*Weight*
1 pound = 0.4536 kilogram	1 kilogram = 2.2046 pounds
1 hundredweight = 45.359 kilograms	100 kilograms = 2.2046 hundredweight
Temperature	*Temperature*
0°Fahrenheit = −17.8° Centigrade	0° Centigrade = 32° Fahrenheit
100° Fahrenheit = 37.8° Centigrade	100° Centigrade = 212° Fahrenheit

6. SILAGE CAPACITY TABLES FOR ESTIMATING APPROXIMATE FARM SILO CAPACITY
(Upright Silos, Trench Silos)

To find the tons remaining in a top unloading silo after part of the silage is removed: (1) find the tons of silage when the silo was filled, (2) find the tons of silage filled to the height equal to the depth of silage removed, (3) subtract the number of tons in Step 2 from the number of tons in Step 1.

Example: A 20-ft. silo was filled to a settled depth of 60 ft., and 22 ft. was fed off. (1) 20 × 60 = 507 tons, (2) 20 × 22 = 126 tons, (3) 507 tons − 126 tons = 381 tons of remaining silage.

Approximate Silage Capacity (70% Moisture)

Depth of Settled Silage	INSIDE DIAMETER OF SILO											
	10	12	14	16	18	20	22	24	25	26	28	30
(ft.)												
2	1	1	2	3	3	4	5	6	6	7	8	9
4	3	4	5	7	9	11	13	16	17	19	22	25
6	5	7	10	13	16	20	24	28	31	33	39	44
8	7	11	15	19	24	30	36	43	46	50	58	67
10	10	15	20	26	33	41	50	59	64	69	80	92
12	13	19	26	34	43	53	64	76	83	90	104	119
14	17	24	32	42	54	66	80	95	103	112	130	149
16	20	29	39	51	65	80	97	115	125	135	157	180
18	24	34	46	61	77	95	115	137	148	160	186	213
20	28	40	54	71	89	110	133	159	172	186	216	248
22	32	45	62	81	102	126	153	182	197	213	248	284
24	36	52	70	92	116	143	173	206	224	242	280	322
26	40	58	79	103	130	160	194	231	251	271	314	361
28	45	64	87	114	144	178	216	257	279	301	350	401
30	49	71	96	126	159	197	238	283	308	333	386	443
32	54	78	106	138	175	216	261	311	337	365	423	486
34	59	85	115	151	191	235	285	339	368	398	461	530
36	64	92	125	164	207	255	309	368	399	432	501	575
38	69	99	135	177	224	276	334	397	431	466	541	621
40	74	107	146	190	241	297	359	428	464	502	582	668
42	80	115	156	204	258	318	385	459	498	538	624	717
44	85	123	167	218	276	340	412	490	532	575	667	766
46	91	131	178	232	294	363	439	522	567	613	711	816
48	96	139	189	247	312	385	466	555	602	651	756	867
50	102	147	200	262	331	409	494	588	639	691	801	920

(Continued)

Approximate Silage Capacity (70% Moisture) (Continued)

Depth of Settled Silage (ft.)	INSIDE DIAMETER OF SILO											
	10	12	14	16	18	20	22	24	25	26	28	30
52	107	154	210	274	347	428	518	617	669	724	839	964
54	112	161	219	287	363	448	542	645	700	757	878	1,008
56	117	168	229	299	379	468	566	673	731	790	916	1,052
58	122	175	239	312	395	487	590	702	761	823	955	1,096
60	127	182	248	324	411	507	613	730	792	857	993	1,140
62			258	337	426	526	637	758	823	890	1,032	1,185
64			268	350	442	546	661	786	853	923	1,070	1,229
66			277	362	458	566	685	815	884	956	1,109	1,273
68			287	375	474	585	708	843	915	989	1,147	1,317
70			296	387	490	605	732	871	945	1,022	1,186	1,361
72					506	625	756	899	976	1,056	1,224	1,405
74					522	644	780	928	1,007	1,089	1,263	1,450
76					538	664	803	956	1,037	1,122	1,301	1,494
78					554	684	827	984	1,068	1,155	1,340	1,538
80					570	703	851	1,013	1,099	1,188	1,378	1,582
82							875	1,041	1,129	1,222	1,417	1,626
84							898	1,069	1,160	1,255	1,455	1,671
86							922	1,097	1,191	1,288	1,494	1,715
88							946	1,126	1,221	1,321	1,532	1,759
90							970	1,154	1,252	1,354	1,571	1,803
92							993	1,182	1,283	1,387	1,609	1,847
94							1,017	1,211	1,313	1,421	1,648	1,891
96							1,041	1,239	1,344	1,454	1,686	1,936
98							1,065	1,267	1,375	1,487	1,725	1,980
100							1,088	1,295	1,406	1,520	1,763	2,024

Approximate Dry Matter Capacity

Depth of Settled Silage (ft.)	INSIDE DIAMETER OF SILO											
	10	12	14	16	18	20	22	24	25	26	28	30
2	0	0	1	1	1	1	1	2	2	2	2	3
4	1	1	2	2	3	3	4	5	5	6	6	7
6	1	2	3	4	5	6	7	9	9	10	12	13
8	2	3	4	6	7	9	11	13	14	15	17	20
10	3	4	6	8	10	12	15	18	19	21	24	28
12	4	6	8	10	13	16	19	23	25	27	31	36
14	5	7	10	13	16	20	24	29	31	34	39	45
16	6	9	12	15	19	24	29	35	38	41	47	54
18	7	10	14	18	23	28	34	41	44	48	56	64
20	8	12	16	21	27	33	40	48	52	56	65	74
22	9	14	19	24	31	38	46	55	59	64	74	85
24	11	15	21	27	35	43	52	62	67	73	84	97
26	12	17	24	31	39	48	58	69	75	81	94	108
28	13	19	26	34	43	54	65	77	84	90	105	120
30	15	21	29	38	48	59	71	85	92	100	116	133
32	16	23	32	41	52	65	78	93	101	109	127	146
34	18	25	35	45	57	71	85	102	110	119	138	159
36	19	28	38	49	62	77	93	110	120	130	150	172
38	21	30	41	53	67	83	100	119	129	140	162	186
40	22	32	44	57	72	89	108	128	139	151	175	200
42	24	34	47	61	77	96	116	138	149	161	187	215
44	26	37	50	65	83	102	124	147	160	173	200	230
46	27	39	53	70	88	109	132	157	170	184	213	245
48	29	42	57	74	94	116	140	167	181	195	227	260
50	31	44	60	78	99	123	148	177	192	207	240	276
52	32	46	63	82	104	128	155	185	201	217	252	289
54	34	48	66	86	109	134	163	194	210	227	263	302
56	35	50	69	90	114	140	170	202	219	237	275	316
58	37	53	72	94	118	146	177	210	228	247	286	329
60	38	55	75	97	123	152	184	219	238	257	298	342
62			77	101	128	158	191	227	247	267	310	355
64			80	105	133	164	198	236	256	277	321	369
66			83	109	137	170	205	244	265	287	333	382
68			86	112	142	176	212	253	274	297	344	395
70			89	116	147	182	220	261	284	307	356	408

(Continued)

Approximate Dry Matter Capacity (Continued)

Depth of Settled Silage	INSIDE DIAMETER OF SILO											
	10	12	14	16	18	20	22	24	25	26	28	30
(ft.)												
72					152	187	227	270	293	317	367	422
74					157	193	234	278	302	327	379	435
76					161	199	241	287	311	337	390	448
78					166	205	248	295	320	347	402	461
80					171	211	255	304	330	357	413	475
82							262	312	339	366	425	488
84							270	321	348	376	437	501
86							277	329	357	386	448	514
88							284	338	366	396	460	528
90							291	346	376	406	471	541
92							298	355	385	416	483	554
94							305	363	394	426	494	567
96							312	372	403	436	506	581
98							319	380	412	446	517	594
100							327	389	422	456	529	607

Corn Silage in Trench Silo

Tons = average width × length × depth of silage (in ft.) × tons per cu. ft. of depth (see the following tabulation).

Depth of Settled Silage	Tons per Cu. Ft.	Depth of Settled Silage	Tons per Cu. Ft.
(ft.)		*(ft.)*	
1	0.00925	9	0.01320
2	.00985	10	.01365
3	.01040	11	.01405
4	.01090	12	.01445
5	.01140	13	.01490
6	.01190	14	.01530
7	.01235	15	.01565
8	.01280		

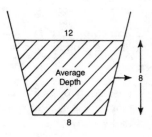

7. ESTIMATING CORN VOLUME

General Directions

In estimating corn volume, multiply the length times the width times the height (all in feet) to get cubic feet. If the storage unit is round, use the formula πr^2 times height equals cubic feet. To get bushels, multiply cubic feet times 0.4 *or* divide cubic feet by 2.5.

To calculate bushels of small grain or shelled corn, multiply by 0.8 *or* divide by 1.25. If wet corn is stored, use the following table.

Volume of a Bu. of Wet Corn
Shelled or Ear—at Specific Moisture Levels

Moisture Content	Cu. Ft.			
	Shelled Corn		Ground Ear Corn	
	×	÷	÷	×
15.5	.800	1.25	1.94	.515
16	.794	1.26	1.96	.510
17	.787	1.27	1.97	.508
18	.781	1.28	2.00	.500
19	.775	1.29	2.02	.495
20	.769	1.30	2.05	.488
22	.758	1.32	2.10	.476
24	.741	1.35	2.15	.465
26	.725	1.38	2.20	.455
28	.709	1.41	2.25	.444
30	.694	1.44	2.30	.435
32	.680	1.47	2.34	.427
34	.667	1.50	2.38	.420

For example: $\pi r^2 h$ for a 20 × 40 ft. silo = 12,560 cu. ft. If this is filled with 30% moisture ground ear corn, divide by 2.3. Thus, 12,560 ÷ 2.3 = 5,460 bu.

or

Multiply by .435, thus 12,560 × .435 = 5,463 bu. Divide cubic feet by the factor across from the moisture content and under the column of corn type and division sign.

or

Multiply cubic feet by the factor across from the moisture content and under the column of corn type and multiplication sign.

Two Moisture Content Corrections[1]

1. If dry: Bu. = volume in cu. ft. $\times$ $4/9$ ($4/9$ = 0.4444).
   If new: Bu. = volume in cu. ft. $\times$ $4/10$ ($4/10$ = 0.4000).
   If damp: Bu. = volume in cu. ft. $\times$ $4/11$ ($4/11$ = 0.3636).

2. Following are correction factors for converting gross bushels of ear corn to net bushels.

Percent Moisture Content		Factor	Percent Moisture Content	Factor	Percent Moisture Content	Factor
15	or less	1.030	22	0.925	29	0.820
16		1.015	23	0.910	30	0.805
17		1.000	24	0.895	31	0.790
18		0.985	25	0.880	32	0.775
19		0.970	26	0.865	33	0.760
20		0.955	27	0.850	34	0.745
21		0.940	28	0.835	35	0.730

1. Example: 10,000 cu. ft. of storage.

   Dry ....10,00 cu. ft. $\times$ $4/9$ = 4,444 bu.
   New ....10,000 cu. ft. $\times$ $4/10$ = 4,000 bu.
   Damp .....10,000 cu. ft. $\times$ $4/11$ = 3,636 bu.

2. Example: 10,000 cu. ft. of storage.

Percent Moisture Content	Cu. Ft.	Gross Bu. Standard Factor		Bu.		Moisture Factor		Net Bu.
15	10,000	$\times$	0.4	=	4,000	$\times$	1.030	=	4,120
17	10,000	$\times$	0.4	=	4,000	$\times$	1.000	=	4,000
19	10,000	$\times$	0.4	=	4,000	$\times$	0.970	=	3,880
21	10,000	$\times$	0.4	=	4,000	$\times$	0.940	=	3,760
23	10,000	$\times$	0.4	=	4,000	$\times$	0.910	=	3,640
25	10,000	$\times$	0.4	=	4,000	$\times$	0.880	=	3,520
27	10,000	$\times$	0.4	=	4,000	$\times$	0.850	=	3,400
29	10,000	$\times$	0.4	=	4,000	$\times$	0.820	=	3,280
31	10,000	$\times$	0.4	=	4,000	$\times$	0.790	=	3,160

[1]*Farmer's Handbook of Financial Calculations*, Agricultural Handbook No. 230, USDA, November 1966, pp. 44 and 49.

8. ESTIMATING GRAIN AND HAY VOLUME

Grain

A bushel of grain contains 1.25 cubic feet. Multiply the length of the bin by the width by the depth (all in feet) to get cubic feet. Then divide cubic feet by 1.25. A quicker way is to multiply the cubic feet by 0.8. If the storage unit is round, use the formula $\pi r^2 \times$ height = cu. ft.

Example: A bin $10' \times 4' \times 3' = 120$ cu. ft.; $120 \times 0.8 = 96$ bu.

Storage Space Requirements for Feed and Bedding*

Material	Weight per Cu. Ft.	Cu. Ft. per Ton
	(lbs.)	
Hay—long loose, in shallow mows	3.6–4.2	475–550
long loose, in deep mows	4–5	400–500
baled, loosely	5.5–6.6	300–360
baled, tightly	6.6–8.3	240–300
chopped, 3″ machine cut	5.3–6.1	330–380
chopped, 1½″–2″ machine cut	5.6–6.7	300–360
Straw—loose	3.5–4.5	450–570
baled	6–10	200–330
chopped	5.7–8.0	250–350
Shavings, baled	20	100
Mixed ground feed	30–40	50–67

*"Planning Stall Barns," Special Bulletin 4, Experiment Station, University of Wisconsin–Madison, October 1954.

Index

Index